Conceiving Cosmopolitanism

Theory, Context, and Practice

edited by

STEVEN VERTOVEC

and

ROBIN COHEN

OXFORD

UNIVERSITY PRESS

This book has been printed digitally and produced in a standard specification
in order to ensure its continuing availability

OXFORD QM LIBRARY
UNIVERSITY PRESS (MILE END)

Great Clarendon Street, Oxford OX2 6DP

Oxford University Press is a department of the University of Oxford.
It furthers the University's objective of excellence in research, scholarship,
and education by publishing worldwide in

Oxford New York

Auckland Cape Town Dar es Salaam Hong Kong Karachi
Kuala Lumpur Madrid Melbourne Mexico City Nairobi
New Delhi Shanghai Taipei Toronto
With offices in
Argentina Austria Brazil Chile Czech Republic France Greece
Guatemala Hungary Italy Japan South Korea Poland Portugal
Singapore Switzerland Thailand Turkey Ukraine Vietnam

ISBN 978-0-19-925228-2

CONTENTS

III. Contexts of Cosmopolitanism

IV. Practices of Cosmopolitanism

NOTES ON CONTRIBUTORS

Rainer Bauböck is a political scientist at the Austrian Academy of Science. He also teaches at the Universities of Vienna and Innsbruck and was Willy Brandt Professor in International Migration and Ethnic Relations at the University of Malmö in 2000/2001. His research interests are in normative political theory and comparative research on citizenship, migration, nationalism and minority rights. His publications include *Transnational Citizenship: Membership and Rights in International Migration* (1994), *Blurred Boundaries: Migration, Ethnicity, Citizenship* (co-edited, 1998) and *The Challenge of Diversity: Integration and Pluralism in Societies of Immigration* (co-edited, 1996).

Ulrich Beck is Professor of Sociology at the University of Munich, and the British Journal of Sociology Professor at the London School of Economics. His interests focus on 'risk society', 'individualization' and 'reflexive moderniza-tion'. His books (all translated into many languages) include *Risk Society* (1992), *Democracy without Enemies* (1998), *World Risk Society* (1999), *What is Globalization?* (1999) and *Future of Work and Democracy* (2000). His most recent research activities include working on a sociological framework to analyse the ambivalences and dynamics of 'cosmopolitan societies'.

Ayse Caglar is a Turkish-born scholar trained in Anthropology at McGill University, Montreal. She has lived and worked for the last decade in Berlin, where she has been widely recognized for her sensitivity and insights into the situation facing 'German Turks', particularly in post-reunification Germany. She has published extensively on citizenship and cultural matters, a recent pub-lication being 'Popular Culture, Marginality and Institutional Incorporation', *Cultural Dynamics* 10 (3): 243–61. She is currently interested in how 'ethno marketing' is targeting particular minorities in Germany and thereby redefining their cultural and social space.

Craig Calhoun is President of the US Social Science Research Council and Professor of Sociology and History at New York University. His books include *The Question of Class Struggle: Social Foundations of Popular Radicalism during the Industrial Revolution* (1982), *Neither Gods nor Emperors: Students and Struggle for Democracy in China* (1994), *Critical Social Theory: Culture, History and the Challenge of Difference* (1995) and *Nationalism* (1997).

Chan Kwok-bun is Professor and Head of the Department of Sociology and Director of the David C. Lam Institute for East-West Studies, Hong Kong Baptist University. His research areas include transnationalism, identities and diasporas, ethnic and immigrant entrepreneurship, and ethnic Chinese business networks. His publications include 'A Family Affair: Migration, Dispersal and the Emergent Identity of the Chinese Cosmopolitan', *Diaspora* 6 (2): 195–214 (1997), *Stepping Out: The Making of Chinese Entrepreneurs* (co-authored, 1994) and *Chinese Business Networks* (2000). He is currently working on two forthcoming books on the *Chinese of Thailand* and the *Social History of Singapore* (using archival photographs).

Robin Cohen is Dean of the Faculty of Humanities at the University of Cape Town while on long leave from his Chair in Sociology at the University of Warwick. He has published widely on issues concerning development, migration, globalization and social identity. His books include *Frontiers of Identity: The British and the Others* (1994), *Global Diasporas: An Introduction* (1997, 1999) and (with Paul Kennedy) *Global Sociology* (2000). With Alisdair Rogers and Steven Vertovec he edits the new journal *Global Networks*.

Robert Fine is Reader in Sociology at the University of Warwick. His books include *Civil Society: Democratic Perspectives* (co-edited, 1997), a socio-historical study of the relation between labour and nationalism in South Africa, called *Beyond Apartheid: Labour and Nationalism in South Africa* (1991) and a theoretical study of the relation between liberal and Marxist legal thought titled *Democracy and the Rule of Law: Liberal Perspectives and Marxist Critiques* (1986). He is currently researching in two areas: Hegel's political thought and post-Auschwitz political philosophy.

Stuart Hall is widely recognized as one of Britain's foremost public intellectuals. He was Director of the Centre for Contemporary Cultural Studies at the University of Birmingham before becoming Professor of Sociology at the Open University. Notable publications include *Policing the Crisis: Mugging, the State, and Law and Order* (with others, 1978), *Questions of Cultural Identity* (co-authored, 1996) and *Representation: Cultural Representation and Signifying Practices* (edited, 1997). A volume compiled in tribute to his achievements and influence is titled *Without Guarantees: In Honour of Stuart Hall* (2000).

David Held is Graham Wallas Professor of Political Science at the London School of Economics and was previously Professor of Politics and Sociology at the Open University. His research interests include rethinking democracy at transnational and international levels and the study of globalization and global governance. He has strong interests both in political theory and in the more empirical dimensions of political analysis. Among his books are *Democracy and the Global Order: From the Modern State to Cosmopolitan Governance* (1995), *Models of Democracy* (1996), and *Global Transformations: Politics, Economics and Culture* (co-author eds, 1999).

Daniel Hiebert is a social geographer at the University of British Columbia, and specializes in immigrant settlement in Canadian cities. He coordinates research on immigration, housing and neighbourhood change in the Vancouver Centre of Excellence for Research on Immigration and Integration in the Metropolis (RIIM), a large project funded by the government of Canada. His recent publications include: 'Immigration and the Changing Canadian City', *The Canadian Geographer* 44 (2000) 25–43, 'Local Geographies of Labour Market Segmentation: Montréal, Toronto and Vancouver', *Economic Geography* 75 (1999): 339–69 and, with Ian Burnley, 'Emerging Patterns of Immigrant Settlement at the Metropolitan Scale: The Need for New Concepts and Models', *Planning Perspectives* (2001).

David A. Hollinger is Professor of History at the University of California, Berkeley. He has made his reputation particularly in American Studies and the history of ideas. His notable books include *The American Intellectual Tradition: A Sourcebook* (co-edited, 1989 and now in its fourth edition) and *In the American Province: Studies in the History and Historiography of Ideas* (1989). His *Postethnic America: Beyond Multiculturalism* has produced an extensive intellectual and political debate on the limits of identity politics.

Mary Kaldor joined the London School of Economics in 1999 as Director of the Programme on Global Civil Society at the Centre for the Study of Global Governance. She previously researched and taught at the University of Sussex for thirty years. Her publications include *The Imaginary War: Understanding the East-West Conflict* (1990), *Democratization in Central and Eastern Europe* (co-edited, 1999), and *New and Old Wars: Organised Violence in a Global Era* (1999), a book already translated into five languages. She was a founder member of European Nuclear Disarmament and is currently Co-chair of the Helsinki Citizen's Assembly.

Andrew Linklater is Woodrow Wilson Professor of International Politics at the University of Wales, Aberystwyth. His most recent book is *The Transformation of Political Community: Ethical Foundations of the Post-Westphalian Era* (1998). His current research includes a reassessment of the 'English School' of International Relations and the study of cosmopolitan harm conventions in different international systems.

Richard Sennett was Professor of Sociology at New York University and now teaches at the London School of Economics. He specializes in research on cities, work and social theory. He is an accomplished musician and has written a novel on Brahms. His books include *The Conscience of The Eye: The Design and Social Life of Cities* (1990), *The Fall of Public Man* (1986) and *The Corrosion of Character: The Personal Consequences of Work in the New Capitalism* (1998). He is currently writing a book on the future of socialism.

John Tomlinson is Professor of Cultural Sociology and Director of the Centre for Research in International Communication and Culture (CRICC), Nottingham Trent University. He is the author of *Cultural Imperialism* (1991) and *Globalization and Culture* (1999). He has published on issues of globalization, cosmopolitanism, media and culture in a wide range of books and journals in disciplines from communications and cultural studies to geography, urban studies and development studies.

Peter Van der Veer is Professor of Comparative Religion at the University of Amsterdam and Director of the Research Centre on Religion and Society. His extensive publications include *Gods on Earth* (1988) and *Religious Nationalism* (1994), *Nation and Migration* (1995) and *Conversion to Modernities* (1996).

Steven Vertovec is Director of the ESRC Centre on Migration, Policy and Society at the University of Oxford and Fellow of the Wissenschaftskolleg/ Institute for Advanced Study, Berlin. His books include *Hindu, Trinidad* (1992), *Islam in Europe* (co-edited, 1997), *Migration and Social Cohesion* (1999), *Migration, Diasporas and Transnationalism* (co-edited, 1999), and *The Hindu Diaspora* (2000).

Sami Zubaida is Reader in Sociology at Birkbeck College and Research Associate at the Centre for Near and Middle East Studies, School of Oriental and African Studies, of the University of London. His research and writing are on religion, ethnicity and nationalism in the Middle East, and on food and culture. His publications include *Islam, the People and the State: Essays on Political Ideas and Movements in the Middle East* (1993), *Taste of Thyme: Culinary Cultures of the Middle East* (co-edited, 2000) and 'Is there a Muslim Society? Ernest Gellner's Sociology of Islam', *Economy and Society* 24 (2): 1995.

LIST OF ACRONYMS AND ABBREVIATIONS

ASEN	Association for the Study of Ethnicity and Nationalism
ATV	Aktif Television (Turkish TV channel in Germany)
AYPA	Turkish TV and radio channel in Berlin
BCE	before common (or Christian) era
CEE	Central and Eastern Europe
CERIS	Centre of Excellence for Research on Immigration and Settlement
CHCs	cosmopolitan harm conventions
CMS	Church Missionary Society
CNN	Cable News Network
DM	Deutschmark (German currency used until January 2002)
ESL	English as a second language
EU	European Union
G7	Group of Seven (leading industrial nations)
G8	Group of Eight (leading industrial nations)
GE	General Electric
GfK	Gesellschaft für Konsumforschung
IGO	intergovernmental organization
IMF	International Monetary Fund
INGO	international non-governmental organization
IP Arbo	marketing firm in Germany (formerly IP Plus)
KLA	Kosovo Liberation Army
LMS	London Missionary Society
NATO	North Atlantic Treaty Organization
NGOs	non-governmental organizations
OECD	Organization for Economic Cooperation and Development
OED	Oxford English Dictionary
OSCE	Organization for Security and Co-operation in Europe
RPF	Rwanda People's Front
RTL	Radio Tele Luxembourg
SFB	Sender Freies Berlin (A radio station in Germany)
TD1	Transponder 1 (Radio station in Berlin)
TEU	Treaty of the European Union
TMM	marketing branch within IP Arbo
TRT–INT	Turkish Radio Television—International

UN   United Nations
UNESCO United Nations Educational, Scientific and Cultural Organization
WTO   World Trade Organization
Zft   Zentrum für Türkeistudien

1

Introduction: Conceiving Cosmopolitanism

STEVEN VERTOVEC AND ROBIN COHEN

'Cosmopolitanism' is a long-sidelined concept recently reactivated by a wide range of social and political theorists. For various reasons, as David Harvey (2000: 529) puts it, 'cosmopolitanism is back'.

In most cases the re-emergence of cosmopolitanism arises by way of a proposed new politics of the left, embodying middle-path alternatives between ethnocentric nationalism and particularistic multiculturalism. For some contemporary writers on the topic, cosmopolitanism refers to a vision of global democracy and world citizenship; for others it points to the possibilities for shaping new transnational frameworks for making links between social movements. Yet others invoke cosmopolitanism to advocate a non-communitarian, post-identity politics of overlapping interests and heterogeneous or hybrid publics in order to challenge conventional notions of belonging, identity and citizenship. And still others use cosmopolitanism descriptively to address certain socio-cultural processes or individual behaviours, values or dispositions manifesting a capacity to engage cultural multiplicity.

What are the processes and conditions that have led to a call to conceive cosmopolitanism afresh? Globalization, nationalism, migration, multiculturalism and feminism are prominent among these (Held 1995*a*; Heater 1996; Hutchings 1999; Pollock *et al.* 2000). Again, the secular protests against corporate-led globalization, such as those seen in the dramatic demonstrations in Seattle in December 1999, as well as the excesses displayed and atrocities committed by those who evince narrow religious and ethnic identities, have led to the urgent reposing of two basic cosmopolitan questions: Can we ever live peacefully with one another? What do we share, collectively, as human beings?

Cosmopolitanism: International and Social Levels

While a growing awareness of common risks, such as climate change, is arguably fostering a sense of a globally shared collective future (Beck 1996*a*; Chapter 6, this volume), many emergent political issues (including human rights, crime and terrorism) are beyond the capacity of individual states to control. Further, the political and economic processes of globalization and regionalization, along with various perceived external challenges to national security, increasingly impact upon the accustomed sovereignties of the nation-state. New alliances between countries—whether for regularizing free trade, harmonizing social policies or combating crime—can be described as modes of cosmopolitanism superseding the nation-state model. Over the past decade there has been a new, post-cold war tendency for multinational military inter-ventions such as the Gulf War, the North Atlantic Treaty Organization (NATO) actions in former Yugoslavia and the international 'coalition against terrorism' following the events of 11 September 2001. These are sometimes described as 'cosmopolitan' institutions and initiatives since they are multilateral and seem to supplant the nation-state model. Indeed, they represent examples of 'cosmopolitan war' (Zolo 1997).

There are observers who claim that such developments fundamentally chal-lenge the Westphalian system of sovereign nation-states that is underpinned by tradition, convention and, not least, by the United Nations (UN) (see Lyons and Mastanduno 1995; Biersteker and Weber 1996; Sassen 1996). Today, we are witnessing new tendencies towards interventionism (Mayall 1996) and 'proac-tive cosmopolitanism', or what Paul Taylor (1999: 540) defines as the 'deliber-ate attempt to create a consensus about values and behaviour—a cosmopolitan community—among diverse communities'.

Yet, calls for an emergent cosmopolitan order beyond the nation-state system have not been accepted without challenge. As summed up by Kimberly Hutchings (1999: 25), 'The criticisms tend to be of two kinds: either they depend on a reassertion of realist claims about the continuing significance of state power in relation to global governance, or they stress a pessimistic reading of the post-Westphalian order as the dominance of global capital over both state and inter-state politics'. Several contributors to this volume (Held, Bauböck, Linklater and Kaldor) engage realist and idealist perspectives on the nation-state and question what kinds of institutions and processes purport to transcend it.

At the other extreme—at a social, or more intimate personal level—many individuals now seem to be, more than ever, prone to articulate complex affilia-tions, meaningful attachments and multiple allegiances to issues, people, places and traditions that lie beyond the boundaries of their resident nation-state. This holds especially for migrants, members of ethnic diasporas and other transnational communities (Vertovec and Cohen 1999). People who are active in global social movements also orient their politics and identities toward agen-das outside, as well as within, their resident nation-states (Cohen and Rai 2000).

Such a 'pluralization' of political orientations is coexistent with the nation-state's struggle to maintain a singular political identity in the face of globalization

(Held, Chapter 5, this volume). Multiculturalism has been one notion embodying both a kind of broad vision of society and often a set of specific policies, whereby both specific ethnic and religious identities could be maintained alongside a common national one. However, multiculturalism has received broad criticism for resting upon and reproducing rather rigid notions of culture and group belonging (see *inter alia* Taylor *et al.* 1994; Modood and Werbner 1997; Baumann 1999; Parekh 2000). In contrast to multiculturalism, cosmopolitanism is now increasingly invoked to avoid the pitfalls of essentialism or some kind of zero-sum, all-or-nothing understanding of identity issues within a nation-state framework (Clifford 1998).

In this introduction we commence by looking at the multi-layered ways ('windows') in which cosmopolitanism has entered our world. We continue with socially profiling various sorts of cosmopolites or 'cosmopolitans'.[1] We next review the major theoretical interventions of recent years, using six ideas and approaches ('perspectives') to synthesize a complex body of literature. We then review the other major themes considered by the contributors to this book by discussing the contexts and practices of cosmopolitanism. Finally, we provide a cautiously optimistic conclusion regarding the future of the concept and its relevance to the twenty-first century.

Windows on Cosmopolitanism

The need to foreshadow and open up new ways for understanding cosmopolitanism sets the primary purpose of this book. No single conceptualization is adequate. In the first part of the book we seek to gain a first taste of the multilayered character of cosmopolitanism. We call this part 'windows' partly to evoke the switches in screens that are characteristic of computer operating systems, such as the one ubiquitously marketed by Mr Gates of Seattle. But more pertinently, 'windows' is a reference to the insights of the German sociologist Georg Simmel who, when looking through a window into the Potsdamer Platz in Berlin in 1908, first understood that the relationships between the Self and the Other were being newly articulated in contemporary urban settings. As Richard Sennett (Chapter 4, this volume) recalls, Simmel saw people whom he simply could not classify in conventional ways—Poles different from those from Warsaw, peasants coming from the south of Germany and others. He discerned that this 'unknown other' provoked and enticed those dependent on a more monocultural background. Similar effects arise today. As Stuart Hall

---

[1] Older dictionaries prefer the term 'cosmopolites', which indeed is clearer and more elegant, but 'cosmopolitans' has passed into general use and here we use the terms interchangeably.

(Chapter 2, this volume), drawing on Waldron's (1992) argument suggests, people are no longer inspired by a single culture that is coherent, integrated and organic. Instead, the arrival of transnational migrants has enriched and altered the cultural repertoires of many people. As he (below) explains:

> It is not that we are without culture but we are drawing on the traces and residues of many cultural systems, of many ethical systems—and that is precisely what cosmopolitanism means. It means the ability to stand outside of having one's life written and scripted by any one community, whether that is a faith or tradition or religion or culture—whatever it might be—and to draw selectively on a variety of discursive meanings.

This widening of consciousness and confrontation with alterity can be found not only on the streets of cosmopolitan cities, but in the living rooms of more prosaic locales. As David Held notes in his 'window' (Chapter 5, this volume), the recent generations of people brought up with Yahoo and Cable News Network (CNN)—not to mention exposure to relentless 'We are the World'-type advertising, the rise of 'world music' and decades of high profile environmental campaigns by Greenpeace and the like—are tending to manifest a sense of global identification. Their inherent sense of 'globality', or 'consciousness of the world as a single place' (Robertson 1992: 132), is consistent with many of the meanings of cosmopolitanism that have been voiced by philosophers. This growing consciousness fosters what Beck (2001) calls a 'banal cosmopolitanism', in which everyday nationalism is circumvented and we experience ourselves as integrated into global processes and phenomena. For many people, then, a sense of global commonality is emerging.

The global, national and social/personal discursive levels represent but three points along a conceptual spectrum. At all positions along this spectrum, some notion of cosmopolitanism has acquired appeal because the term seems to represent a confluence of progressive ideas and new perspectives relevant to our culturally criss-crossed, media-bombarded, information-rich, capitalist dominated, politically plural times. Cosmopolitanism suggests something that simultaneously: (a) transcends the seemingly exhausted nation-state model; (b) is able to mediate actions and ideals oriented both to the universal and the particular, the global and the local; (c) is culturally anti-essentialist; and (d) is capable of representing variously complex repertoires of allegiance, identity and interest. In these ways, cosmopolitanism seems to offer a mode of managing cultural and political multiplicities.

Since it has been around for a long time, the term cosmopolitanism has attracted many understandings and uses over the years (cf. Fine and Cohen, Chapter 9, this volume). Recently, such mixed meanings have been elaborated and extended in a burgeoning body of literature in political philosophy and sociology. Yet, as Sheldon Pollock and his Chicago colleagues (2000: 577) point out, 'cosmopolitanism is not some known entity existing in the world, with a clear genealogy from the Stoics to Immanuel Kant, that simply awaits a more detailed description at the hands of scholarship'. There is much scope for conceiving cosmopolitanism theoretically, practically and in terms of the people and contexts that the term might illuminate.

Who are the Cosmopolitans?

Despite the danger of a small overlap between our later discussion of theories and what follows in this section, it may none the less be helpful to provide some sociological characterization of both those who practise cosmopolitanism (who may not always be the same as those who preach it) and those who are labelled as 'cosmopolitans'.

The earliest advocates of cosmopolitanism in ancient Greece were often *metics*, non-citizens, who attracted criticism from no less a figure than Homer. He attacked those who were 'clanless' and 'hearthless'. Yet Homer's most enduring hero, Odysseus, celebrates someone seeking adventure and valuing the unfamiliar and the strange. We can see in this earliest of literary examples the powerful tension between the exciting, stimulating and even arousing attractions of the exotic, and the converse desire for the support, consolation and warmth of the local and familiar (see Chan, Chapter 12, this volume for further discussion). These contradictory pulls are often projected onto the cosmopolitans who are simultaneously or successively figures of emulation, envy, hatred and fear.

A frequent attack on cosmopolites is that cosmopolitanism is only available to an elite—those who have the resources necessary to travel, learn other languages and absorb other cultures. This, historically, has often been true. For the majority of the population, living their lives within the cultural space of their own nation or ethnicity, cosmopolitanism has not been an option. However, in the contemporary world, cultural and linguistic diversity is omnipresent, and the capacity to communicate with others and to understand their cultures is available, at least potentially, to many (Poole 1999: 162). Travel and immigration have led to the necessity of cheek-by-jowl relationships between diverse peoples at work or at street corners, and in markets, neighbourhoods, schools and recreational areas. Some of the most fascinating social research in the field is now generating countless examples of so-called 'everyday' or 'ordinary' cosmopolitanism, where (as Hiebert puts it in Chapter 13, this volume) 'men and women from different origins create a society where diversity is accepted [and] rendered ordinary'.

Such everyday cosmopolitanism might be regarded as a newly recognized form of behaviour. However, in more commonly described settings, cosmopolites have been seen as deviant—refusing to define themselves by location, ancestry, citizenship or language (Waldron 1992). 'Cosmopolite or cosmopolitan in mid-nineteenth century America', for example, meant 'a well-travelled character probably lacking in substance' (Hollinger 1995: 89). Here 'substance' likely referred to a readily identifiable provenance, an integrated and predictable pattern of behavioural practice, including loyalty to a single nation-state or cultural identity. In situations of extreme nationalism or totalitarianism, such as those of the Soviet Union, Nazi Germany or Fascist Italy, cosmopolites were seen as treacherous enemies of the state. It is not coincidental that the Jews and gypsies—'rootless' peoples without an attachment to a particular land— were the first to be shunted to the charnel houses of the holocaust and the bleak camps of the Gulag.

Even where the reactions were not so extreme, the common stereotype of cosmopolitans suggested the privileged, bourgeois, politically uncommitted elites. They have been associated with the wealthy jet setters, corporate managers, intergovernmental bureaucrats, artists, tax dodgers, academics and intellectuals, all of whom maintained their condition 'by virtue of independent means, expensive tastes, and a globe-trotting lifestyle' (Robbins 1998*b*: 248). As Craig Calhoun (Chapter 7, this volume) notes, cosmopolitanism still often refers to 'the class consciousness of frequent travellers'. It is embodied in the emergent culture of the transnational capitalist class described by Leslie Sklair (2000). In his posthumous collection of essays, the US commentator, Lasch (1995: 46), echoed this pejorative use referring to the privileged classes or 'elites' said to be in revolt against the nation-state:

In the borderless global economy, money has lost its links to nationality. ... The privileged classes in Los Angeles feel more kinship with their counterparts in Japan, Singapore, and Korea than with most of their countrymen. This detachment from the state means they regard themselves as 'world citizens' without any of the normal obligations of national citizenship. They no longer pay their share of taxes or contribute to democratic life.

The members of such a class are people whom John Micklethwait and Adrian Wooldridge (2000) label as a new global economic elite, a meritocratic but elusive ruling group, the 'cosmocrats'. They are 'people who attend business-school weddings around the world, fill up the business-class lounges at international airports, provide the officer ranks of most of the world's companies and international institutions, and, through their collective efforts, probably do more than anyone else to make the world seem smaller' (Micklethwait and Wooldridge 2000: 229). Rather wildly, Micklethwait and Wooldridge estimate their numbers as amounting to some twenty million people worldwide. 'Cosmocrats', they say, 'are defined by their attitudes and lifestyles rather than just their bank accounts. That separates them from the widest class of winners from globalization' (Micklethwait and Wooldridge 2000: 230). However, such financial experts, corporate personnel and the like embody a bounded and elitist version of cosmopolitanism, marked by a specialized and—paradoxically—rather homogenous transnational culture, a limited interest in engaging 'the Other', and a rather restricted corridor of physical movement between defined spaces in global cities (Monaci *et al.* 2001).

By being associated with such elites, cosmopolitanism is conceived largely as a matter of consumption, an acquired taste for cultural artefacts from around the world. The high-flying 'cosmocrats' take the lead: 'Fresh sea bass from Chile is now old hat for Manhattan cosmocrats; the fish displays in restaurants groan with *loups de mer* from the Mediterranean, *hamachi* from New Zealand.... Magazines such as *Wallpaper, Condé Nast Traveler*, and *Cigar Aficionado* all act as informal cosmocrat search engines, scouring the world to explain where the best cushions, holidays, and smokes can be found' (Micklethwait and Wooldridge 2000: 233). In an amusing comment on the concept of 'cosmocrats' in a popular magazine, Helen Kirwan-Taylor (2000: 190–1) suggests that the city of London is inhabited by Ethno-Yars (smart people without roots). They have American MBAs and law degrees and know nothing about Britain beyond Heathrow airport. 'Going out of town' means a three-day weekend break in Bali with McKinsey's *Index of Members*—the cosmocrats' functional equivalent of the *Burke's Peerage*—as their reading material. Not surprisingly, cosmocrats 'get up many people's noses'. She suggests they can be relabelled 'cosmoprats'—floating above the world and treating everybody living in a small community 'as though they were wearing a loincloth and clutching a handful of glass beads'.

The growth in the number and reach of global connoisseurs, elite or not, is sometimes taken as a sign of growing cosmopolitanism. The tendency is linked to John Urry's (1995) notion of 'aesthetic cosmopolitanism'. Not only elites, but also tourists of all kinds have developed more cosmopolitan or far-reaching aesthetic tastes. This can be directly linked with (as both the driving force and outcome of) the enhanced popular trend over the past few decades towards the 'consumption' of foreign places. Cosmopolitan tourism includes the search for varied experiences, a delight in understanding the contrasts between societies rather than a longing for uniformity or superiority, and the development of some skills at interpreting cultural meanings. It is a trend arguably based on exoticism, commodification and consumer culture. Considering where most global tourists come from, such a trend may contribute to an image of cosmopolitanism as 'a predominantly white/First World take on things' (Massey, in Tomlinson 1999: 187; cf. Zubaida and Chan, Chapters 3 and 12, this volume).

Aesthetic cosmopolitanism can be found at home, too, through other forms of consumption. The growth in 'world music' represents such a case (Frith 2000), while a routine exposure to global cultural difference through the television creates the possibility of people becoming cosmopolitans in their own living rooms (Hebdige, in Tomlinson 1999: 202). A sure sign of this is the fact that advertising firms have sought to capitalize on people's growing cosmopolitan views. These kinds of campaigns were probably launched by Coca-Cola's 'I'd like to teach the world to sing' commercial in the 1970s. Now, such ads are ubiquitous and formulaic. This point is captured by a critique of one firm's adverts, which have 'proffered the usual pick-and-mix stock shots: grinning people of mixed race, new dawns, foreign climes, hot air balloons, all swathed in a saccharine glow of nauseating mawkishness' (*Private Eye* 1020, 8 February 2001).

Certainly in the current age of post-national or post-Westphalian political trends, transnational flows, diasporic attachments and multiple identity politics, it is even harder to pin down the 'substance' of cosmopolitans. 'Exactly what it means to be a post-national cosmopolitan is far from clear', writes Gerard Delanty (2000: 138), 'particularly given the diffuse nature that nationalism is taking and the fact that the new media of communication and consumption have made everybody cosmopolitan'. Obviously a bit of dabbling in, or desire for, elements of cultural otherness in itself does not indicate a very deep sense of cosmopolitanism. Ulf Hannerz (1990) addresses this when he distinguishes true cosmopolitans from merely globally mobile people—tourists, exiles, expatriates, transnational employees and labour migrants. The 'true' cosmopolitans exhibit a culturally open disposition and interest in a continuous engagement with one or other cosmopolitan project. The other category, Hannerz suggests, simply (and understandably) want some experience of 'home plus' a bit of exoticism when going abroad. In addition to a specific disposition, John Tomlinson (1999) also insists that real cosmopolitans should have a sense of commitment to belonging to the world as a whole.

Despite this attempt to draw lines between the 'real' and 'fake' cosmopolites, there is increasing recognition that the 'cosmopolitan' philosophies, institutions, dispositions and practices—expressions of 'actually existing cosmopolitanism' (Robbins 1998*a*)—exist among a wide variety of non-elites, especially migrants and refugees. This approach to cosmopolitanism underlines the positive, socioculturally and politically transformative meanings of the term (see Schein 1998*a,b*; Werbner 1999; Zachary 2000*a*). And it is this sense that James Clifford employs to describe how the term cosmopolitanism helps to undermine the 'naturalness' of ethnic absolutisms, recognizes 'worldly, productive sites of crossing; complex, unfinished paths between local and global attachments' and 'presupposes encounters between worldly historical actors willing to link up aspects of their complex, different experiences' (Clifford 1998: 362, 365).

Theories: Six Perspectives on Cosmopolitanism

Examining the question of who now identifies with the label 'cosmopolitan' and who is so identified provides a 'first pass' at the subject-matter, but next we have to turn explicitly to the proliferation of recent theories of cosmopolitanism. The rapidly expanding literature on the concept represents a considerable variety of descriptive uses, political discourses and levels of concern. These can be outlined under at least six rubrics. Drawing upon Vertovec (2000*a*), we argue that cosmopolitanism can be viewed or invoked as: (a) a socio-cultural condition; (b) a kind of philosophy or world-view; (c) a political project towards building transnational institutions; (d) a political project for recognizing multiple identities; (e) an attitudinal or dispositional orientation; and/or (f) a mode of practice or competence.

A Socio-Cultural Condition

While ethnic pluralism and cultural admixture has historically been the norm for most parts of the world (cf. McNeill 1986), several aspects of contemporary globalization combine to make current conditions rather different. The relative ease and cheapness of transportation across long distances, mass tourism, large-scale migration, visible multiculturalism in 'world cities', the flow of commodities to and from all points of the compass and the rapid development of telecommunications (including cheap telephone calls, satellite television, email and the Internet) have all wrought a socially and culturally interpenetrated planet, on a scale and intensity hitherto unseen. This is the sense of a mounting contemporary 'cosmopolitanism' described by a number of commentators.

'The world of the late twentieth century', observe Arjun Appadurai and Carol Breckenridge (1988: 5–9) for instance, 'is increasingly a cosmopolitan world. More people are widely travelled, are catholic in their tastes, are more inclusive in the range of cuisines they consume, are attentive to worldwide news, are exposed to global media-covered events and are influenced by universal trends in fashion'. In other words, as Clifford Geertz (1986: 121) foresaw, 'that the world is coming at each of its local points to look more like a Kuwaiti bazaar than like an Englishmen's club . . . seems shatteringly clear'.

For many, such a socio-cultural condition, loosely called 'cosmopolitanism' is to be celebrated for its vibrant cultural creativity as well as its political challenges to various ethnocentric, racialized, gendered and national narratives. There are critics, on the other hand, who are highly sceptical of what is perceived to be an emergent global, hybrid and 'rootless' cosmopolitan culture marked by 'a pastiche of traditional, local, folk and national motifs and styles; a culture of mass consumerism consisting of standardized mass commodities, images, practices and slogans; and an interdependence of all these elements across the globe, based upon the unifying pressures of global telecommunications and computerized information systems' (Smith 1995: 20). This view reflects widespread fears, among many professional commentators and members of the public associated with the death of local and national identities. Such resonant tension is found among political thinkers as well.

A Philosophy or World-View

A number of authors suggest that contemporary political philosophers tend to divide themselves into *communitarians*, who believe that moral principles and obligations are grounded in specific groups and contexts, and *cosmopolitans*, who urge that we live in a world governed by overarching principles of rights and justice (Cohen 1992; Waldron 1992; Hollinger 1995; Bellamy and Castiglione 1998). In this latter sense, largely following Kant, cosmopolitanism refers to a philosophy that urges us all to be 'citizens of the world', creating a worldwide community of humanity committed to common values. Thomas Pogge (1992) suggests that such a general cosmopolitan philosophy can take the form of either a broad *moral* cosmopolitanism, urging that all persons have a certain respect for one another, or a *legal* cosmopolitanism that sets forth universal rights and duties. Further, the citizen-of-the-world philosophy can take various forms or slants. Michael Ignatieff (1999: 142) distinguishes the Marxist cosmopolitans, who stand for the brotherhood of workers, 'gentlemanly' cosmopolitans who feel at home everywhere and regard nationalism as vulgar, and liberal cosmopolitans who proclaim universal standards. Despite such differences, all these cosmopolitans appeal to ideals that are broader than the national one.

However, drawing on their strong views on the political need for a moral grounding in groups, communitarians say that commitments to broad cosmopolitan ideals represent a view that 'embodies all the worst aspects of classical liberalism—atomism, abstraction, alienation from one's roots, vacuity of commitment, indeterminacy of character, and ambivalence towards the good' (Waldron 1992: 764–5). Perhaps the distinction is overplayed. As Ross Poole (1999: 156), for one, argues, 'there need be no inconsistency between affirming the cosmopolitan ideal and also recognizing the importance of particular attachments and the commitments they carry with them'. A degree of moral priority is often appropriate and justified in specific cases of human action, obligation and responsibility: as most people will see it, family and neighbourhood come first, humanity as a whole comes second.

A variant of this argument is found in the question of whether this sense of cosmopolitanism, and its proposed world citizens, can be reconciled with patriotism or loyalty to a single nation-state (see especially Nussbaum *et al.* 1994). There seem to be at least two ways to solve this conundrum. One is advocated by Kwame Anthony Appiah (1998), who raises the possibility of being a 'cosmopolitan patriot' through celebrating different human ways of being while sharing commitment to the political culture of a single nation-state. Another is suggested by Georgios Varouxakis (1999: 7) who believes that 'patriotism can be expressed in a cosmopolitan language and can seek to promote pride in what one's nation is contributing to the universal fund of humanity'; this could be demonstrated, for example, through participation in the UN peace missions. As Fine and Cohen (Chapter 9, this volume) point out, this attempt to reconcile cosmopolitanism and patriotism was implicitly at the heart of the contemporary 'moment' in the US debate before 'September 11'. But the bombing of the World Trade Center has now propelled a number of the US public intellectuals with established universalistic positions into overt displays of loyalty to the US state.

Other theorists effectively seek to transcend the national scale altogether. For example, in his 'Cosmopolitan Manifesto' Ulrich Beck (1998: 29–30) argues for 'a new dialectic of global and local questions which do not fit into national politics'. 'For this', Beck continues, 'there has to be a reinvention of politics, a founding and grounding of the new political subject' that puts 'globality at the heart of political imagination, action and organization'. Such a perspective informs most political scientists who envision a new order of transnational political structures that exercise what is now often described as 'cosmopolitan democracy' (Archibugi and Held 1995; Archibugi *et al.* 1998).

Political Project I: Transnational Institutions

A 'cosmopolitan' or global perspective can be said to be at the heart of political initiatives to establish frameworks and institutions that bridge or overtake the conventional political structures of the nation-state system (see especially Held 1995*a*). Mary Kaldor suggests that when applied to political institutions, the term cosmopolitan implies 'a layer of governance that constitutes a limitation on the sovereignty of states and yet does not itself constitute a state. In other words, a cosmopolitan institution would coexist with a system of states but would override states in clearly defined spheres of activity' (Kaldor 1999: 216). Foremost examples here are the UN and the European Union (EU). In this sense, cosmopolitan political institutions should address policy quandaries surrounding a host of problems that spill over national borders (such as pollution and crime).

Another transnational site of cosmopolitan democracy is that which is increasingly described as an emerging global civil society (for instance, Walzer 1995; Köhler 1998; Delanty 2001; see also Kaldor, Chapter 17, this volume). This is to be seen in an exponential growth in the number, size and range of activities of transnational social movements and networks concerned with issues including the environment, labour conditions, human rights, women and peace (see Smith *et al.* 1997; Smith 1998; Cohen and Rai 2000). The possibilities for developing a global civil society, according to Gerard Delanty (2000, 2001), are dependent on the emergence of what he describes as a cosmopolitan public sphere of communication and cultural contestation that is necessary for any large-scale shift in values (cf. Bohman 1998).

Bringing together these kinds of democratic activity, Kaldor (1996) describes processes creating (a) cosmopolitanism from the above, in the form of international organizations, complex partnerships and cooperative agreements between states, and (b) cosmopolitanism from below through the activities of new transnational social movements. The fact that individuals can continue their roles and identities as national citizens while directly engaging in political activities aimed at a sphere beyond the nation-state, points toward an understanding of the cosmopolitanism of individuals conveying complex political interests.

Political Project II: Multiple Subjects

On a far more immediate level than the global political agendas addressed by some political theorists, others who invoke a concept of cosmopolitanism do so to describe the variegated interests of political actors. Using this interpretation of the term, David Hollinger (1995: 86) suggests that 'Cosmopolitanism is more oriented to the individual, whom it is likely to understand as a member of a number of different communities simultaneously'. Mitchell Cohen (1992: 482) also advocates an understanding of cosmopolitanism as 'a multidimensional conception of political society and human relations, one that implies an important democratic principle: the legitimacy of plural loyalties'.

In fact this view of cosmopolitanism is an age-old one. It can be traced to the ancient Greek Stoics and their proposal that 'we think of ourselves not as devoid of local affiliations, but as surrounded by a series of concentric circles' (Nussbaum 1994: 4). In this view, each circle is considered to represent a different kind or level of attachment or identification: from self, family, group, city and country, to humanity at large. Accordingly, a person's specific political interests and activity are bound to shift from one 'circle' or another. Present-day processes, however, such as diasporic identification and the rise of identity politics, have multiplied people's interests and affiliations. Now gender, sexuality, age, disability, 'homeland', locality, race, ethnicity, religion—even cultural hybridity itself—are among the key identifications around which the same person might at one time or another politically mobilize.

A cosmopolitan politics, in this understanding, emphasizes that people have—and are encouraged to have—multiple affiliations. Political institutions catering to this would include civil and voluntary associations, networks and coalitions providing the expression of various interests and voices (Hirst 1994; Held 1995a; Vertovec 1999). Such a project entails the idea that 'each citizen of a state will have to learn to become a "cosmopolitan citizen" as well: that is, a person capable of mediating between national traditions, communities of fate and alternative forms of life' (Held *et al*. 1999: 449). As these authors continue:

The core of this project involves reconceiving legitimate political authority in a manner which disconnects it from its traditional anchor in fixed borders and delimited territories and, instead, articulates it as an attribute of basic democratic arrangements or basic democratic law which can, in principle, be entrenched and drawn on in diverse self-regulating associations—from cities and subnational regions, to nation-states, regions and wider global networks. It is clear that the process of disconnection has already begun as political authority and legitimate forms of governance are diffused 'below', 'above' and 'alongside' the nation-state (Held *et al*. 1999: 450).

An Attitude or Disposition

In addition to having multiplex identifications, cosmopolitans and cosmopolitanism are often said to embody a unique outlook or 'mode of engaging with the world' (Waldron 1992). In this way Ulf Hannerz views cosmopolitanism as 'a perspective, a state of mind, or—to take a more processual view—a mode of managing meaning' (Hannerz 1990: 238). Hannerz further suggests that 'The perspective of the cosmopolitan must entail relationships to a plurality of cultures' and that this entails 'first of all an orientation, a willingness to engage with the Other' (Hannerz 1990: 239). It is an intellectual and aesthetic stance of openness toward divergent cultural experiences (cf. Vertovec 1996). Cosmopolitanism here represents a desire for, and appreciation of, cultural diversity—a view that Pierre-André Taguieff (1990) has deemed 'heterophilia'.

The cosmopolitan, then, develops 'habits of mind and life' through which he or she can end up anywhere in the world and be 'in the same relation of familiarity and strangeness' to the local culture, and by the same token 'feel partially adjusted everywhere' (Iyer 1997: 30, 32). Such an outlook or disposition is largely acquired through experience, especially travel. It entails not only respect and enjoyment of cultural difference, but also a concomitant sense of 'globality' or global belonging that can be integrated into everyday life practices (Tomlinson 1999: 185).

A Practice or Competence

Along with a particular disposition or orientation towards the world and others, Hannerz (1990: 239) suggests that cosmopolitanism can be a matter of 'competence' marked by 'a personal ability to make one's way into other cultures, through listening, looking, intuiting and reflecting' as well as by a built-up skill of manoeuvring through systems of meaning. Jonathan Friedman (1994: 204), too, sees cosmopolitanism as characterized by a mode of behaviour that 'in identity terms [is] betwixt and between without being liminal. It is shifting, participating in many worlds, without becoming part of them'. For Waldron, it is such partial cultural competencies that comprise 'the cosmopolitan self'. 'If we live the cosmopolitan life,' he writes, 'we draw our allegiances from here, there, and everywhere. Bits of cultures come into our lives from different sources, and there is no guarantee that they will all fit together' (Waldron 1992: 788–9).

There is a qualitative difference, however, between the kind of cosmopolitan competence highlighted by Hannerz and people's practices that amount to a mere cultural mix-and-match. The latter may often comprise simply what Craig Calhoun (Chapter 7, this volume) describes as 'consumerist cosmopolitanism'. Such is manifested in the globalization of tastes: the massive transfer of food-stuffs, artworks, music, literature and fashion. Such processes represent a multi-culturalization of society, but also the advanced globalization of capitalism.

A key question of our age is: can or does exposure to other cultures—from buying bits of them to learning to partake in their beliefs and practices—lead to a fundamental change in attitudes? That would seem to be the *raison d'être* of most multicultural education, though the jury is out on whether people exposed to it have become 'more tolerant'. Surely it is a good thing to be exposed to, or even relish, some customs, habits, lifestyles, values and languages other than those of one's own locality or country? Like being multilingual, individuals themselves can be multicultural, or develop a personal repertoire that provides them with a multiple cultural competence (Vertovec and Rogers 1998). The opportunities for such exposure, learning and practice—even if initially only by way of a coarse consumerism—present themselves today as never before.

Contexts: More Than a 'Western' Concept

Even if we can refute an attack on cosmopolitanism from those who believe it can only be a preoccupation of an elite, is there a more legitimate question that it cannot easily transcend its 'Western' origins? Are the voices of the poor, the weak, the minorities and the cultural marginal being ignored—drowned by the babble of those who control or acquire privileged access to the airwaves, TV channels and printed media of the rich world? Though these questions are understandable, a number of the contributors to this volume demonstrate that they are unwarranted. It is perhaps a mere debating point to allude to the fact that many of the founders of cosmopolitanism, the Stoics in ancient Athens, were Phoenicians or Semites from the 'wrong' (non-European) side of the Mediterranean. By contrast, whereas there is no gainsaying that Kant was the crucial figure in the evolution of European ideas of cosmopolitanism, he was riddled with the racist prejudices of his age (Harvey 2000). In any case, cos-mopolitanism has a much wider and more complex genealogy than that arising from either Kant or ancient Greece.

We can identify the more multifarious provenance and spread of cosmopolitanism by alluding, for example, to the Arab and Muslim cultures. As Zubaida (Chapter 3, this volume) shows, the Abbasid court of the eighth and ninth centuries mixed Islam with Persian culture and statecraft. Arab Spain ('al-Andalus') married Greek and Jewish philosophy with Arab science and medicine. Later, during the zenith of the Ottoman Empire, Middle Eastern cities, especially Istanbul, Cairo and Alexandria, became celebrated cosmopolitan milieus. For Van der Veer (Chapter 10, this volume) cosmopolitanism was embedded in what he calls 'colonial modernity', where the imperial mission joined evangelical Christianity in its encounters with the colonized peoples. However, such interactions were by no means unidirectional. Religious leaders like Swami Vivekananda saw Hinduism as the pinnacle of universal spirituality and Theosophists like Madame Blavatsky and Annie Besant supported his claims. Buddhism, Judaism, Islam, Shinto, Confucianism, Taoism and Jainism also preached a universal message. In short, as Van der Veer avers, a popular, nineteenth-century cosmopolitan consciousness based on universal spirituality emerged, quite different from the secular rationalism of the western European Enlightenment.

Also discrete from European cosmopolitanism were the attempts by Chinese philosophers to find the enriching and elevating elements of alien discourses that could then be adapted for local use. Christianity, Buddhism, Confucianism and Moism (not Maoism), as well as more familiar concepts like democracy and less familiar ones like 'supreme realization' were incorporated into the Chinese systems of thinking. As Chan (Chapter 12, this volume) shows, Chinese cultures show a continuous process of mutation, adaptation and transformation all set within a 'moral injunction against the violence of hegemony, of making the other the same as self'. Though the ideal was harmonious adaptation, there were of course inevitable conflicts—for example, between Confucian this-worldliness and Buddhist other-worldliness. None the less, the process of continuous interrogation shows a cosmopolitan consciousness and practice that is comparable to, but distinct from, Western cosmopolitanism.

Ironically, another 'exotic' variant of cosmopolitanism is presently emerging in Kant's homeland, Germany. In her analysis of how the media and advertising agencies are targeting Turks in Berlin, Ayse Caglar (Chapter 11, this volume) demonstrates that the language and culture has shifted well beyond a narrowly ethnic construction. Broadcasting is in Turkish, but not Turkish as Turks would know it. 'Playful and creative' sets of crossovers between German and Turkish have generated a new language. Instead of reinforcing the idea of an original homeland, replete with nationalism and an attachment to the land, the *city* (in this case Berlin) has intervened to create an 'unmoored' or 'unbound' identity. These 'weak', multiple and deterritorialized attachments are what Caglar understands as cosmopolitan openings, ties and spaces.

We can see in these examples that Western cosmopolitanism has itself become decoupled, even derailed, from any notion of a unilinear heritage stemming from the Enlightenment. Even in Western and white settler societies (Canada is represented in Chapter 13, in this volume), the arrival of visibly different transnational migrants in sufficient numbers and with distinct heritages has led to new syncretic, creolized or hybridized cultures, some of which are the seedbeds of an incipient cosmopolitanism distinct from the Enlightenment tradition.

There is one final issue we must clarify in this discussion of the 'contexts' of cosmopolitanism—namely whether we are engaging in a contradiction in terms in qualifying the concept of cosmopolitanism. The word in itself implies universality. To talk, therefore, of a Western, Islamic, Arabic, Ottoman, colonial, Chinese or European cosmopolitanism seems to imply the recognition of a difference or, indeed, a cultural relativism. This is not what we intend. In refuting the notion that cosmopolitanism is exclusively 'Western' we have had to show that the idea can find fertile soil in many cultures and many contexts. The idea itself remains universal though the language, idiom and form in which it is expressed may differ. Again, the locale in which cosmopolitanism finds a friendly home may change over time. Athens in the ancient world and Istanbul and Venice in the early modern period gave way to cities like Paris, Berlin and London in the modern period. Nowadays Singapore and the Republic of Ireland are important cosmopolitan places and settings.

Practices: Between, Within and Beyond the State

Because this volume either alludes to or covers in detail so many experiences of cosmopolitanism, it is difficult to be entirely comprehensive in summarizing the varied practices described. One, perhaps somewhat schematic, way of classifying the diverse practices involved is to advance a trichotomy, distinguishing between inter-state, intra-state and ultra (beyond)-state practices.

Inter-State Practices

The first category takes in writers such as Held (1995*a* and Chapter 5, in this volume), Linklater and Kaldor (Chapters 16 and 17, this volume) who have been preoccupied mainly with new 'international', 'transnational', 'supranational' or 'global'—the choice of vocabulary implies subtly different positions—institutions that are replacing or paralleling the nation-state system. Held's starting point is to examine how the neat coincidence between nationalism, the modern nation-state and political community is gradually being subverted by the evolution of global cultural movements and communications. As the nation-state system evolved, a political community and a national identity emerged out of the military and bureaucratic requirements of statehood itself. Social relations became embedded in this political community. Held argues that while the 'globalists' can present convincing evidence of the leap in global connectivity and cultural pursuits, national cultures remain robust and capable of adapting and reinterpreting foreign imports. Cosmopolitanism, therefore, becomes a means whereby national and global cultures can be mediated, where dialogues can be initiated and transboundary issues resolved by those who can see above their national parapets.

These processes of mediation and dialogue can be seen as a 'civilizing process' (Elias 1982), an expression usefully reintroduced in Kaldor's contribution in Chapter 17 (this volume). For her, legitimate authority and the management and prevention of conflict must replace the callous disregard for civilian life and the old rules of engagement characteristic of the 'new wars' of the late twentieth century. However, the Westphalian nation-state system cannot do this alone—global, regional and local layers of authority also have to become activated. It is this necessity that dictates a cosmopolitan approach. The cosmopolitan law (human rights laws, the Geneva Convention, the Law of War) needs to be evoked to protect civilians and to save lives. Whereas 'old' wars were (at least in theory) meant only to target the enemy's infrastructure and armed forces, new wars destroy lives and livelihoods and create the pathetic streams of refugees whose images haunt our TV screens. Only by respecting the claims of 'global justice' can human dignity be restored. Nor is this plea entirely theoretical. A 'global civilizing process' can be seen, for example, in the humanitarian aid workers who have risked their lives to save others. As Kaldor pointedly asks, 'Can their experience offer a moral basis for future forms of cosmopolitan governance?'

A number of Kaldor's preoccupations are echoed in Linklater's (Chapter 16, this volume) specific attention to 'cosmopolitan harm conventions' (CHCs). These are laws or conventions that protect the individual or substate communities from the evils perpetrated by states (like war, conquest and other forms of damage caused by aggressive states in pursuit of their trade, investment, environmental and political interests). Though there are undoubted limitations in the practice of such 'global' or international law, occasioned partly by the fact that many of the drafters and implementers of such laws are in the rich world, Linklater argues that CHCs are both evidence and part of the process of developing a post-national world. In the post-national world human (as opposed to state) security is also considered, as are universal human rights. Globally governed environmental spaces (a 'global commons'), the increasing evolution of regional identities and a notion of world citizenship also mark this phase of cosmopolitanism. Only a rash person would suggest that state laws will be supplanted by CHCs, but they certainly both parallel and limit state sovereignty.

Intra-State Practices

We have already referred to a number of ways in which nation-states have been transformed in recent years by transnationalism, globalization, regionalization and by the increasing number and variety of international migrants demanding entry. We must, of course, remember that a number of important nation-states (the United States of America, Australia, Canada and Argentina among them) are 'nations of immigrants' (Freeman and Jupp 1992). However, even if this task was never entirely achieved, the rationale of admitting more immigrants was historically predicated on the assumption that they would conform to the existing mores or create a new, distinct national identity—American, Australian, and so forth. As the limits of this form of social engineering became apparent, goals retreated. Hyphenated Americans (like Polish-Americans or African-Americans) became acceptable, the first half of the appellation signifying a continuing or reinvented ethnic identity, the second a loyalty to the new nation-state. However, this formula, as well as comparable attempts to create 'multicultural' social policies in Australia and Canada, never satisfied the old 'monocultural' nation-builders on the one side, or addressed the increasing fragmentation of ethnicities on the other.

This all too quickly describes the contested intellectual territory into which a number of key commentators, some represented in this book, stepped. David Hollinger's (1995) account of *Postethnic America* created one of the most important interventions. His contribution to this volume (Chapter 14) sharpens the distinctions between those advocating multiculturalism and those advancing cosmopolitan ideas. If we take, for the purposes of this argument, the synonymy between 'pluralism' and 'multiculturalism',[2] Hollinger shows that while both perspectives favour tolerance and diversity, pluralism accepts ethnic segmentation as normal while cosmopolitanism makes a decisive break with the celebration of 'communities of descent' in favour of individual choice and multiple affiliations. As an intra-state practice, cosmopolitanism does not recognize cultural segmentation. It assumes complex, overlapping, changing and often highly individualistic choices of identity and belonging.

In the face of criticism, Hollinger concedes that his notion of 'postethnicity' does not easily apply to black Americans; nor is the story that simple when it comes to distinguishing between immigrant groups, indigenous peoples and national minorities (some of whom, like the Quebecois or the Basques have the attributes of a nation). Bauböck (Chapter 8, this volume) makes a similar point in his distinction between transborder national minorities, indigenous minorities and immigrant minorities. Like Held (discussed above) he is concerned

---

[2] The differences would need to take into account not only the 'pluralism' used by Hollinger in the sense commonly understood in the United States of America, but also the more complex Caribbean, Dutch, colonial and African uses (M. G. Smith 1969). This is an unnecessary diversion here.

with how the shape of a political community is transformed by the unusual or recalcitrant alternatives to nativism, seeing this as a moment when state-based notions of citizenship have to yield to the new realities. The state, he surmises, will have to yield to multicultural demands, devolve regional power (in multi-national states), recognize some element of self-determination by indigenous peoples and grant some degree of dual citizenship for certain transnational migrants. This can be conceived as an intra-state set of cosmopolitan practices, and one that will provide a major problem for the politicians to solve. Already in states like Germany (especially in Bavaria), Australia, France, the United States of America (especially after 11 September), the United Kingdom and Austria, the politicians who are espousing 'one-nation' ideologies are getting re-elected or gaining in popularity. In the face of economic necessity, economic immigration is often conceded—asylum seekers are fiercely resisted—but immigrants are told to *conform*. The battle lines are being drawn up between the mono and multiculturalists and between nationalist and cosmopolitan views of the future.

Ultra-State Practices

In our earlier work we have written a great deal about how migrants, ethnic dia-sporas and other transnational communities have either revived or created global ties that have largely escaped their national locations and affiliations (Cohen 1997; Vertovec and Cohen 1999; Vertovec 2000*b*). In association with Shirin Rai one of us has considered how those active in global social movements also orient their politics and identities toward agendas outside their resident nation-states (Cohen and Rai 2000). Finally, with the help of yet another colleague, Alisdair Rogers, the current authors have launched a journal, *Global Networks*, with an editorial statement that includes the following passage (Rogers *et al.* 2001: 1–2):

We see global networks as constituted by dynamic and flexible types of connection between individuals, groups or organizations that span the world. The structure of such global networks conditions the interactions, strategies and identities of their members. These networks have burst across territorial borders, rupturing the degree of cultural and economic self-sufficiency once experienced by nations. The cumulative impact of these interconnections has meant that societies, along with their cities and regions, have tended to spread outwards so as to merge and become coextensive with other societies. This has vast implications for the way we understand the world and how it is governed. ... The once clear-cut separation between the domestic sphere of national life and the external or international sphere has largely broken down. Transnational processes present profound challenges and opportunities to states, corporations, cities and terri-torially based actors of all kinds. People and firms, places and communities, can be switched in and out of the global circuit board. For those who are beneficiaries of global corporatism or have cosmopolitanism preferences this erosion of the world we have known is to be welcomed.

In short, without repeating previous arguments *in extensio* we have strongly argued that transnational ethnic, religious and even virtual communities, global social movements and global networks have already massively subverted state structures by going around and beyond them. Important as these social changes are, they do not necessarily constitute cosmopolitanism. Faith communities (like some militant sections of Christianity, Hinduism, Islam or Judaism) can be narrowing, rather than broadening, despite working in a transborder fashion. Right-wing movements drawing on Nazism and Fascism have been revived through global connections. And global networks (as we all know now) can promote terrorism, crime and the drugs trade. In a similar way Beck (2001) warns against 'a possible cosmopolitan fallacy':

The fundamental fact that the experiential space of the individual no longer coincides with the national space, but is being subtly altered by the opening to cosmopolitanism should not deceive one into believing that we are all going to become cosmopolitans. Even the most positive development imaginable, an opening of cultural horizons and a growing sensitivity to other unfamiliar, legitimate geographies of living and coexistence, need not necessarily stimulate a feeling of cosmopolitan responsibility. The question, how this might at all be possible, has hardly been properly put so far, never mind investigated. Actually cosmopolitization is about a dialectics of conflict: cosmopolitization *and its enemies* (Beck 2001, emphasis in original).

Its enemies remain and sometimes gather strength. Nationalism, along with a paradoxical combination of postmodern relativism (which celebrates identity) and fundamentalism (which celebrates exclusivity) are all reactions to the ultra-state practices of transnational communities, movements and networks. Transnational practices are, in short, a necessary but insufficient condition for the growth of a successful cosmopolitanism. Conviction, enthusiasm, organization and action are all needed to ratchet up a set of cosmopolitan practices to a new level. Only then can cosmopolitanism have a serious chance of superseding the old foci of loyalty.

The Futures of Cosmopolitanism

We need now to return to the primary purpose of this book. We have suggested that the revival of the term 'cosmopolitanism' has been marked by a considerable degree of conceptual and theoretical diversity, even confusion. So our first task was to provide a full conspectus of views on the nature, definition and prospects for cosmopolitanism as well as a clarification and explication of different cosmopolitan traditions. This task has been addressed in a number of ways, for example, by advancing new analytical frameworks and challenging old assumptions and representations.

Indeed, much literature surrounding the recent revitalization of the term has been produced precisely to displace the aloof, globetrotting bourgeois image of cosmopolitanism, in order to propose more progressive connotations. To do this, various writers have employed a range of adjectives to modify or refine the term (cf. Harvey 2000). Such qualified notions include 'discrepant cosmopolitanisms' (Clifford 1992, 1998), 'exclusionary cosmopolitanism' and 'inclusionary cosmopolitanism' (A. Anderson 1998), 'rooted cosmopolitanism' (Cohen 1992), 'oppositional cosmopolitanism' (Schein 1998*a,b*), 'eccentric or ex-orbitant cosmopolitanism' (Radhakrishnan 1995) and the seemingly strange hybrid notion, 'cosmopolitan communitarianism' (Bellamy and Castiglione 1998). We have generated a similarly long list when discussing the contexts in which cosmopolitanism, old and new, arises.

While the trend towards positively reappropriating notions of cosmopolitanism is to be welcomed for its socially and politically transformative potential, practically all the recent writings on the topic remain in the realm of rhetoric. There is little description or analysis of how contemporary cosmopolitan philosophies, political projects, outlooks or practices can be formed, instilled or bolstered. In short, there are few recipes for fostering cosmopolitanism (Vertovec 2000*a*). One important exception has been Nussbaum's (1994: 4) call for 'cosmopolitan education'. Such an educational agenda, forming the basis for shaping attitudes as well as institutions, would have among its goals to appreciate how common ends are variously instantiated in many cultures, to imagine vividly 'the different' based on a mastery of facts, and to stimulate in every person an overall 'process of world thinking'. In addition to the educational system, the fostering of cosmopolitanisms (that is cosmopolitanism understood through each rubric above and through their combination) is a process that would need to be located among a number of intermediary institutions in public space, including journals, conferences and political discussions (cf. Delanty 2001). The media, in their variety, also represent obvious sites for stimulating cosmopolitan awareness and highlighting cosmopolitan practices. To date, this has mostly been addressed through the media structures and programmes surrounding the presentation of cultural diversity or multiculturalism.

This lacuna, this lack of a political programme, is only briefly and imperfectly addressed (though at least it is recognized!) in Beck's (1998) three-page 'Cosmopolitan Manifesto', a conscious reference to the Communist Manifesto of 1848. Despite the undeveloped nature of its political project, we none the less are of the view that only a cosmopolitan outlook can accommodate itself to the political challenges of a more global era, marked by the overlapping communities of fate, multi-layered politics and new identity formations. Unlike political nationalism, cosmopolitanism registers and reflects the multiplicity of issues, questions, processes and problems that affect and bind people, irrespective of where they were born or reside. The theory and practice of cosmopolitanism have at least the potential to abolish the razor-wired camps, national flags and walls of silence that separate us from our fellow human beings.

Acknowledgements

Not only for help on this introduction, but for help on the book at large, warm thanks are due to the following: Our publisher at Oxford University Press, Dominic Byatt; the Press's anonymous readers; and to Anna Winton, Emma Newcombe and Selina Cohen for their editorial assistance. Our fellow editor at *Global Networks*, Alisdair Rogers, provided a creative mixture of practical suggestions and sage comments. This book arises from a conference and set of related activities associated with the Transnational Communities Research Programme of the Economic and Social Research Council (see www.transcomm.ox.ac.uk).

I

Windows on Cosmopolitanism

2

Political Belonging in a World of Multiple Identities

STUART HALL

Outlining some of the background thinking to the conference that preceded this volume, the editors identified what they called two strands within cosmopolitanism. They said, 'for some theorists, envisioning a politics of cosmopolitanism refers to possibilities surrounding global democracy and world citizenship. For some it means fostering new frameworks of alliance-making among social movements, locally and globally. Others who have invoked cosmopolitanism advocate a non-communitarian, post-identity politics of overlapping interest and heterogeneous or hybrid publics, and still others draw upon the term to challenge the conventional notions of belonging, identity and citizenship'.

The remarks that I want to make are really directed to the second concern. I am interested in what stands as a definition of political community and what stands as a definition of political belonging in a world in which transnational communities and transnational relations obviously bear directly and limit the possibilities of conceiving of those things within the framework of the nation-state alone. I am sensitive to the questions of global governance, but I want to address the consequences of that for thinking about the strategies of belonging-ness and identification within those political communities that are still left behind at the local and national level. I am thinking very much of the societies that arose as a consequence partly of globalization, partly of other economic factors, partly as a consequence of the end of the pressures of decolonization. In a world of constant movement, both forced and free, both at the centre and at the periphery of the global system, communities and societies are increasingly multiple in their nature. They are composed of communities with different origins, drawing on different traditions, coming from different places, obliged to make a life together within the confines still of a fixed territorial boundary or space while acknowledging that they are making a common life, not living a form of apartheid or separatism. They want, nevertheless, to retain in some sense the distinctiveness of their historical roots in the place in which they have ended up.

Is cosmopolitanism an alternative aspiration for the way in which political community and belongingness might be adequately expressed in that context? Here I want to say that I think there may be at least two versions of cosmopolitanism in play and I want to distinguish between the two of them. This may sound a bit like this weird experience of constantly being in search of 'the third way', but since there are so many 'third ways' around—this is about the fourteenth way—but whatever it is, it is a way that lies somewhere in between the two established alternatives.

What I want to call the strong or hard version of cosmopolitanism might run something like this, and I am basing myself on a classic article by Jeremy Waldron (1992), which looks at the cosmopolitan alternative in the context of migrants and migrating societies. It is an article that begins with his reflections on Salman Rushdie's *The Satanic Verses* (1988). In paraphrase, Waldron says of Rushdie:

> Here is someone that comes from what might be thought an ethnic or minority community. The whole thrust of his work and life is to refuse being bound by those definitions. The figures in Rushdie's book but what Rushdie has himself said about it, emphasises that this is a world in which only hybridity, mongrelization and the crossing of traditions are the sources of novelty. That is how newness enters the world. We are destined to live in that more decultured cosmopolitan universe and that is the only alternative we have.

Obviously this is a very important witness for Waldron—because it is all very well to be a cosmopolitan if you are a white American academic. However, to find a good Third World novelist, living in the First World, who affirms the cosmopolitan ideal so positively seems to kind of clinch the argument.

From the case that Waldron develops from this in favour of a kind of cosmopolitanism, I will try to identify the main points that he makes. He does not deny the importance of the role of culture, and thinking about choice, that is the choices we make (it would be impossible to think about that except embedded within a framework of cultural meanings). But, he adds, the world is not divided up neatly into particular distinct cultures wedded to every community. People need access to cultural meanings in order to live a life that is meaningful, but everyone does not need just one of these cultures, which is single, coherent, integrated and organic. Though he affirms that choice does take place in a cultural context, he argues that our cultural vocabularies and discourses are now drawn from a variety of cultural repertoires. It is not that we are without culture but we are drawing on the traces and residues of many cultural systems, of many ethical systems—and that is precisely what cosmopolitanism means. It means the ability to stand outside of having one's life written and scripted by any one community, whether that is a faith or tradition or religion or culture—whatever it might be—and to draw selectively on a variety of discursive meanings.

Waldron further affirms that in the context of that kind of cosmopolitanism, there is something artificial and absurd about the attempts to preserve and keep intact a single culture. One cannot preserve in full cultural identity and cultural rights. We need attachments but each person can have a variety, a multiplicity of these at their command. They need to stand outside them, to reflect on them and to dispense with them when they are no longer necessary. And this is a view of 'the cosmopolitan self', which is the only kind of self that is adequate to a modern cosmopolitan environment.

We can reflect for a minute on some of the points just made. I agree with Waldron about the centrality of the role of culture in choice and identity. We cannot establish identity without a cultural vocabulary, we are in that sense always culturally situated and embedded—embodied beings—but, equally, the world increasingly does not divide up neatly into particular, distinct cultures any longer. And I am certain that everyone, or most people, do not any longer need just one of them. So that in fact I would grant a great deal of the underlying framework of the cosmopolitan framework. Why then do I not simply say that the best thing for a mixed post-transnational community like the British one is to accept the waning of all the forms of the cultural community, which have been inherited from the past? Whether these forms are internal to the system or brought by those who have migrated to it they point people increasingly towards a more cosmopolitan way of living, of understanding themselves in this way and of appreciating their insertion into the outside world.

Liberal Universalism: A Critique

I do not go that far in pressing this case and the question is why not? If the argument in its simplest terms is not dressed up in a cosmopolitan framework, we can recognize that it has some clear antecedents. It is not very different from the framework of liberal universalism. It is, broadly speaking, assimilationist in its thrust, it does not say that people are not embedded in culture but it does say that as far as the public political culture is concerned the state should operate behind the veil of ignorance. It does say the state should be neutral with respect to the particularity of any culture or the particularity of any definition of the good life. It does, therefore, assume the ethical neutrality of the state, the unencumbered nature of the artificial liberal citizen, and so on. That is to say this is a recipe for a certain kind of cosmopolitan modernity. The question that I want to counterpose is this: 'Is this framework of liberal universalism the only and the best possible shell for cosmopolitan modernity'? Are there any other ways of societies being in the kind of world that we are in and accepting some of the premises behind the cosmopolitan case, and not as if it were living that within the broad framework of an assimilationist, liberal, universalist frame? I think there are.

I have two sets of objections to liberal universalism, one theoretical or conceptual and one empirical. I will start with the conceptual. Let us leave aside the problems that we know about the actual operations of such a system of liberal universalism in actually guaranteeing either freedom or equality to all the citizens from whatever background they came. I take that as read so we would have to do something about that, before cosmopolitan modernity was an advance on what we have in existence at the moment. I would add, however, that in spite of what Waldron says about all choice being embedded, this remains a notion of the individual and of communities that has an extremely thin and reductive notion of the nature of culture. It does not go so far as to see the individual self as not simply related in some cultural meanings but as dialogically constituted by the existence of the other. This is a much more radical conception of what individuality is about. Liberal universalism is also, I think, weak in its conception of tradition. It takes a kind of fixed notion of tradition as already constituted in authority, whereas in fact in the world that we know, traditions do not on the whole function like that. There are conditions in which traditions actually lose their main purpose, which is to provide a framework within which argument and exploration can take place. Instead of promoting a kind of conceptual or dialogical discursive framework, traditions become immured in authority; they become doctrinal. That is when tradition has lost its efficacy. Instead of sustaining the discursive exploration of life, it is drawing life to a halt. Liberal universalism does not sufficiently recognize that healthy tradition is continuously changing, responding to the new circumstances in which it is embedded and finds itself, and is constantly revising itself in the light of those conditions.

As to the neutral state, one could discuss this at great length. I simply want to say that I do not believe and I have never believed in the pure notion of the civic national state. I do not know a single national state that evinces a fully civic nationalism. Every civic nationalism I know requires belongingness on the part of its citizens; it requires identification. Identification cannot be constructed in relation to a political system alone; it has to be constructed on cultural meanings. It has to be embedded, that is to say, in an imagined community. As well as the loyalty that they evoke on the part of the citizen (that is rational loyalty to the political institutions), states also call on the imaginative identification with certain cultural particularities. It is not possible to understand 'American' without understanding 'the American way of life'. In the same way it is not possible even now to understand what Britain could be without trying to understand, with increasing difficulty, what indeed Englishness ever was or can be, or shall be in the future. So, the notion that civic nationalism can proceed as it were, cutting itself off from any understanding of the cultural embeddedness of the citizens on whom its legitimacy rests, just seems to me to be nonsensical. I'm not suggesting that everybody is immured inside his or her own particularity, but I am suggesting that this is the kind of abstractional fantasy at a social level.

I will halt the critique a little prematurely. I have not got to the point where I wanted to show how Western societies rewrite their particularity as universalism.

Despite claims to the contrary, even in Western societies there was no mass global conversion to the universal rule of reason. Instead we can observe a much dirtier, Foucaultian, power–knowledge kind of game. The particularities find themselves exalted into what all rational human beings want to do or think is right. Think about this society [Britain] in this respect. Think about the degree to which this society is founded on a Protestant ascendancy in spite of the fact that it is not supposed to have a religious basis. Without understanding the Protestant ascendancy of the formation of the United Kingdom we could not explain why Englishness has never been able, imaginatively, to encompass Irishness. Nor could we explain why the Anglo-Saxon rather than the Celtic tradition has always been favoured, or Englishness over Britishness. The moment you get into how these societies actually operate to hold the allegiances of their citizens together, you get into the complexity of their particularities.

I am not suggesting that, therefore, all societies and states are just the open play of rival interests, let alone that we go back to the wars of religious intolerance. I am not suggesting that we have not moved as a consequence of requiring the state to hold itself apart from simply being at the mercy of vested interest. What I am suggesting is that there is a kind of artificial fantasy about the notion that the state could ever, in any literal sense, be neutral and abstracted from cultural values. We therefore have a dilemma. We have a form of cosmopolitanism that requires the whole baggage of liberal universalism. Many of the points cosmopolitanism makes in response to a strong version of communitarianism will not hold, but we cannot resolve the problems into a simple acceptance of liberal universalism as the framework within which cosmopolitanism can operate. What is the alternative? I have no time to elaborate in detail but I would say two things very quickly. One is empirical and one is a programmatic sketch.

The empirical question is this. Think about the communities that migrated into Britain in the 1950s. While they are strongly culturally marked, they have never been separatist, they have never formed ghettos, their relation to their formal traditions and places of origin are still extremely important in terms of their self understanding. At the same time they have the widest lateral connections with everyday life around them, with the secular life around them, with neighbourhood life, with economic life, with political life, and so forth. They require many of the same things of the state at the same time as requiring their capacity in their own domestic, private, religious and other circumstances, to maintain their differences. That is to say we are no longer in a world in which liberal universalism can dominate, but we are also not in a world that is segmented in terms of specific, well-bounded, tightly knit, organic, isolated cultures or communities either. We are in that absolutely, extremely difficult, open situation to characterize where the communities matter but could not possibly be enfranchised in their own right, because that would simply mean that they started to police everybody. From the inside of these communities many people now hold exactly the double consciousness one would expect. What they say is: 'Our parents are perfectly right to maintain the customs and religious beliefs that they have; it is just not for me. But they have a right to their ways. I simply don't want all my life to be bounded by that. I don't want them to police me with communal norms, but that is not because community doesn't matter'.

(You may say this is like having your cake and eating it and I do believe that is what it is.)We witness the situation of communities that are not simply isolated, atomistic individuals, nor are they well-bounded, singular, separated communities.(We are in that open space that requires a kind of vernacular cosmopolitanism, that is to say a cosmopolitanism that is aware of the limitations of any one culture or any one identity and that is radically aware of its insufficiency in governing a wider society, but which nevertheless is not prepared to rescind its claim to the traces of difference, which make its life important.)

How can such a mixed situation, which is in transition and constantly moving from one generation to the next, be expressed in political terms? I would simply say that I think one could find a way of doing this if one is prepared to venture beyond the existing political vocabularies(What such a situation requires is what political theorists tell us is impossible, the combination of equality and difference.)Now you cannot have all the equality or all the difference but you can have programmes and strategies of self-government and of governments in general, of the provision of resources, which are sensitive to the double demand of equality and difference. You can have societies that recognize the importance of community and culture at the same time as acknowledging the liberal limit on communitarianism—that is to say the right of individuals to say no to the cultures they think should continue to exit while maintaining their communities' viability. This should not be so surprising because for most of us cosmopolitanism has involved and has a continued relationship to our family cultures. You think they are tremendously important, you would not dream of being bound by them any longer, you prize the moment when you left them but you know that as you leave them they continue to support you. They continue to be what you are. You could not be what you are without that struggle both to defend them and to exit from them. So, though this is not a logical political position, it is actually an existential political position we all perfectly well understand.

In addition to that there are only two other things that you need to do. One is you have to decide that if there is some way in which these different communities have to live together you do have to say what is the framework within which one is going to be judged to be good or right and the other put down. What is the framework in which this society is going to negotiate the compromises between difference and equality, which enables society to enhance life's choices? That means a certain requirement of forms of agnostic democratic process is absolutely intrinsic to this position because without them there would be no way of coming to some decision as to how you might find a horizon within which the

contending or contesting differences could be reconciled. And the other requirement would be, of course, that everybody should have access to this process of
democratic negotiation. Consequently, the vestiges of exclusion, whether racial,
ethnic, religious, sexual or gendered, would have to be the principal way in which
such a cosmopolitan vernacular society underpins the ability of all its citizens to
enter the dialogue about what the political good might be.

3

Middle Eastern Experiences of Cosmopolitanism

SAMI ZUBAIDA

Arab and Muslim empires, like their predecessors and successors, brought together many peoples and cultures and established imperial centres that in their heydays comprised thriving artistic, literary and commercial cultures, aspects of which can be described as cosmopolitan. The Abbasid court, for instance, at its golden age in the eighth and ninth centuries, created such a cosmopolitan milieu mixing the Arab religion with the Persian culture and statecraft, patronizing poets and philosophers. It was this cosmopolitan milieu that scandalized the pious Arabs who constructed the 'legalist' *shari'a* tradition. The conflict between the philosophers, with wide cultural horizons, and the jurists insisting on the authority of scriptures and traditions, which arose in that period, was to constitute the paradigm for contests to follow through much of Muslim history.

Cosmopolitan milieux also arose at various points of the Muslim period in Spain (the eighth to the fifteenth centuries). Especially poignant in the subsequent nostalgic romance of al-Andalus (as Arab Spain was called) was the twelfth century Cordova of Ibn Rushd (Averros), who translated Aristotle (a translation that was to be eagerly followed in contemporary Christian Europe), and incorporated Greek philosophy into the Muslim sciences. Ibn Rushd and his milieu were the subject of the recent Franco–Egyptian film *Destiny* (1998) by Yusuf Shahin, a romantic (and idealized) celebration of cosmopolitan and liberal moments of the Muslim past, in which the zealous fundamentalists are ultimately defeated (allegories on the present), and the values of social and cultural mixing between the religions and the cultures are upheld. The Jewish philosopher and medic Maimonides of thirteenth-century Spain and Egypt is another such figure of cosmopolitan celebration, as is the later (fourteenth century) Ibn

This 'window' is extracted from earlier papers published by the author as 'Cosmopolitanism in the Middle East' *Amsterdam Middle East Papers* 12: Dec. (1997); and in Meijer (1999) *Cosmopolitanism, Identity and Authenticity in the Middle East*. London: Curzon.

Khaldun, the author of the *Muqaddima*, a much admired philosophy of history, considered by many, including Ernest Gellner, to be a forerunner of sociology and political science, much like Machiavelli. These were not solitary figures but the products of a particular milieux of cultural effervescence and hybridity.

Did the processes of modernity also succeed in creating cosmopolitan milieux in the Middle East, similar or parallel to those in Europe? Did a process of deracination from caste, community and religion occur in the modern Middle East along the lines described by Mannheim (1936/1960) in the European case? We know that the closures of religio-communal boundaries have continued in the region, much as they have done elsewhere, including many parts of Europe (witness the tragedy of the former Yugoslavia). The question is: were there sufficient breaks in these boundaries to allow the development of what may be identified as cosmopolitan milieux? My answer is affirmative, and what follows is a sketchy exploration of these processes.

The Ottoman Empire included many peoples and lands, for the most part organized in self-regulating communities, guilds, military units (such as the Janissaries) and groupings of scholars, scribes and functionaries. While there was a fair degree of social mobility, these were occupational rather than across communal lines, and mostly confined to Sunni Muslims. This mobility, however, was into well-defined and bonded groupings, such as guilds, bureaucracies and scholarly occupations with their distinctive discourses, practices and loyalties, much like the guilds and the scholarly stratum in Medieval Europe. Until the nineteenth century, any small pockets of what may be seen as cosmopolitan milieux must have been confined to the higher echelons of Istanbul society (and maybe to some other centres in the Empire, such as Salonika) of patrician merchants, diplomats and courtiers.

It was the 'European impact' (a euphemism for conquest and military-economic dominance) that made its effect felt in particular corners of Ottoman societies in the nineteenth century. Particular aspects of this impact led to the formation of social milieux and personalities that may be identified as cosmopolitan. The attempt of the Ottoman rulers to 'catch up' with European technico-military and economic superiority included European education and training for new or transformed elites of the military and of the high functionaries. Some of these were sent to European centres (mostly France where they established an Ottoman school in Paris); others were educated in new European-style schools in Constantinople. Education, of course, cannot be confined to its technical aspects, but inevitably leads to exposure to sociopolitical and cultural ideas and models. The Ottoman ethos, like that of any other imperial civilization, was based on a firm conviction of the superiority of Islam, both as a religion and in the wider civilizational/cultural sense, over the Christian civilizations of Europe, its historical antagonists. The realization of the economic and military superiority of Europe by the nineteenth century shook this conviction, at least for sectors of the intelligentsia. Those who got to know

Europe, though critical of some aspects of its societies, were mostly dazzled, not only by its material achievements, but also crucially by its forms of order and what lay behind that order in philosophy and political organization (Mitchell 1988). Responses varied from the wish for a wholesale incorporation of European models to the assertion of the superiority of some original pure Islam, corrupted and subverted by tyranny and superstition, but whose restoration to original purity would bring about reforms and transformations to rival Europe (and look remarkably like its models of constitutionalism and liberty).

Aside from the ideologico-political debates and conflicts that surrounded the reform measures (*Tanzimat*) and Mehmet-Ali's more authoritarian reforms in Egypt, were the social and cultural milieux, which emerged as a result of transformations of elites and the mixing with European models. Serif Mardin's (1962) account of the intellectuals and functionaries in the middle decades of the nineteenth century, who came to be known as Young Ottomans, shows a pattern of associations, ideas and movements (including much travel to Europe and elsewhere, whether on business or exile) that suggests a cosmopolitan milieu. Some of Mannheim's (1936/1960) factors can be found here: intellectuals who are culturally deracinated from confident traditional perspectives on the world, yet unhappy with the dominant European perspectives, trying to invent their own world, but in the middle of sociopolitical upheavals in which they actively participate. All this occurred with styles of life, which oscillate between the Ottoman and the European, with patterns of personal relationships, cultural mixes and a geographic compass that suggests 'cosmopolitanism'.

Most of the Young Ottomans started their careers at the Translation Bureau of the Porte, products of modern schools and foreign environments. Some of them, like Namik Kemal, were from traditional scholarly families that were impoverished by the sweeping socio-economic transformations. Kemal was a poet, essayist and political philosopher, deeply influenced by European currents: he translated Montesquieu, debated Voltaire and Condorcet, followed the nationalist models of Garibaldi and Mazzini (the Young Turks had personal and political connections with Italian nationalists). Kemal, and many of the others, spent periods of exile in Paris, London and Geneva, where they published the journals that were prohibited in Istanbul, intriguing with patrons and factions in and out of government. Intellectually and politically this is cosmopolitan by any definition. Yet, Kemal was firmly attached to the idea that a revived Islam and its *Shari'a* must form the basis of society and government. He tried to find Islamic idioms for expressing the main ideas and concepts of the Enlightenment, of Rousseau, Montesquieu and the Natural Law tradition. He was highly critical of the ruling functionaries of the Porte for their blind imitation of Europe, in parties and balls in which their women dressed in *décolletée* gowns. Yet, Kemal himself was known for his drinking, and alcoholism was one of the risks of his circle.

Jamaleddin al-Afghani

Many members of the Ottoman elites, politicians and high functionaries and including some Young Ottomans, became members of Freemason lodges, first started by Europeans with rival lodges in which political and personal factions and intrigues and European powers' interests were pursued.[1] A similar situation prevailed in Egypt in the nineteenth and twentieth centuries. The most renowned Muslim reformer of the time, Jamaleddin al-Afghani, Asadabadi to the Iranians, (1838–97) was a member (by some reports a Master) of such a lodge in Egypt. We have in the figure of Jamaleddin a remarkable cosmopolitan.

There is some mystery surrounding the figure of Afghani. The designation 'Afghani' has been widely challenged by historians, in favour of an Iranian origin, hence Asadabadi (Keddie 1968/1983). It is thought that he adopted an Afghani identity to dissimulate his Shi'i origins in the Sunni world in which he operated. He first appeared on the scene in British India, where he acquired some European education and formed his political and philosophical orientations. He then set off on a career of religious and political preaching and agitation. He proceeded from Afghanistan to Istanbul to Iran, then Egypt, then London and Paris, then back to Iran and ultimately to Istanbul where he spent the last years of his life. He exerted his greatest influence in Egypt in the 1870s. Like the Young Ottomans, Afghani's pan-Islamism was aimed at the restoration of Islam to its pristine origins, which would then make it superior to European creeds in political order and civilization. The reforms aimed for, however, would result in the polity, the law and society looking remarkably like idealized European models. Politically, his objective was a pan-Islamic unity, which, armed with reformed religion, society and polity, would stand up to European domination, and revive the strength and glory of historical Islam. Like all reformers of his time, he sought to influence elites, primarily the princes and kings of Islam. These welcomed him at first, flattered by his attentions, but soon realized the import of his advocacy and sought to get rid of him. At this point he turned to the dissident intellectuals and constitutionalists to propagate his ideas, which landed him in exile.

The cosmopolitanism of Afghani spans not only the European–Muslim boundaries, but also inter-Muslim cultures. He operated between British India, Iran, Egypt and Turkey, as well as the European capitals and knew Persian, Turkish and Arabic, as well as English and French. He debated with the Indian Muslim reformers and the Arab Azharites (the leading Muslim university, located in Cairo), and his best-known work was a polemic with the French

---

[1] Note that at that time Freemasonry in the Middle East was associated with freethinking and political dissent. Its secrecy made it ever more suspect to the traditional authorities of state and religion, though many princes and ministers became members to further their political intrigues.

Ernest Renan. In this work, Afghani advances a rationalist explanation of the formation and history of religion and of its social functions, arguments that led to accusations of 'atheism' by opponents in the Muslim world and by European commentators who sought to detract from the reformist project (see Kedourie 1966/1997). His cosmopolitanism extended to elements in the style of life and culture. Apart from his membership of Masonic lodges, he was also known to frequent cafés and clubs, to drink alcohol (he was fond of cognac) and rumoured to have illicit sexual encounters. Recent Arab historians who wrote on these aspects of his life, specially his Freemasonry, have been attacked by orthodox Muslims who still claim him as an ancestor of their reforms.

Afghani was only a prominent example of this genre of cosmopolitanism that thrived in the late nineteenth and into the first half of the twentieth century in the major metropoles of the Middle East, especially Istanbul, Cairo and Alexandria. Let us turn to the mixes that made this phenomenon.

Cosmopolitanism in the Nineteenth and Early Twentieth Centuries

In the course of the nineteenth and early twentieth centuries, the processes of opening up formerly closed communities, of education, printing and migrations, created new spaces and ingredients for cosmopolitanism, primarily in Istanbul and the Egyptian cities.

First, the *millet*s, the corporate communities of Christians and Jews, underwent dramatic transformations. Part of the *Tanzimat* legislation decreed the formal equality of the subjects of the Sultan before the law irrespective of their religion. This was the culmination of a long period of 'protection' by the European powers of these communities, and the participation of many of their richer and more educated members in European consulates and enterprises, some acquiring European nationalities and the privileges that went with them. The formal equality before the law, however, though a dead letter for most of the poorer members of these communities on the fringes of the empire, was nevertheless an avenue for the participation of the intelligentsias of these communities in Ottoman public life. This was accompanied by a process of the 'secularization' of some Christian communities from control by religious authorities and traditional elders to democratically elected councils in which the intelligentsia and the rich came to prominence.

The intellectual and business milieux produced by these mixes were located in a wide range of institutions and circles. Missionary schools (specially Protestant missions, which were subversive of the traditional authorities of Orthodox and Catholic prelates) did not only bring European languages and ideas, but, in Syria-Lebanon, stimulated the revivals in Arabic language and letters, and founded the first printing presses in that language (see Hourani 1983).

The journals, reviews and books produced by these milieux were marked by the excitement of discovery and renewal through the stimulus of European ideas and technique and the renewal (or invention) of past glories. Consulates, enterprises and partnerships played similar roles for the business communities, and the lowering (but never demise) of communal barriers allowed the social and cultural confluence of personnel, ideas and institutions across the communal divides.

It was also during this period that many Syrian Christians, intellectuals and entrepreneurs, migrated to the freer domains of British dominated Egypt. Some played an important part in nascent Egyptian journalism, and played their part in the political effervescence of the time, between Ottomanism and Islam, and the pro-British versus Egyptian nationalist camps.

The cosmopolitan enclaves of Egypt had been formed over the course of the nineteenth century. Mehmet Ali imported cadres of European experts and entrepreneurs, as well as instituting elite European schools and scholarships to European destinations. The cultivation, manufacture and trade in cotton as well as of the military industry, attracted further influxes of resident foreigners. European, as well as Syrian-Lebanese and Turkish influxes into Egypt were stimulated later in the century, especially with the ambitious construction and urban projects of Khedive Ismail, including the building of the Suez Canal and the rebuilding of Cairo. Concessions to the dominant European powers, now also the debtors of an increasingly bankrupt state, resulted in many privileges for European and foreign businesses, including the Mixed Tribunals, civil courts with judges and lawyers from the different powers involved to adjudicate in cases involving mixed transactions. The subsequent British occupation and rule of Egypt (starting in 1882) gave rise to many more cultural, legal and institutional mixes, as well as stimulating further European and Levantine migrations. It was the cumulation of these processes that established the legendary cosmopolitan enclaves in Cairo, but specially Alexandria, the paradigm case of Middle Eastern cosmopolitanism, celebrated in many literary and artistic works, notably Durrell's famous *Alexandria Quartet* (1962), the stuff of subsequent nostalgia.

This was the golden age of Middle Eastern cosmopolitanism. The political context was that of European imperial dominance. The First World War, the defeat of the Ottomans, the occupation of Istanbul and much of its old territories by the triumphant allies may have given a further twist to this imperial-linked cosmopolitanism. It also illustrates the reason for the nationalist and religious reactions against it. The subsequent nostalgia for this golden age conveniently forgets its imperial context. Cosmopolitan Alexandria, for instance, included a rigorous system of exclusions for native Egyptians, including segregation or exclusion on buses and trams, and certainly from clubs, some bars and cafés and many social milieux. Native Egyptian society provided servants, functionaries and prostitutes for the cosmopolitan milieu. They were inferior-ized and despised. It was no coincidence then that the Muslim Brotherhood was founded in 1928 in Ismailiya, in the Canal Zone, and had as its founding pro-gramme the rescue of Muslim youth from the corruption of European domi-nance, of drink and prostitution, and it is no wonder that it found an echo in Egyptian society.

Egypt in the first half of the twentieth century thus witnessed a flourishing of intellectual and artistic movements and milieux as well as religious and nativist reactions against them. The new Egyptian university, a lively press, the film industry, an artistic and musical renaissance and intellectual opening, all looked to the wider world for inspiration and innovation. Taha Hussein, a prominent figure in Egyptian letters, declared the Pharaonic and Hellenistic roots of Egyptian culture: it was to the Mediterranean world that it must look for its future. The 1932 Congress of Arab Music in Cairo, attended by musicians and theorists from the Arab world, but also major European figures such as the composers Bela Bartok and Paul Hindemith, debated the links between tradition and modernity, particularism and universality. Paradoxically, it was Bartok who defended traditional music against the Arab modernists who proclaimed the decadence of the old, and the necessity to innovate and evolve in line with the general progress of society and the opening to universal trends and values. The British anthropologist E. Evans-Pritchard gave his seminal lectures on primitive religion at the Egyptian University. The films portrayed a universe of romance and music in social settings contrasting the old and the new, the popular quarters and the Europeanized suburbs. This cultural mix and excitement was cosmopolitan in a much more profound sense than the celebrated European–Levantine milieu of Alexandria.

Cosmopolitanism in the Contemporary Period

Our own time is marked by the most profound technical revolution in global communications, which transcends national and cultural boundaries. At the level of the common people, television soaps from Hollywood, Bombay and South America are beamed into every home and followed with passion. This is accompanied by international patterns of mass consumption with global brand names that have become symbolic (Levi Jeans, McDonald's and Coca-Cola being the most prominent). At the technical and institutional levels the Internet is conquering ever more frontiers: even the most repressive and isolationist Middle Eastern states are looking into ways of participating with controls. Add to that the enormous explosion in tourism, travel, commerce, international media and the translation/publishing industries to arrive at impressive cross-cultural transactions and mixes.

Side by side with this cultural globalization, we have the most xenophobic and intolerant manifestations of narrow nationalisms and religious revivals, of which political Islam is the most prominent in our region. Does cultural globalization represent heightened cosmopolitanism? And is the xenophobia of political Islam a reaction?

I would argue that the manifestations of cultural globalism have transcended the 'problematique' of cosmopolitanism. The context of the cosmopolitanisms of the first half of this century were networks and milieux of intellectuals, artists, dilettantes and *flaneurs* in urban centres, deracinated, transcending recently impermeable communal and religious boundaries, daring and experimenting. Or, at least, that was the projected image, one that defined identities and outlooks. These kinds of networks and milieux persist, and are probably more extensive than ever before. In the age of cultural globalism, however, they have been 'routinized', lost their special identities and charismatic images. At the same time, global communications of television, the Internet and other media, do not necessarily breach communal and particularistic boundaries and spaces. People receive foreign soap operas in their own homes or neighbourhood cafés, dubbed into their own language. They consume them in terms of their own constructions of meanings and life worlds.

In another global context, international business creates its own uniform milieux, with its executives and personnel travelling the world and residing in diverse centres, but always in the same hotel rooms, apartments, served by Filipina maids, and networks of sociability of colleagues and associates of the same formations. Tourism similarly creates its own milieux: at the cheaper levels, resorts, hotels, entertainments and food, which strive for standardization from Benidorm to Bodrum. Up-market tourists pay for a touch of exoticism and local colour, often constructed within the safe and hygienic confines of their hotels: witness the constructions of popular cafés and souks in the Cairo Nile Hilton, complete with Ramadhan nights if you happen to stay during the blessed month. What is intriguing is that these constructions are not just for tourists but attract the native prosperous classes, who also like to engage in ersatz exoticism without rubbing shoulders with their poor compatriots.

Where does political Islam stand in relation to these developments? There are, of course, many ideological varieties of political Islam with widely varying stances on what is to be included under 'Western cultural invasion'. Mainstream groups have generally maintained that science, technology and, for some, business relations, are to be welcomed, whereas cultural values and products are to be excluded. Broadcasting, the media, computers and the Internet have been actively embraced by Islamists for propagation of materials and for organization, often at an international level. At the same time, like the tyrants of the region, they have deplored the uses of these media for the diffusion of disapproved items. But the nature of these media, specially satellite broadcasting and the Internet, are making censorship increasingly difficult.

Like all nationalisms, political Islam rejects old-fashioned cosmopolitanism: the personal and cultural mixing across communal boundaries, the cultural products of this mixing, the urban spaces utilized, often with drink and the mixing of the sexes (with suspected sexual laxity), all anathema to religious Puritanism and the quest for communal authenticity. Examples from Turkey will illustrate some interesting confrontations in these respects.

In the 1994 municipal elections the Islamist Refah Partisi gained control in many major cities, including Istanbul and Ankara. Beyoglu, the central entertainments and arts quarter of Istanbul, elected a Refah mayor, to the shock and disgust of the Istanbul bourgeoisie. The electorate were predominantly poor people, Anatolian migrants, in the marginal habitations that have spread throughout the city, including Beyoglu. The first worry was that the new regime would try to restrict the bars and entertainments that thrive in the area and that are the home to many artistic and 'Bohemian' circles, the stuff of old-fashioned cosmopolitanism. Indeed, in the first weeks of the Refah regime, there were attempts to prevent drinking on the street terraces of bars and cafés, and to force bars to erect thick curtains that would hide the spectacle of drinking from passers-by. These measures were greeted with loud expressions of indignation, culminating in defiant demonstrations of street drinking. Eventually, the mayor had to withdraw quietly in the face of influential secular (*laiklik*) opinion (and some say the threats from the mafias that protect the bars). But this was in the context of the weakness of municipal authorities facing the watchful Kemalist interests in the army, the state and the media, a balance that may change in future years. In Egypt, where there are no such powerful secular forces and where the government is ever appeasing conservative and respectable Islamism, the Islamic censors have been much more successful in restricting drinking and cultural production alike, and the urban spaces that go with them.

Nostalgia for the cosmopolitanism of previous decades is a notable feature of the response of the secular intelligentsia and the Europeanized bourgeoisie to the ruralization of their cities and the concomitant challenge of Islamic advocacy. A striking example is the Tunisian film *Summer at la Goulette*, made in the 1990s and portraying the life of a cosmopolitan seaside suburb of Tunis in the early 1950s. The story is of the life of three families and their teenage children, one Muslim, one Jewish and one Italian, their work, love, celebrations and conflicts, all good fun. The only 'bad' character is the rich and religious uncle of the Muslim family who is a ruthless and greedy landlord and a lecher, lusting after the sexy young daughter and persecuting the family for refusing his offer of marriage. The thrust of the film is clearly directed against the xenophobia and (hypocritical) Puritanism of nationalism and then Islamism, which brought this idealized cosmopolitanism to an end. In the streets of Beyoglu in 1994, with the

Islamists in the electoral ascendance, the music blaring from the record stores was Rebetika, the Taverna and low-life Greek songs from the Istanbul of the 1930s and 1940s. Many voices in the cafés and bars were to be heard protesting the cosmopolitan destiny of Istanbul and denouncing the 'barbarian' invasion of Anatolians and their brand of Islam.

Conclusion

Cosmopolitanism in the Middle East, in the old-fashioned sense of communally deracinated and culturally promiscuous groups and milieux, continues to exist in particular corners of urban space. These, however, are submerged by the two major forces of the metropolis: the recently urbanized masses and their transformation of the city and its politics; and forces of international capital, of business and tourism and their towering buildings, hotels and offices, their media and the consumption goods and images for which they cater.

Mass higher education produces a proletarianized, poorly educated intelligentsia, poor and resentful, directing its 're-sentiment' against the Westernized elites, seen as the agents of cultural invasion. These are the main cadres of nationalist and religious xenophobia, currently so powerful in the region. While some degree of liberalization has benefited the cultural production in Egypt and elsewhere in recent decades, these limited gains have been very insecure, specially now that they are threatened by religious censorship and intimidation, which also extend to the urban spaces, such as cafés and bars, which form the social milieux of intellectuals and artists. It is not surprising, therefore, that the main cultural flourishing of Middle Eastern cosmopolitanism now occurs in London and Paris.

4

Cosmopolitanism and the Social Experience of Cities

RICHARD SENNETT

Cosmopolitanism has a very different cast when you think about it in terms, not so much of political theory, but of social experience and particularly in terms of the social experience of cities. The dynamics of what we mean by cosmopolitanism, its opposites and its internal contradictions are very differently structured. Once you actually take an institution like the city, the link between cosmopolitan and cosmopolitanism is obviously a very particular one.

Here, I am concerned with how the concept or understanding of cosmopolitanism has changed within the context of urban life during the course of this century. I want to peg the problematics of cosmopolitanism that appeared to people like Georg Simmel or the founding members of the Chicago School of Urban Studies—people like Robert Park and Louis Wirth at the beginning of the twentieth century—to the kind of dynamics of cosmopolitanism that face urbanists like myself today.

Basically, I want to argue that when the first modern, urban discussions of cosmopolitanism began there was an attempt to sort out a dialectic between what could be called strangeness and rigidity or, to put it in technical jargon, between alterity and bureaucratic rationalization. How did these two phenomena coexist in this city?

That dialectic has in the course of time achieved something quite different, namely the dialectic between flexibility and indifference. What I want to argue about this is that changes in modern capitalism have made this shift occur in the urban formulations of cosmopolitanism. The capitalism that the generation of Simmel or Walter Benjamin in Germany, or Simmel's students Park and Wirth in the United States of America knew, was an increasingly bureaucratizing capitalism, a capitalism that set the terms for the kinds of experiences of cosmopolitanism in the city that a very different kind of capitalism today, a more flexible anti-bureaucratic capitalism, is setting for a different kind of dynamic in modern urban discussions of cosmopolitanism.

Readers of Simmel will know that when he looked into the Potsdamer Platz in Berlin, he wrote in a letter to a friend: 'As I look out into this teeming square what I understand is that the city is the site of strangeness'. The word he uses in German should really be translated into our English term 'alterity'. This is because what he saw when he looked into the Potsdamer Platz in 1908 was a world of people he could not classify. The migrants who came to Berlin at that time were, to Berliners who had lived in the city before, a people who were unknown—Poles who did not look like the Poles they knew from Warsaw, peasants coming from the south of Germany who spoke dialects they could not understand, and so on. The distinction between difference and alterity has to do with the possibility of classifying strangers in terms of difference versus the possibility of the unknown other. What Simmel understood about this stranger, understood as a force of alterity, was that this had a profoundly provoking quality to it. As Benjamin would later argue, the notion of the unknown had a kind of force, a kind of power of arousal in crowds. It was much greater than a crowd of differences in which one knew who was there, what class they belonged to, where they came from, their race, their styles of life and so on. When these first urbanists talked about cosmopolitanism, they understood that the problematic character of urban crowds was created by the emotional charge that people felt in them. For example, the *flaneur* in Benjamin's account immerses himself in a Paris that is both a puzzle that cannot be deduced and something that is compellingly attractive. Thus, the quality of cosmopolitanism for these urbanists at that time had to do with the notion of being engaged by the unknown. That is what cosmopolitanism meant.

What they had to set against this was that, for Simmel and in a different way for Joyce or Proust, the stranger is a bearer of a new kind of freedom. When you plunge into a crowd of people who cannot be categorized, you are dislodged from your own subjective categories of difference. You are released from your own mental set of reading social relations. The cosmopolitan adds the quality of a bringer of freedom through a kind of dislocation wrought by virtue of experiencing the stranger.

This is not an analoid condition. The dialectic for Simmel, as for his American students Park and Wirth, was that curiously, we almost could say paradoxically, the experience of alterity is taking place in a city whose capitalistic forum is working towards an ever-greater bureaucratic rigidification and solidification of capitalist enterprise. I love quoting Simmel's letters because they are so beautiful. In another letter Simmel looks outside another window, this time into the Pariser Platz: 'I look at buildings that signal to me that they ought to be about government but they are insurance agencies'. The physical constitution of the solid form of the city now begins to realize these rationalized bureaucracies, as Max Weber called them, which find a kind of physical location and institutionalization in this city.

Weber famously compared the structure of army life with the development of capitalism at the end of the nineteenth century. In fact, one reason why he contested Marx's image of capitalism was because all that is solid melts into air. What Weber was seeing under the growth of monopoly capitalism and large-scale bureaucracy was just the physical opposite of that, which was the same thing for the students of Weber and Simmel who started the Chicago School. A skyscraper for them was a monument not to the instability of capitalism but to its physical implantation—a giant object of a scale and determination unlike any form of building known before. The unfolding of this bureaucratic capitalism, this monopoly capitalism that planted itself in the city so physically, was a paradox for these urbanists because this form of bureaucratic capitalism was also seen as a form of cosmopolitanism. In other words, it was a revelation of the division of labour, articulated, defined, made literally solid in these building types. We seldom think about cosmopolitanism with reference to the accounts provided by Adam Smith. But for Smith the division of labour was a principle of differentiation and of difference making in the economy. And for Weber and Simmel that articulation of difference was now solidified in the city and made permanent in these bureaucracies. This created another kind of definition of cosmopolitanism.

So, at the beginning of the formal understanding of the city as a capitalist city a century ago there were two contrasting orders of cosmopolitanism, one based on alterity, the other on rigidity or rational bureaucracy. The problems those urbanists had were both tangible. One was constituted by the crowds of the city, which were unreadable and illegible. They were also inaudible with people speaking languages nobody understood. The same would have been true of New York in 1910 when English was a language spoken only by 18 per cent of the population. So that dimension of the unknown constituted one kind of cosmopolitanism smack up with a second notion. The capitalist system has an entirely different dialectic, a dynamic of difference embodied in its bureaucratic rigidity. The problem was how to put these two forms of cosmopolitanism together.

Urbanists today face a very different set of understandings and problematics in the notion of cosmopolitanism. The resolution come to by someone like Louis Wirth, who in my view is probably the most under-recognized social theorist of the twentieth century, was that one reconciles alterity and rigidity, or alterity and rationality, with a notion of temporary identification. People moved through the offices or zones of the city that were articulated in this rationalized fashion and temporarily took on the attributes of the places in which they worked, shopped or lived, but there would be no single durable identity. Wirth called this the segmented role theory of passage through the city, so basically the mediator of these two versions of cosmopolitanism is the notion of not what Stuart Hall would call a hybrid identity so much as a kind of temporal limit on identity. This posits that identities are 'short' in cities. This is a very interesting idea.

Flexibility and Indifference

Now the kind of world of migration from country to city, from country to country, from nation to city, and certainly the economic world of capitalism that Weber saw, is a world that is undoing itself in the modern city. In place of this dialectic between alterity and rationality or rigidity there is another kind of dialectic coming into being that really sets the terms for modern urbanists' thinking about what we mean when talking about the cosmopolitan. This is the dialectic between flexibility and indifference.

To understand this duality, I have to say that to understand modern capitalism simply in terms of globalization, in terms of global labour and capital flows, is insufficient to account for what has happened. There has also been a kind of revolution in the organization of institutions that cannot simply be explained by migration of labour or capital, which is a kind of revolt against the Weberian world of fixed organizations. One way of thinking about this is in terms of the search for flexible capitalist forums, in which there are some of the same qualities in the economy of alterity. There are high degrees of risk taking in which you do not know what the outcomes will be, groups of workers feeling comfortable about working short term with unknown or unknowable colleagues whom they are only going to work with on that task. This kind of institutional revolution in the conditions of modern capitalism seems to me to be as important, though it is often overlooked in talking about the effect of modern capitalism on cities, as the more obvious features of global flows of labour and capital.

So, when I use the term 'flexibility' I am not merely talking about the capacity to transmit labour and capital easily across borders from city to city; I am also talking about the institutional structures of both work and welfare in the city itself in which there is an attempt to break down this Weberian notion of a kind of fixed division of labour.

I would like to advance three ideas about what this new dialectic between flexibility and indifference looks like. The first is something that is very familiar to us in terms of discourses of globalization and it is a crisis in citizenship; particularly at the top of this new capitalist system, the global inhabitants of modern cities tend to use the city as a space for economic activity without any desire to participate in it as citizens. There is a kind of crisis of democratic participation in the city that originates in globalization itself. I can make this clear by contrasting a set of statistics from Wirth's Chicago in 1925 with New York today.

In Wirth's Chicago in 1925, political and economic power in the city was coextensive in the following ways. The presidents of the city's top 80 corporations sat on 142 hospital boards and composed 70 per cent of the trustees of colleges and universities. The 18 largest corporations in the city gave out an estimated 85 per cent of all the money that went to political organizations in the city and the tax revenues of these same 18 largest corporations in the city formed 23 per cent of the municipal budgets. What this means is that, in that old style capitalism, control of the political machinery of the city and economic power in the city were coextensive. This is not the case in New York city today. My research group has done a study of major global organizations in the city and of their civic, or indeed political, involvement in the city. All these numbers are in single digits.

This, in my mind, is what it means to talk about the crisis of citizenship in modern cities. The global corporations that are in it are indifferent to ruling the city in which they operate. That is one dimension of indifference.

The second dimension of this problem has to do with the proliferation of 'flexibilized' institutions and their relationship to physical urban forms. A few years ago I took the head of the General Electric Corporation, a man named Jack Welch, a sort of new-style global commando flexible leader, through a building in New York called the Channon Building. It is a building, dripping with art deco offices and with very articulate functions about where people work and where the social spaces are located. He looked at me and said, 'Well, if the General Electric (GE) Corporation were here you know I would tear this building down because it would give people a sense that they actually belong here'.

There is a profound meaning to that story, for what we are seeing appear under the weight of highly flexibilized corporations is a great deal of standardization in the urban environment and we could talk about this at great length. The reasons for it are fairly simple. One is the notion that place does not matter in the context of business; so flexibilized offices have no quality. A deeper structural reason is that these buildings, which people inhabit and then leave and then are inhabited by somebody else, are also sold on the global capital market; for example, in Singapore you can buy 1000 square feet of office space in London. For this property exchange to operate, 1000 square feet in New York or London has to be something that somebody in Singapore understands. In other words, you create the flexibilization of work, where you have impermanent residents in a spot with a market in impermanent office space. Flexibilization leads to standardization. Look at the monuments of modern capitalism. They look absolutely insidious, nothing architecturally like the kinds of buildings that say Simmel or Weber looked at in early twentieth-century Berlin, and that were to impose such a distinctive corporate identity on physical space.

In turn, this creates a sort of indifference about physical place. That line from flexibility to standardization to indifference, that is 'I could be here or any-where', 'I don't care', is something that is deeply embedded in the flexibilized order. It also has its reflection in the realm of flexible consumption, which is also highly standardized. It is a problem for cosmopolitanism that there is a kind of 'no place' relationship, produced precisely by the churning instability of cap-italism. It produces a more standardized environment to which people have fewer attachments.

The third thing I wanted to say about this is that sociologically, and here we come back to the issue of public sociability, in places like this there is, as a sub-stitute for alterity, a regime of differences that are non-interactive. You get a regime of geographical, educational, even to some extent leisure, segregation in which class, race and ethnic differences are managed in the city by principles of non-interaction. Crowds become mono-functional, levels of violence go down, non-interaction becomes a guarantor of public order; so the way to manage the constant churning over of populations is to have less contact. Once again you produce a system that is flexible in its population, in which alterity of the popu-lation is replaced by the marking of difference, and the result is that difference produces indifference. From my generation of urbanists, it seems to me that these three phenomena create the kind of dilemmas and paradoxes of cos-mopolitanism with which we have to deal—the paradox of a flexible social world that produces social relations of indifference.

The last thing I want to say about this is that, for most urbanists, the propos-ition between the cosmopolitan and the local is a false distinction. For us the problem is to get some of the benefits people have in mind when they talk about what the locality requires, so that rather than engaging in a kind of opposition they return to understanding the notion of engagement in the other. In other words, how do you intensify rather than localize social interaction? It is a clas-sic problem in urban design when we look at how to design streets. By defin-ition, a street is a local operation. The problem is how do you get intensity of interaction on the street?

I would like to conclude with this problem. It seems to me that with the terms with which we are dealing, cosmopolitan versus local, when you actually go into a city and lose the modern reality, you are left with a completely different set of dialectics.

5

Culture and Political Community: National, Global, and Cosmopolitan

DAVID HELD

This 'window' explores the impact on national culture of the globalization of communications and cultural life. It is in four parts. In the first part, the historical background to the debate about the nature and prospects of national culture is explored. The second and third sections examine the debate in an era of increasing transborder cultural interchange. Two positions are set out: the traditionalist or modern, territorial, state-based conception of the enduring significance of national identity and the cultural globalist position—the view that global popular culture, consumption orientations and hybrid identities are transforming cultural life. These positions are related to the development of political community and, in particular, to accounts about the proper nature and locus of the political good. The fourth and final part draws on aspects of both accounts, and points toward an alternative formulation, which appears a better fit with, and more appropriate to, cultural and political life in the contemporary age.

Historical Backdrop

The globalization of culture has a long history. The formation and expansion of the great world religions are profound examples of the capacity of ideas and beliefs to cross great distances with decisive social impacts. No less important are the great pre-modern empires such as the Roman Empire, which, in the absence of a direct military and political control, held its domains together through a shared and extensive ruling class culture (Millar *et al.* 1967; Mann 1986). For most of human history, these extensive ruling cultures passed through a fragmented mosaic of local cultures and particularisms; little stood between the political centre and the village. It was only with the emergence of nation-states and national cultures that a form of cultural identity coalesced between these two poles.

With the rise of nation-states and nationalist projects, the spatial organization of culture was transformed. Nation-states took control of educational practices, linguistic policies, postal systems, and so on. However, from the eighteenth century, as European empires expanded and as a series of technological innovations began to have far-reaching practical effects (regularized mechanical transport and the telegraph most notably), new forms of cultural globalization crystallized. The most important ideas and arguments to emerge from the West during this era were science, liberalism and socialism (Held *et al.* 1999: chapter 7). Each of these modes of thought—and the practices that went with them—transformed the ruling cultures of almost every society on the planet. They have certainly had a more considerable impact on national and local cultures than Nike, Coca-Cola, McDonalds and a host of pop groups.

However, in the period since the Second World War, the extensity, intensity, speed and sheer volume of cultural communication are unsurpassed at a global level (UNESCO 1950, 1986, 1989; OECD 1997). The global diffusion of radio, television, the Internet, satellite and digital technologies has made instantaneous communication possible, rendered many border checks and controls over information ineffective, and exposed an enormous constituency to diverse cultural outputs and values. A telling example is the viewing figures for *Baywatch*; over two billion people are estimated to have watched each episode. While linguistic differences continue to be a barrier to these processes, the global dominance of English provides a linguistic infrastructure that parallels the technological infrastructures of the era. In contrast to earlier periods in which states and theocracies were central to cultural globalization, the current era is one in which corporations are the central producers and distributors of cultural products. Corporations have replaced states and theocracies as the key producers and distributors of cultural products. Private international institutions are not new but their mass impact is. News agencies and publishing houses in previous eras had a much more limited reach than the consumer goods and cultural output of the global corporations today.

Though the vast majority of these cultural products come from the USA, this does not amount to a simple case of 'cultural imperialism'. One of the surprising features of our global age is how robust national and local cultures have proved to be. National institutions remain central to public life; while national audiences constantly re-interpret foreign products in novel ways (see Thompson 1995). The central question is the future impact of communication and cultural flows on local and national cultures, and on our sense of personal identity, national identity and politics. The next section turns to the debate on this.

National Culture and its Presuppositions

The rise of the modern nation-state and nationalist movements altered the landscape of political identity. The conditions involved in the creation of the modern state often helped generate a sense of nationhood. In particular, the military and administrative requirements of the modern state 'politicized' social relations and day-to-day activities (Giddens 1985; Mann 1986). Gradually, people became aware of their membership in a shared political community, with a common fate. Although the nature of this emergent identity was often initially vague, it grew more definite and precise over time (Therborn 1977; Turner 1986; Mann 1987).

The consolidation of the ideas and narratives of the nation and nationhood has been linked to many factors including the attempt by ruling elites and governments to create a new identity that would legitimize the enhancement of state power and the coordination of policy (Breuilly 1992); the creation, via a mass education system, of a common framework of understanding—ideas, meanings, practices—to enhance the process of state coordinated modernization (Gellner 1983); the emergence of new communication systems—particularly new media (such as printing and the telegraph), independent publishers and a free market for printed material—which facilitated interclass communication and the diffusion of national histories, myths and rituals, that is a new imagined community (Anderson 1983); and building on an historic sense of homeland and deeply-rooted memories, the consolidation of ethnic communities via a common public culture, shared legal rights and duties and an economy creating mobility for its members within a bounded territory (Smith 1986, 1995).

Even where the establishment of a national identity was an explicit political project pursued by elites, it was rarely their complete invention. That nationalist elites actively sought to generate a sense of nationality and a commitment to the nation—a 'national community of fate'—is well documented. But 'it does not follow', as one observer aptly noted, that such elites 'invented nations where none existed' (Smith 1990: 180–1). The 'nation-to-be' was not any large, social or cultural entity; rather, it was a 'community of history and culture', occupying a particular territory, and often laying claim to a distinctive tradition of common rights and duties for its members. Accordingly, many nations were 'built up on the basis of pre-modern "ethnic cores" whose myths and memories, values and symbols shaped the culture and boundaries of the nation that modern elites managed to forge' (see Smith 1986; 1990: 180). The identity that nationalists strove to uphold depended, in significant part, on uncovering and exploiting a community's 'ethno-history' and on highlighting its distinctiveness in the world of competing political and cultural values (cf. Hall 1992).

Of course, the construction of nations, national identities and nation-states has always been harshly contested and the conditions for the successful development of each never fully overlapped with that of the others (see Held *et al.* 1999: 48–9, 336–40). The fixed borders of the modern state have generally embraced a diversity of ethnic, cultural and linguistic groups with mixed leanings and allegiances. The relationships between these groups, and between these groups and states, has been chequered and often a source of bitter conflict. In the late nineteenth and twentieth centuries, nationalism became a force that supported and buttressed state formation in certain places (e.g., in France) and challenged or refashioned it elsewhere—for instance, in multiethnic states such as Spain or the United Kingdom (Held *et al.* 1999: 337–8).

However, despite the diversity of nationalisms and their political aims, and the fact that most national cultures are less than two hundred years old, these 'new' political forces created fundamentally novel terms of political reference in the modern world—terms of reference that appear so well rooted today that many, if not the overwhelming majority, peoples take them as given and practically natural (see Barry 1998). In fact, advocates of the primacy of national identity juxtapose its enduring qualities and the deep appeal of national cultures with the ephemeral and ersatz qualities of the products of the transnational media corporations (Smith 1990; Brown 1995). Since national cultures have been centrally concerned with consolidating the relationships between political identity, self-determination and the powers of the state, they are, and will remain, so the argument runs, formidably important sources of ethical and political direction.

The political significance of nationalism, along with the development and consolidation of the state, has been at the heart of modern political theory. Political theory, by and large, has taken the nation-state as a fixed point of reference and has sought to place the state at the centre of interpretations of the nature and proper form of the political good (Dunn 1990: 142–60). The theory and practice of liberal democracy has added important nuances to this position. For within the framework of liberal democracy, while territorial boundaries and the nation-state demarcate the proper spatial limits of the political good, the articulation of the political good is directly linked to the national citizenry. The political good is inherent in, and is to be specified by, a process of political participation in which the collective will is determined through the medium of elected representatives (Bobbio 1989: 144).

The theory of the political good in the modern territorial polity rests on a number of assumptions that repay an effort of clarification (see Held 1995*a*: chapter 10; Miller 1995*a*, 1999*b*). These are that a political community is properly constituted and bounded when:

1. its members have a common socio-cultural identity; that is, they share an understanding, explicit or implicit, of a distinctive culture, tradition, language and homeland, which binds them together as a group and forms a (if not the) basis (acknowledged or unacknowledged) of their activities;
2. there is a common framework of 'prejudices', purposes and objectives that generates a common political ethos, namely an imagined 'community of fate' that connects its envoys directly to a common political

project—the notion that they form a people who should govern themselves;

3. an institutional structure exists—or is in the process of development—that protects and represents the community, acts on its behalf and promotes the collective interest;

4. 'congruence' and 'symmetry' prevail between a community's 'governors' and 'governed', between political decision-makers and decision-takers. That is to say, national communities 'programme' the actions, decisions and policies of their governments, and governments determine what is right or appropriate for their citizens; and

5. members enjoy, because of the presence of the above conditions, a common structure of rights and duties, namely they can lay claim to and can reasonably expect certain kinds of equal treatment, that is certain types of egalitarian principles of justice and political participation.

According to this account, appropriate conceptions of what is right for the political community and its citizens follow from its cultural, political and institutional roots, traditions and boundaries. These generate the resources—conceptual and organizational—for the determination of its fate and fortunes. And the underlying principle of justification involves a significant communitarian thought: ethical discourse cannot be detached from the 'form of life' of a community; the categories of political discourse are integral to a particular tradition; and the values of such a community take precedence over or trump global requirements (MacIntyre 1981, 1988; Walzer 1983; Miller 1988).

The Globalization of Communications and Culture

Globalists take issue with each of these propositions, and they mount a sustained critique of them. First, shared identity in political communities historically has been the result of intensive efforts of political construction; it has never been a given (cf. Anderson 1983; Gellner 1983; Smith 1986, 1995). Even within the boundaries of old-established communities, cultural and political identity is often disputed by and across social classes, gender divisions, local allegiances, ethnic groupings and the generations. The existence of a shared political identity cannot simply be read off vociferously proclaimed symbols of national identity. The meaning of such symbols is contested and the 'ethos' of a community frequently debated. The common values of a community may be subject to intense dispute. Justice, accountability and the rule of law are just a few terms around which there may appear to be a shared language and, yet, fiercely different conceptions of these may be present. In fact, if by a political consensus is meant normative integration within a community, then it is all too rare (Held 1996: part 2; and see below).

Political identity is only by exception, for instance during wars, a singular, unitary phenomenon. Moreover, contemporary 'reflexive' political agents, subject to an extraordinary diversity of information and communication, can be influenced by images, concepts, lifestyles and ideas from well beyond their immediate communities and can come to identify with groups beyond their borders—ethnic, religious, social and political (Keck and Sikkink 1998; Thompson 1998; Held *et al.* 1999: chapter 8). Further, while there is no reason to suppose that they will uncritically identify with any one of these, self-chosen ideas, commitments or relations may well be more important for some people's identity than 'membership in a community of birth' (Thompson, 1998: 190; cf. Giddens 1991; Tamir 1993). Cultural and political identity today is constantly under review and reconstruction.

Second, the argument that locates cultural value and the political good firmly within the terrain of the nation-state fails to consider or properly appreciate the diversity of political communities that individuals can appreciate, and the fact that individuals can involve themselves coherently in different associations or collectivities at different levels and for different purposes (Thompson 1998). It is perfectly possible, for example, to enjoy membership and voting rights in Scotland, the United Kingdom and Europe without necessarily threatening one's identification or allegiances to any one of these three political entities (see Archibugi *et al.* 1998). It is perfectly possible, in addition, to identify closely with the aims and ambitions of a transnational social movement—whether concerned with environmental, gender or human rights issues—without compromising other more local political commitments. Such a pluralization of political orientations and allegiances can be linked to the erosion of the state's capacity to sustain a singular political identity in the face of migration, the movement of labour and the globalization of communications. Increasingly, successful political communities have to work with, not against, a multiplicity of identities, cultures and ethnic groupings. Multiculturalism, not national culture, is increasingly the norm.

Third, globalization has 'hollowed-out' states, eroding their sovereignty and autonomy. State institutions and political agents are, globalists contend, increasingly like 'zombies' (Beck 1992; Giddens 1999*b*). Contemporary political strategies involve easing adaptation to world markets and transnational economic flows. Adjustment to the international economy—above all to global financial markets—becomes a fixed point of orientation in economic and social policy. The 'decision signals' of these markets, and of their leading agents and forces, become a, if not the, standard of rational decision-making. States no longer have the capacity and policy instruments they require to contest the imperatives of global economic change; instead, they must help individual citizens to go where they want to go via the provision of social, cultural and educational resources (Giddens 1999*a*). Accordingly, the roles of the state as a protector and representative of the territorial community, as a collector and (re)allocator of resources among its members, as a promoter of an independent, deliberatively tested shared good are all in decline.

Fourth, the fate of a national community is no longer in its own hands. Regional and global economic, environmental and political processes profoundly redefine the content of national decision-making. In addition, decisions made by quasi-regional or quasi-supranational organizations such as the EU, the World Trade Organization (WTO), the International Monetary Fund (IMF) or NATO diminish the range of political options open to given national 'majorities'. In a similar vein, decisions by particular states—not ust the most economically or militarily powerful nations—can ramify across borders, circumscribing and reshaping the political terrain. Political communities are, thus, embedded in a substantial range of processes that connect them in complex configurations, making them all too often decision-takers, not decision-makers.

Fifth, national communities are locked into webs of regional and global governance that alter and compromise their capacity to provide a common structure of rights, duties and welfare to their citizens. From human rights to trade regimes, political power is being re-articulated and re-configured. Increasingly, contemporary patterns of globalization are associated with a multi-layered system of governance. Locked into an array of geographically diverse forces, national governments are having to reconsider their roles and functions. Although the intensification of regional and global political relations has diminished the powers of national governments, it is recognized ever more that the nurturing and enhancement of the political good requires coordinated multilateral action, for instance to prevent global recession and enhance sustainable growth, to protect human rights and intercede where they are grossly violated and to act to avoid environmental catastrophes such as ozone depletion or global warming. A shift is taking place from government to multi-level global governance. Accordingly, the institutional nexus of the political good is being reconfigured.

Each of the five propositions set forth by the theorists of national culture and of the modern national state can be contrasted with positions held by the globalists. Thus, the political community and the political good need, on the globalists' account, to be understood as follows:

1. Individuals increasingly have complex loyalties and multi-layered identities, corresponding to the globalization of economic and cultural forces and the reconfiguration of political power.
2. The continuing development of regional, international and global flows of resources and networks of interaction, along with the recognition by growing numbers of people of the increasing interconnectedness of

political communities—in domains as diverse as the social, cultural, economic and environmental—generates an awareness of overlapping 'collective fortunes' that require collective solutions. Political community begins to be re-imagined in regional and global terms.

3. An institutional structure exists comprising elements of local, national, regional and global governance. At different levels, individual communities (albeit often imperfectly) are protected and represented; their collective interests require both multilateral advancement and domestic (local and national) adjustment if they are to be sustained and promoted.

4. Complex economic, social and environmental processes, shifting networks of regional and international agencies and the decision outcomes of many states cut across spatially delimited, national locales with determinate consequences for their agendas and policy options. Globalization alters decisively what it is that a national community can ask of its government, what politicians can promise and deliver, and the range of people(s) affected by government outputs. Political communities are 'reprogrammed'.

5. The rights, duties and welfare of individuals can only be adequately entrenched if they are underwritten by regional and global regimes, laws and institutions. The promotion of the political good and of egalitarian principles of justice and political participation are rightly pursued at regional and global levels. Their conditions of possibility are inextricably linked to the establishment of transnational organizations and institutions of governance. In a global age, transnational organizations and institutions are the basis of cooperative relations and just conduct.

Accordingly, what is right for the individual political community and its citizens, in the globalists' account, must follow from reflection on the processes that generate an intermingling of national fortunes. The contemporary world 'is not a world of closed communities with mutually impenetrable ways of thought, self-sufficient economies and ideally sovereign states' (O'Neill 1991: 282). Not only is ethical discourse separable from forms of life in a national community, it is also developing today at the intersection and interstices of overlapping communities, traditions and languages. Its categories are increasingly the result of the mediation of different cultures, communication processes and modes of understanding. There are not enough good reasons for allowing, in principle, the values of individual political communities to trump or take precedence over global principles of justice and political participation. While for the traditionalists ethical discourse is, and remains, firmly rooted in the bounded political community, for the globalists it belongs squarely to the world of 'breached boundaries'—the 'world community' or global order.

Cosmopolitan Alternatives

There is insufficient space here to appraise all the claims of these two positions. But by way of a conclusion, I would like to make a number of additional points, and indicate the plausibility of a third position—neither traditionalist, nor globalist, but cosmopolitan.

The leading claims of the globalists are at their strongest when focused on institutional and process change in the domains of economics, politics and the environment, but they are at their most vulnerable when considering the movements of people, their attachments and their cultural and moral identities. For the available evidence suggests that national (and local) cultures remain robust; national institutions continue in many states to have a central impact on public life; national television and radio broadcasting continue to enjoy substantial audiences; the organization of the press and news coverage retain strong national roots and imported foreign products are constantly read and re-interpreted in novel ways by national audiences (Miller 1992; Liebes and Katz 1993; Thompson 1995). Moreover, the evidence indicates that there is no simple common global pool of memories, no common global way of thinking, and no 'universal history' in and through which people can unite. There is only a manifold set of political meanings and systems through which any new global awareness, or multicultural politics, or human rights discourse must struggle for survival (see Bozeman 1984). Given the deep roots of national cultures and ethno-histories, and the many ways they are often re-fashioned, this can hardly be a surprise. Despite the vast flows of information, imagery and people around the world, there are only a few signs, at best, of a universal or global history in the making, and few signs of a decline in the importance of nationalism.

There has been a shift from government to multi-level governance, from the modern state to a multi-layered system of power and authority, from relatively discrete national communication and economic systems to their more complex and diverse enmeshment at regional and global levels. Yet, there are few grounds for thinking that a concomitant widespread pluralization of political identities has taken place. One exception to this is to be found among the elites of the global order—the networks of experts and specialists, senior administrative personnel and transnational business groups—and those who track and contest their activities, the loose constellation of social movements, trade unionists and (a few) politicians and intellectuals. The globalists' emphasis on the pluralization of political identities is overstated. What one commentator has written about the EU applies, in many respects, to the rest of the world: 'The central paradox . . . is that governance is becoming increasingly a multi-level, intricately institutionalized activity, while representation, loyalty and identity remain stubbornly rooted in the traditional institutions of the nation-state' (Wallace 1999: 521).

Hence, the shift from government to governance is an unstable shift, capable of reversal in some respects, and certainly capable of engendering a fierce reaction—a reaction drawing on nostalgia, romanticized conceptions of political community, hostility to outsiders (refugees, immigrants), and a search for a pure national state (e.g., in the politics of Haider in Austria). But this reaction itself is likely to be highly unstable, and a relatively short-term phenomenon. To understand why this is so, nationalism has to be desegregated. As 'cultural nationalism' it is, and in all likelihood will remain, central to people's identity; however, as political nationalism—the assertion of the exclusive political priority of national identity and the national interest—it cannot deliver many sought-after public goods and values without seeking accommodation with others, in and through regional and global collaboration. In this respect, only a cosmopolitan outlook can, ultimately, accommodate itself to the political challenges of a more global era, marked by overlapping communities of fate and multi-layered politics. Unlike political nationalism, cosmopolitanism registers and reflects the multiplicity of issues, questions, processes and problems that affect and bind people together, irrespective of where they were born or reside.

Cosmopolitanism is concerned to disclose the cultural, ethical and legal basis of political order in a world where political communities and states matter, but not only and exclusively. It dates at least to the Stoics' description of themselves as cosmopolitans—'human beings living in a world of human beings and only incidentally members of polities' (Barry 1999: 35). The Stoic emphasis on the morally contingent nature of membership of a political community seems anachronistic after 200 years of nationalism. But what is neither anachronistic nor misplaced is the recognition of the necessary partiality, one-sidedness and limitedness of 'reasons of political community' or 'reasons of state' when judged from the perspective of a world of 'overlapping communities of fate'— where the trajectories of each and every country are tightly entwined. Cosmopolitanism today must take this as a starting point, and build a robust conception of the proper basis of political community and the relations among communities. The Kantian understanding of this, based on a model of human interaction anchored in co-presence, cannot be an adequate basis of this (Held 1995a: chapter 10). Cosmopolitanism needs to be reworked for another age.

What would such a cosmopolitanism amount to? In the little space available here, I cannot unpack what I take to be the multi-dimensional nature of cosmopolitanism. But I would like to end with a few words about cultural cosmopolitanism. Cultural cosmopolitanism is not at loggerheads with national culture; it does not deny cultural difference or the enduring significance of national tradition. It is not against cultural diversity. Few, if any, contemporary cosmopolitans hold such views (see, e.g., Waldron 1999; Barry 2000). Rather, cultural cosmopolitanism should be understood as the capacity to mediate between national cultures, communities of fate and alternative styles of life. It encompasses the possibility of dialogue with the traditions and discourses of others with the aim of expanding the horizons of one's own framework of meaning and prejudice (Gadamer 1975). Political agents who can 'reason from the point of view of others' are better equipped to resolve, and resolve fairly, the challenging transboundary issues that create overlapping communities of fate. The development of this kind of cultural cosmopolitanism depends on the recognition by growing numbers of peoples of the increasing interconnectedness of political communities in diverse domains, and the development of an understanding of overlapping 'collective fortunes' that require collective solutions—locally, nationally, regionally and globally.

Cultural cosmopolitanism emphasizes the possible fluidity of individual identity— 'people's remarkable capacity to forge new identities using materials from diverse cultural sources, and to flourish while so doing' (Scheffler 1999: 257). It celebrates, as Rushdie put it, 'hybridity, impurity, intermingling, the transformation that comes of new and unexpected combinations of human beings, cultures, ideas, politics, movies, songs' (quoted in Waldron, 1992: 751). But it is *the ability to stand outside a singular location (the location of one's birth, land, upbringing, conversion) and to mediate traditions* that lies at its core. However, there are no guarantees about the extent to which such an outlook will prevail. For it has to survive and jostle for recognition alongside deeply held national, ethnic and religious traditions (Held and McGrew 2000: 13–18 and part 3). It is a cultural and cognitive orientation, not an inevitability of history.

The core requirements of cultural cosmopolitanism include:

1. recognition of the increasing interconnectedness of political communities in diverse domains including the social, economic and environmental;
2. development of an understanding of overlapping 'collective fortunes' that require collective solutions—locally, nationally, regionally and globally; and
3. the celebration of difference, diversity and hybridity while learning how to 'reason from the point of view of others' and mediate traditions.

Like national culture, cultural cosmopolitanism is a cultural project, but with one difference: it is better adapted and suited to our regional and global age.

II

Theories of Cosmopolitanism

6

The Cosmopolitan Perspective: Sociology in the Second Age of Modernity

ULRICH BECK

The cosmopolitan gaze opens wide and focuses—stimulated by the post-modern mix of boundaries between cultures and identities, accelerated by the dynamics of capital and consumption, empowered by capitalism undermining national borders, excited by the global audience of transnational social movements and guided and encouraged by the evidence of worldwide communication (often just another word for misunderstanding) on central themes such as science, law, art, fashion, entertainment and, not least, politics. Worldwide public debate and perception of global ecological danger or global risks of a technological and economic nature ('Frankenstein food') have laid open the cosmopolitan significance of fear. And if we needed any proof that even genocide and the horrors of war now have a cosmopolitan aspect, this was provided by the Kosovo war in the spring of 1999 when NATO bombed Serbia in order to enforce the implementation of human rights.[1]

In the face of this widening cosmopolitan perspective, social scientists and social theorists find themselves embracing contrary views and starting points. The nation-state society is the dominant societal paradigm. The mainstream considers that the concept of society is applicable only to the nation-state. Accordingly, the sociological perspective or gaze (the sociology of inequality, of the family, of politics and so on) is geared to and organized in terms of the nation-state. On the whole, sociology observes, measures and comments on its

Translated by Martin Chalmers. This article was previously published in the *British Journal of Sociology*, 15: 1 (2000). Reproduced by kind permission of Taylor and Francis Ltd. P.O. Box 25, Abingdon, Oxfordshire, OX14 3U6. There is some minor stylistic editing in the version printed here.

[1] This war is post-national (and therefore can no longer be grasped by the concept of war developed by von Clausewitz) because it is neither waged in a national interest—the continuation of politics by other means—nor can it be seen in the context of older rivalries between more or less hostile nation-states. What makes the war in Kosovo post-national is in fact the opposite of this, namely the global weakening of the sovereign order of the nation-state, the debilitation, even barbarization of the state guilty of the expulsion and genocide of its own citizens and, at the same time, the belief in the morality of human rights as a source of civility.

phenomena, for example, poverty and unemployment within a national context rather than in the context of world society. Within this frame, the theme of globalization means that an increasing number of social processes are indifferent to national boundaries. This is based on an understanding of globalization that decodes it as a 'time–space compression' (Harvey 1989; Appadurai 1990; Featherstone 1990; Lash and Urry 1994; Albrow 1996; Giddens 1996; Adam 1998). Accordingly, for empirical purposes globalization is operationalized as interconnectedness (Zürn 1998; Held *et al.* 1999) between state societies. All three criteria—the indifference to national boundaries, space–time compression and an increasing network-like interconnectedness between national societies—are exemplified primarily by economic globalization. But there are many more examples. As more processes show less regard for state boundaries—people shop internationally, work internationally, love internationally, marry internationally, research internationally, grow up and are educated internationally (that is multilingually), live and think transnationally, that is combine multiple loyalties and identities in their lives—the paradigm of societies organized within the framework of the nation-state inevitably loses contact with reality. These changing circumstances have prompted a never-ending debate on the condition of the nation-state. Does it still exist or has it already gone? Is the scope of its activity even growing as its autonomy—state sovereignty—is shrinking? Perhaps it has long since been converted into a super/supra/inter/post/neo/trans/nation-state? Or have politics and the state become zombies—dead long ago but still haunting peoples minds? The heat generated by this debate derives in some degree from the premise that it is only in the framework of the nation-state that the essential achievements of Western modernity, including democracy, the legitimation of state action, the welfare state and the state of law (*Rechtsstaat*) are possible, real and thriving.

By contrast, within the paradigm of world society, globalization is considered normal and the perspective of the nation-state gives rise to continual bafflement. Why are the social sciences still dominated by a secret Hegelianism that sees society as derived from a state's claim to embody the principle of order? How is it that the theorists of the nation-state invariably identify society with a piece of land, like animals identifying with their territory or like the gangs of youths in Central Park who get ready to repel the intruder as soon as someone comes too close and trespasses on their territory? Why are societies seen as 'somehow rooted in the land, as if they needed the soil'? (Kieserling 1998: 65; on this territorial bias of the social sciences—the container theory of society—see Beck 2000*a*: 23.)

In this chapter, I will develop and discuss the opposing theories, real conflicts and transition between the cosmopolitan perspective and that of the nation-state within the framework of an epochal distinction between the familiar image of the first age of modernity and the indistinctness and ambivalence of a second

age of modernity. The choice of words is in fact programmatic. First, by distinguishing between a first and second age of modernity, I distance myself from
the theoretical schema of postmodernism. While the followers of postmodernism emphasize destructuring and the end of modernity, my concern is
with what is beginning, with new institutions and the development of new social
science categories. Second, the distinction between a first and second age of
modernity also challenges theories that suggest that the unfolding of modernity
at the end of this millennium should be seen as a linear process of differentiation based on 'evolutionary universals' (Talcott Parsons) or modern 'basic
institutions' (Wolfgang Zapf). Third, the distinction between a first and second
age of modernity is intended to clarify misunderstandings that have emerged in
the debate on 'reflexive modernization' (Beck *et al.* 1994). The reference to a
second age of modernity is intended to make it clear that there is a structural and
epochal break—a paradigm shift—and not merely a gradual increase in the
significance of knowledge and reflection as is mistakenly suggested by the term
'reflexive modernization'.

The theory and sociology of the second age of modernity, therefore, elaborate the basic assumption that towards the end of the twentieth century the *con-
ditio humana* opens up anew—with fundamentally ambivalent contingencies,
complexities, uncertainties and risks, which, conceptually and empirically, still
have to be uncovered and understood. A new kind of capitalism, a new kind of
economy, a new kind of global order, a new kind of politics and law, and a
new kind of society and personal life are in the making, which both separately
and in context are clearly distinct from earlier phases of social evolution.
Consequently, a paradigm shift in both the social sciences and in politics is
required.[2] In this chapter, however, I can only investigate one aspect of this shift,
namely which social science categories make the cosmopolitan perspective
possible?

From the First to the Second Age of Modernity

There is an excellent example that illustrates the need to understand and decode
the transition from the first to the second age of modernity as a paradigm shift,
a change in the coordinate system. And that is the difficult relationship between
the international law and human rights, characteristic of the first as well as the
second age of modernity, which has come to the fore again with the Kosovo war,

---

[2] See Beck and Bonß (1999) where the question of the change of a paradigm between the first and the
second age of modernity in many areas of the social sciences is formulated at the initiation of a research
centre (funded by the Deutsche Forschungsgemeinshaft for an extended period). This also applies to the
other basic distinctions of the first age of modernity such as work and non-work (Beck 2000*b*), society
and nature (Adam 1998; Beck 1999*b*; Latour 1999), family and non-family (Beck and Beck-Gernsheim
1995; Giddens and Pierson 1998: 118–50; see Beck and Bonß 1999).

if not before. Within the paradigm of the first age of modernity—where the field of international relations is mainly elaborated and represented by the realist school of political theory—the interconnectedness of an increasingly complex world society remains subject to the order of sovereign independent states, which came into being with the Treaty of Westphalia in 1648. This means that none of the serious problems that states can only solve through cooperation— the increasing authority and materiality of supranational organizations, the development of transnational regimes and regulations to legitimize decisions, the economization or even ecologization of foreign policy and, in conjunction with this, the blurring of the classical boundary between domestic and foreign policy in general—affect the international legal principle of non-intervention in the internal affairs of foreign states.

In this framework, the NATO bombing in response to the genocide in Kosovo appears to be a striking breach of international law, even a war of aggression, which is, for example, forbidden by the German constitution. A small country is attacked militarily by a world power in pursuit of selfish capital interests and, in a display of moral perversion as it were, this is legitimized as the defence of human rights.

In the conflict of values between the authority of the sovereign state and the protection of human rights, Western governments, led by the United States of America, place a higher value on opposing the genocide against the Kosovars than on the UN Charter procedures based on international law. The basis for this decision was a twofold critique of the legal system, which the states agreed upon among themselves and institutionalized in the United Nations Organization. International law does admittedly contain rules concerning the international use of violence and it also distinguishes between what is permit- ted and what is forbidden. But it does so inadequately because the question of whether the state authorities themselves have a legitimate existence, or, to be more precise, whether they satisfy the Human Rights Charter and the demands arising from it, is not examined. The former US Secretary of State Madeline Albright established a link between a very American, that is national, foreign policy and a human rights policy that is primarily guided by normative stand- ards. However, the promotion of human rights is not just a form of international social work. It is indispensable for our safety and well being because govern- ments that fail to respect the rights of their own citizens will in all likelihood also not respect the rights of others. In this century, almost every major act of international aggression was carried out by a regime that suppressed political rights. Such regimes are also more likely to trigger unrest by persecuting minorities, offering a safe haven to terrorists, smuggling drugs or clandestinely manufacturing weapons of mass destruction (Albright 1998: 2).

There has always been a tension between national sovereignty and human rights, the two sources of national legitimacy, but the relationship has now been given a new twist, which is bound to have significant consequences. A government may now forfeit the recognition of its sovereignty under international law by a blatant violation of the human rights of its own citizens and on its own territory. Thus, the transition from a nation-state world order to a cosmopolitan world order brings about a very significant priority shift from international law to human rights. The principle that *international law precedes human rights*, which held during the (nation-state) first age of modernity, is being replaced by the principle of the (world society) second age of modernity, that *human rights precede international law*. As yet, the consequences have not been thought through, but they will be revolutionary. The result is a collapse of the distinctions—between war and peace, domestic (policy) and foreign (policy)—on which the previous order was based.[3] No one really knows which poses the greater danger: the disappearing world of sovereign subjects of international law who have long since lost their innocence, or the indistinct mix of supranational institutions and organizations that act on a global level but remain dependent on the goodwill of powerful states and alliances, or a self-appointed hegemonic power defending human rights on foreign territory under the banner of military humanism. Regardless of how one judges and assesses this highly ambivalent constellation, it is precisely in this muddle between the old order based on international law and the new order based on human rights that the epochal distinction between the first and second age of modernity can be pinned down and illustrated.

As has already been noted, the principle that 'international law precedes human rights' characterizes the international coordinate system of the first age of modernity. It is based on principles of collectivity, territoriality and boundary. The aim of the concept and development of international law was to secure peace. It regulates relations between states, namely collective subjects, and not between individuals. That is how Hugo Grotius saw it, and that is how it still appears today in the paragraphs of the UN Charter and the final agreement of

---

[3] That international law is dissolving the world's borders is an idea that has been growing since the end of the Second World War. The Nüremberg tribunal introduced the concept that the leaders' treatment of their own people was subject to international prosecution and the UN created the 1948 Universal Declaration of Human Rights. Nations also signed the Geneva Convention and a treaty promising to punish genocide carried out anywhere in the world. These laws were never enforced because the cold-war politics intervened. In 1998, 120 nations, excluding the United States of America, signed a treaty to establish an international criminal court in which international law could trump national sovereignty. One might even say that the G7 states (Group of seven leading industrial nations) are forming an embryo-like world government. But the attacks in 1999 on sovereignty did have two victims: first, of course, Serbia and its prime minister Milosevic, but second the NATO member states as well—France, Italy, the United States of America, Germany, Spain, Poland and others—who somehow lost their sovereignty by becoming actively involved in the Kosovo war without being able to decide autonomously on the issue of life and death. Who actually did decide to start bombing Serbia? None of the attacking nations on their own: NATO? But who is NATO? One could say that it is a military organization of post-sovereign, post-national nation-states.

the Organization for Security and Co-operation in Europe (OSCE). The high-flown words of the 'creation of a world free from fear and misery ... [as] the greatest endeavour of mankind', proclaimed in the preamble to the Human Rights Convention of 1948, could therefore not be followed by deeds against the will of the states concerned because they were protected by international law. Even if the Security Council had taken the Kosovo issue into its own hands, the wording of the UN Charter would have denied it the right to give direct help to the suffering population of Kosovo, but merely allowed it to safeguard world peace and international security.

The principle that human rights precede international law refers, however, to international relations in the cosmopolitan paradigm of the second age of modernity. The categorical principles of the first age of modernity—collectivity, territoriality, boundary—are replaced by a coordinate system in which individualization and globalization are directly related to each other and establish the conceptual frame for the concepts of state, law, politics and individuals, which have to be redefined. The bearers of human rights are individuals and not collective subjects such as a 'nation' or 'state'. In essence, human rights are *subjective* rights. These rights grant individuals the legal basis to act according to their own motives. The crucial point, however, is that they do away with a moral code binding the individual. At any rate, within the limits of what is legally permitted, no one is obliged to publicly justify his or her actions. With the introduction of subjective liberties, modern law, in contrast with traditional legal systems, endorses Hobbes's principle that everything is permitted that is not explicitly forbidden. Hence, law and morality diverge. While the moral code posits duties, the law establishes rights without reciprocal obligations. All this serves to create a space in which institutionalized individualism can thrive.

At the same time, human rights have to be seen not only in individualized terms but also in a globalized context. They are, however, inconceivable if they are not endowed with a claim to universal validity, which grants these rights to all individuals, independent of status, class, gender, nationality and religion.

If, in relations between individual states, standards and legal conceptions develop in which human rights are no longer among the matters that are, by their nature, part of the internal affairs of a state, this is more revolutionary than any re-interpretation of Article 2 of the UN Charter would be. Intervention would not only be permitted, it would be required. That amounts to a paradigm shift from nation-state societies to cosmopolitan society in so far as international law goes over the heads of nations and states and addresses individuals directly, thereby positing a *legally binding world society of individuals*.

This is made manifest in what has been stated as the most diverse consequence of globalization: the political and constitutional loss of power of the nation-state. But as soon as national sovereignties are undermined, conventional international law forfeits its classic subjects. However distant the actual vanishing point of this process may be, a foreign-policy based international law will develop along its line of flight into the constitution of a world domestic policy. Subjective human rights cannot be distinguished from domestic legal claims. They do not postulate border guards between individuals, as does the old international law; they make them redundant.[4] Accordingly, Habermas (1999: 6) is calling for world citizenship rights so that the intervention on behalf of persecuted individuals and nations does not remain a matter of morality alone:

The proposed establishment of a status of world citizenship would mean that violations of human rights would not be judged and combated directly from a moral viewpoint but prosecuted like criminal offences within a national legal code. A thorough going legalization of international relations is not possible without established procedures of conflict resolution. In the institutionalization of these procedures a juridically controlled approach to human rights violations will prevent a moral de-differentiation of the law and a direct and sweeping discrimination of enemies. This can be achieved without the monopoly of force of a world state and a world government. A minimum requirement, however, is a functioning Security Council, the binding jurisdiction of an international criminal court and the supplementing of the General Assembly of government representatives by the second level of a representation of world citizens. Since such a reform of the United Nations is unlikely in the foreseeable future, reference to the distinction between legalization and moralization remains a correct but ambiguous response. As long as the institutionalization of human rights on a global level is relatively weak, the boundary between law and morality can easily be blurred as in the case at hand. Because the Security Council is blocked, NATO can only appeal to the moral validity of international law, to standards for which there are no effective authorities to apply and enforce laws recognized by the community of nations.

But how do Western states respond to the criticism that it is basically the Western interpretation of human rights that NATO embraces, promotes and wants to enforce by military means, breaching the valid international law as it does so? The African, Asian and Chinese scholars, intellectuals and politicians counter the individualistic nature of the human rights with three arguments: (1) the priority of rights, in principle, has to be balanced by duties; (2) this in turn would provide for a communitarian ranking of human rights with the purpose of (3) establishing the priority of the common good and of community values against a primarily negative, individualistic system of human rights. But what will happen if one day the military alliance of another region, for example, in Asia, starts to pursue an armed human rights policy based on its own, very different interpretation of communitarian-based human rights? In other words, the military humanism of the West is founded on an uninterrogated world monopoly

---

[4] This implies a prediction that, in the global age, the dominant polarization between political programmes and parties will be on behalf of the challenges of cosmopolitan movements and counter-movements and not (as it was in the first age of modernity) in relation to the economy—capital versus labour.

of power and morality that, especially in the course of the transition to the second age of modernity, has become extremely questionable.

Circles of Globalization

This, however, leads to a dangerous confusion. The two images of world society—a patchwork quilt of nation-states (the sum of sovereign nation-states) or a world society, at once individualized and globalized, conceived of as a cosmopolitan order of human rights—clash and spark a worldwide intellectual and political conflict from which emerges, one way or another, some element of a world public, some degree of conscious globality. But in both cases—and this idea is no less crucial—we are dealing with a specific system of world power. Hence, the principle that human rights precede international law must be understood and decoded not only as a system of values but also as a system of power. Whoever wants to enforce this principle assumes three things: first, the end of the cold war and the end of a bipolar world order; second, the military and political hegemony of the United States of America; and third, the conciliation or inclusion of third powers such as Russia and China.

There is no question that after the collapse of the Eastern bloc, the Western democracies suddenly found themselves without an enemy and in need of new and reviving sources of legitimation. In the era of globalization these sources must enable them to establish justifications for the activity and the self-representation of success. Put very cautiously, the military humanism the West has taken up by embracing human rights fills the vacuum perfectly by providing institutions that have been deprived of an enemy with a cosmopolitan mission.

It is probably no exaggeration to talk of the democratic crusades the West will conduct in the future to renew its own self-legitimation. Precisely because the worldwide demand for fundamental human rights is entirely legitimate and the resulting interventions are regarded as disinterested, it often remains unnoticed how neatly they can be dovetailed with old-fashioned aims of imperialist world politics (bringing into play the UN, mentor and client relationships, and market interests), while internally they simultaneously encourage the creation of stage roles that give lame ducks—politicians and military men—the opportunity to bathe in the glamour of renewed activity and legitimacy.

This new form of humanitarian disinterest and imperial logic of power is preceded by developments that can be described as globalization circles in the sense that, with the erosion of territorially-based state power, the hour has come for 'global responsibility'. Globalization—however the word is understood—implies the weakening of state sovereignty and state structures. The collapse of the nation-state institutions has, however, led to the very bad human tragedies and wars of the 1990s, not only in former Yugoslavia but also in Somalia,

West Africa, and in parts of the former Soviet Union. With the financial crisis in Southeast Asia, there appears to be a threat of something similar there, particularly in Indonesia. Even if the influences of global capital markets are not the sole or primary causes of the weakening of centralized state power, it is evident that they can exacerbate a concealed power and legitimation vacuum and bring it out into the open with explosive force. This includes the possibility that nation-state based compromises between ethnic groups can lose their binding force and hitherto latent conflicts may explode into civil wars. Since this is happening before the eyes of the world, within a perceived framework of global responsibility, the possibility of military intervention by the West increases with the looming eruption of violence and chaos.

In the 'circle of globalization', the 'needs' of the world market and the 'good intentions' of a society of world citizens combine with a chain of unintended side effects to form a civil–military–humanitarian threat (inclusive of all the dilemmas this threat raises on all sides). The more successfully the prophets of the free-world market act on a global scale, which also means undermining the structures of the territorial nation-state, the more an ever larger proportion of the world's population is exposed to the threat of 'humanitarian intervention' by the West, an intervention that is now motivated by cosmopolitan concerns. In a world system of weak states, as propagated and established in the course of the development of neo-liberal world politics, there are no further obstacles in the way of an imperialist abuse of the cosmopolitan mission.

Thus, in Moscow there is a continuing debate on the question of whether the Kosovo war can be taken as a dress rehearsal in the event of Russia collapsing and the nuclear power at the centre of ethnic conflicts becoming the source of a new world war. In the Arab states and also in China and Israel, people are asking themselves whether the war in Kosovo could become a precedent. What is happening to the Serbs today may happen tomorrow to the Chinese, the Arab states or even to Israel. There are plenty of reasons for humanitarian intervention. Almost every state has a couple of minorities that it does not treat properly. It is becoming clear that the mere threat, the possibility of such a military human rights policy, is already shaking the very foundations of the exercise of power in world politics. Even if nothing happens, a lot is happening: the military humanism of the West must also be decoded (neo-realistically as it were) as a strategy, a calculation of world power politics.

Non-Western Countries

In the cosmopolitan paradigm of the second age of modernity, therefore, new power strategies and rifts are emerging between the champions of the new democratic world order—the original countries of the West and the global underdogs, countries that do not or cannot satisfy these requirements. But this is only one side of the development. On the other side, in the transition from the first (nation-state) age of modernity to the second (cosmopolitan) age of modernity, the Western claim to a monopoly on modernity is broken and the history and situation of diverging modernities in all parts of the world come into view. In the paradigm of the first modernity, world society is thought of in terms of the nation-state and nation-state society. Accordingly, globalization is seen as an additive and not a substitute. In other words, globalization appears to come from outside, a process in which the territorial principle of the social and the political is assumed as a given. This view of globalization as a matter of increasing links between nations, between states and between societies, does not call into question the distinctions between the First and Second Worlds, between tradition and modernity, but confirms them.

Within the paradigm of the second modernity, however, globalization alters not only the interconnectedness of nation-states and national societies but also the internal quality of the society. Whatever constitutes society and politics in itself becomes questionable because the principles of territoriality, collectivity and frontier are being questioned. More precisely, the assumed congruence of state and society is broken down and suspended; economic and social ways of acting, working and living no longer take place within the container of the state. The categories framing world society—the distinction between highly developed and underdeveloped countries, between tradition and modernity— are collapsing. In the cosmopolitan paradigm of the second modernity, the non-Western societies share the same time and space horizon with the West. Moreover, their position as provinces of world society is derived from the same challenges posed by the second modernity, which are variously perceived, assessed and processed in a variety of cultural contexts and locations.

The epochal break results from the fact that the guiding ideas and, with them, the interdependent institutionalized core answers of the first age of modernity are no longer self-evident and persuasive. Seen from the dimension of globalization, it is the idea of territoriality; at the level of work in society, it is full employment; from the dimension of individualization, it is a given, communal collectivity and hierarchy; from the dimension of gender relations, it is the natural division of labour between men and women; and from the dimension of the ecological crisis, it is the exploitation of nature as the basis of unlimited growth. This entails a significant consequence: the guiding ideas, the foundations and, ultimately, the claim to a monopoly on modernity by an originally western European modernism are shattered.

In the first age of modernity, non-Western societies were defined by their foreignness and otherness, their 'traditional', 'extra-modern' or 'pre-modern' character. In the second age of modernity, all people have to locate themselves in the same global space and are confronted with similar challenges, and strangeness is replaced by the amazement at the similarities. This implies a degree of self-criticism of the Western project of modernity, which can defend neither its role as a spearhead of progress nor its claim to a monopoly on modernity. The extra-European world is defined by its own history and is no longer regarded as the opposite or absence of modernity (even today many social scientists believe that it is only necessary to study pre-modern Western societies to make useful statements on the situation and problems of non-Western societies). In the second age of modernity, various cultures and regions of the world are proceeding along various routes to various ideas of modernity, and they may not achieve them for various reasons. Hence, the transition to the second age of modernity raises the problem of a comparison of cultures within the different, world-regional (national) frames of reference in a radical way. It also makes necessary, on the basis of the recognition of multiple modernities, dialogue between them (Jameson and Miyoshi 1998).

It is therefore mistaken to exclude non-Western countries from the analysis of Western society. This applies to the history of Europe as well as to the present. Shalini Randeria turns the evolutionary hierarchy of progress between the Western and non-Western countries upside down: 'Putting Marx's judgment on its feet and not on its head, one can say that in many ways the "Third World" today holds up a mirror in which Europe can see its own future' (Randeria 1998). Set out in more detail, this means that the West should listen to non-Western countries when they have something to say about the following experiences.

1. How can coexistence in multi-religious, multiethnic and multicultural societies work?
2. Can Western societies obtain realistic, non-utopian, namely disappointment-proof, answers to the question: 'How is tolerance possible in a confined space and in the face of cultural differences being prone to lead to violence'?
3. Also non-Western countries are highly developed when it comes to dealing with legal and judicial pluralism. Finally, even a previous lack proves to be an advantage: Non-Western countries are experienced in dealing with multiple sovereignties on an everyday basis, a situation that will become normal, for example, in a multinational Europe with one currency.

On the other hand, Western societies are beginning to adopt non-Western standards of reality and normality that do not bode well.

1. The deregulation and flexibilization of wage labour normalize something that used to be regarded as a surmountable disgrace: the informal economy and the informal sector.

2. In addition, the deregulation of the labour market leads to an abandonment of the cooperatively organized employee society that froze the class conflict between work and capital by harmonizing a capitalist supply dynamic with a system of privileges for the 'working citizen'. Consequently, with the casualization of labour relations and contractual conditions, trade-union free zones are spreading in the centres of Western post-work society.

3. Many countries of the non-Western world are regarded as weak states. If the neo-liberal revolution perseveres, state legitimation crises, accompanied by civil war-like eruptions of violence, such as are rife in countries of the South, could well become part of the future of the West.

The current situation of the world can perhaps be summed up—ironically—in a single image. During the first age of modernity, capital, labour, and the state played at making sand castles in the sandpit (a sandpit limited and organized in terms of the nation-state) and during this game each side tried to knock the other's sand castles off the spade in accordance with the rules of institutionalized conflict. Now, suddenly, business has been given a present of a mechanical digger and is emptying the whole sandpit. The trade unions and the politicians, on the other hand, have been left out of the new game, have gone into a huff and are crying for mummy.

The Politics of Post-Nationalism

The crucial question of the second age of modernity is, therefore, what happens to the territorially bounded politics in world society? How do collective binding decisions become possible under post-national conditions? Will politics wither away? Or will it undergo a transformation? If so, what will it be like? Will the transformation be evolutionary or will it be seen as a political process in itself? That is to say, it does not happen but is rather a function of the opening out of the cosmopolitan perspective. If this transformation of the political dimension can only be understood politically, will it emerge from the worldwide conflict over the cosmopolitanization of nation-state societies? This is, in fact, the direction that is presented and sketched out—hypothetically—in this chapter. The cosmopolitan project contradicts and replaces the nation-state project.[5] An essential difference between the discourses of the world society and cosmopolitan

---

[5] For this, see discussions by Herder, Fichte, Schelling, Schlegel, Novalis, Schiller, Goethe, Heinrich, Heine, Nietzsche and many others. Heine, interestingly, dreaded a German national feeling without cosmopolitanism. But this is precisely what came to pass in the course of the twentieth century's history of madness and still continues today in a certain sense, because the tradition of German cosmopolitanism as a reservoir of ideas for political philosophy and theory is nowhere present. Here also, it holds true that the nation-state epoch has buried what must be rediscovered.

society is that in the latter globality becomes reflexive and political, which is to say that it is present in or even governs thinking and political action. In other words, the term 'world society' is not only too big but also too apolitical and undefined because it fails to address the key question of how people's cultural, political and biographical self-awarenesses change or have to change if they no longer move and locate themselves in a space of exclusive nation-states but in the space of world society instead. So the question is how does one re-image post-national political communities?

As far as I can see this question has not, as yet, really been analysed and discussed, either in political theory and science or in social theory and sociology. For example, in their brilliant work *Global Transformations*, Held *et al.* (1999) give stimulating analyses of globalizing politics, economics and culture, but they fail to enquire how society or the concept of political community changes under conditions of cosmopolitanization, or ask what cosmopolitanization means in terms of the images of the political community, social structure, political programmes, transnational parties and conflicts.

So the theme of this chapter is not (once again) the transformation of the inter-state system, not governance and democracy in a globalizing world, not the prospects of cosmopolitan democracy; neither is it the statelessness of the world society nor the proposition that the world society models are copied and so give a shape to the nation-state identities, structure and behaviour as part of a global cultural and associational process (Meyer *et al.* 1997). The question I want to put on the agenda is, how are we to imagine, define and analyse post-national, transnational and political communities? How are we to build a conceptual frame of reference in which to analyse the coming of a cosmopolitan society (behind the façade of nation-state societies) and its enemies.

Neither Habermas nor Luhmann provide an answer to this question. Luhmann does not do so because he posits world society as a post-political world society without enquiring into the political and cultural self-awareness of world citizens, as opposed to the citizens of the nation-states (Luhmann 1975: 51–63; 1997: 145ff.). He sees politics in terms of a millennial antithesis and dismisses it: the world society that undermines the paradigm of the nation-state has its counterpart in nation-state politics, which is condemned to die for this very reason. To be more precise, Luhmann formulates the zombie theory of the nation-state politics in world society—politics becomes one of the living dead and is unable to die; it is at the same time a theory of worldwide false consciousness. We are still playing democracy, but it is an epochal phantom sensation and it happens under false pretences. The place of politics in the paradigm of the nation-state is taken by a vacuum, which is (not) filled by the theory of functional differentiation on a world scale.

Habermas, on the other hand, does stress the overall importance of the question of how politics and democracy will be possible in the post-national constellation. He is looking for the 'possibilities of a political closure of a glob-ally networked, highly interdependent world society without regression' (Habermas 1998*b*: 130, 133ff., 153ff.) What he is ultimately talking about, however, is the question of a 'European people' as the subject of a post-national democracy, which is conceived in terms of an 'extended closure' of national democracy.

In both cases, politics is thought of exclusively in the model of the nation-state. In Luhmann's case it is negated: transnational politics can only be thought of as zombie politics or remainder politics (non-governmental organizations (NGOs) are a prime example); in Habermas's case, it is extended national poli-tics, one historical size bigger as it were (European democracy, European nation-state, European welfare state). Ultimately, Habermas gets caught in the contradictions of the theory of a post-national nation.

In the paradigm of the second age of modernity, however, the questions become acute and are addressed (Beck 2000*a*: 26–113): what transformations do society and politics undergo in the course of the transition from a national to a cosmopolitan society and politics? Which political categories and theories, which actors, which political institutions and ideas, which concept of the state and of democracy correspond to the epoch of world society? Who inhabits the transnational space—not only the capital and knowledge elites but also the blacks, immigrants, the excluded? Is there only a class of cosmopolitans or a cosmopolitanization of classes? How do global problems and opportunities for the development of transnational associations affect the individual conscious-ness and how can these associations become part of individuals' understanding of themselves? And which indicators and processes of the cosmopolitanization of national societies can be identified, analysed or commented on by the social sciences?

The old-fashioned modernists believe (positively or negatively) that only an all-embracing national project, held together by language, military service and patriotism (with or without a constitution) makes possible and guarantees the integration of modern society. Cosmopolitanization, by contrast, means that the ethnic identities within a nation become plural and relate in a plural and loyal way to the different nation-states. Nathan Sznaider (1999) argues that being an Israeli, for example, can mean that one reads Russian papers, watches Russian television, goes to a Russian theatre and listens to Russian rock music. But being an Israeli means equally that one takes one's Jewish-oriental identity seriously and, paradoxically, thanks to the influence of Western multicultural-ism, rejects everything Western. And, last but not least, being an Israeli also means that non-Jewish Israelis, Palestinians with an Israeli passport, claim multicultural autonomy for themselves.

For the inhabitants of the first (nation-state) age of modernity, who recognize patriotic identity as the only true and legitimate one, this ethnic conflict is no more than a primitive tribal war that will be resolved by modernization in an all-embracing state. The inhabitants of the second, post-national, age of modernity, however, are constantly reformulating and abandoning new categorizations. The resulting mixture is not a sign of the failure of integration; it is rather precisely the specific individuality determining identity and integration in this global society (Beck-Gernsheim 1999).

Thus, individuality is a result of the overlaps and conflicts with other identities. For each individual this is a creative achievement. The national public sphere becomes a space in which divisions can be overcome through conflict and in which certain kinds of indifference and social distance make a positive contribution to social integration. Conflict is the driving force of integration. A world society comes into being because it is divided. Tensions within the national public spheres are immediately buffered by indifference and relativized by transnational identities and networks. The cosmopolitan project both entails the national project and extends it. From the perspective of transnational identities and ways of life this means that it will be easier to try out and rearrange various combinations. One chooses and weights different overlapping identities and lives on the strength of the combination (Bauman 1996). The effect is of central importance: the enclosed space of the nation-state is no longer extant in the cosmopolitan project. The various groups remain in touch beyond the boundaries of the state, not only for the benefit of business and the development of scholarship but also in order to contain and control national divisions and conflicts by embedding them in intersecting transnational loyalties.

The question remains as to what extent collectively binding decisions are possible under these conditions. It is no longer a matter of solidarity or obligation but of a conflict-laden coexistence side by side in a transnationally neutralized space.

Migration and Transnational Risk Communities

In the first, nation-state, age of modernity, solidarity is always limited to one's own nation; it has degenerated into solidarity among equals. In the second age of modernity, therefore, the question to be asked is not how to revive solidarity, but how solidarity with strangers, among non-equals can be made possible. I will first explore the relationship between mobility and migration in this context and then develop the concept of transnational risk communities.

In the societal project of cosmopolitan modernity, the significance of mobility and migration also changes. In the nation-state paradigm of the first age of modernity there is a very clear-cut distinction between mobility and migrations in the sense that they are associated with diametrically opposite values. The movement within nation-states is called mobility and is highly desirable. The movement between nation-states is called migration and is extremely undesirable. At the

borders of nation-states the virtue of flexibility mutates into the vice of potentially criminal immigration. The paradigm of cosmopolitan society can now be
explained on the basis of the post-national distribution of labour and wealth
(Elkins 1995).

1. *Global population movements*: Increasing inequalities on a world scale and
   the differences between the sparsely populated wealthy states of the North
   and the densely populated poor states of the South will, as many argue, lead
   to new mass migrations from the overpopulated areas of the world to the
   sparsely populated regions with their tempting standard of living.
2. *Migration of labour*: Not the people but the workplaces move. Jobs
   (combined with corresponding training opportunities) are exported to
   places where the poor and the unemployed live, namely the overpopulated
   regions of the world.
3. *Transnational job-sharing between the rich and poor countries*:
   New ways of sharing work and wealth across borders and continents
   develop—without migration. In the long term this means that the elimination of distance—made possible by modes of production based on
   information technology—facilitates a cosmopolitan distribution of work
   and wealth. The rich countries would then export low skill jobs to poor
   countries, while jobs requiring greater skills would be located in sparsely
   populated but highly skilled countries.

Within the paradigm of the nation-state, the first scenario is regarded as a nightmare. The metaphor of the boat, which is allegedly full, fans the flames of xenophobia. The second scenario has been a reality for at least twenty years, but it
meets with considerable resistance from the states and trade unions of the job
exporting countries. The third scenario of international job sharing deserves to
be discussed as an alternative to mass emigration and Western protectionism.
David J. Elkins argues that in a cosmopolitan society two contrary questions are
posed: assuming that transnational audiences and communities do in fact
develop on the basis of a division of labour, which implies a distribution of life
chances, will this lead to a decrease in the pressure leading to emigration? Does
the cosmopolitan project contain a model to ease world tensions because the
need to seek one's happiness on another continent is diminished? To put the
question differently: if territoriality and nationality no longer define one's identity and life chances, why should one emigrate?

But one can also ask precisely the opposite question. If staying in one place
becomes less and less important for social relations and context, why should
migrants remain migrants and not be welcomed as mobile? If a pattern of social
relations establishes itself in which transnational identities and networks
dominate, that is in which people also live and work across borders, why should
they be prevented from emigrating to the places where they want to go?

The crucial question therefore is, to what extent are the forms of the division of labour and distribution of wealth linked to the cosmopolitan project? The protectionist double standard, distinguishing between undesired migration and desired mobility would become meaningless if such a link were established. The idea of mobility, not only in the spatial sense but also culturally and intellectually, which was originally linked to modernity, is detached from the constraints of geographical labour mobility and the mobility of wealth. Consequently, in a cosmopolitan society it will be possible to rediscover and explore the specific cultural meaning of 'mobility'. At the same time, it may become possible to reduce and overcome the tyranny of the spatial mobility of traffic.

What becomes evident in this context is that the cosmopolitan project also involves a new division of labour between business and politics. Business becomes, whether wittingly and willingly or not, the location and arm of transnational politics. Big companies determine the conditions and situations of people in society—usually unnoticed, often narrow-mindedly and thus exclusively pursuing their own economic interests. In the future, much will depend on whether they—under state guidance—perceive and accept the politically formative role in world society that has become theirs. Since the companies determine the distribution of labour and income through their investment decisions, they create the basis for inequality, justice, freedom and democracy on a worldwide scale. Why not, for example, privatize both the profits and the costs of unemployment and ecological destruction so that businesses are held responsible for the social consequences of their decisions and have to anticipate those consequences in their own economic interest?

The Socialization of Risk

In the second age of modernity the relationship between the state, business and a society of citizens must be redefined. The state-fixated perspective of a nationally defined society seems to have particular difficulty in recognizing and exploring the benefit of the scenario of a society of citizens for the transnational revival and encouragement of politics and democracy. One thing, however, is certain. Without stronger citizen elements, solidarity with foreigners and a corresponding extension and restructuring of national institutions (trade unions and consumer movements) is impossible. Trade unions, for instance, would no longer be tied to plants and industries in a national frame, but must adapt to fragile, risky labour conditions and operate along global chains of value creation.

This raises a key question. On what basis do transnational community ties, which are no longer supported by place (neighbourhood), origin (family) or nation (state organized solidarity of citizens), have their material foundation and sense of obligation? How can decisions be made that are at once post-national and collectively binding, or, in other words, how is political activity possible in the age of globalization?

Whoever poses the question, how modern societies, having dissolved all givens and transformed them into decisions, handle the uncertainties of their own making, encounters a core invention of modern times: the socialization of shared risks or shared risk definitions (Beck 1992, 1996*b*, 1999*b*). Risks presuppose decisions, definitions and permit individualization. They relate to individual cases here and now. At the same time, however, they set an organizational pattern of formulae of community formations and bonds, which is separate from individual cases, and allows the establishment of mathematical calculable probabilities and scenarios, on the one hand, and negotiable standards of shared rights and duties, costs and compensation, on the other. In a world risk society, the risk regime also implies a hidden, community building aspect and force (Elkins 1995). If, for example, the states around the North Sea regard themselves as a risk community in the face of the continuing threat to water, humans, animals, tourism, business, capital, political confidence and so on, then this means that an established and accepted definition of threat creates a shared space for values, responsibilities and actions that transcends all national boundaries and divisions. By analogy with the national space, this can create an active solidarity among strangers and foreigners. This is the case if the accepted definition of a threat leads to binding arrangements and responses. The accepted definition of a risk thus creates and binds—across national boundaries—cultural value frameworks with forms of more or less compensatory, responsible counter activities. It is a transnational answer to the key question of active solidarity. From whom can I expect help if and when necessary and to whom will I have to give help in an emergency? Risk communities, therefore, combine what is apparently mutually exclusive.

- They are based on culturally divergent values and perceptions.
- They can be chosen.
- They can be regulated informally or by contract.
- They conform to or create definitions of community.
- In culturally divided and socially constructed definitions of risk, they establish socially binding cross-frontier neighbourliness.
- They are not comprehensive but affectual, linked to certain themes and priorities.
- They create a moral space of mutual commitments across frontiers.
- This space is defined by answers to the question, from whom can I expect help? To whom will I have to give help if this or that happens? What kind of help can I expect or do I have to give?

The realities that are perceived and assessed as risks are the secondary realities of civilization and not fate. The defining element of risk communities is, therefore, not a common destiny that has to be accepted but their covert political character, the fact that they are based on decisions and questions that can be made and answered differently. Who is responsible? What has to be done and changed on a small and on a large scale, locally, nationally and globally in order to avert risks?

Indicators of Cosmopolitanization

With that we once again come to the key question of this chapter: what does cosmopolitanization and/or cosmopolitan society mean? A further step towards answering this question is to specify and investigate the empirical indicators of cosmopolitanization (without any claim to comprehensiveness and systematic exposition).

1. *Cultural commodities*: Developments in the import and export of cultural commodities, transnationalization of the book trade, developments in the import and export of periodicals, in the number and proportion of local and foreign productions in the cinema, in the proportion of local and foreign productions in television, corresponding radio broadcasts and so on.

2. *Dual citizenship*: Legal basis and official practice in dealing with migrants, asylum seekers; how are 'foreigners' defined statistically, in the media and in everyday (administrative) practice?

3. *Political intensities*: To what extent are various ethnic groups represented and present in the centres of national power—parties, parliaments, governments, trade unions?

4. *Languages*: Who speaks how many languages? (Recently, for example, a news item was widely reported in the German media, according to which in a small town in Bavaria—Landshut—more than 20 different languages were spoken by children in one secondary modern school class).

5. *Mobility*: Permanent immigration, development of immigration, development of labour migration; temporary immigration, development of refugee numbers, development in the number of foreign students.

6. *Routes of communication*: Development of items sent by letter post, nationally and internationally; development of telephone conversations, nationally and internationally, of the corresponding data exchange through the electronic network and so on.

7. *International travel*: Development of international passenger air travel, development of international tourism, the number and proportion of journeys abroad.

8. *Activity in transnational initiatives and organizations*: Short or long-term involvement in campaigns by Greenpeace, Amnesty International and

NGOs, or participation in international collections of signatures, consumer boycotts and so on.

9. *Criminal activity*: Development of international (organized) criminality; development of politically motivated acts and/or acts of violence by transnational terrorism.

10. *Transnational ways of life*: Diaspora communities and their cross-border private and public networks and decision-making structures, number and kind of transnational marriages, births of transnational children, new emerging 'hybrid' cultures, literatures, languages.

11. *Transnational nexus coverage*: For example of wars on television; to what extent is a change in perspective taking place?

12. *National identities*: What is the relationship of the number and kind of national identities to citizenship identity? Does cosmopolitanism cancel national identity? Or is there something like a cosmopolitan nation and what does that mean?

13. *Ecological crisis*: Development in the (stratospheric) ozone layer, development of world climate, development of worldwide fish resources, development of cross-border air and water pollution, development of attitudes to local, national and global world crises, environmental legislation, environmental jurisdiction, environmental markets, environmental jobs.

The quantitative development of these indicators is of course difficult to assess simply because of the available statistics and the immense problems of comparability. And yet, an initial survey shows that cosmopolitanization can be understood and represented empirically, although it varies considerably by country and dimension (see Beisheim *et al.* 1999; Held *et al.* 1999). Since the 1990s, however, the breadth and intensity of cosmopolitanization has acquired a new quality, and surpassed by far what could be observed at the beginning of the twentieth century. Parallel with cosmopolitanism on the micro level in the life worlds, ways of life and everyday institutions of society (such as school or municipality), a process of cosmopolitanization is also taking place on the macro level. This is occurring not solely as a result of the world market dependencies, but also in the international and supranational network of institutions (Kaldor 1995*b*; Lapid and Kratochwil 1997; Falk 1998; Rosenau 1998; Held *et al.* 1999).

But that does not answer the question, what is a cosmopolitan society? It is probably easier to say what it is not. It is certainly not useful to talk about a cosmopolitan society if the process of cosmopolitanization has begun and is continuing exclusively on an objective level, but is at the same time being (actively) masked by a dominant national project and a national self definition of society—in the political parties, in the government, in the media and in the educational system. It follows that it is only meaningful to talk of cosmopolitanization once this process is not only objectively indicated but is also reflexively known, commented on and institutionalized. But that in turn means that only through the contrast and conflict between cosmopolitan and national projects does the former become real and effective. Included in the social locations in which the specific space–time dimension and the new subjects of the global become concentrated and self aware are not only the privileged capitalists and intellectual professions, but also the various ethnic groups, women, immigrants, in fact all those who are marginalized in the national space. Here too a politics informed by cosmopolitanism can discover zones of activity that belong neither to the state nor to business.

Roland Robertson (1992) was probably the first to make becoming aware and awareness of one world the indicator of cosmopolitanism, as does Martin Albrow in his book *The Global Age* (1996). Armin Nassehi (1998) pursues a similar argument when he links cosmopolitanism to the Thomas theorem and thus to the self-definition and public reflexivity of transnational ways of life and situations, not only at the top but also at the bottom and in the middle of an emerging society of world citizens.

The process concept 'cosmopolitanization' must therefore be understood as a relational concept, a relational process, in which, on the one hand the connections between cosmopolitan changes and movements and on the other the resistances and blockades triggered by them are analysed together. Cosmopolitanization, therefore, by no means indicates 'a' cosmopolitan society, but the interactive relationship of de-nationalization and re-nationalization, de-ethnicization and re-ethnicization, de-localization and re-localization in society and politics (Miller 1995*b*; Eade 1997; Bauman 1999).

This gives rise to a twofold reproach of the conspicuous popularity of the term identity (Meyer and Geschiere 1999). Identity denies ambivalence, pins things down and attempts to draw boundaries in a process of cosmpolitanization that suspends and blurs boundaries. There is a corresponding nostalgia on the part of social scientists (not forgetting anthropologists) for an ordered world of clear boundaries and the associated social categories. In such a world, theoretical reflection simply assumed the existence of boundaries rather than questioning them, with a high degree of reflexivity, as problematic constructs are done today.

Bearing this in mind, it is very tempting to develop the argument of cosmopolitanization as a phased model in which progressive cosmopolitanization develops in tandem with its ambivalences, that is to say a cosmopolitan society and its enemies. The phases of blocked cosmopolitanization overlap with the phases and movements of cosmopolitan reflexivity in which the self-awareness and the political aims of the cosmopolitan movements within and between national societies and nation-states articulate and organize themselves

(Cheah and Robbins 1998). Where this is the case, cosmopolitanization is no longer merely an objective process but is also a publicly reflected one in which rebellious groups break out of the shell of their dependence on nation-state identity. The symbolism of the melting pot—the model of integration in the first age of modernity—is replaced by the symbolism of the 'salad bowl', an image that anticipates the elements of a deterritorialized concept of society, but also becomes caught up in a web of contradictions (Beck-Gernsheim 1999).

Self-reflection points to a blind spot in the current talk of space–time compression. What does the deterritorialization of time mean? Or, putting the question differently, what does global memory, namely remembering, mean in the world society? In the cosmopolitan project historical time is no longer conceived as a national culture of memory, with individual remembering enclosed within it, but as fragmented and plural, in other words, a cosmopolitan and therefore optional remembrance and memory with all the resulting contingencies, complexities and contradictions of individual memory. The place of publicly reflected national history and historiography—which includes the time and becoming of self—is taken by staged landscapes of memory, which can only be deciphered transnationally. These landscapes of memory can no longer be dismissed as national absent-mindedness. They pave the way for forms of de-territorialized memory and remembrance in the world society. The liberation movements and African Americans who have broken the spell of the national memory provide exemplary illustrations of this process. Likewise, in their historiography, the blacks in the United States of America are discovering their roots by developing fragmented and staged transatlantic forms of memory and remembrance and related historiographies and self-discoveries (Beck-Gernsheim 1999).

Accordingly, we have to distinguish between the different forms of expression of cosmopolitan self-reflection. There is first of all the pattern of minority revolution under majority dominance. In the course of this publicly conducted conflict, the national monopoly on remembrance collapses, and a variety of loosely connected, boundary-transcending layers of memory emerge, unfold (and are invented). This critique of collective memory allows the various minorities to get a clearer picture of their history of oppression and detaches it from the nation-state equation of space, time and society. In the media and in the social sciences, these struggles over remembrance, memory and identity are debated under the heading of multiculturalism. The increasing self confidence of the 'multicultural'—by now on a transnational level—shatters the frame of reference of national integration and with it a key principle of the societal organization of the first age of modernity. As this entails questioning the cultural and political claim to power of the state-determining minority, this kind of reflexive cosmopolitanism is dramatized as an identity crisis and a political crisis of the nation-state. The United States of America, as well as the United Kingdom, France, Germany and Israel exemplify this.

A retrospective historical view may be instructive here. In the context of the first nation-state epoch of modernity, an illuminating debate took place on the connections between cosmopolitanism, nation and state. This debate must be reopened to address the challenges of this second age of modernity. For example, in the eighteenth century, the idea of the citizen of the world was one of the programmatic, indeed fashionable phrases of the Enlightenment. It developed in close relationship with transnational organizations (such as Freemasonry), served the promotion of tolerance, was closely linked to the concept of humanity and not least to a universal eternal peace (from Kant to Croce) encompassing all the states of the earth. Even then there was a lively discussion about how the world citizenship and nationality could be combined, that is the degree to which cosmopolitan orientations in particular formed the basis and limit of a national consciousness.[6] The idea was born of a 'cosmopolitan nation'.

Against this background, a few at least of the basic features of the ideal type of 'cosmopolitan society' can be determined; this is a type of deterritorialized society that is: (1) essentially structured by an objective process of cosmopolitanization (as given by the corresponding indicators and their empirical significance and interpretations); is (2) on its way to a reflexive cosmopolitanism; and (3) simultaneously an institutionalized reflexive learning process is gaining in importance, perhaps even becoming dominant. The aim of this learning process is to test how in one's own life, in a world without distance, ways of relating to the otherness of others can be learned. This includes, in particular, issues of a shifting perspective and transnational conflict resolution:

- a society in which the cosmopolitan values rate more highly than the national values;
- a society in which the national–cosmopolitan parties, identities, institutions are invented, tested and developed;
- and in this way they gain increasing power by comparison with the national and nationalist counter-movements, and can assert themselves on a worldwide scale.

In other words, a cosmopolitan society means a cosmopolitan society and its enemies.

---

[6] As Manuel Castells (1997: 11–131) points out, there may be various oppositions to globalization: religious fundamentalism, nationalism, and ethnic or territorial identities. I propose the hypothesis that the constitution of subjects at the heart of the process of social change takes a different route from the one we knew during modernity, namely subjects, if and when constructed, are not built any longer on the basis of civil societies (as in the case of socialism on the basis of the labour movement) but as a prolongation of the communal resistance against globalization. But Castells misses the importance of cosmopolitanization (objective and reflexive) and the coming of cosmopolitan movements and ideologies—namely the inside–outside politicization of nation-state societies—from which counter-cosmopolitan movements like ethnic nationalism, fundamentalism and territorial identities derive and must be understood.

Final reflections

A congenital defect of the first age of modernity, which may become a dramatic problem in the second modernity, is that thus far the institutionalization of conflict has almost only been developed within nation-states. Procedures have not been developed in those places in a world society where explosive sources of conflict will arise out of the mix of protectionist reactions, the constraints of cooperation and the oversize questions of the second age of modernity, which demand concrete and radical changes in the economy, administration, politics and everyday life. For sure, the global and transnational have their address and jurisdictions: the General Assembly of the UN, the International Court of Justice in the Hague or also—with reference to Europe—the supranational institutions of the EU. And yet it is not hard to demonstrate that, on the one hand, a striking and growing imbalance exists between the new and intensifying sources of conflict between the nations, regions and cultures and, on the other, there are the few, rather non-obligatory, relatively weak institutions of transnational or even global conflict resolution floating somehow above things, with large moral claims but without the power to make decisions binding.

The old–new sources of conflict are more quickly named than exorcized. First, the establishment of free world markets itself must be stressed, for at least two reasons. Within nation-states, wherever there existed strong working-class parties, welfare state social security systems and forms of trades union negotiating power, this led to a de-institutionalization of the conflict between capital and labour. The demand for flexibility, which is heard on all sides, means nothing other than the relaxation or abolition of rules on how the collective labour contracts, codetermination standards and industrial health and safety requirements are negotiated. At the same time, the neo-liberal revolt aims at an internal and international minimization of the state. However, this can easily turn into a militarization of internal and interstate conflicts.

Other new areas of conflict, the results of which are likewise very far from foreseeable, can only be mentioned here: ecological crises, catastrophes and wars. The conflicts of the divergent modernities over the old and new fundamentalisms are already casting dark shadows over the future. It is precisely in the opening out and compression of the world, in the spaces without distance of the mass media, and in the new production and labour forms of transnational companies spreading over frontiers and across continents that new sources of conflict are emerging, which are difficult to assess. Their force must be seen in an overlapping combination of virtuality and reality. They include the global risks and processes of possible mass migrations from the poor to the rich regions of the world; the nuclear power stations that may explode tomorrow or in a thousand years; and the new (deliberately) hidden internationally organized crime. Characteristic of these global threats is that they can develop a society-changing power precisely in places where they have not appeared and put into action the underlying political meaning of risk dramaturgy (not) to act before it is too late.

In future, those transnational conflicts that emerge from the triumphal march of neo-liberal policies, and hence develop a capacity for political irritation, will substantially affect the everyday life of business, politics and people. Closely regulated industries have been liberalized in recent years: telecommunications, energy, food and finance. The worldwide competitiveness released as a result has brought conflict between the national standardization bodies. With the free movement of goods the problem has meanwhile become a global one. And all this is only the beginning. Further sources of conflict are already becoming apparent, for example over agreements on global food, environmental or labour market standards, and over regulation in fields in which conflicts are even more difficult to manage because they are politically highly sensitive.

The first wave of national deregulation makes necessary a second wave of transnational regulation. Thus, the state and politics, which were devalued in the 1980s, now become revalued. What is needed is the complete opposite of neo-liberal deconstruction, that is to say strong, transnationally active states so that the global market regulations can be established internally and externally. To the extent that such agreements are found, invented and negotiated, globality will become a theme and an axis of conflict not only in politics and business but also in the everyday life of people around the world.

What follows from all of this? In a world without distance, which is consequently becoming more crowded and susceptible to conflict, it is the task of political action and activity to establish and test—with all the available human creativity and political–institutional imagination—the transnational forums and forms of a regulated, namely acknowledged, non-violent resolution of conflicts between mutually exclusive and often mutually hostile national and cosmopolitan movements. For this idea of transnational institutions, transnational conflict recognition and resolution—a centrepiece of cosmopolitan democracy—to assume a shape and power, a new political subject needs to be legitimated and founded: the movements and parties of world citizens. The sociology of the second age of modernity can make a contribution to this by both widening the cosmopolitan perspective and focusing it more sharply.

7

The Class Consciousness of Frequent Travellers: Towards a Critique of Actually Existing Cosmopolitanism

CRAIG CALHOUN

Some claim that the world is gradually becoming united, that it will grow into a brotherly community as distances shrink and ideas are transmitted through the air. Alas, you must not believe that men can be united in this way.

—Fyodor Dostoevsky (1981: 379)

A certain attenuated cosmopolitanism had taken place of the old home feeling.

—Thomas Carlyle (1888: 369)

Among the great struggles of man—good/evil, reason/unreason, etc.—there is also this mighty conflict between the fantasy of Home and the fantasy of Away, the dream of roots and the mirage of the journey.

—Salman Rushdie (2000: 55)

On 11 September 2001, terrorists crashing jets into the World Trade Center and the Pentagon struck a blow against cosmopolitanism—perhaps more successfully than against their obvious symbolic targets, the unequal structures of global capitalism and political power. They precipitated a renewal of state-centred politics and a 'war on terrorism', seeking military rather than law enforcement solutions to crime. Moved by Wahabi Islamic Puritanism and sheltered by Afghanistan's Taliban, they seemed to exemplify a simplistic

Earlier versions of this chapter were presented to the conference, 'Conceiving Cosmopolitanism', University of Warwick, April 2000; to the International Studies Association in February 2001; to the University of North Carolina Conference on Local Democracy and Globalization in March 2001; and at Candido Mendes University in May 2001. I am grateful for comments on all these occasions and especially from Pamela DeLargy, Saurabh Dube, Michael Kennedy, Laura MacDonald, Thomas McCarthy, and Kathryn Sikkink. A similar version of this chapter will be published in the *South Atlantic Quarterly* 101: 3 (2002) and its inclusion in this collection is with the permission of the author and publisher.

opposition between backward traditionalists and Western modernism. That Muslims had long been stereotyped as the bad Other to globalization only made it easier for Westerners to accept this dubious framing of the events, and made it harder for them to see a clash between different modernist projects and to miss the evidently popular message that 'technology can be our weapon too'.

One need be no friend to terrorism to be sorry that the dominant response to the terrorist attacks has been framed as a matter of war rather than crime, an attack on America rather than an attack on humanity. What could have been an occasion for renewing the drive to establish an international criminal court and the multilateral institutions needed for law enforcement, quickly became an occasion for America to demonstrate its power and its allies to fall into line with the 'war against terrorism'. Militarism gained and civil society lost not only on '11 September' but also in the response that followed (see Kaldor 2002 for a good analysis of this). This was true domestically as well as internationally, as the United States of America and other administrations moved to sweep aside protections for the rights of citizens and immigrants alike and strengthen the state in pursuit of 'security'.

In this context, the cosmopolitan ideals articulated during the 1990s seem all the more attractive but their realization much less imminent. It is important not only to mourn this but also to ask in what ways the cosmopolitan vision itself was limited—over-optimistic, perhaps, more attentive to certain prominent dimensions of globalization than to equally important others. In the wake of the Cold War, it seemed to many political theorists and public actors that the moment had finally arrived not just for Kantian perpetual peace but also for cosmopolitanism to extend beyond mere tolerance to the creation of a shared global democracy. It seemed easy to denigrate states as old-fashioned authorities of waning influence and to extol the virtues of international civil society. It was perhaps a weakness of this perspective that the myriad dimensions of globalization all seemed evidence of the need for a more cosmopolitan order, and therefore the tensions among them were insufficiently examined. Likewise, the cosmopolitanism of democratic activists was not always clearly distinct from that of global corporate leaders, though the latter would exempt corporate property from democratic control. Just as protesters against the WTO often portrayed themselves as being 'anti-globalization', even though they formed a global social movement, the advocates of cosmopolitan institutions often sounded simply pro-globalization rather than sufficiently discriminating among its forms.

In a sense, the non-cosmopolitan side of globalization struck back on 11 September. Migrants whose visions of their home cultures were more conservative and ideological than the originals figured prominently. Indeed, most of the terrorists were Arabs who had spent considerable time studying in the

West—even at seemingly cosmopolitan Oxford, in the case of Osama bin Laden. A dark side to globalization was brought to light: criminal activity and flow of weapons, people, ideas, money and drugs that challenged the state authority but hardly in the name of the international civil society, and sometimes financed terrorist networks. At the same time, the sharp inequalities masked by cosmopolitan ideals—and especially the use of cosmopolitan rhetoric by neo-liberal corporate leaders whose actions contribute to those inequalities—challenged efforts to 'solve' terrorism as a problem separate from others.

This chapter is an effort to examine some of the limits and biases of the cosmopolitan theory that flourished in the 1990s. It is written not as a rejection of cosmopolitanism but as a challenge to think through more fully what sorts of social bases have shaped cosmopolitan visions and what sorts of issues need more attention if advances in democracy are to be made. What experiences make cosmopolitan democracy an intuitively appealing approach to the world? What experiences does it obscure from view? I also want to consider how much the political theory of cosmopolitanism is shaped by liberalism's poorly drawn fight with communitarianism and thus left lacking a strong account of solidarity. This impedes efforts to defend the achievements of previous social struggles against neo-liberal capitalism, or to ground new political action. Finally, I wish to offer a plea for the importance of the local and particular—not least as a basis for democracy and no less important for being necessarily incomplete. Whatever its failings, 'the old home feeling' helped to produce a sense of mutual obligations, of 'moral economy', to borrow the phrase Edward Thompson (1971) retrieved from an old tradition.

Cosmopolitanism, Old and New

Cosmopolitanism today partly resumes its own old tradition. Cosmopolitan ideals flourished as calls for unity among the ancient Greek city-states, though in fact these were often at war. Rome was more cosmopolitan if less philosophical than Greece. Cosmopolitanism has been a project of empires, of long distance trade and of cities. Christianity offered a cosmopolitan framework to medieval Europe, though it equally informed a non-cosmopolitan rejection of those it deemed heretics and heathen. The Ottoman Empire offered a high point of cosmopolitanism, and European empires their own often less tolerant versions. But the cosmopolitanism of the Church and the empire depended on the distinction of the merchants and clerics from the rulers. It is, thus, an innovation to see cosmopolitanism as a political project and especially to speak of 'cosmopolitan democracy'. The tolerance of diversity in great imperial and trading cities has always reflected, among other things, precisely the absence of need or opportunity to organize political self-rule.

A new cosmopolitanism flourished in the Enlightenment. This once again involved relative elites without a responsibility for ruling. It did none the less influence rulers, not least by encouraging a courtly cosmopolitanism in the later years of the ancient regime. There were also cosmopolitan links among the democrats and the other insurgents, and these contributed to the ideals of the late eighteenth-century public sphere. Nationalism and cosmopolitanism met in certain strands of the American and French revolutions and linked to democracy in figures like Thomas Paine. But eighteenth-century cosmopolitanism, especially its elite variants, was hostile to religion, and in opposing reason to prejudice often imagined a collective life free of traditional loyalties, rather than incorporating them in a heterogeneous form. The philosophical cosmopolitans of the Enlightenment imagined a world reflecting their lives and intellectual projects. During the same period, though, European colonial projects were becoming increasingly important. They informed both the development of nationalism and that of cosmopolitanism, the view of both home and away. While some nineteenth-century thinkers embraced cosmopolitanism as an urban aesthetic ideal, others, like Thomas Carlyle, were ambivalent about cosmopolitanism. They worried that it was somehow an 'attenuated' solidarity by comparison with those rooted in the more specific local cultures and communities.

Today's cosmopolitans need to confront the same concerns. Many rightly point to the limits and dangers of relying on nation-states to secure democracy in a world that is ever more dramatically organized across state borders. Yet they—we—imagine the world from the vantage point of frequent travellers, easily entering and exiting polities and social relations around the world, armed with visa-friendly passports and credit cards. For such frequent travellers cosmopolitanism has considerable rhetorical advantage. It seems hard not to want to be a 'citizen of the world'. Certainly, at least in Western academic circles, it is hard to imagine preferring to be known as parochial. But what does it mean to be a 'citizen of the world'? Through what institutions is this 'citizenship' effectively expressed? Is it mediated through various particular and more local solidarities? Does it present a new, expanded category of identification as better than older, narrower ones (as the nation has frequently been opposed to the province or village) or does it pursue better relations among a diverse range of traditions and communities? How does this citizenship contend with global capitalism and with non-cosmopolitan dimensions of globalization?

A thoroughgoing cosmopolitanism might indeed bring concern for the fate of all humanity to the fore, but a more attenuated cosmopolitanism is likely to leave us lacking the old sources of solidarity without adequate new ones. Much cosmopolitanism focuses on the development of a world government or at least global political institutions. These, advocates argue, must be strengthened if democracy is to have much future in a world where nation-states are challenged by global capitalism, cross-border flows and international media, and accordingly

; able to manage collective affairs (see Archibugi and Held 1995; Held 1995a; Archibugi *et al.* 1998).[1] At the same time, these advocates see the growing domestic heterogeneity and newly divisive sub-national politics as reducing the efficacy of the nation-states from within. While most embrace diversity as a basic value, they simultaneously see multiculturalism as a political problem. In the dominant cosmopolitan theories, it is the global advance of democracy that receives most attention and in which most hopes are vested. But cosmopolitanism without the strengthening of local democracy is likely to be a very elite affair. And advances in global democracy are challenged by fragmented solidarities at both the intermediate and local levels.

Place and Perspective

Cosmopolitanism is often presented simply as global citizenship. Advocates offer a claim to being without determinate social bases, which is reminiscent of Mannheim's idea of the free-floating intellectual. In offering a seeming 'view from nowhere', cosmopolitans commonly offer a view from Brussels (where the post-national is identified with the strength of the EU rather than the weakness of, say, African states), or from Davos (where the post-national is corporate), or from the university (where the illusion of a free-floating intelligentsia is supported by a relatively fluid exchange of ideas across national borders).

Cosmopolitanism is a discourse centred in a Western view of the world.[2] It sets itself up commonly as a 'third way' between rampant corporate globalization and reactionary traditionalism or nationalism. If Giddens's account of the third way is most familiar, the trope is still more widespread. Barber's notion of a path beyond 'Jihad vs. McWorld' is an example brought to renewed prominence (and the best-seller lists) following the 11 September attacks.[3] Such oppositions oversimplify at best though, and often get in the way of actually

---

[1] Archibugi and Held (1995), and their contributors, conceptualize democratic cosmopolitan politics as a matter of several layers of participation in discourse and decision-making, including especially the strengthening of institutions of global civil society, rather than an international politics dominated by nation-states. Less layered and complex accounts appear in Falk's (2000) call for a global governance and Nussbaum's (1997b) universalism.

[2] One is reminded of Malaysian Prime Minister Mahathir Mohamad's account of human rights as the new Christianity. It makes Europeans feel entitled, he suggested, to invade countries around the world and try to subvert their traditional values, convert them and subjugate them. Mahathir was of course defending an often-abusive government as well as local culture, but a deeper question is raised.

[3] Jihad and McWorld operate with equal strength in opposite directions, the one driven by parochial hatreds, the other by universalizing markets, the one re-creating ancient sub-national and ethnic borders from within, the other making war on national borders from without. Yet Jihad and McWorld have this in common: they both make war on the sovereign nation-state and thus undermine the nation-state's democratic institutions' (Barber 1995: 6). In his opening remarks to the Warwick University Conference on 'Conceiving Cosmopolitanism', David Held similarly opposed 'traditional' and 'global' in positioning cosmopolitanism between the two.

achieving some of the goals of cosmopolitan democracy. In the first place, they reflect a problematic denigration of tradition, including ethnicity and religion. This can be misleading in even a sheer factual sense—as for example Barber's description of Islamism as the reaction of small and relatively homogeneous countries to capitalist globalization. The oppositions are also prejudicial. One should note, for example, the tendency to treat the West as the site of both the capitalist globalization and cosmopolitanism, but to approach the non-West through the category of tradition. More generally, cultural identities and communal solidarities are treated less as creative constructions forged amid globalization than as inheritances from an older order. They should be available to people, much cosmopolitan thought implies, as lifestyle choices. As Brennan (2001: 76) puts it, cosmopolitanism 'designates an enthusiasm for customary differences, but as ethical or aesthetic material for a unified polychromatic culture—a new singularity born of a blending and merging of multiple local constituents'.[4] This vision of unity amid difference echoes on a grander scale that of great empires and great religions, and it underwrites the cosmopolitan appeal for an all-encompassing world government.[5]

Cosmopolitanism also reflects an elite perspective on the world. Certainly, few academic theories escape this charge, but it is especially problematic when the object of theory is the potential for democracy. The top ranks of capitalist corporations provide exemplars of a certain form of cosmopolitanism, though not of democracy. Likewise, a large proportion of the global civil society—from the World Bank to the NGOs setting accountancy standards—exists to support capitalism not pursue democracy. Even the ideas of cosmopolitan democracy and humanitarian activism, however, reflect an awareness of the world that is made possible by the proliferation of NGOs working to solve environmental and humanitarian problems, and by the growth of media attention to these problems. These are important—indeed vital—concerns. None the less, the concerns, the media and the NGOs need to be grasped reflexively as the basis for an intellectual perspective. It is a perspective, for example, that makes nationalism appear one-sidedly as negative. This is determined first, perhaps, by the prominence of ethno-nationalist violence in recent humanitarian crises, but also by the tensions between states and international NGOs. It is also shaped by specifically European visions and projects of transnationalism. Nationalism looks different from, say, an African vantage point. And it is often the weakness of states that seems the most pressing problem, even if tyrants control these relatively weak states.

---

[4] Arguing against Archibugi's account of the nation-state, Brennan rightly notes the intrinsic importance of imperialism, though he ascribes rather more complete causal power to it than history warrants.

[5] The call for world government is more important to some cosmopolitans—notably Richard Falk—than others. See, for example, Falk (2000).

The cosmopolitan ideals of a global civil society can sound uncomfortably like those of the civilizing mission behind colonialism, especially when presented as a programme from the outside borne by global NGOs rather than an opportunity for local development. In this connection, we should recall how recent, temporary and ever incomplete the apparent autonomy and closure of 'nation' is. In Europe, the invocation of 'nation' may sound conservative and traditional (though it was not always so). Looked at from the standpoint of India, say, or Ethiopia, it is not at all clear whether 'nation' belongs on the side of tradition or on that of developing cosmopolitanism. Or is it perhaps distinct from both—a novel form of solidarity and a basis for political claims on the state, one that presumes and to some extent demands the performance of internal unity and external boundedness?

The very idea of democracy suggests that it cannot be imposed from above, simply as a matter of a rational plan. Democracy must grow out of the life world; it must empower people not in the abstract but in the actual conditions of their lives. This means to empower them within communities and traditions, not in spite of them, and as members of groups not only as individuals. This does not mean accepting the old definitions of all groups; there may be a struggle over how groups are constituted. For example, appeals to aboriginal rights need not negate the possibility of struggle within 'traditional' groups over such issues as gender bias in leadership.[6] Cosmopolitan democracy—refusing the unity of simple sameness and the tyranny of the majority—must demand attention to differences—of values, perceptions, interests and understandings.

Yet, it is important we recognize that legitimacy is not the same as motivation. We need to pay attention to the social contexts in which people are moved by commitments to each other. Cosmopolitanism that does so will be variously articulated with locality, community and tradition, and not simply as a matter of common denominators. It will depend to a very large extent on local and particularistic border crossings and pluralisms, not universalism.

Such cosmopolitanism would both challenge the abandonment of globalization to neo-liberalism (whether with enthusiasm or a sense of helpless pessimism), and question the impulse to respond simply by defending nations or communities that experience globalization as a threat. None the less, the power of states and global corporations and the systemic imperatives of global markets suggest that advancing democracy will require struggle. This means not only a struggle against states or corporations, but also struggle within them to determine the way they work as institutions, how they distribute benefits, what kinds of participation they invite. The struggle for democracy, accordingly, cannot be only a cosmopolitan struggle from social locations that transcend these domains; it must also be a local struggle within them. It would

---

[6] This is a central issue in debates over group rights. See for example Kymlicka (1995).

be a mistake to imagine that cosmopolitan ethics—universally applied—could somehow substitute for a multiplicity of political, economic and cultural struggles. Indeed, the very struggle may be an occasion and source for solidarity.

Liberalism and Belonging

Contemporary cosmopolitanism is the latest effort to revitalize liberalism.[7] It has much to recommend it. Aside from world peace and more diverse ethnic restaurants, there is the promise to attend to one of the great lacunae of more traditional liberalism. This is the assumption of nationality as the basis for membership in states, even though this implies a seemingly illiberal reliance on inheritance and ascription rather than choice, and an exclusiveness that is hard to justify in liberal terms.

Political theory has, surprisingly, often avoided addressing the problems of political belonging in a serious, analytic way by presuming that nations exist as the pre-political bases of state-level politics. I do not mean that the political theorists are nationalists in their political preferences, but rather that their way of framing analytic problems is shaped by the rhetoric of nationalism and the ways in which this has become basic to the modern social imaginary.[8] 'Let us imagine a society', theoretical deliberations characteristically begin, 'and then consider what form of government would be just for it'. Nationalism provides this singular and bounded notion of society with its intuitive meaning.

Even so Kantian, methodologically individualistic and generally non-nationalist a theorist as John Rawls exemplifies the standard procedure, seeking in *A Theory of Justice* to understand what kind of society individuals behind the veil of ignorance would choose—but presuming that they would imagine this society on the model of a nation-state. Rawls modifies his arguments in considering international affairs in *Political Liberalism* and *The Law of Peoples* (1999), but continues to assume something like an idealized nation-state as the natural form of society. As he (Rawls 1993: 41) writes:

We have assumed that a democratic society, like any political society, is to be viewed as a complete and closed social system. It is complete in that it is self-sufficient and has a place for all the main purposes of human life. It is also closed, in that entry into it is only by birth and exit from it is only by death.

Rawls is aware of migration, war and global media, of course, even while he rules them out of theory and even though it is striking how little he considers the

---

[7] Liberalism of course embraces a wide spectrum of views in which emphases may fall more on property rights or more on democracy. So too cosmopolitanism can imply a global view that is liberal not specifically democratic. Archibugi prefers 'cosmopolitics' to 'cosmopolitan' in order to signal just this departure from a more general image of liberal global unity. See Archibugi (2000).

[8] On the predominance of nationalist understandings in conceptions of 'society', see Calhoun (1999).

globalization of economic foundations for his imagined society. For Rawls, questions of international justice seem to be just as that phrase and much diplomatic practice implies: questions 'between peoples', each of which should be understood as unitary. Note also the absence of attention to local or other constituent communities within this conception of society. Individuals and the whole society have a kind of primacy over any other possible groupings. This is the logic of nationalism (Calhoun 1997).

This is precisely what cosmopolitanism contests—at least at its best—and rightly so. Indeed, one of the reasons given for the very term is that it is less likely than 'international' to be confused with exclusively intergovernmental relations (Archibugi 1998: 216). The advocates of cosmopolitanism argue that people belong to a range of polities of which nation-states are only one, and that the range of significant relationships formed across state borders is growing. Their goal is to extend citizenship rights and responsibilities to the full range of associations thus created. In David Held's (1995a: 233) words, 'people would come, thus, to enjoy multiple citizenships—political membership in the diverse political communities which significantly affected them. They would be citizens of their immediate political communities, and of the wider regional and global networks which impacted upon their lives'.[9] Though it is unclear how this might work out in practice, this challenge to the presumption of nationality as the basis for citizenship is one of the most important contributions of cosmopolitanism (and cosmopolitanism is strongest when it takes this seriously, and weakest when it recommends the leap to a more centralized world government).

The cosmopolitan tension with the assumption of nation as the prepolitical basis for citizenship is domestic as well as international. As Jurgen Habermas (1998a: 115) puts it,

the nation-state owes its historical success to the fact that it substituted relations of solidarity between the citizens for the disintegrating corporative ties of early modern society. But this republican achievement is endangered when, conversely, the integrative force of the nation of citizens is traced back to the prepolitical fact of a quasi-natural people, that is, to something independent of and prior to the political opinion and will-formation of the citizens themselves.

But pause here and notice the temporal order implied in this passage. *First* there were local communities, guilds, religious bodies and other 'corporative bonds'. *Then* there was republican citizenship with its emphasis on the civic identity of each citizen. *Then* this was undermined by ethno-nationalism. What this misses is the extent to which each of these ways of organizing social life existed simultaneously with the others, sometimes in struggle and sometimes symbiotically.

---

[9] Held's book remains the most systematic and sustained effort to develop a theory of cosmopolitan democracy.

New 'corporative ties' have been created, for example, notably in the labour movement and in religious communities. Conversely, there was no 'pure republican' moment when ideas of nationality did not inform the image of the republic and the constitution of its boundaries.

As Habermas (1998a: 117) goes on, however, 'the question arises of whether there exists a functional equivalent for the fusion of the nation of citizens with the ethnic nation'.[10] We need not accept his idealized history or entire theoretical framework to see that this raises a basic issue. That is, for polities not constructed as ethnic nations, what makes membership compelling? This is a question for the EU, certainly, but also arguably for the United States of America itself, and for most projects of cosmopolitan citizenship. Democracy requires a sense of mutual commitment among citizens that goes beyond mere legal classification, holding a passport, or even respect for particular institutions. As Charles Taylor (2002: 1) has argued forcefully, 'self-governing societies' have need 'of a high degree of cohesion'.

Cosmopolitanism needs an account of how social solidarity and public discourse might develop enough in these wider networks to become the basis for active citizenship. So far, most versions of cosmopolitan theory share with traditional liberalism a thin conception of social life, commitment and belonging. They imagine society—and issues of social belonging and social participation—in a too thin and casual manner. The result is a theory that suffers from an inadequate sociological foundation. Communitarianism is more sociological in inspiration, but often suffers from an inverse error, a tendency to elide the differences between local networks of social relationships and broad categories of belonging like nations.

The cosmopolitan image of multiple, layered citizenship can helpfully challenge the tendency of many communitarians to suggest not only that community is necessary and/or good, but that people normally inhabit one and only one community.[11] It also points to the possibility—so far not realized—of a rapprochement between cosmopolitanism and communitarianism. As Bellamy and Castiglione (1998) write, hoping to bridge the opposition between cosmopolitanism and communitarianism, 'a pure cosmopolitanism cannot generate the full range of obligations its advocates generally wish to ascribe to it. For the proper acknowledgement of "thin" basic rights rests on their being specified and overlaid by a "thicker" web of special obligations'. They would strengthen Held's suggestion that persons inhabit not only rights and obligations, but also

---

[10] Note that Habermas tends to equate 'nation' with 'ethnic nation'.

[11] It is this last tendency that invites liberal rationalists occasionally to ascribe to communitarians and advocates of local culture complicity in all manner of illiberal political projects from restrictions on immigration to excessive celebration of ethnic minorities to economic protectionism. I have discussed this critically in Calhoun (1999).

relationships and commitments within and across groups of all sorts including the nation.

More often, however, cosmopolitans have treated communitarianism as an enemy, or at least used it as a foil (see, e.g., Thompson 1998). Despite this, advocates of cosmopolitan democracy find themselves falling back on notions of 'peoples' as though these exist naturally and prepolitically. They appeal, for example, for the representation of peoples—not only states—in various global projects including an eventual world parliament (Archibugi 1998: 146). This poses deeper problems than is commonly realized. Not only is the definition of 'people' problematic, the idea of representation is extremely complex. Representing peoples has been one of the primary functions of modern states—however great the problems with how they do it. The advocates for 'peoples' represent them in the media and claim to represent them even in terrorist action. But it is the legal and political procedures of states and the relatively cohesive public spheres associated with them that provide effective checks on unstated claims to represent others and tie mediatic images to concrete policy choices. In the absence of state-like forms of explicit self-governance, it is not clear how the representation of peoples escapes arbitrariness.

Cosmopolitan democracy requires not only a stronger account of representation, but also a stronger account of social solidarity and the formation and transformation of social groups. If one of its virtues is challenging the idea that nationality (or ethnic or other identities understood as analogous to nationality) provides people with an unambiguous and singular collective membership, one of its faults is to conceptualize the alternative too abstractly and vaguely. Another is to underestimate the positive side of nationalism, that is the virtues of identification with a larger whole. This can indeed be oppressive and anti-democratic. But it can also be the source of mutual commitment and solidarity underpinning democracy and uniting people across a range of differences. Moreover, whatever its limits, the nation-state has proved to be more open to democratization than religions or some other kinds of large groupings.

Solidarity

In cosmopolitanism as in much other political theory and democratic thought, generally, there is a tendency to assume that social groups are created in some prepolitical process—as nations, for example, ethnicities, religions or local communities. They reflect historical accident, inheritance and necessity. They result perhaps from the accumulation of unintended consequences of purposive action, but they are not in themselves chosen. Surely, though, this is not always so.

The social solidarity that makes social commitments compelling is indeed shaped by forms of integration, like markets, that link people systemically, by force of necessity, or as it were 'behind their backs'. It is also shaped by material power; as for example, modern economic life is a matter not only of markets but also of corporations and state regulation. Clearly, it is informed by a shared culture and by categorical identities like race, ethnicity, class and nation. And crucially it is built out of networks of directly interpersonal social relations, such as those basic to local community. The last already suggests the importance of choice: community is not just inherited, it is made and remade—and interpersonal relationships are also basic to social movements. More generally, though, we should recognize the importance of public discourse as a source of social solidarity, mutual commitment and shared interest. Neither individuals nor social groups are fully or finally formed in advance of public discourse. People's identities and understandings of the world are changed by their participation in public discourse. Groups are created not just found and the forms of group life are at least potentially open to choice.[12]

Public discourse is not simply a matter of finding pre-existing common interests, in short, nor of developing strategies for acting on inherited identities; it is also in and of itself a form of solidarity. The women's movement offers a prominent example; it transformed identities, it did not just express the interests of women whose identities were set in advance. It created both an arena of discourse among women and a stronger voice for women in discourses that were male dominated (even when they were ostensibly gender neutral). The solidarity formed among women had to do with the capacity of this discourse to meaningfully bridge the concerns of private life and large-scale institutions and culture. We can also see the inverse, namely the extent to which this gendered production of solidarity is changed as feminist public discourse is replaced by mass marketing to women and the production of feminism's successor as a gendered consumer identity in which liberation is reduced to the freedom to purchase.

In short, there are a variety of ways in which people are joined to each other, within and across the boundaries of states and other polities. The theorists of cosmopolitan democracy are right to stress the multiplicity of connections. But we need to complement the liberal idea of rights with a stronger sense of what binds people to each other. One of the peculiarities of nation-states has been the extent to which they were able to combine elements of each of these different sorts of solidarity. They did not do so perfectly, of course. Markets flowed over their borders from the beginning, and some states were weak containers of either economic organization or power. Not all states had a populace with a strong national identity, or pursued policies able to shape a common identity among citizens. Indeed, those that repressed public discourse suffered a particular liability to fissure along the lines of ethnicity or older national identities

---

[12] I have further developed this argument about public discourse as a form of or basis for solidarity and its significance for transnational politics in Calhoun (2002).

weakly amalgamated into the new whole; the Soviet Union is a notable case. Conversely, though, the opportunity to participate in a public sphere and seek to influence the state was an important source of solidarity within it.

Actually existing international civil society includes some level of each of the different forms of solidarity I listed. In very few cases, however, these are joined strongly to each other at a transnational level. There is community among the expatriate staffs of NGOs; there is public discourse on the Internet. But few of the categorical identities that express people's sense of themselves are matched to strong organizations of either power or community at a transnational level. What this means is that the international civil society offers a weak counterweight to systemic integration and power. If hopes for cosmopolitan democracy are to be realized, they depend on developing more social solidarity.

As I have emphasized, such solidarity can be at least partially chosen through collective participation in the public sphere. It is unlikely, however, that solidarity can be entirely a matter of choice. This is the import of Habermas's question about whether the nation of citizens can fully replace the ethnic nation. It is a problem to rely heavily on a purely political conception of human beings. Such a conception has two weak points. First, it does not attend enough to all the ways in which solidarity is achieved outside of political organization, and does not adequately appreciate the bearing of these networks on questions of political legitimacy. Second, it does not consider the extent to which high political ideals founder on the shoals of everyday needs and desires—including quite legitimate ones. The ideal of a civil society has sometimes been expressed in recent years as though it should refer to a constant mobilization of all of us all the time in various sorts of voluntary organizations.[13] But in fact one of the things people quite reasonably want from a good political order is to be left alone some of the time—to enjoy a non-political life in civil society. In something of the same sense, Oscar Wilde famously said of socialism that it requires too many evenings. We could say of cosmopolitanism that it requires too much travel, too many dinners out at ethnic restaurants, too much volunteering with *Médecins sans frontières*. Perhaps not too much or too many for academics (though I would not leap to that presumption) but too much and too many to base

---

[13] This hyper-Tocquevillianism appears famously in Putnam (2000), but has in fact been central to discussions since at least the 1980s, including prominently Bellah *et al.* (1984). The embrace of a notion of civil society as centrally composed of a 'voluntary sector' complementing a capitalist market economy has of course informed public policy from America's first Bush administration with its 'thousand points of light' forward. Among other features, this approach neglects the notion of a political public sphere as an institutional framework of civil society; see Habermas (1989). It grants a high level of autonomy to markets and economic actors; it is notable for the absence of a political economy from its theoretical bases and analyses. As one result, it introduces a sharp separation among the market, government, and voluntary association (non-profit) activity that obscures the question of how social movements may challenge economic institutions, and how the public sphere may mobilize the government to shape economic practices.

a political order on the expectation that everyone will choose to participate—even if they acknowledge that they *ought* to.

A good political order must deal fairly with the fact that most people will not be politically active most of the time. That actually existing politics turn many people off only makes the issue more acute. But for cosmopolitan democracy, scale is the biggest issue. The participation rates are low in local and national politics; there is good reason to think that the very scale of the global ecumene will make participation in it even narrower and more a province of elites than participation in national politics. Not only does Michels's law of oligarchy apply, if perhaps not with the iron force he imagined, but the capacities to engage cosmopolitan politics—from literacy to computer literacy to familiarity with the range of acronyms—are apt to continue to be unevenly distributed. Indeed, there are less commonly noted but significant inequalities directly tied to locality. Within almost any social movement or activist NGO, as one moves from the local to the national and global in either public actions or levels of internal organization, one sees a reduction in women's participation. Largely because so much labour of social reproduction—child care, for instance—is carried out by women, women find it harder to work outside of their localities. This is true even for social movements in which women predominate at the local level.[14]

Rationalism and Difference

Contemporary cosmopolitan theory is attentive to the diversity of people's social engagements and connections. But this cosmopolitanism is also rooted in seventeenth and eighteenth century rationalism with its ethical universalism.[15] Modern cosmopolitanism took shape largely in opposition to traditional religion and more generally to deeply rooted political identities. Against the force of universal reason, the claims of traditional culture and communities were deemed to have little standing. These were at best particularistic, local understandings that grasped universal truths only inaccurately and partially. At worst, they were outright errors, the darkness that Enlightenment challenged. Certainly, the sixteenth- and seventeenth-century wars of faith seemed to cry out for a universalistic reason and a cosmopolitan outlook. Yet, nationalism was as important a result as cosmopolitanism and the two often developed hand-in-hand.

[14] On how global NGOs actually work, see Keck and Sikkink (1998).
[15] See Stephen Toulmin's (1990) analysis of the seventeenth-century roots of the modern liberal rationalist worldview. As Toulmin notes, the rationalism of Descartes and Newton may be tempered with more attention to sixteenth-century forebears. From Erasmus, Montaigne and others we may garner an alternative but still humane and even humanist approach emphasizing wisdom that included a sense of the limits of rationalism and a more positive grasp of human passions and attachments.

Religion sometimes divided nations, but nations also provided a secular frame-work for achieving unity across religious lines.

Early modern rationalism was also rich with contractarian metaphors and embedded in the social imagination of a nascent commercial culture. It approached social life on the basis of a proto-utilitarian calculus, an idea of individual interests as the basis of judgement, and a search for the one right solution. Its emphasis on individual autonomy, whatever its other merits, was deployed with a blind eye to the differences and distortions of private property. The claims of community appeared often as hindrances on individuals. They were justified mainly when the community was abstracted to the level of a nation, and the wealth of nations was made the focus of political as well as eco-nomic attention. Much of this heritage has been absorbed into contemporary liberalism, including the political theory of cosmopolitan democracy.

Like the earlier vision of cosmopolis, the current one responds to international conflict and crisis. It offers an attractive sense of shared responsibility for devel-oping a better society and transcending both the interests and intolerance that have often lain behind war and other crimes against humanity. However, this appears primarily in the guise of ethical obligation, an account of what would be good actions and how institutions and loyalties ought to be rearranged. A connection is seldom established to any idea of political action rooted in the imminent contradictions of the social order. From the liberal rationalist tradi-tion, contemporary cosmopolitanism also inherits a suspicion of religion and rooted traditions; a powerful language of rights that is also sometimes a blinder against recognition of the embeddedness of individuals in culture and social relations; and an opposition of reason and rights to community. This last has appeared in various guises through 300 years of contrast between allegedly inherited and constraining local community life, on the one hand, and the osten-sibly freely chosen social relationships of modern cities, markets, associational life and more generally cosmopolis, on the other.

Confronting similar concerns in the mid-twentieth century, Theodor Adorno (1974: 103) wrote:

An emancipated society ... would not be a unitary state, but the realization of univer-sality in the reconciliation of differences. Politics that are still seriously concerned with such a society ought not, therefore, propound the abstract equality of men even as an idea. Instead, they should point to the bad equality today ... and conceive the better state as one in which people could be different without fear.

This is very inadequately achieved at the level of the nation-state, to be sure, but it seems harder, not easier, to develop in a global polity. Indeed, the projection of nationality to a global scale is a major motivation behind the repression of dif-ference. This is not to say that cultural and social differences provoke no conflict in villages or urban neighbourhoods. They do, but face-to-face relations also provide for important forms of mediation. Ethnic violence in cities and villages commonly reflects organized enmity on a larger scale rather than being its basis.

The tension between abstract accounts of equality and rooted accounts of difference has been renewed in the recent professional quarrels between liberal and communitarian political theorists. For the most part, cosmopolitans model political life on a fairly abstract, liberal notion of a person as a bearer of rights and obligations.[16] This is readily addressed in rationalist and indeed proceduralist terms. And however widely challenged in recent years, rationalism retains at least in intellectual circles a certain presumptive superiority. It is easy to paint communitarian claims for the importance of particular cultures as irrational, arbitrary and only a shade less relativist than the worst sort of postmodernism.[17] But an immanent struggle for a better world always builds on particular social and cultural bases.[18] Moreover, rationalist universalism is liable not only to shift into the mode of 'pure ought' but to approach human diversity as an inherited obstacle rather than as a resource or a basic result of creativity.

Entering this quarrel on the liberal side, but with care for diversity, Held suggests that national communities cease to be treated as primary political communities. He does not go so far as some and claim that they should (or naturally will) cease to exist, but rather imagines them as one sort of relevant unit of political organization among many. What he favours is a cosmopolitan democratic community: 'a community of all democratic communities must become an obligation for democrats, an obligation to build a transnational, common structure of political action which alone, ultimately, can support the politics of self-determination' (Held 1995*a*: 232). In such a cosmopolitan community, 'people would come ... to enjoy multiple citizenships—political membership in the diverse political communities which significantly affected them' (Held 1995*a*: 233). Sovereignty would then be 'stripped away from the idea of fixed borders and territories and thought of as, in principle, malleable time–space clusters ... it could be entrenched and drawn upon in diverse self-regulating associations, from cities to states to corporations' (Held 1995*a*: 234). Indeed, so strong is Held's commitment to the notion that there are a variety of kinds of associations within which people might exercise their democratic rights that he imagines 'the formation of an authoritative assembly of all democratic states

---

[16] Amartya Sen (2000) lays out an account of 'capacities' as an alternative to the discourse of rights. This is also adopted by Martha Nussbaum (2000). While this shifts emphases in some useful ways (notably from 'negative' to 'positive' liberties in Isaiah Berlin's terms), it does not offer a substantially 'thicker' conception of the person or the social nature of human life. Some cosmopolitan theorists, notably David Held, also take care to acknowledge that people inhabit social relations as well as rights and obligations.

[17] See, for examples, Habermas's (1994) surprisingly sharp-toned response to Charles Taylor's *The Politics of Recognition* (1994); or Janna Thompson's (1998) distorting examination of 'communitarian' arguments.

[18] This has been an important theme in the work of Ashis Nandy (see especially Nandy 1993, 1998).

and agencies, a reformed General Assembly of the UN' with its operating rules to be worked out in 'an international constitutional convention involving states, intergovernmental organizations (IGOs), NGOs, citizen groups and social movements' (Held 1995*a*: 273–4). The deep question is whether this all-embracing unity comes at the expense of cultural particularity—a reduction to liberal individualism—or provides the best hope of sustaining particular achievements and openings for creativity in the face of neo-liberal capitalism.

Various crises of the nation-state set the stage for the revitalization of cosmopolitanism. The crises were occasioned by the acceleration of global economic restructuring in the 1990s, new transnational communications media, new flows of migrants and the proliferation of civil wars and humanitarian crises in the wake of the cold war. The last could no longer be comprehended in terms of the cold war, which is one reason why they often appeared in the language of ethnicity and nationalism. Among their many implications, these crises all challenged liberalism's established understandings of (or perhaps wilful blind spot towards) the issues of political membership and sovereignty. They presented several problems simultaneously: (1) Why should the benefits of membership in any one polity not be available to all people? (2) On what bases might some polities legitimately intervene in the affairs of others? (3) What standing should organizations have that operate across borders without being the agents of any single state (this problem, I might add, applies as much to business corporations as to NGOs and social movements) and conversely how might states appropriately regulate them?

Enter cosmopolitanism. Borders should be abandoned as much as possible and left porous where they must be maintained. Intervention on behalf of human rights is good. The NGOs and transnational social movements offer models for the future of the world. These are not bad ideas, but they are limited ideas.

Capitalism

The current enthusiasm for global citizenship and cosmopolitanism reflects not just a sense of its inherent moral worth but also the challenge of an increasingly global capitalism. It is perhaps no accident that the first cited usage under 'cosmopolitan' in the Oxford English Dictionary (OED) comes from John Stuart Mill's *Political Economy* in 1848: 'Capital is becoming more and more cosmopolitan'.[19] Cosmopolitan, after all, means 'belonging to all parts of the world; not restricted to any one country or its inhabitants'. As the quotation from Mill reminds us, the latest wave of globalization was not required to demonstrate

---

[19] This is a point made also by Robbins (1993: 182). See also Robbins (2001).

that capital fits this bill. Indeed, Marx and Engels (1976: 488) wrote in the *Communist Manifesto*:

the bourgeoisie has through its exploitation of the world market given a cosmopolitan character to production and consumption in every country.... All old-established national industries have been destroyed or are daily being destroyed.... In place of the old local and national seclusion and self-sufficiency, we have intercourse in every direction, universal inter-dependence of nations. And as in material so also in intellectual production. The intellectual creations of individual nations become common property. National one-sidedness and narrow-mindedness become more and more impossible, and from the numerous national and local literatures, there arises a world literature.

This is progress, of a sort, but not an altogether happy story. 'The bourgeoisie', Marx and Engels (1976: 488) go on,

by the rapid improvement of all instruments of production, by the immensely facilitated means of communication, draws all, even the most barbarian, nations into civilisation. ... It compels all nations, on pain of extinction, to adopt the bourgeois mode of production; it compels them to introduce what it calls civilization into their midst, i.e. to become bourgeois themselves. In one word, it creates a world after its own image.[20]

It is not clear that these new commonalties are necessarily a basis for harmony, though, and Marx and Engels stressed the contradictions within capitalism and the inevitable clashes among capitalist powers.

The rise of the modern capitalist world system was not simply a progress of cosmopolitanism. It marked a historical turn against empire, and capitalist globalization has been married to the dominance of nation-states in politics (a central point of Wallerstein 1974). Capitalist cosmopolitans have indeed traversed the globe, from early modern merchants to today's World Bank officials and venture capitalists. They have forged relations that cross the borders of nation-states. But they have also relied on states and a global order of states to maintain property rights and other conditions of production and trade. Their passports bear the stamps of many countries, but they are still passports, and good cosmopolitans knew which ones would get them past the inspectors at borders and airports.

Not least of all, capitalist cosmopolitanism has offered only a weak defence against reactionary nationalism. This was clearly *déclassé* so far as most cosmopolitans were concerned. But Berlin in the 1930s was a very cosmopolitan city. If having cosmopolitan elites were a guarantee of respect for civil or human rights, then Hitler would never have ruled Germany, Chile would have been spared Pinochet, and neither the Guomindang nor the communists

---

[20] Marx and Engels, remarkable as their insight is, were fallible observers. Not much later in the *Communist Manifesto* (1976: 494) they reported that the modern subjection to capital had already stripped workers of 'every trace of national character'.

would have come to power in China. Cosmopolitanism is not responsible for empire or capitalism or fascism or communism, but neither is it an adequate defence.

Even while the internal homogeneity of national cultures was being promoted by linguistic and educational standardization (among other means), the great imperial and trading cities stood as centres of diversity. Enjoying this diversity was one of the marks of the sophisticated modern urbanite by contrast to the 'traditional' hick. To be a cosmopolitan was to be comfortable in a heterogeneous public space (Sennett 1977: 17). Richard Sennett cites (and builds on) a French usage of 1738: 'a cosmopolite ... is a man who moves comfortably in diversity; he is comfortable in situations which have no links or parallels to what is familiar to him'. Yet, there is a tendency for commercial capitalism and political liberalism to tame this diversity. While cities can be places of creative disorder, jumbling together ethnicities, classes and political projects, most people claim only familiar parts of the diversity on offer. The difference between a willingness to enter situations truly without parallels or familiarity, and a willingness to experience diversity as packaged for consumer tastes is noteworthy. While Sennett's strong sense of cosmopolitanism calls for confrontation with deep and necessarily contentious differences between ways of life, there is a tendency for a soft cosmopolitanism to emerge. Aided by the frequent flyer lounges (and their extensions in 'international standard' hotels), contemporary cosmopolitans meet others of different backgrounds in spaces that retain familiarity.

The notion of cosmopolitanism gains currency from the flourishing of multiculturalism—and the opposition that those who consider themselves multiculturally modern feel to those rooted in monocultural traditions. The latter, say the former, are locals with a limited perspective, if not outright racists. It is easier to sneer at the far right, but too much claiming of ethnic solidarity by minorities also falls foul of some advocates of cosmopolitanism. It is no accident either that the case against Salman Rushdie began to be formulated among diasporic Asians in Britain or that cosmopoliticians are notably ambivalent towards them. Integrationist white liberals in the United States of America are similarly unsure what to make of what some of them see as 'reverse racism' on the part of blacks striving to maintain local communities. The debates over English as a common language reveal a related ambivalence towards Hispanics and others. It is important for cosmopolitan theorists to recognize, though, that societies outside the modern West have by no means always been 'monocultural'. On the contrary, it is the development of the European nation-state that most pressed for this version of unity. And it is often the insertion of migrants from around the world into the Western nation-state system that produces intense 'reverse monoculturalism', including both the notion that the culture 'back home' is singular and unified and pure, and sometimes the attempt by political leaders on the home front to make it so. Such projects may be simply reactionary, but even when proclaimed in the name of ancient religions, they often pursue alternative modernities. An effectively democratic future must allow for such different collective projects—as they must allow for each other. It must be built in a world in which these are powerful and find starting points within them; it cannot be conceptualized adequately simply in terms of the diversity of individuals.

This complexity is easy to miss if one's access to cultural diversity is organized mainly by the conventions of headline news or the packaging of ethnicity for consumer markets. In the world's global cities, and even in a good many of its small towns, certain forms of cosmopolitan diversity appear ubiquitous. Certainly Chinese food is now a global cuisine—both in a generic form that exists especially as a global cuisine and in more 'authentic' regional versions prepared for more cultivated global palates. And one can buy Kentucky Fried Chicken in Beijing. Local taste cultures that were once more closed and insular have indeed opened up. Samosas are now English food just as pizza is American and Indonesian curry is Dutch. Even where the hint of the exotic (and the uniformity of the local) is stronger, one can eat internationally—Mexican food in Norway, Ethiopian in Italy. This is not all 'McDonaldization' and it is not to be decried in the name of cultural survival. None the less, it tells us little about whether to expect democracy on a global scale, successful accommodation of immigrants at home or respect for human rights across the board. Food, tourism, music, literature and clothes are all easy faces of cosmopolitanism. They are indeed broadening, literally after a fashion, but they are not hard tests for the relationship between local solidarity and international civil society.

Despite the spread of consumerist cosmopolitanism, too many states still wage war or take on projects like ethnic cleansing that an international public might constrain or at least condemn. Profit, moreover, is pursued not only in 'above board' trading and global manufacturing, but in transnational flows of people, weapons and drugs. The 'legitimate' and 'illegitimate' sides of global economic life are never fully separable—as is shown, for example, by the role of both recorded and unrecorded financial transfers in paving the way for the 11 September attacks. The cosmopolitan project speaks to these concerns, suggesting the need not only for multilateral regulatory agreements but also for new institutions operating as more than the sum—or net outcome—of the political agendas of member states. It may be that 'legitimate' businesses have an interest in such institutions and that this will help to compensate for their weak capacity to enforce agreements. Trying to secure some level of democratic participation for such transnational institutions will remain a challenge though, for the reasons suggested above. So too will avoiding a predominantly technocratic orientation to global governance projects. Not least, there will be important tensions between liberal cosmopolitan visions that exempt property relations from democratic control and more radical ones that do not. If this is not addressed directly, it is easy for the rhetoric of cosmopolitanism—and indeed cosmopolitan democracy—to be adopted by and become a support for neo-liberal visions of global capitalism.

Cosmopolitanism—though not necessarily cosmopolitan democracy—is now largely the project of capitalism, and it flourishes in the top management of multinational corporations and even more in the consulting firms that serve them. Such cosmopolitanism often joins elites across national borders while ordinary people live in local communities. This is not simply because common folk are less sympathetic to diversity—a self-serving notion of elites. It is also because the class structuring of public life excludes many workers and others. This is not an entirely new story. One of the striking changes of the nineteenth and especially twentieth centuries was a displacement of cosmopolitanism from cities to international travel and mass media. International travel, moreover, meant something different to those who travelled for business or diplomacy and those who served in armies fighting wars to expand or control the cosmopolis. If diplomacy was war by other means, it was also war by other classes who paid less dearly for it.

Deep inequalities in the political economy of capitalism (as earlier of empire) mean that some people labour to support others whose pursuit of global relations focuses on acquisition and accumulation. Cosmopolitanism does not in itself speak to these systemic inequalities, any more than did the rights of bourgeois man that Marx criticized in the 1840s. If there is to be a major redistribution of wealth, or a challenge to the way the means of production are controlled in global capitalism, it is not likely to be guided by cosmopolitanism as such. Of course, it may well depend on transnational—even cosmopolitan—solidarities among workers or other groups. But it will have to contend with both capitalism's economic power and its powerful embeddedness in the institutional framework of global relations.

The affinity of cosmopolitanism to rationalist liberal individualism has blinded many cosmopolitans to some of the destructions neo-liberalism—the cosmopolitanism of capital—has wrought and the damage it portends to hard-won social achievements. Pierre Bourdieu has rightly called attention to the enormous investment of struggle that has made possible relatively autonomous social fields—higher education, for example, or science—and at least partial rights of open access to them (see essays in Bourdieu 1999, 2001). Such fields are organized largely on national bases, at present, though they include transnational linkages and could become far more global. This might be aided by the 'new internationalism' (especially of intellectuals) that Bourdieu proposes in opposition to the globalization of neo-liberal capitalism. The latter imposes a reduction to market forces that undermines both the specific values and autonomy of distinctive fields—including higher education and science—and many rights won from nation-states by workers and others. In this context, the defence of existing institutions including parts of national states is not merely reactionary. Yet, it is commonly presented this way, and cosmopolitan discourse too easily encourages the equation of the global with the modern and the national or local with the backwardly traditional.

Neo-liberalism presents one international agenda simply as a force of necessity to which all people, organizations and states have no choice but to adapt. Much of the specific form of integration of the EU, for example, has been sold as the necessary and indeed all but inevitable response to global competition. This obscures the reality that transnational relations might be built in a variety of ways, and indeed that the shifting forces bringing globalization can also be made the objects of collective choice. Likewise, existing national and indeed local institutions are not mere inheritances from tradition but—at least sometimes—the hard won achievements of social struggles. To defend such institutions is not always backward.

The global power of capitalism, among other factors, makes the creation of cosmopolitan institutions seem crucial. But it would be a mistake for this to be pursued in opposition to more local solidarities or without an adequate distinction from capitalism. Appeals to abstract human rights in themselves speak to neither—or at least not adequately as currently pursued. Building cosmopolitanism solely on such a discourse of individual rights—without a strong attention to diverse solidarities and struggles for a more just and democratic social order—also runs the risk of substituting ethics for politics. An effective popular politics must find roots in solidary social groups and networks of ties among them.

Conclusion

The current pursuit of cosmopolitan democracy flies in the face of a long history in which cosmopolitan sensibilities thrived in market cities, imperial capitals, and court society, while democracy was tied to the nation-state. Cosmopolitanism flourished in Ottoman Istanbul and old regime Paris partly because in both the members of different cultures and communities were not invited to organize a government together. It was precisely when democracy became a popular passion and a political project that nationalism flourished. Democracy depends on strong notions of who 'the people' behind phrases like 'we the people' might be, and who might make legitimate the performative declarations of constitution-making and the less verbal performances of revolution (see Taylor 2001: 1).

One way of looking at modern history is as a race in which popular forces and solidarities are always running behind. It is a race to achieve social integration, to structure the connections among people and organize the world. Capital is out in front. The workers and ordinary citizens are always in the position of trying to catch up. As they get organized on local levels, capital and power integrate on larger scales. States come close to catching up, but the integration of nation-states is an ambivalent step. On the one hand, state power is a force in its own right—not least in colonialism—and represents a flow of organizing capacity away from local communities. On the other hand, democracy at a national level constitutes the greatest success that ordinary people have had in catching up to capital and power. Because markets and corporations increasingly transcend states, there is new catching up to do. This is why cosmopolitan democracy is appealing.

Yet, as practical projects in the world (and sometimes even as theory), cosmopolitanism and democracy have both been intertwined with capitalism and Western hegemony. If cosmopolitan democracy is to flourish and be fully open to human beings of diverse circumstances and identities, then it needs to disentangle itself from neo-liberal capitalism. It needs to approach both cross-cultural relations and the construction of social solidarities with a deeper recognition of the significance of diverse starting points and potential outcomes. It needs more discursive engagement across lines of difference, more commitment to the reduction of material inequality, and more openness to radical change. Like many liberals of the past, advocates of cosmopolitan democracy often offer a vision of political reform that is attractive to elites partly because it promises to find virtue without a radical redistribution of wealth or power. This is all the more uncomfortable for the left in the advanced capitalist countries because those advocating more radical change typically challenge Western culture and values—including much of liberalism—as well as global inequality.

The answer clearly does not lie with embracing illiberal nationalisms or 'fundamentalisms'. These may be the voices of the oppressed without being voices for good. But not all nationalism is ugly ethno-nationalism; not all religion is fundamentalism. Both can be sources of solidarity and care for strangers as well as xenophobia or the persecution of heretics. They are also in conflict with each other as often as they are joined together. But, if cosmopolitan democracy is to be more than a good ethical orientation for those privileged to inhabit the frequent traveller lounges, it must put down roots in the solidarities that organize most people's sense of identity and location in the world. To appeal simply to liberal individualism—even with respect for diversity—is to disempower those who lack substantial personal or organizational resources. It is also disingenuous if would-be cosmopolitans do not recognize the extent to which the cosmopolitan appreciation of global diversity is based on the privileges of wealth and perhaps, especially, citizenship in certain states. Cosmopolitan democracy depends on finding ways to relate diverse solidarities to each other rather than trying to overcome them.

This is surely a matter of robust public communication in which ordinary people can gain more capacity to shape both the societies within which they live and the global forces that shape the options open to them. But it is important to recognize that relations across meaningful groups are not simply matters of rational-critical discourse, but involve the creation of local hybrid cultures, accommodations, collaborations and practical knowledge. Equally, it is important to see that attenuated cosmopolitanism will not ground mutual commitment and responsibility. Not only tolerance but also solidarity is required for people to live together and join in democratic self-governance.

Still, feeling at home cannot be enough of an adequate basis for life in a modern global society. Exclusive localism is neither empowering nor even really possible, however nostalgic for it people may feel. Cosmopolitanism by itself may not be enough; a soft cosmopolitanism that does not challenge capitalism or Western hegemony may be an ideological diversion; but some form of cosmopolitanism is needed.

8

Political Community Beyond the Sovereign State, Supranational Federalism, and Transnational Minorities

RAINER BAUBÖCK

A cosmopolitan perspective needs not only a conception of global identities and global governance, but also of forms of political community beyond state borders. We can imagine the relations between political communities within a larger supranational context in four different ways: as separate, nested, multi-level or overlapping. The Hobbesian paradigm in international relations imagines sovereign states as separate communities; Kant's vision of eternal peace promoted a confederation of free republics; the EU moves towards a regional model of multi-level governance and citizenship. These three ways of constructing a political community beyond the state, use existing state-based polities as building blocks for the larger structure. This is different from the transnational minorities whose political membership or aspirations for self-government cut across the boundaries of state-based communities. I discuss three types of such groups: transborder national minorities, indigenous minorities and immigrant minorities. For each of them their transnationalism is not necessarily a vehicle for a cosmopolitan alternative to the present global political order. However, they generate overlapping forms of political community that may pave the way for a greater responsiveness of state-based policies towards the multiple political identities of their citizens.

Where is the *Polis* in a Cosmopolis?

When academic discourses go public there is always a danger that they will become subject to the laws of infotainment. Media discourses are not cumulative, as academic ones ought to be, but follow the dictates of fashion. Globalization was the buzzword of the 1990s and behind the outpouring of popular literature on this phenomenon there was a serious academic debate. Now there are signs of globalization discourse fatigue and it will without doubt affect the social sciences as well. Political philosophy, however, is always a latecomer. It usually discovers a new field only when the other disciplines are about to abandon it. Multiculturalism, for example, was a big theme in the social sciences a decade before political theory developed a serious literature on cultural minority rights. The theories of cosmopolitan democracy might then similarly build on the globalization literature and enjoy a greater longevity. Cosmopolitanism is certainly not a novelty in political philosophy. It can draw on a venerable tradition stretching back to the Sophists and the Stoics. Globalization creates a new context for testing the consistency and practical implications of this old ideal. As a political theorist I believe that such a belated but systematic rethinking of the normative issues has some virtues. It allows one to ground normative approaches in empirical research that is already there and it helps to avoid the facile partisan polemics in which many social scientists, who eschew value judgements in their research, engage so easily when switching into the role of public intellectuals.

A question that political theorists are likely to raise about cosmopolitanism concerns the concept of political community that corresponds with this term. Cosmopolitanism may refer to an individual life style, to a universalist morality, or to global political institutions. What is strange about these uses of the term is that they generally seem to do without a vision of a cosmo-*polis*, namely a global community of citizens.

The first interpretation attributes cosmopolitanism to the 'man without country'. This figure is not, as one might believe, the stateless refugee who is desperately in search of a country. It is, rather, the person who can live well without a country. What comes to one's mind is the corporate manager who shuttles back and forth across the continents and whose life is increasingly similar to that of a diplomat, except that he represents a company rather than a country. We might characterize him as 'a real nowhere man, living in a nowhere land' (the Beatles). But a nowhere land is not a polis and a nowhere man is not a citizen. In reply to Martha Nussbaum's plea for cosmopolitanism, Michael Walzer stated dryly that he was 'not even aware that there is a world such that one could be a citizen of it. No one has ever offered me citizenship' (Walzer 1996: 125). Certainly, citizenship becomes less important (or at best instrumentally important) for life-style cosmopolitans. One does not need a world citizenship if one can cash in on the benefits of national citizenship in many different countries and shirk its obligations in all of them. Yet, Walzer's point remains a sound one. A non-political cosmopolitanism is almost a contradiction in terms. This brand of cosmopolitanism is purely negative in its contrast with the existing political communities, and moreover parasitic with regard to their citizenship.[1]

---

[1] At the 2000 Davos world economic forum, Fareed Zakaria declared the end of the Westphalian state system and Lester Thurow explained in an interview that the new world will be ruled by the global corporations that will collect taxes from governments that compete for their investment (*Der Standard*, 28 January 2000).

The second interpretation is political in a way. In this view, cosmopolitanism is a universalistic morality that negates the priority of compatriots (or coreligionists, co-ethnics and so forth). One might think that every perspective that starts from the basic premise of moral equality of all human beings is by implication cosmopolitan. But that would make cosmopolitanism rather uninteresting. To give some edge and added value to the term, the distinctive point of a cosmopolitan morality must be a stronger one of denying special obligations towards those with whom one shares a common membership in a political community. This is a step few liberal philosophers have been willing to take.[2] Some forms of utilitarianism may qualify as cosmopolitan in this narrow sense. It is now generally recognized that Bentham's principle of the greatest happiness of the greatest number is an inconsistent idea because it requires maximizing two variables simultaneously. One can either maximize the happiness of a given number, or maximize the number of persons who enjoy a given level of happiness but not both at the same time (Kymlicka 1990: 47, n.1). The former reading undermines the claim of utilitarianism that it defends a universal moral principle, because the determination of the number would then be arbitrary and outside the scope of application of the utilitarian principle. The latter view seems to be more consistent. Political decisions about the provision of public goods or the redistribution of private goods could then always be criticized as immoral as long as there are outsiders whose happiness could be increased by including them.[3] However, such a cosmopolitan morality is again a 'view from nowhere' (Nagel 1986) that negates special obligations,[4] rather than a view from the vantage point of a world polity. The moral imperative applies to all human beings and political institutions everywhere, but it remains an open question whether human needs are best served by building global political institutions.

The third brand of cosmopolitanism starts from an affirmative answer to this latter question. It is a political theory rather than more broadly a moral one and it combines normative arguments for globalizing democracy with empirical accounts of an emerging set of political norms, organizations and movements that are no longer international but supranational and sometimes genuinely global in character. I locate my inquiry in this chapter within this field of theories of cosmopolitan democracy and I will selectively discuss some of their insights. My main point is, however, that even these approaches, which are

---

[2] For example, Kwame Anthony Appiah defends a 'cosmopolitan patriotism' that regards the fact of being a fellow-citizen . . . [as] not morally arbitrary at all' (Appiah 1996: 28).

[3] For an application of this latter approach to refugee admission policies, see Singer and Singer (1988).

[4] Robert Goodin has suggested a more sophisticated utilitarian approach of 'assigned responsibility'. In his view, we have only general moral duties towards other human beings. Special duties such as those of citizenship are 'merely devices whereby the moral community's general duties get assigned to particular agents' (Goodin 1986: 678).

explicitly political and institutional in their focus, generally avoid the polity question. They discuss the emergence of global political regimes; they propose to strengthen them and they want to make them accountable through democratic procedures. There are many convincing arguments for this case: the need for new arrangements to secure international peace in the post-cold war era, for averting global threats to the environment, for re-regulating financial markets. A cosmopolitan response to these and other global challenges need not argue for a unitary world state, or a central world government. Neo-institutionalists have demonstrated that at supra state levels we already find emerging forms of 'governance without government' (Rosenau and Czempiel 1992). Others regard these as halfway solutions that will ultimately have to give way to real statehood (Höffe 1999). Yet, the project of *democratic* cosmopolitanism requires more than the building of powerful institutions that can exercise legislative, executive and jurisdictional tasks on a global scale. It must spell out how these institutions will be constrained by the rule of law and be accountable both to the states that form the international order as well as to citizens who are the ultimate subjects of their decisions. Neo-realists like Danilo Zolo (1997: 15) ask, 'Can any cosmopolitan project ever be anything other than an inherently hegemonic and violent undertaking'? The current economic and military hegemony of the United States of America on a world scale and the blatantly undemocratic rules of the UN Security Council seem to support such scepticism. Democratic cosmopolitans reply to this that, given the increasing global interdependence, we are likely to see a growing concentration and exercise of global political power anyway. The project of bringing it under democratic control may ultimately be more realistic than the futile desire of normative realism to dismantle it and disperse it among sovereign states.

However, there is still this nagging doubt. Democratic cosmopolitanism must also ask what kind of *demos* these institutions will represent and be accountable to. One strategy might be to adopt a purely formal conception of the demos as the aggregate of persons who happen to be subject to a given political authority. In this case, a global demos exists by definition as soon as there are global political institutions that are exposed to democratic procedures of representation. The *polis* of cosmopolis could then be constructed from above, almost by fiat through institutional design. Of course this is a daunting task and one may well be sceptical about the prospects of overcoming the countervailing national interests of states.[5] But for a normative theory the problem would greatly be reduced if it would suffice to show why governments, political parties and NGOs *ought* to commit themselves to building global democratic institutions. The alternative

---

[5] Bellamy and Castiglione (1998: 160) aptly characterize this view: 'What defines the *demos* is largely functional, making the parcelling out of popular sovereignty theoretically unproblematic, even though there are numerous practical difficulties'.

view is that the demos not only conceptually precede the institutions that represent it, but must also correspond to a social reality: a significant status of membership, a widespread sense of belonging and a historical trajectory of community. Liberal democracy is not exhaustively characterized by the rule of law, the division of powers and a periodic opportunity of citizens to dismiss their government. Sustainable democratic institutions require a shared sense of a political identity among citizens. Cosmopolitans who accept this latter perspective have to show how the existing forms of political community at the state and substate levels could be transformed, bundled into greater aggregates or shifted beyond the state so that individuals could in a meaningful way conceive of themselves as the citizens of a global *polis*. For this latter perspective it is a sense of commonness that 'defines the *demos*, as it were, for whom a form of democratic rule appears appropriate and plausible' (Bellamy and Castiglione 1998: 163).

This second view accepts the communitarian critique 'that attempts to expand democracy and distributive justice across borders of states is not something that can be accomplished by an appeal to morality or reason, or even the creation of appropriate institutions' (Thompson 1998: 186). As he explains (p. 90):

For principles . . . will not necessarily be acceptable as the basis for transnational political authority if individuals have loyalties and interests which are threatened by the exercise of authority. Equally unsatisfactory is a theory that concentrates on defining the political institutions that should be adopted by a cosmopolitan society. For institutions are empty shells without the motivations which underwrite their authority. World citizenship requires the creation of a new political identity, and cosmopolitanism must concern itself with how this identity might be constructed.

Thompson concludes (p. 194) that cosmopolitanism needs stories about how social changes might affect individual self-understandings, encourage participation in transnational democratic practices and provide a motivation to support transnational or global political formations.

The stories that are currently on offer cannot arouse much optimism. One such story is about the global economy and its effect on undermining state sovereignty. There is much debate about the novelty, extent and impact of economic globalization.[6] Setting aside such questions of assessment, most observers agree that these developments undermine political community rather than expanding it from the national into a global space. This is not to say that global markets develop outside any legal and political framework. Every market regime needs a legal regime to back up property rights, enforce contracts and resolve disputes. Economic globalization generates the need for a whole range of regulatory mechanisms involving international organizations (the WTO, the IMF and the World Bank), legal norms (international private law)

---

[6] For a critical assessment see Hirst and Thompson (1996).

and specialized courts and private law firms. Global markets are thus not completely unregulated, but supposedly sovereign states are 'losing control' (Sassen 1996) over this regulation and find their scope for self-determination of economic and fiscal policies severely constrained. We may characterize the new global economic regime as a form of 'governance without government' that generates some functional equivalents for democracy in a global space (Rosenau 1998). One may even—in my view more contentiously—regard the power of global corporations 'to extract accountability from governments' as a new form of economic citizenship (Sassen 1996: 34). But nobody can seriously believe that economic globalization and its current regulatory regime contribute to the emergence of a global sense of political community, except by way of triggering resistance of the type we have recently witnessed at the 1999 WTO summit in Seattle.

Such resistance is part of the second story, which is about the global civil society and human rights. The number and political impact of transnational NGOs and associations has dramatically increased over the last three decades. They address issues ranging from environmental concerns to the rights of women or indigenous peoples. There is again an expanding legal regime of international human rights conventions, commissions and courts that back up these activities—both the freedom to engage in such practices and the general political goals that they pursue. And in this story, too, the legal regime increasingly constrains the law-making power of sovereign states. One important difference with economic globalization is that we can find here the germs of a global polity. International human rights may be understood as a universalized core of liberal citizenship (Bauböck 1994: 239–40), and transnational associations can be regarded as precursors of a nascent worldwide civil society. The other difference is, however, that the scope of protection afforded by the human rights regime and the extent of popular involvement in transnational associations are still rather marginal compared with the pervasive impact economic globalization has on the life-worlds and identities of people everywhere.

The human rights revolution after 1945 is certainly the most important cosmopolitan achievement so far. It overturned the previous conception of states as the exclusive subjects of international law and normatively disconnected rights from national membership. Yet, this doctrinal change is hardly enough to promote a strong sense of cosmopolitan identity. Those living in non-democratic states find their human rights constantly in jeopardy, and the residents of liberal democracies regard them as a benefit of national rather than of global citizenship.[7] If human rights lack teeth, global civil society lacks participants. Although there are many more transnational associations and NGOs

---

[7] David Beetham (1998) presents a carefully balanced assessment of the contribution of human rights development to cosmopolitan democracy.

than ever before (Rosenau 1998: 31), the number of individuals actively engaged in them is minuscule compared with the vast mass of consumers exposed to the global flows of commodities and information. Moreover, the associations of civil society are necessary, but not sufficient as building blocks for modern democratic polities. The former are divided by their orientation towards particular interests and issues, whereas the latter are integrated by a public discourse about the common good. Even a global civil society with many more participants would not by itself create a sense of shared political identity that makes for mutual recognition and a willingness to compromise or to accept temporary defeat. It could very well lead instead to an exacerbated conflict between social groups that pursue incompatible goals.

Neither of the two globalization stories provides a satisfactory answer to the political community question. To understand the dimensions of this task we must compare it with the emergence of such communities in the Westphalian state system, and that means with a theory of nationalism. Nationalism is the dominant manifestation of political community in the modern world and also the greatest antagonist of cosmopolitan democracy. I will briefly highlight the challenges that normative and explanatory theories of nationalism raise for cosmopolitanism.

John Stuart Mill was the first important political theorist to spell out the view that liberal democracy would best flourish if citizens shared a common nationality, that is 'common sympathies which do not exist between them and others—which make them cooperate with each other more willingly than with other people, desire to be under the same government, and desire that it should be government by themselves, or a portion of themselves exclusively' (Mill 1972: 391). The problem with Mill's liberal nationalism is that it gives up on the task of building larger multinational polities that must be the starting point for a cosmopolitan project. He advocates the assimilation of the smaller and less civilized populations and the separation of those who are equally developed into different states (Mill 1972: 396–8). The contemporary liberal nationalists still face this dilemma of either denying nationhood to many potential contenders, or accepting frequent revisions of borders, which undermine the integration of the political community that the shared nationality is supposed to guarantee. The cosmopolitan liberals react to this by denouncing ethnic nationalism and promoting instead a civic and constitutional patriotism that is cleansed from any particularistic traits and can therefore easily be transposed to larger units. Yet, it remains unclear how universal principles could possibly ground particular political identities (Yack 1996; Kymlicka 1998a: 173). There are only two plausible ways of building political communities that transcend existing national identities: assimilation into a larger community that replicates the particularistic traits of nationhood, or federalization that generates loyalties to the encompassing unit grounded in recognition of its constituent parts. Once coercive assimilation is ruled out as incompatible with liberal democracy, multinational federalism appears as the most promising way, first, for maintaining unity in liberal states faced with internal demands for self-government and, second, for creating larger entities from states with their own strong national identities. Devolution in Spain, Belgium and Britain provides recent West-European illustrations for the first task; the second one is likely to emerge as a challenge for the EU. The further the EU moves beyond economic and towards political integration, the more demands for recognition of national and cultural diversity will be raised. Yet multinational federalism is no easy formula. There are three difficulties that cosmopolitan projects have to consider: asymmetry, enlargement and democratization.

First, most multinational federations are plagued by the problem that a linguistic or religious majority constructs for itself a national identity that encompasses the whole federation and regards the internal borders between states or provinces as merely regional, but not national. For minorities, however, the federation is not itself a nation, but composed of distinct national communities. Such asymmetry is likely to arise also in the EU project for constructing a regional federation. The larger and more powerful states will push for integration formulas that are formally neutral with respect to cultural and political differences between the constituent parts of the union, but actually tend to homogenize them. The smaller constituent states are more likely to insist on the specific recognition of their particularities, which the bigger players regard as costly and cumbersome. Moreover, a multinational mode of integration raises expectations among national minorities within the member states to have their languages and cultural traditions recognized as well. This creates a further asymmetry between the intergovernmental construction of the EU as a confederation of equal member states and the demand of substate minorities to be directly represented at the Union level.

Second, multinational federalism as we know it operates with a limited and stable set of units. Canada is bilingual, Belgium has three official languages and Switzerland has four. If, in these countries, the new languages of immigrants were given the same status this would upset the carefully crafted federal balance. The smaller minorities are likely to interpret this as a weakening of their position and a breach of an implicit federal contract concluded between the original partners only. Multinational arrangements are often characterized by a certain rigidity that is difficult to reconcile with high rates of demographic change (differential fertility, intergroup mobility or immigration from outside). This problem is greatly exacerbated for externally expanding federations like the EU. For example, the current EU language regime with its principle of equal recognition of official languages of member states will come under severe strain with Eastern enlargement (Kraus 1998). Theoretically, it is obvious that multinational recognition is a socially scarce commodity (Hirsch 1976)—with an expanding number of beneficiaries its value diminishes towards zero. A world federation could therefore hardly be multinational in the same sense as Canada or Belgium. The enlargement dilemma will not arise if we think of the cosmopolitan project as a top-down federal transformation of the existing UN system. Yet, this approach is unlikely to answer the polity question with which we are concerned. Supranational federations that are built from below, that is from existing nation-states, will have to become more thickly multinational the more they integrate internally but will have to thin out the more they expand externally. The EU tries to do both at the same time and this is creating considerable tensions.

Third, the cases of Central and Eastern Europe (CEE) since 1989 show how the need for political community becomes stronger with the transition towards democracy. Any such transition is likely to exacerbate the conflicts in society that had been suppressed by an authoritarian regime. National identities become a resource for rebuilding communities within which these conflicts are mitigated by norms of solidarity and Mill's 'common sympathy'. The move towards democracy in CEE states was therefore accompanied by a nationalizing dynamic (Brubaker 1996) that often worsened the position of ethnic minorities. In the formally multinational federations of the Soviet Union, Yugoslavia and Czechoslovakia, national identities were not an integrating force but instead became the fault-lines along which these states broke apart. The implication of these experiences for a cosmopolitan project is that one ought to expect a heightening rather than an attenuation of conflicts with supranational political integration, with the emergence of a global civil society and with a broader participation of individual citizens in supranational elections and political decisions. The international society of states and supranational government in the EU operate so far in a rather undemocratic manner. Cosmopolitan democracy means that conflicts that had hitherto been negotiated in the sheltered environments of diplomatic meetings and intergovernmental conferences will create deep rifts in society. Already established national identities will not simply fade away in this process but will more likely be mobilized. The question is whether a sense of supranational political community can emerge at the same time and promote the integration of these identities into an expanding multinational conception.

This question moves us beyond normative theories that ask how existing national identities ought to be taken into account towards a broader historical perspective. According to most contemporary theorists, nationalism is a phenomenon of the modern world. If we understand the conditions under which it emerged we might also be able to envisage its eventual demise. Ernest Gellner, whose theory of nationalism (Gellner 1965, 1983) is probably the most influential one, argued that the industrial division of labour required standardized national cultures in which individuals could communicate with each other in a context-free manner. Only the modern bureaucratic state was able to organize the socialization of the mass of the population into these national cultures. National loyalties are essentially a by-product of the value of belonging to a cultural pool that provides its members with economic opportunities. The theory highlights the structural forces that made nation building both possible and imperative. And it rejects the belief shared by nationalists and liberal cosmopolitans alike that nationalism is grounded in some pre-modern attachment of human beings to blood and soil.

On the one hand, this account may raise cosmopolitan hopes. National communities are not rooted in ancient cultures, but are constructed by modern political elites and state bureaucracies in the transition to modernity and they make fairly arbitrary use of the available cultural material. Another historical transition might then create a new type of global political community that finally separates political authority from cultural belonging. On the other hand, this is also a sobering perspective. While individual national communities are constructed and deconstructed through a political agency, the basic *pattern* of community emerges from the structural characteristics of a whole historical era. Constructing a global polity is a task entirely different from nation building—it requires changing the pattern rather than adding new patches to the existing one. Gellner himself thought that there were only three fundamental types of human societies: pre-agrarian, agrarian and industrial. Of course there are many indicators (such as the growing service sector and the revolution in information technology) that ours is already a post-industrial era. But it is still an open question how these changes in the economic structure and knowledge base of society will affect the future patterns of political community. Are we heading towards a new medievalism with overlapping political authority and multiple loyalties (Bull 1977: 254) or towards a well-ordered world federal republic (Höffe 1999), towards a formation of regional civilizational blocks (Huntington 1996) or rather a further fragmentation of the world into ever more nation-states (Hobsbawm 1990; Nairn 1997: 143–9)? Instead of proclaiming prematurely the end of the nation (Guéhenno 1994) we ought to be attentive to contradictory trends and gather more evidence about those transformations that are already under way. The normative theory of democracy must then consider how the allocation of membership, rights and obligations must be altered in response to these changes so that individuals can still see themselves as equal participants in collective self-government.

The general conclusion from these sketchy considerations is that it is not enough for cosmopolitans to maintain that building a global political community would be desirable or even morally required. All such prescriptions are subject to the constraint of 'ought implies can'. Political communities cannot be wished into existence if their emergence is a historically contingent process. We have to examine first whether the new context of globalization will itself create the preconditions for forming a worldwide political community before we can jump to constitutional designs for cosmopolitan democracy that already pre-suppose the existence of such a polity. To me it seems wiser to adopt a sceptical attitude in this regard. Even if our generation might be witnessing a change as fundamental as the transition from agrarian to industrial societies, only future generations would be able to perceive its grand patterns from the vantage point of historical hindsight. What we can do instead is to consider the various pat-terns of political community beyond the nation-state that are already emerging before our eyes and discuss their impact on democratic citizenship. Political legitimacy for cosmopolitan citizenship 'has to be constructed from the bottom up' (Bellamy and Castiglione 1998: 164) and this means from the emerg-ing forms of political community that already transcend the boundaries of nation-state sovereignty.

Four Boundary Regimes

Political communities share distinct historical identities and are separated from each other by boundaries that demarcate jurisdictions over territories or persons. As Hannah Arendt repeatedly pointed out, democratic citizenship is only possi-ble in a world where many such communities coexist with each other. 'A citizen is by definition a citizen among citizens of a country among countries. ... The establishment of one sovereign world state ... would be the end of all citizen-ship' (Arendt 1970: 81–2). This critique of cosmopolitan democracy is, how-ever, not as devastating as Arendt believed. It only rules out a unitary structure of a global polity whose internal boundaries would be merely administrative ones. Any defensible cosmopolitan vision will be pluralistic and federal in the sense that it conceives of a global polity as a composite of many communities in which sovereignty would be widely dispersed or shared both horizontally and vertically. The cosmopolis would then still be a world with many countries, and world citizens would at the same time be citizens of particular communities. But this assertion merely leads to a further question. How will these various political communities relate to each other? What will be the pattern of bound-aries that demarcates their jurisdictions?

Once the nightmare utopia of a unitary and sovereign world state has been discarded, there remain four possible patterns of boundaries between political communities, each of which could satisfy Arendt's requirement of pluralism. First, communities can be separate; second they can be nested so that the more comprehensive units are composed of distinct smaller ones; a third type are multi-level communities in which individuals are members not only of the smaller communities but also of the encompassing larger unit; the fourth pat-tern is one of overlapping communities that share jurisdiction over parts of their territory or population. We can regard these boundary patterns in two different ways: as alternative models for a political world order or as steps in building a combined regime of increasing complexity. I will first consider the ideal type models of each boundary pattern and then suggest that contemporary developments already point towards a mixed regime.

A pattern of strict separation is postulated by the realist paradigm in the international relations theory. States are like billiard balls: internally homogenous and independent of each other. The neo-realist approaches shed the Hobbesian assumption of a permanent international state of nature in order to account for the emergence of international blocks and regimes (Rosenau and Czempiel 1992; Kaldor 1995*a*; Zolo 1997: 107–8). However, they still regard states as unitary rational actors competing with each other in an international environment that is at best an 'anarchical society' (Bull 1977). This theory matches well with the dominant positivistic doctrine in international law. Although there is an international legal order, its exclusive sources are treaties between states and the customary recognition of norms in state practices. The legitimacy of international law is thus not derived from the democratic decision-making within a global political community composed of either states or individual citizens. The individuals are bearers of human rights that have become an important element of international law since 1945, but they are not citizens represented in the making of international laws within a global polity.

The second pattern of nested communities was first extensively described in Johannes Althusius's (1965) conception of confederation. He provided an alternative to Bodin's theory of sovereignty by considering the polity as a composite entity that unites families, professional associations, cities and provinces, so that each level is constituted as an association of its immediate sub-units. In contrast with an international society, a confederation is a sort of political community, but its members are states in their collective capacity representing their citizens rather than individual citizens themselves. Montesquieu went beyond Althusius by proposing that a confederate constitution is specifically suitable for republics because it 'has all the internal advantages of a republican, together with the external force of a monarchical government' (Montesquieu 1748/ 1949: 126). Immanuel Kant used this idea as a vehicle for a cosmopolitan project. He proposed that 'eternal peace' could be only achieved by overcoming the international state of nature and its 'wild (lawless) liberties' through an ever-expanding confederation of free republics that would ultimately comprise all peoples. However, he also thought that states were unwilling to comply with this moral imperative and suggested a mere alliance or non-aggression pact as a 'negative surrogate' (Kant 1795/1995: 296). Kant's preferred solution was still a confederation whose members are peoples rather than a federation with membership for individuals. This becomes obvious once we consider his definition of world citizenship, which he reduces to a mere right to visit other countries, namely international travel and trade (Kant 1795/1995: 297). Kant's world citizens enjoy a limited free movement that does not lead to the mixing of peoples in a global polity because it does not include a right to permanent settlement. There are also no provisions for individuals to participate and be represented in political decisions at the global level.

The idea of the federation as a multi-level system of government takes one step further. It originates in the US constitution adopted at the Philadelphia Convention of 1787. Different from the earlier models of the Swiss and Dutch confederations and the first American constitution (the Articles of Confederation of 1781) the second one established a dual structure of membership. Citizens are simultaneously members of their states and of the federation[8] and the federal community itself is composed of individual citizens as well as of the states. While external sovereignty was located in the federal government, internal sovereignty was divided between the state and federal governments. The current theories of cosmopolitan democracy generally advocate a federal model rather than a confederal one. This does not mean that they imagine a world state as a larger replica of the United States of America with a similar concentration of power at the centre. First, a world federal state is by definition different in one essential respect from any present federal system. In the former, external sovereignty would lose its meaning. Second, internal sovereignty can be divided in various ways without affecting the character of the polity as a federation. Höffe, for example, advocates a principle of subsidiarity that would allocate only those tasks to a world government that cannot be fulfilled by lower level governments—such as the resolution of an interstate conflict (Höffe 1999: 293–4). The distinctive characteristic of democratic federation is not a strong central authority, but a multi-level structure of the polity. Individuals are citizens of a constitutive unit as well as of the federal state, and both individuals and constitutive units are directly represented in a federal legislation.[9] A federal world republic would have to create a similar structure of dual membership.

The fourth boundary pattern can be less easily described as an ideal world order. For most political theorists the very idea of overlapping boundaries of

---

[8] The relationship between the state and federal citizenship, however, remained contentious for a long time and became a major issue in the conflict between the slave-holding Southern states and the North. The ambiguity was only resolved by the Fourteenth Amendment of 1868, which states that 'all persons born or naturalized in the United States of America, and subject to the jurisdiction thereof, are citizens of the United States of America and of the State wherein they reside'. Until then, the status and rights of federal citizenship were still to a large extent mediated through state citizenship.

[9] Dual representation at the federal level as expressed in bicameral legislatures does not necessarily follow from the duality of individual citizenship. Regional sub-units can enjoy a high degree of autonomy without being collectively represented at a federal level. Daniel Elazar (1987) has suggested the term 'federacies' for such arrangements. In other cases, such as Austria, the federal chamber of parliament has no real legislative powers.

polities conveys an image of disorder.[10] However, a political order that requires individuals to be neatly separated into national boxes is quite unattractive both from descriptive and normative perspectives. It is a fact that many groups have multiple affiliations that cut across state borders, and ignoring these in the design of political institutions could mean treating individuals who belong to such groups with less respect and concern than others. Instead of focusing on the grand architecture of a world polity, our attention is then drawn to phenomena such as multiple nationality or international protectorates. These are apparently rather marginal disturbances in the state system that could be easily dismissed as irrelevant for a theory of global political order. However, this first impression may be misleading. Different from political theories of cosmopolitanism, the new sociological and anthropological literature on transnational communities examines how the Westphalian pattern is subverted from the bottom up. A good example is Arjun Appadurai's notion of 'global ethnoscapes', which he describes as 'landscapes of group identity' where 'groups are no longer tightly territorialized, spatially bounded . . . or culturally homogeneous' (Appadurai 1996: 48). For a cosmopolitan project it may be important to consider how cultural communities that are no longer confined within the boundaries of the state system might transform this system in the long run. If we accept Gellner's account of nation building as an attempt to make cultural and political boundaries coincide, then transnational cultural communities pose a quite significant challenge to the nation-state. While the other three patterns describe how existing state-based communities may be used as building blocks for constructing an encompassing global order, an overlapping pattern of political community would increase the permeability of boundaries, not merely for communication, commerce and travel, but also for political membership, identity and loyalty. The theories of post-nationalism interpret this as a trend that will eventually undermine the territorial as well as cultural bases of political legitimation. In contrast with cosmopolitan federalists they regard the erosion of existing national communities as a precondition for the emergence of a global polity.

What is broadly lacking so far is a normative political theory that would regard these phenomena of overlapping boundaries not only as a subversive tendency challenging the dominant architecture of the state system, but would integrate them into positive conceptions of what justice and democracy require. Let me take as a starting point a recent essay by Amartya Sen where he suggests a third alternative to 'grand universalism' and 'national particularism' in the

---

[10] The cosmopolitans are obviously more sympathetic to this idea. David Held emphasizes the 'overlapping spheres of influence, interference and interest' of countries that create 'overlapping communities of fate' (Held 1996: 22). But this notion still refers to the increasing *interdependence* between distinct political communities rather than to overlapping forms of *membership*.

theories of justice. The former espouses a global version of justice, which ignores the national affiliations of individuals, while the second endorses a two-stage conception: just institutions must first be built within states before we can apply principles of justice to relations between political communities. Sen points out that 'we all have multiple identities' (Sen 1999*b*: 120) and these give rise to conflicting obligations. Many of these affiliations and their corresponding institutions 'cut vigorously across national boundaries and do not operate through national polities' (Sen 1999*b*: 123). Issues of justice and fairness arise in various domains that do not encompass all humanity but are also not confined within national boundaries. Acknowledging this multiplicity has implications for our view of persons and of institutions. Somebody who is a medical doctor, an environmentalist and a member of a church will have affiliations and obligations not all of which can or should be subordinated to one overarching identity as a human being or as a member of a national polity. If 'justice is the first virtue of social institutions' (Rawls 1971: 3), then specific demands of justice will have to be developed not only for states and international bodies, but also for organizations such as business corporations or NGOs that operate beyond national borders.

While I fully agree with Sen's broadening of the scope of theories of justice,[11] I would still like to emphasize the specific place occupied by the basic institutions of a political community. As Sen himself points out, Rawls's device of the original position is used 'to yield the choice of the basic political and social structure for each society, which operates as a political unit and in which the principles of justice find their application' (Sen 1999*b*: 119). Resolving the Hobbesian problem of a just political order in the domestic and international realm is a task prior to determining the norms of justice that apply within other areas of social life. In the absence of such a political order, we may still feel bound by general moral norms that apply between individual persons but we cannot even think about developing norms for larger organizations such as business corporations or professional associations. Once the principles of justice for relations within and between political communities have been found, it will then be possible to develop more specific accounts of ethical principles that reflect our multiple and often competing affiliations.[12] The problem with Sen's approach is that it is not radical enough. People do not only have many social, cultural, ideological or economic affiliations that cut across their membership in political communities, but sometimes this very membership itself cuts across state boundaries as well. This

---

[11] Jon Elster (1992) explores a similar route in his account of pluralistic norms of 'local justice' embedded in substate institutions.

[12] Saying that political justice is in this sense prior to social justice does not at all imply that our national affiliations always take priority over our membership in other kinds of communities and associations. A stable and just global political order may require abandoning the general priority of obligations to compatriots defended by nationalists.

raises the problem within the heart of political theory. What would a just political order look like in which individuals are members of overlapping political communities? Grand universal cosmopolitanism cannot answer this question because it disregards the importance of affiliation to all kinds of political community; national particularism cannot answer it because it builds on the premise of exclusive membership. Federalist cosmopolitanism allows for the multiple levels of nested membership but not for the horizontal multiplicity that blurs the boundaries of jurisdictions. There is not yet a cosmopolitan theory that would permit or promote a global pattern of overlapping membership.

Combined Patterns

So far I have described the four patterns as alternative and (with the exception of the first one) utopian conceptions of a global order. I now want to question this interpretation and suggest that we are already witnessing a transformation of the state system through a combined emergence of the second, third and fourth pattern. I also regard such a rather messy combination as preferable to an exclusive realization of the confederal, the federal or the post-national vision. This is, however, a slow and uneven process and it is important to keep in mind the limitations of each of the three cosmopolitan dynamics with regard to their scope and their community-building potentials.

The pattern of an international society of states is clearly still the dominant one. It is almost universal in scope. Today, nearly all populations and territories (with the notable exception of Antarctica) are formally allocated to state jurisdictions. Only the high seas have remained outside their reach and since the beginnings of international law they have been a testing ground for its capacity to contain the global state of nature. The UN and its affiliated international organizations represent a cautious step towards a world confederation. Different from Kant's idea, its membership is not limited to republics or democratic states. Although Switzerland still stays outside, the scope of the UN regime is truly global. Permanent membership and veto rights for five states in the Security Council counterbalance the danger that such indiscriminate membership might undermine the capacity to build an effective common political order. At its hard core, where the UN aspires to state-like functions by claiming a monopoly of legitimate violence in the international arena, this organization resembles an alliance of unequal powers more than a confederation of equal states.[13] At its soft edges, on the other hand, the UN regime moves beyond the

---

[13] The 1999 NATO intervention in Kosovo without a mandate from the Security Council demonstrated that even the claim itself is rather spurious given the present monopolar structure of global military power.

confederal framework. In its decision-making institutions this regime basically represents only states, but it has also adopted a principle of self-determination of peoples that is not strictly confined to existing states (Cassese 1995). Stateless nations like the Palestinian people and a global network of indigenous peoples have based their claims to international recognition on this principle. Moreover, the UN activities have provided a global public arena for NGOs to campaign for global environmental policies or women's rights. The basic reason why the overall UN architecture must be unattractive for cosmopolitan democracy derives, however, from the deficiencies of the confederal model itself. In the present UN world there is simply no place for global citizenship in the strict sense of the word. Its human rights treaties promise individuals protection against their governments, but not representation in global institutions. This fault is not beyond repair. Creating a second chamber directly elected by citizens alongside the UN General Assembly, where only states are represented, would be a significant move towards a democratic world federation (Childers and Urquhart 1994; Held 1995*b*: 111; Bienen *et al.* 1998: 297–8; Höffe 1999: 333–4). Yet, such reforms are not merely blocked by the authoritarian members of the UN. So long as there is no emerging sense of global political community, they are unlikely to arouse much enthusiasm among the citizens of democratic states as well.

Until now there is only one example of a supranational membership that transcends the limitations of a confederal model and this is the citizenship of the EU. The EU is also closer to the Kantian idea than the UN in the sense that it is a gradually expanding union that admits only democratic states. Yet its scope is obviously quite limited. The borders of Europe are not naturally fixed and may eventually extend not only towards the east but could also include the southern and eastern shores of the Mediterranean Sea. But the European dreams of building empires that encompass the globe have long been abandoned. However far the EU might stretch, it will remain a regional association of states that coexists with other states and regional formations. There is nothing inherently cosmopolitan in the attempt to build a strong regional economic block that can successfully compete with the United States of America and Southeast Asia in global markets. What makes the EU attractive from a cosmopolitan perspective is a still fledgling conception of supranational citizenship that has emerged as a by-product of market-driven integration. The citizenship, formally established by the Maastricht Treaty of 1992, did little more than bring together under a new name the various rights that citizens of member states had previously enjoyed as benefits derived from intergovernmental agreements (Shaw 1997; Weiler 1999). The core rights of political participation remain limited because of the lack of legislative power in the European Parliament and because the crucial franchise in national elections is not included in the rights of European citizenship. Moreover, through their laws on nationality the member states remain the gatekeepers of admission to the Union citizenship. Current plans for an EU charter of fundamental rights, which would be directly adjudicated by the European Court of Justice, would greatly strengthen the civil rights component of citizenship in Europe. For the foreseeable future political and social rights will, however, remain primarily attached to national membership. The Eurosceptics argue that the main obstacle for the transformation of the EU into a federal polity is the strength of the distinct national and linguistic identities of the member states. This objection looks to the United States of America or Germany as model federations but ignores that in countries like Canada, Belgium, Switzerland or India where federalism has been a constitutional mechanism to accommodate diversity of just this kind. What makes the task of the European federation different and difficult is not in the salience of national differences *per se* but the fluid nature of boundaries. I have already pointed out above in the first section that existing models of multinational federalism establish a stable balance between the constitutive national and linguistic groups. As the EU keeps expanding new states join the club and demand that their national identities shall be respected.[14] And as its political integration deepens, the regional national minorities demand recognition and representation alongside the member states. The EU is the most advanced model of a multi-level supranational government, but it has so far failed to create a robust form of a multi-level citizenship with the direct representation of individuals in decisions at the Union level, and has not found a formula on how to integrate the plural national identities into a larger polity.

The fourth boundary pattern of overlapping affiliations to political communities exists in three major manifestations that I want to discuss briefly in the rest of this chapter: these are transborder national minorities, global networks of indigenous groups and transnational migrant communities.

Three Kinds of Transnational Communities

Theoretically, one can imagine two different types of overlapping political communities: a first where a common territory is shared between several polities and a second where membership is shared across territorial divisions. As examples for the first type we might think of the special status of non-sovereign territories such as postwar Germany and Austria or today's northern Iraq, Bosnia and Kosovo where foreign powers or representatives of the international community exercise control over the local government. Plans for a special status of Jerusalem as the capital for both Israel and a future Palestinian state provide another illustration. These cases show the limitations of the scope and

---

[14] See Article 6 (3) Treaty of the European Union (TEU) as amended by the Treaty of Amsterdam.

transformative impact of such a territorial model of overlapping boundaries. Deviations from a rule of exclusive territorial jurisdiction emerge only temporarily in the aftermath of a breakdown of political order and are regarded as means for re-establishing clearly defined territorial sovereignties. Where several external powers are involved in governing an occupied country or international protectorate they usually avoid problems of coordination among themselves by further subdividing the territory into zones, each of which is controlled by one foreign state.[15] There are no indications that the territorial structure of the state system is gradually dissolving under the pressures of globalization. We are not moving towards a neo-medieval world of overlapping territorial sovereignties and constantly shifting state borders. In the present state system there is still no toleration for ambiguities of this sort. From a cosmopolitan perspective it would also be unwise to promote them in order to overcome the rigidities of the Westphalian structure. Stable and internationally respected territorial borders of states are a precondition for federal as well as for transnational models of building larger political communities.

This leaves us with the second type of overlap where populations in the territories of several states share a political community. The first and most obvious instance of this phenomenon are national minorities linked to a neighbouring state or region, in such a state with whose population they share a common language, history and ethnic identity. The national minority demands for self-government may generally be accommodated in two different ways: by granting autonomy within the territory of a state or by revising state borders so that the minority can form its own state or join a neighbouring one. From a liberal perspective, the former solution should be preferred unless the minority has a serious and justified grievance that can only be redressed through territorial separation (Buchanan 1991). Territorial autonomy can be achieved through the devolution of power within the federal states or through creating a special status for a self-governing territory within a unitary state. The cultural autonomy of a non-territorial kind over matters such as public education may sometimes provide an alternative solution for national minorities who live dispersed throughout a state (Bauer 1907). Many Western democracies have a bad record of coercive assimilation, segregation, expulsion or genocide of indigenous and national minorities who had been settled in their territories at the time of nation building. A growing number of liberal theorists recognize that accommodating aspirations of national minorities to self-government is a question of justice that cannot be ignored for the sake of unity (Kymlicka and Norman 2000). There are

---

[15] In the case of Jerusalem, making it the capital of two independent states would almost certainly involve dividing the city. Alternatively, if it were indeed to be governed jointly, this would be a viable solution only if it led towards creating a binational federal state for the Jewish and Palestinian populations.

three kinds of reasons for respecting national minority rights.[16] First, these are sometimes grounded in historical agreements that promised autonomy as a condition for voluntary integration. Second, even in the absence of actual treaties, minorities may have strong claims because of the persistent disadvantage resulting from the dominance of a hegemonic majority culture. Finally, there is an argument that applies to national majorities as well as to minorities. Liberal democracies ought to recognize the general value of a secure membership in cultural and political communities for individual autonomy and well being (Kymlicka 1989; Margalit and Raz 1994).

These reasons support the claims for minority rights, which are articulated at the global, international, domestic and transnational levels. First, at the global level there is an individual human right for persons belonging to minorities 'in community with the other members of their group, to enjoy their own culture, to profess and practice their own religion, or to use their own language'. This right ought to be respected in the same way in all 'those states in which ethnic, religious or linguistic minorities exist' (International Covenant on Civil and Political Rights, Article 27). Second, a claim for secession involves a prima facie violation of the principle of territorial integrity of existing states and a demand for the recognition of new international borders. If the state from which a group wants to secede does not agree to a peaceful separation, a secession demand becomes a matter of concern for the international community. Developing adequate standards for mediation, arbitration and adjudication in such conflicts is an important task for international law and international organizations. Third, there is a broad range of minority claims that fall somewhere in between universal human rights and legitimate secession. These are demands for various collective arrangements and rights ranging from official status for a minority language to territorial autonomy and special representation at federal level. These can only be assessed contextually within a domestic framework. The particular history of a country and its constitutional traditions matter for normative judgements on minority policies, but they should be critically evaluated in the light of the three general reasons for recognizing minority claims that I have listed above.

The minority rights articulated in the three arenas discussed so far fit well into a federalist cosmopolitan project for strengthening the universal legal norms and international organizations, while respecting the self-governing rights of the historically established political communities. However, strengthening such rights will hardly contribute to the emergence of a global citizenship. Quite the contrary, their dynamic appears to produce a further differentiation and

---

[16] I discuss these three reasons in Bauböck (1999) where I also add the value of diversity for the wider society as a fourth argument. I do not include this latter reason here because I regard it as irrelevant for the collective autonomy claims of national minorities.

fragmentation of the existing state-based citizenship. From a cosmopolitan perspective the more interesting cases are those located at a fourth transnational
level. If the members of a minority think of themselves as belonging to a group
living in a neighbouring state, how should such an attachment be taken into
account? Gidon Gottlieb has suggested an internationally recognized 'special
regime for a national or ethnic community in a historical homeland that lies
across an international border'. Such a homeland regime 'would permit a soft
exercise of national rights that does not entail a territorial rearrangement among
states'. 'It could provide that no national would have the status of an alien in his
or her national home even though not all might have the right to settle there'
(Gottlieb 1994: 106, 107).

There are three ways in which a state may include an external minority in a
broader national community: by granting its members immigration rights or
access to citizenship in its own territory, by establishing an external citizenship
that involves the minority in political decisions in the 'homeland' (through
absentee ballots) or by assuming the role of a protecting power for the group's
rights in the state where it resides. The first among these is fairly common.
Germany, Israel, Japan, Greece and Italy are among the countries that privilege
the immigrants whom they regard as belonging to their national community
although they are not formally nationals of the state. Such ingathering of an ethnic diaspora belongs plainly to a territorial conception of nation building. In the
case of the German-speaking minority in Romania this safety valve has led to
the vanishing of the whole group from its traditional area of settlement. In other
instances, this policy may, however, transform local minorities into transnational ones who orient politically, culturally and economically towards an external homeland. From a liberal perspective the problem with this approach is that
it creates different standards for admission that are difficult to sustain and justify when immigration becomes more diverse.

The second way of giving a special role to external minorities by enfranchiz-
ing them in the homeland is regarded as more problematic because it reinforces
the impression of disloyalty not only through exit but also through voice. In
order to include minorities abroad in elections at home they must first be made
nationals, which usually is only possible for the descendants of emigrants who
acquire it at birth through *jus sanguinis*.

The third strategy of acting as a protecting power in the international arena is
the most contentious one because the state where the minority lives generally
regards such external protection as an interference in its domestic affairs. The
failure of the interwar regime of minority treaties under the League of Nations,
which eventually served as a pretext for Hitler's claim to all lands inhabited by
the Germans in Eastern Europe, created a general international reluctance to
endorse claims of this sort. An exceptional and rather successful example is the
role Austria assumed with regard to the German-speaking minority in South

Tyrol/Alto Adige. The language and regional autonomy rights were originally laid down in a 1946 bilateral agreement between Austria and Italy. When the Italian government appeared to stall on its promises and redrew the provincial boundaries so as to turn the German-speaking group into a minority in the region as well, the Austrian government raised the issue at the UN General Assembly in 1960. In 1992 the long negotiated 'package' on group rights and regional autonomy was accepted by Italy and both countries declared the dispute to be terminated. Such an outcome is only possible where the external homeland refrains from sponsoring an irredentist movement and where the country of residence does not enforce a unitary conception of the polity. Both preconditions are unlikely to be met by new states involved in nation-building exercises. Roger Brubaker has studied the triadic relation between national minorities, nationalizing states where they live and their external homelands in CEE.[17] His conclusion is that the structure of this triangle creates a potential for the escalation of conflict, but that contingent factors of social and political agency determine what the outcome will be (Brubaker 1996: 76).

There is indeed very little that could be said in general about the virtues or disadvantages of an international regime of 'soft borders' between the national minorities and their 'homelands', except that liberal democratic states will find it much easier to tolerate when they integrate themselves into larger supranational federations. While supranational federation makes it less likely that border revisions between states would lead to violent conflict, it reduces also the plausibility of such claims in the first place. Free movement across borders, a common citizenship and the recognition of many different languages diminish the need for external minorities to sustain formal links with their homelands.[18] In this sense, the demands of transnational minorities may be compatible with a cosmopolitan project and may even contribute to overcoming rigid Westphalian conceptions of mutual non-interference and exclusive territorial sovereignty.

Indigenous groups are a second type of minority whose demands may have a special significance for a transnational conception of community. In their case it is even more important, than with the other national minorities discussed so far, to emphasize the wide range of different historical experiences and of political and social organization among such groups. What they share in common is

---

[17] A similar triadic relation exists between Northern Ireland, the Irish Republic and Britain, with the difference that the external minority of Ulster Unionists has kept Northern Ireland within the United Kingdom. The Good Friday Agreement of 10 April 1998 provided for several layers of nested and overlapping jurisdictions: a Northern Irish dimension of self-government within the province, an all Irish dimension bringing together the executives of the South and the North, and a British Isles dimension with a council including members of all the devolved administrations within the United Kingdom and representatives of the Isle of Man and the Channel Islands as well as the British and Irish governments.

[18] Austria's joining the EU in 1995 might have been seen as lowering the barriers for nationalist demands to reunite the South and North Tyrol, but has actually led to a de-escalation.

an experience of colonial settlement that has turned them into minorities in their traditional homelands, has deprived them of natural resources and traditional means of subsistence and has marginalized their cultural traditions. Like the demands of other national minorities, indigenous claims focus on self-government. They do not merely claim equal citizenship and freedom to prac-tise their culture and religion, but want a large measure of political autonomy. And as with national minorities, self-government is for them not merely an instrument to preserve a traditional culture, but expresses their desire to deter-mine their own future and is an intrinsic value attached to their collective identity as distinct peoples. Yet the kind of self-government they desire is spe-cial in several respects. On the one hand, it is in practically all cases an internal autonomy within the states where they reside and not a demand for territorial secession and independence. On the other hand, indigenous political leaders make it clear that they do not only direct their demands at the political authori-ties of the state where they live, but ground their rights in international law and its principle of self-determination of peoples. Moreover, they have formed an impressive global network for deliberating about common concerns and lob-bying international organizations. The indigenous minorities for whom land has a religious significance are apparently the most territorially rooted of all minorities. Yet, paradoxically, they have developed a much more cosmopolitan form of political orientation and mobilization than other minorities that engage in traditional nation-building policies. Today indigenous claims are being reconsidered in the international arena and there is a UN Draft Declaration on the Rights of Indigenous Peoples waiting to be presented to the General Assembly.

Both the national and linguistic minorities in federal states and the indigen-ous minorities in settler societies often refer to historical agreements that ori-ginally recognized their statuses and rights. Yet there is another important difference here: for the former these agreements have constituted the political community as a joint enterprise of equal partners. During an initial period of colonization the white settler societies in North America concluded treaties with the native communities as well. The indigenous groups were recognized as independent peoples whose title to the land under natural law could be relin-quished only through voluntary cessation or as a consequence of acts of war against the settlers (Anaya 1996: 9–19). However, these first treaties were essentially about separation rather than integration into a common polity. When the natural law doctrines were gradually replaced by the positivist theory, the international law became by definition a law created by states and applying only between them. The indigenous peoples lost their international legal standing and were turned into mere subjects of the colonizing states (Anaya 1996: 19–23). In the United States of America their status as 'domestic dependent nations' became a pretext for excluding them from full citizenship until 1924. In referring back to the first agreements that recognized their status as peoples, indigenous groups refuse to be seen as constitutive communities of the present state where they reside and demand a direct relation to the international community that is unmediated by their individual citizenship. This is a challenge to the dominant 'paradigm of domestication', which affirms 'that treaty claims... can be dealt with satisfactorily and justly within the doctrinal framework and legal system of one party only, namely the state party' (Schulte-Tenckhoff 1998: 259). Liberal democracies have recently reaffirmed the validity of old treaties[19] or offered new ones to those groups who were subjected without a treaty.[20] Yet the condition attached to these offers is that indigenous groups would thereby accept domestic jurisdiction and abandon their claims to a special status under international law. For these reasons a recognition of indigenous rights to self-determination under international law would be a major shift away from the traditional state-centred paradigm.

The migrant communities are a third type of minorities who do not easily fit into a territorial framework of political boundaries. They have received the most attention in the literature on transnationalism. There are two developments that appear to create new forms of political community beyond the nation-state. One is the fact that immigrants in Western receiving states enjoy an increasing range of rights that have historically been connected to citizenship but are now extended to foreign residents. The other observation is that some migrant communities retain a long-term political orientation towards their countries of origin and form transnational networks defined by their ethnic origin. On the first point Yasemin Soysal (1994) has suggested that immigrants now enjoy universal human rights of personhood that are disconnected from their nationality. David Jacobson (1996) regards this trend as a devaluation of citizenship. Tomas Hammar (1990) has introduced the term 'denizenship' to characterize the status of permanent foreign residents as quasi-citizens. I have analysed this development as a move towards 'transnational citizenship', which expands the range of membership and rights by taking into account the societal ties emerging from long-term residence and from links between sending and receiving countries (Bauböck 1994).[21] The second trend has generated a new interest in migrant diasporas (Cohen 1997; Vertovec and Cohen 1999). Nina Glick-Schiller and her associates have studied migrant communities that participate intensely in the political life of their homelands and argue that the

---

[19] A prominent example is the re-interpretation of the 1840 Treaty of Waitangi in the discussion about Maori rights in New Zealand.

[20] A recent case is the creation of the autonomous Inuit territory of Nunavut in the Canadian North-West Territories in 1999.

[21] For an excellent critical discussion of the recent literature, see Bosniak (2000).

political leaderships of these countries 'are engaged in a new form of nation-building' (Basch *et al.* 1994: 3) so that 'both the political leaderships of sending nations and immigrants from these nations are coming to perceive these states as "deterritorialized"' (Basch *et al.* 1994: 8).

I would once again plead for some caution in the interpretation of these phenomena. First, the rights of immigrants disconnected from nationality have certainly grown but they are still precarious and frequently exposed to the whims of changing governments and parliamentary majorities.[22] The most important right for denizens is their guaranteed access to citizenship itself through naturalization and *jus soli*. There is a slow and hesitant movement among democratic immigration countries to recognize such a norm, but such a reform of nationality laws is still regarded as a purely domestic matter and is not covered by the universal legal norms. Denizenship is thus not an alternative to citizenship, but a condition that must include the offer of full citizenship. As a corollary of guaranteed access, liberal states should also tolerate dual nationality. Multiple citizenships are the most visible illustration of overlapping membership in political communities. For migrants it carries the essential benefit of free movement between two societies to which they are linked by residential and family ties. Yet, even this formal overlap does not generally imply a full and simultaneous participation in the legal order and political life of two states. In most cases only the rights attached to the nationality of the country where the person presently resides are active, while the second citizenship remains dormant until the migrant enters this other country. Second, the transnational political communities of migrants are a generally transitory phenomena. The ambiguities of membership are frequently resolved over time through the return migration to countries of origin or full assimilation into the polity of the receiving country. The traditional political communities are bounded in space but unlimited in time. In contrast, the transnational communities of migrants are territorially dispersed but normally do not extend over more than two or three generations (Bauböck 1998). This is all the more so in liberal democracies, which do not segregate the migrants from the native population but permit them to intermarry and assimilate. On the other hand, the dynamic of migratory chains linking specific countries of origin with particular destinations can also generate an ongoing new influx of first-generation immigrants who reproduce the transnational, ethnic and linguistic character of communities. Even if the migrant communities themselves do not form stable transnational communities of a diaspora type, the receiving society and its conception of political community may be durably changed when it accommodates them.

---

[22] A major illustration is the denial of federal welfare benefits for legal resident aliens introduced in the United States of America through the Welfare Reform Act of 1996.

Conclusions

I have argued that democratic cosmopolitanism needs a conception of political community that is not merely derived from the functional imperatives of globalization or the normative postulates of political philosophy. Economic globalization is a dissolvent for citizenship rather than a motor for its cosmopolitan transformation. Political theorists are therefore right to insist on the normative rather than the prognostic nature of their projects for global democracy. Still, every political community needs some basis in the real world, a set of common experiences and positions *vis-à-vis* political power that sustain a desire for collective self-government. The test for cosmopolitan democracy is whether the boundary shifts in the present international state system have the potential for creating a sense of a global political community. I have examined the nested, multi-level and overlapping patterns of political boundaries that transcend the dominant structure of a state sovereignty. The UN regime is ideally conceived as a confederal model but lacks any significant element of global citizenship. The EU is so far the only supranational regime that has formally established a common citizenship, but it remains plagued by the notorious democratic deficit and the lack of a vision of how to integrate the firmly entrenched national identities into a federal polity.

The overlapping pattern of minority communities whose political and cultural affiliations transcend the national framework of the state where they live offers promising sites for studying the potential of cosmopolitan democracy. However, it would be naïve to attribute to these minorities a special cosmopolitan consciousness. On the contrary, they generally experience their positions in the interstices of the nation-state system as a severe disadvantage that they desire to overcome. The claims of their political leaders are therefore couched in the traditional vocabulary of nationhood that still buys legitimacy in our world.[23] If these minorities can become catalysts for a cosmopolitan transformation of democracy, this is neither due to their ambiguous citizenship nor to their political consciousness. What may bring about such a change is an endogenous development of liberal norms in response to the challenges raised by their claims. The authoritarian regimes do not find it difficult to suppress their national and indigenous minorities and to keep immigrant workers in a state of indentured slavery. The need to take transnational affiliations into account arises only when a regime derives its legitimacy from a norm of equal respect and concern for all those whom it governs.

It is this liberal norm that underpins the politics of multiculturalism, the devolution of regional power in multinational states, the softening of borders

---

[23] A good illustration is the insistence of the indigenous peoples in North America to be regarded as First Nations.

between external minorities and their homelands, the recognition that indigenous peoples have claims to self-determination under international law and the granting of denizenship and dual citizenship for immigrants. All these policy implications of liberal norms are of course controversial in theory and contested in politics. None of the past developments along these lines can be taken for granted. But they still show a profound change in the conception of national community in domestic as well as in international arenas that can pave the path for cosmopolitan projects. I suggest moreover that policies of accommodating transnational minorities carry a much stronger normative force than those of federating existing states into supranational polities. The former is generally a matter of justice whereas the latter is a matter of prudence in the sense of well-understood self-interest. Fortunately, acknowledging the overlapping patterns of political community and promoting the multi-level pattern of supranational federation are two strategies that should well be compatible and could even reinforce each other.[24]

---

[24] A transnational conception of citizenship in the EU member states can, for example, help to correct the exclusionary effects that political integration and the introduction of the EU citizenship has had for migrant minorities. At the Tampere summit in October 1999, the EU Council has for the first time accepted a principle that third country nationals ought to enjoy rights comparable with those of the EU citizens. The recent proposals for an EU Charter of Fundamental Rights would also include these immigrants in an expanding regime of citizenship.

9

Four Cosmopolitanism Moments

ROBERT FINE AND ROBIN COHEN

Why, historically, has 'cosmopolitanism' surfaced from time to time only to become submerged again? In this chapter we consider four contexts or 'moments': the ancient world (Zeno's moment), the Enlightenment (Kant's moment), post-totalitarian thought (Arendt's moment) and late North American thought (Nussbaum's moment). There is no particular theoretical weight attached to the word 'moment': rather it serves as a convenient device to anchor some key debates and antinomies.

Why these particular moments? Our choice is much less than comprehensive, but rather more than arbitrary. By switching between four contexts we plan to reveal the limits and possibilities of certain cosmopolitan ideas/ideals and practices that are of current relevance. We suggest that while cosmopolitanism has many virtues it is unlikely to provide an all-embracing solution or a total antidote to problems of extreme nationalism, racism, ethnic conflict and religious fundamentalism. Many might hope (as we do) that contemporary cosmopolitanism is a harbinger of a new and more benign global ecumene, but might it be possible that it is simply the revival of an old deception? While we do not resolve this central equivocation, we acknowledge it and seek to open up new spaces of argument and contention.

Zeno's Moment

Cosmopolitanism in the ancient world was both more complex and more limited than has often been adduced. Tomlinson (1999: 184) suggests that the etymology is 'clear enough': the Greek words *kosmos*, meaning 'world' and *polis*, meaning 'city'. 'Hence,' he continues 'a cosmopolitan is a citizen of the world'. The 'hence' is not so self-evident. As is well established, for the Athenians citizenship was a form of localized belonging and membership that explicitly excluded slaves, women and resident foreigners (*metics*). For most Athenians over most of the city-state's history, cosmopolitanism did *not* mean the recognition of a universal 'citizen of the world'. Such a notion would have been alien—as it violated the Aristotelian conception of man (we mean 'man') as *zoon politikon*, one whose very nature demands that he live in a particular state. For Aristotle the life of belonging to a *polis* was not a reluctant tie, but a positive embrace of interdependence. Homer too denounced a man who was 'clanless and lawless and heartless'. Such men could never attain happiness or felicity (Waldron 1992: 767). The Athenian citizens conceived of their political community in quite restricted terms. Until Alexander (356–323 BCE) unified the eastern Mediterranean, it is doubtful that Athenians thought of themselves as Greeks, let alone citizens of the world.

Despite its rather narrow pre-Alexandrian notion of citizenship, the Athenian city-state was much more open to external influences than, say, states like Sparta. The conduct of long-distance trade and the promotion of philosophy, culture and mathematics meant that Athens needed to become a more 'open' or 'world city'—namely one that tolerated foreigners, though largely for instrumental purposes. The *metics* were thus usually socially accepted as 'free', but they did not form part of the citizen-body. There was no legal process of naturalization and any *metics* who became fully accepted did so 'by inadvertence or connivance' (Sabine 1961: 5).

Although it was not easy for a stranger to formally become a citizen, the idea of cosmopolitanism had its roots in ancient Greece, in the writings and beliefs of the cynics, Antisthenes and Diogenes. The stoic, Zeno, elaborated the concept. As Gray (1963: 29) remarked, in Zeno's *Republic* 'we have the foreshadowings of [both] anarchism and cosmopolitanism'. For Zeno there was no law, no compulsion, no council, no currency, no temples. All people, he argued, embodied the divine spark and all were capable of *logos*, divine reason (Mason 1999). Zeno imagined an expanding circle of inclusion—from self, to family, to friends, to city, to humanity. In this process of enlargement the state itself would disappear, to be replaced by pure reason. This was a major leap of the imagination—one that boldly elided the self-proclaimed and self-satisfied glories of Athens. It also challenged the widespread and conventional idea that Greeks were different, indeed superior, to all barbarians.

These ideas went down like the proverbial lead balloon. The cynics were social outsiders. The fact that the stoic Zeno was a *metic* from Citium in Cyprus and was sometimes described as a 'Phoenician' (a euphemism for a 'Semite') would hardly have made his ideas popular or mainstream among his contemporaries. Antisthenes, the founder of the cynics, was a Thracian while Diogenes was in exile from Sinope in Pontus. It was Diogenes who suggested that 'all wise men' constituted a single moral community—a city of the world. A 'city' here is to be understood as a meeting of minds, not a spatially delimited settlement. Again it was Diogenes who used the idea of a cosmopolitan in the sense of someone who had no anchorage in any contemporary, real, city-state and was therefore 'a citizen of the world' (Sabine 1961: 136–7). In Diogenes and Zeno we have the first intimations of a universal humanism, a notion of a trans-state community, some imaginative ideas about equal citizenship for women and even the design of unisex clothing.

The stoics and cynics never significantly changed social practices in the ancient world. The influence of their thinking on early Roman jurisprudence was, none the less, important in creating one breakthrough—the idea of equality under the law. Using Zeno's principles, Cicero insisted that all men ('men' again) were equal—not in respect of their wealth ('property') or in terms of their learning, but in terms of their possession of reason and the general consensus of what was honourable or contemptible (Sabine 1961: 164). By using this proposition as a basis for legal reasoning, those who needed to be treated equally by the law needed to be recognized as citizens, whether by birth, long residence or through some process of legal conferment. It was a short step to see citizenship as a more universal possibility that transcended the mere coincidence of birthplace or descent.

Comment

The ancient Greek version of cosmopolitanism was, in sum, quite limited in practice. As a 'world city', cosmopolitanism could legitimately be used as an adjective to describe a more socially diverse setting—rather as we would today talk of 'cosmopolitan London' or 'cosmopolitan New York'. But as a statement of universal humanism or equality, cosmopolitanism was propounded mainly by people who were marginal and powerless—clanless and heartless. It is true that Alexander was able to use 'cosmopolitan' ideas as a form of empire-building, developing a 'pan' movement rather like the nineteenth-century pan-Germanism or pan-Slavism, uniting the Persian and Macedonian peoples through force of arms. The empire soon splintered after his early death, and in any case it is doubtful whether those currently espousing cosmopolitan ideas would wish them to be implemented by military conquest. The idea of equality under the law for legitimate residents/citizens was, however, an enduring legacy, as were the core ideas of universalism and the less well-developed idea of sexual equality. The question of the appropriate unit of 'belonging' is something we will return to in our conclusion.

Kant's Moment

Over 2000 years after Antisthenes first used the term, Kant theorized cosmopolitanism in a series of seminal essays spanning a twelve-year period before and after the French revolution.[1] His ideas have become a focus of contemporary

---

[1] The key essays are all collected in Reiss (1970). The essays are: *Idea for a Universal History from a Cosmopolitan Point of View* (1785), *On the common saying 'This may be true in theory but it does not apply in practice'* (1793), *Toward Perpetual Peace: A Philosophical Sketch* (published 1795, revised 1796), *International Right* in *The Metaphysics of Morals* (1797).

study among those who see a need to revive the idea of cosmopolitanism for our own age.[2] The idea of cosmopolitanism in its modern incarnation is coeval with the rise of nationalism and since its inception has presented itself as an antidote to the ills of nationalism. It presents itself as the standard bearer of the struggle of the universal against the particular, of the interests of humanity against this or that local community.

Criticism of Kant's approach has accordingly taken the form merely of ironing out inconsistencies in his theory and of adapting his theory to modern conditions. The 'other' of this approach is the alliance constituted by the cynical realism of Carl Schmitt, the anti-humanism of the Heideggerian generation and the residual revolutionism of an old Marxist orthodoxy, which sees in the cosmopolitan ideal nothing more than a mask for the pursuit of hidden interests or a spurious moral ground for the idealization of Western power and the depiction of the other as an enemy of humankind itself. Although we do not attempt this here, we consider that what is needed is to look to a critique of Kant that goes further than 'thinking with Kant against Kant'. Later work will also need to provide a critique of the anti-Kantian alliance that is able to take into account the justifications of its discontent. Though these important critical tasks remain, we do briefly discuss Kant's rather unpleasant notions of human geography.

In his *Idea for a Universal History from a Cosmopolitan Point of View*, written in 1785, Kant posed the attainment of a cosmopolitan order as the greatest problem facing the human race—even greater than the achievement of republican civic constitutions within particular nation-states. Kant recognized that it was a 'fantastical' idea, without precedent in world history, but he also argued that it was a 'necessity' if the human race was not to consume itself in wars between nations and if the power of nation-states was not to overwhelm the freedom of individuals. By a 'cosmopolitan order', Kant meant an order in which there are established 'a lawful external relation among states' and a 'universal civic society'.

The idea of 'lawful external relations among states' was a reference to the development of international law and international institutions that treat states as legal subjects with rights and obligations *vis-à-vis* other states, and that aim to enforce peaceful relations among them. The idea of a 'universal civic society' was a reference to the development of what Kant sometimes called 'cosmopolitan law', that is a law that would guarantee the fundamental rights of every individual human being whether or not such rights were respected by their 'own' nation-states. Kant argued that the idea of a cosmopolitan order required the institution of a league or federation of nations that would guarantee with its

---

[2] See in particular the essays by Karl-Otto Apel, Jürgen Habermas, Axel Honneth and David Held in Bohman and Lutz-Bachmann (1997).

'united power' the security and justice of even the smallest states as well as the basic rights of even the most downtrodden individuals.

In his essay *Toward Perpetual Peace*, written ten years later, Kant acknowledged that his idea was looking all the more fantastical. European nation-states continued to relate to one another like individuals in a Hobbesian state of nature, namely as a war of all against all. They continued to treat newly discovered colonies as if they were 'lands without owners', and continued to treat foreigners more like enemies than guests. The immediate occasion for the writing of this essay was an event that was hardly portentous for Kant's cosmopolitan idea: it was the signing of the Treaty of Basel in which Prussia agreed to hand over to France all territories west of the Rhine, in exchange for being allowed to join Russia and Austria in the east in partitioning Poland. It was precisely the sort of *realpolitik* treaty that Kant condemned as a mere 'suspension of hostilities' and as the enemy of true peace.[3] It was to Kant's credit that he did not surrender to the growing nationalistic currents, neither 'enlightened' French nor 'romantic' German, but continued to expound his vision of a cosmopolitan order more strongly than ever.

The analogy between the Hobbesian 'state of nature', characterized by the war of all individuals against all individuals, and existing relations between states was an often repeated theme: 'Each state sees its own majesty precisely in not having to submit to any external legal constraint and the glory of its ruler consists in his power to order thousands of people to immolate themselves for a cause which does not truly concern them, while he need not himself incur any danger whatsoever' (Reiss 1970: 125). Kant argued that this state of affairs was rationally insupportable. Either it displayed 'the depravity of human nature without disguise', or it diminished the concept of international right by interpreting it in a 'meaningless' way as the right to go to war. Kant looked forward to a time when states would renounce their 'savage and lawless freedom' and adapt themselves instead to 'public coercive laws' embracing all the peoples of the earth. Standing armies would be abolished, no national debt would be incurred in connection with the external affairs of state, no state would forcibly

---

[3] We should also not forget the experience of the French revolution by which Kant was confronted. In the flush of its youth, decrees were passed offering French citizenship to all foreigners who had resided in France for five years and had means of subsistence; societies and newspapers for foreigners were encouraged; the use of force against other nations was disavowed; support was given to revolutionaries from other countries to rid themselves of despotic rulers; and certain 'benefactors of humankind', including Tom Paine, Mary Wollstonecraft, Jeremy Bentham and William Wilberforce, were awarded honorary French citizenship. But this new dawn was not to last. With the launching of the 'revolutionary wars', xenophobia became an active political force: campaigns against foreigners abounded as they were held responsible for all that went wrong: military defeats, economic difficulties, political crises, the lot. Foreign clubs and newspapers were disbanded; revolutionary terror was directed primarily against foreigners, and even Tom Paine, 'citizen of the world', the man who signed himself *Humanus*, was impoverished, imprisoned and then expelled. For a fuller account, see Kristeva (1991).

interfere in the constitution and government of other states and no acts of warfare would be allowed that would 'make mutual confidence impossible during a future time of peace' (Reiss 1970: 125). Kant recognized the harsh reality of war but argued that just as the war of all against all in a Hobbesian state of nature necessarily led to the establishment of Leviathan, so too the war of all states against all states would necessarily lead to the cosmopolitan order. Out of evil, or rather out of the 'unsocial sociability of man', would arise the good.

Kant's argument in defence of cosmopolitanism looked to underlying social and political trends to support the viability of his vision. There were four main threads to his argument:

1. The cosmopolitan idea was no more than a recognition of the fact that 'the peoples of the earth have entered in varying degrees into a universal community and it has developed to the point where a violation of rights in one part of the world is felt everywhere'. In this regard it constituted a kind of realism in the modern, globalized age.

2. It corresponded with the necessities of economic life in an age of commerce when peaceful exchange was becoming more profitable than the spirit of war.

3. It corresponded with the interests of nation-states that had been forced to arm themselves in order to encounter other nations as armed powers, but that were now burdened by the increasing costs and risks of war.

4. The spread of republican governments (based on the example set by one 'powerful and enlightened nation'—France) meant both that rulers could no longer declare war without consulting their citizens and that the 'moral maturity' of citizens was higher than in monarchical states. Furthermore, he argued that the constitutional framework of republican forms of government provided a foundation for the development of cosmopolitan law and cosmopolitan institutions.

Kant either believed or hoped that the costs, risks and horrors of war would impel the human species to invent the means to regulate the hostility that prevailed among states and that was a product of their lawless freedom. Behind the scenes, as it were, providence or the plan of nature or the hidden hand of history or the cunning of reason, call it what you will, was working toward the universal end: 'a perfect civil union of humankind'. Beneath the violence of existing relations between states, Kant's faith was that 'the germ of enlightenment always survived, developing further with each revolution and preparing the way for a subsequent higher level of improvement'. In this philosophy of history, progress toward perpetual peace can be discerned taking its course, as it were, behind the backs or over the heads of the actors themselves. Kant wrote that the eventual achievement of a cosmopolitan order was guaranteed 'by no less an authority than the great artist Nature herself'.

Kant's moral argument was that war, in any event, is an evil in itself and that reason therefore 'absolutely condemns war' and sees the achievement of peace as an 'immediate duty' (Reiss 1970: 104). In his metaphysics of morals, the idea of cosmopolitan right is presented as an a priori deduction from the postulates of practical reason, in other words it is a pure idea, based not on experience but on reason, an absolute duty and binding regardless of inclination. Reason proclaims, according to Kant, that 'there shall be no war', that the 'disastrous practice of war' must end forever; this is the 'irresistible veto' of the 'moral, practical reason within us' (Reiss 1970: 194). Kant insists that we have a duty to act in accordance with the idea of perpetual peace, even if there is not the slightest possibility of its realization and even if the idea were to remain forever an 'empty piety'. If Kant in fact justified his claims concerning the evils of war by reference to the experience of war—the 'horrors of violence' and the 'devastation' it causes, the burdens of debt that arise as a result of war, the loss of liberty that often ensues for the vanquished or the moral decline that occurs for the victors—the form of his argument remains. He proclaims a metaphysics of justice, which, on the basis of a priori deductions from the postulates of practical reason, makes the attainment of perpetual peace a categorical imperative and binding duty on rulers and citizens alike.

Kant accepts that provisionally, namely prior to the attainment of perpetual peace, war continues but he argues that there must be certain rules of war, which limit how it is inaugurated and conducted. For example, he says that the traditional 'right' of sovereigns to declare war and then to send subjects to fight on their behalf must be abolished. This so-called right of the ruler was 'an obvious consequence of the right to do what one wishes with one's own property', but it is impermissible to apply it to citizens who are 'co-legislative members of the state' and must therefore give their free consent through their representatives to 'every particular declaration of war'. If war is declared, it must be conducted in accordance with certain principles. These exclude punitive wars and wars of extermination or subjugation, or means of warfare that would render its perpetrators unfit to be citizens, or demands on the enemy for compensation for the costs of war or for the ransom for prisoners. They must also respect the right of other nations to continue to engage in commerce. Kant says that colonization may sometimes be justified in terms of 'bringing culture to uncivilized peoples' and purging the home country of 'depraved characters', but it must be done in such a way as to avoid the plunder, subjugation and extermination of conquered peoples.

To achieve this new cosmopolitan order, Kant advanced three basic conditions: first, that 'the civil constitution of every state shall be republican'; second, that 'the right of nations shall be based on a federation of free states'; and third, that 'cosmopolitan rights shall be limited to conditions of universal hospitality'. By a republican constitution Kant referred to a rights-based state founded on the civil and political freedom of all recognized members of society, namely a state based on features like the rule of law, representative government, a professional executive and the separation of powers. By a federation of free states Kant meant something different both from the domination of a single power (like France) overruling the rest and from a 'world-state', an idea Kant had earlier entertained but now saw as even more likely to lead to a 'universal despotism which saps all man's energies and ends in the graveyard of freedom'. A federation for Kant presupposed the separate existence and vigorous competition of many independent states, and the peace it created could be neither inaugurated nor secured without a general agreement between them. By the term 'cosmopolitan rights' Kant meant those fundamental rights every individual has by virtue of his or her humanity and that will be secured by the federation of free states, regardless of the laws of the nation-state in question. Kant cites here the right of foreigners 'not to be treated with hostility when they arrive on another territory, so long as they behave in a peaceable and lawful manner' and the right of native inhabitants in conquered countries not to be exterminated or 'counted as nothing'. In modern parlance, we might translate this as a call for an international humanitarian framework for major human rights violations.

The greatness of spirit that Kant showed was to stand up to the rising nationalism of his time and to defend the best traditions of enlightenment universalism. By combining a metaphysics of justice with a philosophy of history, Kant abstracted the cosmopolitan ideal both from a dispiriting positivism that declares that the way things are is the way they have to be and from a superficial empiricism that declares that the ways things look on the surface is all there is to the things themselves. Kant did not simply abstract the cosmopolitan ideal from history and society, as is sometimes alleged, but rather he fought against a view of history and society that cannot see beyond what already exists and cannot reach for another form of life. Kant's so-called 'abstract ideal' was his attempt to stem the growing tide of nationalism and harmonize the principle on which the world revolution was turning, namely the independence and sovereignty of the state, with the universalism of enlightenment.

Comment

Kant's argument has been criticized constructively in the sense of ironing out its creases and developing its institutional conclusions. Methodologically, perhaps the most important issue is to bridge the gap between Kant's philosophy of history with its connotation of natural necessity and his metaphysics of morals with its connotation of a priori right, and to link history and morality to one another in less dichotomous ways. Substantively, perhaps the most important substantive issue is to bridge the gap between national sovereignty and cosmopolitan order and recognize that the latter necessitates an incursion into the former. This is particularly evident in cases of 'cosmopolitan right' where defence of the rights of subjects persecuted by their own rulers and punishment of the perpetrators require diminution and revision of the doctrine of national sovereignty and some means of enforcement beyond the nation-state.

There is another criticism of Kant that needs at least some airing—namely the accusation that his cosmopolitan ideals are easily exposed as a sham when notice is taken of his work on geography. Though this had previously been ignored or perhaps deliberately obscured by Kantian scholars, as Harvey (2000) points out, Kant took his geography very seriously (teaching a course on it no less that 49 times, compared with the 54 times he taught a course on logic and metaphysics). Harvey describes the contents of his work in this field, recently published in French (Kant 1999) as 'nothing short of an intellectual and political embarrassment'. Using Harvey as a source and a translator, we have such Kantian gems as: 'Humanity achieves its greatest perfection with the White race. The yellow Indians have somewhat less talent. The Negroes are much inferior and some of the peoples of the Americas are well below them'. The Hottentots are dirty and smelly; the Javanese are thieving, conniving and servile. People of the 'far north' resemble the people of hot lands 'in their timidity, laziness, superstition and desire for strong drink'. Unfortunately, these are not isolated quotations but samples of a continuous discourse.

In short, Kant's views on race would not discomfort the average Nazi—an impression lent greater force by his notion that the German 'has a fortunate combination of feeling, both in that of the sublime and in that of the beautiful'. The English and French were thought only to have half of that feeling (Eze 1967: 48–9). It is interesting that Eze's early exposé, *Race and the Enlightenment*, was widely taught in black studies courses, but is not used by Kantian scholars or cited even by Harvey, who is sympathetic to Eze's outlook. Are we imposing anachronistic notions of race onto an eighteenth-century setting? Was Kant merely reflecting the commonplace ideas of his time? This 'let out' for Kant only goes some way, as is clear in Kant's review of his contemporary Herder's *Ideas on the Philosophy of the History of Mankind*. Herder, unlike Kant, did *not* think it possible to classify various races by skin colour. Again Herder, unlike Kant, thought each culture deserved respect and could not be considered 'inferior' or 'superior' (Eze 1967: 65). Kant systematically attacked Herder's views on these questions.

Arendt's Moment

As we have shown, Kant suggested that cosmopolitanism was necessary to combat the evils of war and the 'horrors of violence' evident in the eighteenth century. The scale of horrors and evils was multiplied many times in the twentieth century and was eventually to generate another moment of cosmopolitanism, particularly in the field of cosmopolitan law. The extreme use of violence is strongly, though regrettably not exclusively, associated with Stalinism and Nazism—the gulag and the holocaust. Both were extreme denials of universal humanism or cosmopolitanism. Both regimes also justified their murderous attacks on the other—be they *kulak*, political dissenter, homosexual, Jew or Roma—in terms of a higher purpose, the fostering of states that would favour some purer, more elevated, subset of humanity, ultimately to humanity's own good. Proletarian internationalism and Aryanism would be good for the world after certain backward-looking and destructive vermin had been exterminated.

It is instructive that the impediments to these new world orders were often identified as 'cosmopolitans'. As is well known, the Nazis reserved their particular hatred for the 'cosmopolitan' Jews—rootless, nationless, without loyalty to anything except some dark conspiracy of their own. The Soviet story is more complicated. Until after the Second World War Soviet dictionaries—a sure guide to official usage—tended to accept Diogenes's definition of a cosmopolitan as 'a citizen of the world'. Thereafter, as with the Nazis, a cosmopolitan was 'a traitor to his country' while cosmopolitanism was thought to be 'a reactionary theory that preaches indifference to the fatherland, to national traditions and to national culture'. It 'expresses the ideology and politics of the bourgeoisie' (Carew Hunt 1957: 36). The Soviet regime sought particularly to associate cosmopolitanism with 'Anglo-American imperialists', who were using notions of world government to weaken legitimate nationalist sentiments. By linking cosmopolitanism with imperialism, the Soviets were able to maintain the ideological purity of an alternative 'proletarian internationalism'. By early January 1949, however, the attack became more swingeing, with cosmopolitanism being associated with international Jewry, Zionism, Pan-Americanism and Catholicism (Carew Hunt 1957: 38). Again, however, the principal internal targets were 'rootless' Jewish intellectuals who were deemed incapable of understanding the commitments and values of the Russian people.

While the Soviets were echoing Nazi sentiments, certain prominent Nazis were on trial in Nuremburg. This was the context for Arendt's moment of cosmopolitanism. The idea of linking the trials to a Kantian vision of cosmopolitanism was, in fact, not Arendt's own, but that of her close friend, Karl Jaspers (1961, first published 1945). He argued that the trials undercut the principle of national sovereignty that put a 'halo' around the heads of state (shades of the current debate about General Pinochet). Guilt must go beyond 'war guilt' and must include 'crimes against humanity', a phrase that was to carry enormous resonance for the next half-century. By treating mass murderers as mere criminals, the trials represented them in 'their total banality', thus depriving them of that 'streak of satanic greatness' with which they otherwise would have been endowed.

Arendt and the Question of Crimes Against Humanity

The legal concept of 'crimes against humanity' came into being in 1945 as a new charge levelled by the Allied powers against Nazi defendants at Nuremberg. It was conceived as a supplement to crimes that already existed under international law, notably 'war crimes' and 'crimes against peace', and as filling a gap in international law that was revealed most horrifically by the extermination of millions of innocent civilians by the Nazi regime in Germany and their accomplices.[4] The Nuremberg Charter defined 'crimes against humanity' in terms of certain specific acts (namely murder, extermination, enslavement and deportation), other non-specific 'inhumane acts', and finally 'persecutions based on political, racial or religious grounds'. The limiting factor in all these cases was that these acts had to be committed against civilian populations, have some connection with war and be carried out as part of a systematic governmental policy.

The Nuremberg Charter advanced a strong notion of personal responsibility. It announced that *individuals*, rather than states, could be held responsible not only for crimes against humanity but also for all crimes under international law. It held that individuals acting within the legality of their own state could nevertheless be tried as criminals. It established a link between people and their actions by treating 'cogs' in the Nazi murder machine as perpetrators and thus as responsible human beings. It stated that service to the state does not exonerate any official in any bureaucracy or any scientist in any laboratory from his or her responsibilities as an individual. It removed from perpetrators the excuse of 'only obeying orders'. It held those who sit behind desks planning atrocities as guilty as those who participated directly in their execution. Not least, it signified that atrocities committed against one set of people, be they Jews or Poles or Roma, were an affront not only to these particular people, but also to humanity as a whole.

The question of crimes against humanity, and that of the personal responsibility of perpetrators, was one aspect of Hannah Arendt's confrontation with the 'burden of events' that she registered under the title of totalitarianism. The issue presented itself to her concretely with the Nuremberg trials, then fifteen years later with the trial of Adolph Eichmann in Jerusalem, indeed with her lifelong efforts to understand the 'frenzy of destruction' into which totalitarian regimes descended. Arendt was confronted both with the 'horrible originality' of the actual crimes committed and with the more uplifting originality of a

---

[4] The term seems to have come from Hersh Lauterpacht, a distinguished professor of international law at Cambridge University, who had been pressing for a war crimes trial since 1943 and was keen to have the court consider atrocities committed against Jews. The pre-history of the term goes back to the allied denunciation of the Turkish government for the massacre of Armenians in 1915, which they held responsible for 'crimes against humanity and civilization'. See Marrus (1997: 185–7).

cosmopolitan law that would hold perpetrators personally accountable for their crimes. There was nothing 'naïve' in her relation to these events in the sense that it was mediated by an engagement with the thinking of others and in particular with three prevailing currents of social theory, which we can call *cosmopolitanism*, *realism* and *postmetaphysics*.[5]

The Relation to Cosmopolitanism

In *The Question of German Guilt*, written in 1945, Karl Jaspers (1961) offered the quintessential cosmopolitan justification of the Nuremberg trials. He stressed the importance of prosecuting 'war criminals' as an element in a more general re-evaluation of responsibility after Nazism and as a rational alternative to the barbarism of collective punishment (which would only mimic the mindset of the Nazis themselves). He argued that the trials undercut that principle of national sovereignty and that they made a necessary distinction between those who were criminally guilty and the indefinite number of others who were merely capable of cooperating under orders. Jaspers rejected the explanations and the defences advanced by the Nazi defendants as amounting only to excuses—to an evasion of their responsibility—and held that the institution of crimes against humanity inaugurated a new organization of human responsibility: politically for how people are ruled, morally for the countless tiny acts of indifference that make injustice possible and metaphysically for all the crimes that are committed in the presence and with the knowledge of other human beings.

From Jaspers's point of view, the trials helped not only to reorient the pariah nation, Germany, back to the tradition of Western humanism, but also to renew the tradition of Western humanism itself. Jaspers acknowledged certain legal defects at Nuremberg, but what interested him most was the future. He described the trials as 'a feeble, ambiguous harbinger of a world order the need of which mankind is beginning to feel' and he maintained that 'as a new attempt on behalf of order in the world', the trial does not 'grow meaningless if it cannot yet be based on a legal world order but must still halt within a political framework'. The new world order might not yet be at hand, but Jaspers celebrated the fact that it has at least come to seem possible to 'thinking humanity' and had appeared on the horizon as 'a barely perceptible dawn' (Jaspers 1961: 60). The spirit of Kant and of the eighteenth-century vision of cosmopolitan law was coming to life before his eyes.[6]

---

[5] We will deal mainly with cosmopolitanism here, though this violates the coherence of Arendt's thought. All three elements are integrated in Fine (1998) and in his forthcoming work.

[6] Kant had written that at the dawn of modernity 'each state saw its own majesty in not having to submit to any external legal constraint and the glory of its ruler consisted in his power to order the death of thousands of its people for causes which did not at all concern them' (Reiss 1970: 103). Kant's hope and

One of the most important achievements of the trials, as Jaspers saw it, was that they revealed the 'prosaic triviality' that characterized the perpetrators. By treating mass murderers as mere criminals, he argued in an idiom that was soon to be picked up by Arendt, the trials represented them 'in their total banality' and deprived them of that 'streak of satanic greatness' with which they might otherwise be endowed. He regarded with horror 'any hint of myth and legend' (Arendt and Jaspers 1992: 62).

Both in her correspondence with Jaspers and in her published articles, Arendt displayed an equivocation that was barely visible in her friend's writings. First, she pointed to the disparity between mere criminality and the facts of mass extermination: it seemed to her that what was distinctive about the enormity of Nazi crimes was that they 'explode the limits of the law' and it was this that constituted their monstrousness. For these crimes, she wrote, no punishment can be severe enough. It may well have been essential to hang Göring and the others but it was totally inadequate to the deed, since 'this guilt, in contrast to all criminal guilt, oversteps and shatters any and all legal systems' (Arendt and Jaspers 1992: 54).

Second, Arendt underlined the disproportion between the relatively few Nazis who were punished and the mass of perpetrators who had committed the crimes in question. In an article first written in 1945 on *Organized Guilt and Universal Responsibility* (1994), she argued that when a machinery of mass murder makes practically everyone complicit, or when the visible signs of distinction between the guilty and the innocent are effaced so that it becomes almost impossible to tell them apart, the allocation of personal guilt is particularly problematic:

The boundaries dividing criminals from normal persons, the guilty from the innocent, have been so completely effaced that nobody will be able to tell in Germany whether in any case he is dealing with a secret hero or with a former mass murderer. In this situation, we will not be aided either by a definition of those responsible or by the punishment of 'war criminals'.... The human need for justice can find no satisfactory reply to the total mobilization of a people to that purpose. Where all are guilty, nobody in the last analysis can be judged (Arendt 1994: 125–6).

Third, when people are prepared to do their jobs as 'cogs in a machine' and see themselves simply as 'doing their job' without responsibility for the consequences of their actions, they do not regard themselves as murderers because they kill only in a professional capacity. For such people, punishment provokes feelings of incomprehension, resentment and betrayal such as those that prevailed

expectation, however, was that states would eventually abandon this 'lawless state of savagery' and introduce in its place a cosmopolitan system of justice based on the recognition that the peoples of the earth have 'entered in varying degrees into a universal community where a violation of rights in one part of the world is felt everywhere' (Reiss 1970: 104–5).

in Germany during the trials, or alternatively among some others a sense of self-consuming guilt. Neither, Arendt wrote, would be of much use.[7] Rather than speak the moral-theological language of guilt, purification and redemption, or the legal language of guilt, prosecution and punishment, Arendt looked to a more political answer: one in which human beings

assume responsibility for all crimes committed by human beings, in which no one people are assigned a monopoly of guilt and none considers itself superior, in which good citizens would not shrink back in horror at German crimes and declare 'Thank God, I am not like that,' but rather recognize in fear and trembling the incalculable evil which humanity is capable of and fight fearlessly uncompromisingly, everywhere against it (Arendt 1994: 132).

The social construction of moral or criminal guilt would exonerate not only the Germans but also humanity from the need for a more profound ethical and political response.

On one issue, however, Arendt expressed her strong agreement with Jaspers: 'I realize', she wrote, 'that I come dangerously close to that "satanic greatness" that I, like you, totally reject . . . we have to combat all impulses to mythologize the horrible' (Arendt and Jaspers 1992: 69). The trials were significant in de-mythologizing as well as publicizing what the Nazis did, and Arendt began to take seriously the notion of 'crimes against humanity' as having a literal truth when she affirmed the difference between 'a man who sets out to murder his old aunt' (a discrete subject of criminal investigation) and 'people who without considering the economic usefulness of their actions at all (the deportations were very damaging to the war effort) built factories to produce corpses' (Arendt and Jaspers 1992: 69). It was in the latter that the substance of 'crimes against humanity' was to be found: 'Perhaps what is behind it all is only that individual human beings did not kill other individual human beings for human reasons, but that an organized attempt was made to eradicate the concept of the human being' (Arendt and Jaspers 1992: 69).

What Arendt pointed to was the *emergence* of crimes against humanity not merely as an expression of a new humanist sensibility but of a radically new form of violence.

Some fifteen years later, in her analysis of the Eichmann trial, there was a discernible shift of emphasis both in Jaspers's and Arendt's writings. Now it was Jaspers who, in his correspondence with Arendt, expressed doubts about the trial. He questioned its legal basis—partly because Eichmann had been

---

[7] Arendt describes the 'mob-man' as the 'end result of the bourgeois' and writes: 'When his occupation forces him to murder people he does not regard himself as a murderer because he has not done it out of inclination but in his professional capacity. Out of sheer passion he would never harm a fly. If we tell a member of this new occupational class, which our time has produced, that he is being held to account for what he did, he will feel nothing except that he has been betrayed' (Arendt 1994: 130).

'illegally' kidnapped from Argentina but mainly because 'something other than law is at issue here' and to address it in legal terms is a mistake. He expressed disquiet over the use of an Israeli court: 'Israel didn't even exist when the murders were committed... Israel is not the Jewish people... Israel does not have the right to speak for the Jewish people as a whole'. He feared that anti-Semitism would find its martyr in Eichmann and that the anti-Semite would say: 'You are acting neither in the name of the law nor in the name of a great political conception. ... you are vengeful... or ridiculous'. He maintained that something was at stake that could not be contained in any national court: 'It is a task for humanity, not for an individual national state, to pass judgement in such a weighty case'. In the absence of such an international body, he thought it better to do without the trial altogether or put in its place some other process of 'examination and clarification'[8] (Arendt and Jaspers 1992: 410–19).

For Jaspers cosmopolitanism had become a reason to doubt the validity of the trial. Arendt, however, countered Jaspers's reservations with some hard-nosed observations. The kidnapping of a man indicted at Nuremberg and charged with crimes against humanity *was* legally justifiable—particularly from a country with a bad record of extradition. The use of an Israeli court was justifiable—neither because it speaks on behalf of all Jews nor because Israel is above criticism, but because many of the surviving victims lived there, because Eichmann was charged exclusively with the killing of Jews, and because in the absence of an international court or a successor institution to the *ad hoc* Nuremberg Tribunal, Israel had as much right as any country to try those apprehended for crimes against humanity. The resort to legal mechanisms of prosecution was justifiable since there were no tools to hand except legal ones with which to judge and pass sentence on Eichmann—even if his deeds could not adequately be represented in legal terms (Arendt and Jaspers 1992: 417). Arendt showed no compunction even about the imposition of the death penalty: 'no member of the human race can be expected to want to share the earth', she wrote, with a man who 'supported and carried out a policy of not wanting to share the earth with the Jewish people and the people of a number of other nations'. She expressed her disagreement with those who cast doubt on the relevance of the trial on the grounds that what was at issue was something much bigger—including German guilt, the nature of evil, technological destructiveness, the beliefs and the structures of modernity.

Arendt now pursued the line of argument that originated in Jaspers's own conception of 'banality of evil'. The achievement of the trial, as she put it, was not only that 'all the cogs in the machinery, no matter how insignificant, are in court forthwith transformed back into perpetrators, that is to say, into human beings' (Arendt 1994: 289); in addition, the benefit of making the perpetrators

---

[8] What, perhaps, one would now know as a Truth and Reconciliation Commission, post-apartheid South Africa being the paradigm case.

'merely criminal' was precisely to subvert the hagiography of satanic greatness that might otherwise surround them. In her view, the trial revealed that Eichmann, except for his extraordinary diligence in looking out for his own advancement, 'had no motives at all'. Nothing was further from his mind than to 'determine with Richard III "to prove a villain"' (Arendt 1994: 287). On the contrary, 'It was sheer thoughtlessness—something by no means identical with stupidity—that predisposed him to become one of the greatest criminals of that period.... That such remoteness from reality and such thoughtlessness can wreak more havoc than all the evil instincts taken together ... that was in fact the lesson one could learn in Jerusalem' (Arendt 1994: 288).[9] The trial revealed that Eichmann was 'terrifyingly normal ... a new type of criminal ... who commits his crimes under circumstances that make it well-nigh impossible for him to know or to feel that he is doing wrong' (Arendt 1994: 276). In *The Life of the Mind*, Arendt reiterated the theme: the Eichmann trial demonstrated the untruth of the proposition that 'evil is something demonic' or that Satan strikes 'like a lightning fall from heaven'. In the trial one could only be struck by the 'manifest shallowness in the doer.... The deeds were monstrous but the doer ... was quite ordinary, commonplace, and neither demonic nor monstrous' (Arendt 1978: 3–4). The thesis concerning the 'banality of evil' originated as a factual judgement on Eichmann's 'quite authentic inability to think' (Arendt 1978: 3).

Through this concept, Arendt reaffirmed the strong notion of personal responsibility that was present within the law: not only among those who committed the deeds with their own hands, but also or especially among the planners and organizers like Eichmann who were remote from the actual killing. It was read, however, as a slogan designed both to trivialize the experience of the holocaust and to diminish the *novum* of this event. Neither was true. Perhaps what really angered Arendt's critics was her resistance—a resistance first fuelled by Jaspers—to what she saw as a growing tendency to depoliticize the extermination of the Jews or indulge in what Gillian Rose later called 'holocaust piety' (Rose 1996: 41). The trial was ultimately justified by Arendt because it testified to the fact that evil is no 'fallen angel', no Lucifer, no 'absolute evil', but the work of human beings—human, all too human.

In her analysis of the political functions of the trial, Arendt was indeterminate: it encouraged the prosecution of leading Nazis in West Germany; it publicized the holocaust to the world; it offered a forum for the testimony of victims; it accomplished a touch of justice. On the negative side, despite her support for

---

[9] Alain Finkielkraut picked up the same theme when he argued in relation to the Barbie Trial that though the holocaust was 'from Eichmann to the engineers on the trains ... a crime of employees ... it was precisely to remove from *crime* the excuse of *service* and to restore the quality of *killers* to law-abiding citizens ... that the category of "crimes against humanity" was formulated' (Finkielkraut 1989: 3–4). We may think here of Hegel's aphorism that to punish an individual is to respect him or her as a rational human being.

Israel's right to try the case, she thought the trial was abused by the Israeli authorities for various nationalistic ends: to support the contention that only in Israel could a Jew be safe; to camouflage the existence of ethnic distinctions in Israeli society; even, controversially to conceal the complicity of certain Jewish leaders, police and speculators in the execution of the holocaust.

As she saw it, the cosmopolitan precedent set by Nuremberg—a precedent that was largely forgotten after the onset of the cold war—was being used to reinforce the very situation it had sought to correct—the breaking up of the human race into a multitude of competing states and nations. Most important of all, perhaps, the nationalistic use of the trial indicated the denial of any equivocation of ethical life: that is, of what Primo Levi called the 'grey zone' in which the dividing line between the executioners and victims becomes blurred and the abused are themselves turned into abusers. Her difficulty was that the institution of crimes against humanity, which had offered hope of release from the elements of totalitarian thought, was being corralled back into a simplistic moral division of the world between 'them' and 'us'. This served as an index of a world purged of all political profundity, or as Arendt put it, of a 'banality that obliterates all distinctions' (Arendt 1983: 30).

Comment

Arendt endeavoured to spell out the substance of crimes against humanity beyond a mere legal definition. If the notion of humanity was a product of the modern age, crimes against humanity were the product of a certain kind of revolution. It was not directed against the modern bourgeois society as such, for the readiness of business to go along with extreme violence was already well established in the imperialist era, and the readiness of the Nazis to do business with business and make use of modern industrial methods is amply documented. Rather, in the name of the 'concrete community', it was directed against the abstract universals of modern bourgeois society, which appeared both false and oppressive and which took their highest form in the idea of 'humanity'. Crimes against humanity were thus aimed at those who personified the dominance of these abstractions—at pariah peoples who were stripped of everything other than their human status as such, and especially at 'rootless, cosmopolitan' Jews. The intent behind these crimes is to destroy not just these people but also the very idea of humanity that they are meant to embody.

Bernstein (1996: 145–6) points out that, while in *The Origins of Totalitarianism* Arendt did not hesitate to write about human nature and its transformation, later in *The Human Condition* (Arendt 1958: 9–10), she repudiated the notion of human nature:

The human condition is not the same as human nature and the sum total of human activities and capabilities which correspond to the human condition does not constitute anything like human nature.... The problem of human nature...seems unanswerable.... It is highly unlikely that we who can know, determine and define the natural essences of all things surrounding us...should ever be able to do the same for ourselves—this would be like jumping over our own shadows.... Nothing entitles us to assume that man has a nature or essence in the same sense as other things.

Bernstein (1996: 146) is absolutely right when he says that Arendt refused the consolation that there is 'something deep down in human beings that will resist the totalitarian impulse to prove that "everything is possible" '. The spectre that haunted her was that the concept of humanity itself could indeed be obliterated or, as she put it in a letter to Jaspers (17 December, 1946), that the organized attempt to 'eradicate the concept of the human being' and bring about a 'total moral collapse' might well succeed (Arendt and Jaspers 1992: 69). For this reason Arendt preferred to speak of crimes against the 'human condition' rather than against 'humanity'.

This existential turn may have solved the problem of 'essentializing' human nature, but at a cost. For it also lost sight of the social and historical character both of humanity and of the attempts to destroy it. The abstraction of 'humanity' is the product of modern political life and would have been meaningless to the ancients. Accordingly, the emergence of 'crimes against humanity' presupposes the prior emergence of humanity as such and is the product of an intentional revolt against this abstract universalism. Because the existential framework of Arendt's analysis could not incorporate socio-theoretical considerations of this kind, the concept of crimes against humanity remained elusive. Perhaps Arendt's achievement was, as she herself put it in *Men in Dark Times*, to make clouds rather than to clear them, and she did not hold herself duty-bound to resolve the difficulties that she created (Arendt 1983: 8). Arendt leaves us with a vision of a new, cosmopolitan order as beautiful as it is necessary, but a vision beset by lost opportunities, tarnished by competition between national memories, degraded by an ideological servitude to particular powers, and corralled into a moral dualism of good and evil, which robs debate of political profundity.

Nussbaum's Moment

Whereas it may seem self-evident to select Zeno, Kant and Arendt as our main *trägers* of key cosmopolitan moments, it may seem a little more idiosyncratic to choose Martha Nussbaum to exemplify late North American thought on the issue of cosmopolitanism. This is no reflection of her status as a philosopher. But there are other US candidates around—notably David Hollinger, who in his often-cited book *Postethnic America* (1995), explicitly seeks to replace the rigidity of American multiculturalism with the multiplicity of cosmopolitanism.

Again, Nussbaum's intervention is primarily about the use of cosmopolitanism in US educational reform—a rather restricted agenda. However, the great advantage of using Nussbaum's intervention for current purposes is that her essay, published in the *Boston Review* (1994), then with replies on the web (Nussbaum *et al.* 1994), then in book form (edited with J. Cohen, 1996) attracted 29 published responses from a wide array of US intellectuals.

Nussbaum starts from a view that 'Americans' have a particular hubris, a pride in American identity and citizenship that blinds them to another primary allegiance, that of being members of a community of human beings spread across the world.[10] Her particular target is Rorty, whom she sees as promoting a rather uncritical patriotism, one that may encourage American students to respect human rights in other countries, but actually places their identity as US citizens at the forefront of their concerns. Nussbaum promotes a radically alternative vision, one that draws explicitly on the ancient cynics and stoics and, less convincingly, on the Indian novelist Rabindranath Tagore.

She explicitly accepts the stoic idea that a self is surrounded by a wider and wider series of concentric circles, ultimately by humanity itself. In her vision (Nussbaum *et al.* 1994), a student in the United States of America

may continue to regard herself as in part defined by her particular loves—for her family, her religious and/or ethnic and/or racial community or communities, even for her country. But she must also, and centrally, learn to recognize humanity wherever she encounters it, undeterred by traits that are strange to her, and be eager to understand humanity in its 'strange' guises. She must learn enough about the different to recognize common aims, aspirations, and values, and enough about these common ends to see how variously they are instantiated in the many cultures and many histories.

World citizenship is favourably contrasted with national citizenship. Nussbaum advances a number of arguments to support this position. A national focus in education leads to a 'false air of moral weight and glory'; only by seeing oneself in the eyes of the other can one recognize what is deep and shared rather than local and unnecessary. Certain global concerns—for example, ecology, food supply and population—have escaped the confines of the national and can only be addressed by global knowledge, global planning and the recognition of a shared future for humanity. Americans should recognize that the high living standards they enjoy are not likely to be universalized so—in the name of Kantian morality—'we' need 'to educate our children to be troubled by this

---

[10] We follow her use of 'Americans' to mean citizens of the United States of America (a common-enough practice), yet it is important in this context to mention that 'American' and 'America' is an appropriation, derived precisely from the hubris Nussbaum attacks. South and Central Americans are also Americans. Note: We have used the web version in this chapter, and as this prints out differently, no page numbers are cited. We allude to Nussbaum *et al.* (1994). Respondents are referred to as Barber in Nussbaum *et al.* (1994), and so forth.

fact'. National boundaries are in any case increasingly incoherent—with international migration the same groups exist 'inside' and 'outside'.

A number of these ideas are commonplace enough, yet they were expressed in trenchant language and seem to have 'got under the skin' of a number of rather eminent commentators and academics. Here are some examples of such responses:

Martha Nussbaum is one of the most eminent female philosophers of time, but when it comes to politics she is a girl scout.... For [the] acrobatic counter-move to Professor Rorty she claims the support, or the authority of the Stoics and of Kant. Why does she ignore the liberalism and constitutionalism of the country in which she lives? . . . Only the philosopher could be a citizen of the world. No possible government could be impartial enough to be truly cosmopolitan (Mansfield in Nussbaum *et al.* 1994).

We must deal with the world we have; and in that world frail and erring mortals give their allegiance not to praiseworthy abstractions but to specific and familiar communities . . . perhaps our best hope for the time being is to follow the precept of Carl Schurz: 'Our country, right or wrong. When right to be kept right; when wrong, to be put right' (Schlesinger in Nussbaum *et al.* 1994).

In the end, Nussbaum's argument reduces to name-calling. Her case is a version of the insult that anyone who takes patriotism seriously must be a crypto-fascist. Her charges range from accusing her opponents of treating their country as a god to their seeking 'a surrogate parent who will do one's thinking for one'. There must be a better way to make the point that we must help those close to us without forgetting those far away (Fletcher in Nussbaum *et al.* 1994).

The bulk of her respondents, even when they are sympathetic to her enterprise, take the view that she had too narrow a notion of American patriotism. Curiously, very few of them are able to demonstrate their argument by reference to a deeper, broader more universal notion of 'Americanness'. On the whole they resort to ritual evocations of the Constitution (which only serve to reinforce Nussbaum's charges of moral piety) or pity her for her foolishness and lack of realism. None even has the wit to evoke Benjamin Franklin's considerable attempts to join French revolutionary thinking to an emergent American version of cosmopolitan nationhood (see Schlereth 1977).

One notable commentator is Benjamin R. Barber, whose heartfelt, even emotional, response strikes a more genuine note, a fact acknowledged by Nussbaum in her riposte to her critics. For Barber, Nussbaum underestimates the 'thinness' of cosmopolitanism and misunderstands the nature of American patriotism. He alludes to St John Crevecoeur's *Letters from an American Farmer*, in which American patriotism is explicitly contrasted with religious parochialism and the ethnic persecutions from which immigrants to the United States of America escaped. In America, said Crevecoeur, they can be 'new men' with 'new laws, a new mode of living, a new social system: here they are becoming men: in Europe they were so many useless plants'. One hesitates even to quote these incantations of manliness to a mixed readership, but we wanted to record the central idea that America is an asylum, a refuge, and an escape—a specifically *territorially defined* safe haven (Barber in Nussbaum *et al.* 1994).

Like other respondents, Barber ritually mentions the Declaration of Independence, the Constitution, the Bill of Rights and the Gettysburg Address, but *also* includes Martin Luther King's sermon at the 1963 March on Washington ('Free at last') and such popular voices as Walt Whitman, Woody Guthrie ('This land is your land...') and the poetry of Langston Hughes. Remember this one from Hughes?

> O, let America be America again—
> The land that never has been yet—
> And yet must be—the land where everyone is free.
> The land that's mine—the poor man's, Indian's
> Negro's, ME—

That this debate stirred such passions, the recollection of childhood civic education lessons and even the recitation of utopian poetry, suggests a hidden anxiety in the public discourse on American patriotism. Some boats of certainty have now slipped their moorings. Though he too is against 'self-congratulatory cosmopolitanism', Wallerstein identifies the cause for this loss of confidence in changes in the behaviour and attitudes of immigrant groups:

Within the United States of America the voice of oppressed groups has become more stridently 'ethnic' using far less appeal to universal values than it previously had. In response to both US geopolitical decline and the more 'ethnocentric' style of US oppressed groups, the defenders of privilege have resorted to demands for an 'integrating' patriotism, and Rorty's arguments simply reflect a cave in this noxious argument (Wallerstein in Nussbaum *et al.* 1994).

Comment

While Wallerstein has clearly spotted the loose ropes that previously just about held American patriotism together, the response has been more complex than he surmised. Certainly, there has been a significant reassertion of the old certainties of integration, even assimilation—Scheslinger, Glazer, Rorty, Hackney and most of the American political class come to mind. The post- 'September 11' manifestations of flag-waving have provided popular support for such views. But it is important not to drown out dissenting views, positioned mainly around the virtues of 'cosmopolitanism' as opposed to 'pluralism'. Of course these words, as it is hoped we established for the first, are not perfectly transportable and we need to understand them in context. Here is Hollinger's (1995: 3–4) key dyad:

Pluralism respects inherited boundaries and locates individuals within one or another of a series of ethno-racial groups to be protected and preserved. Cosmopolitanism is more wary of traditional enclosures and favours voluntary affiliations. Cosmopolitanism promotes multiple identities, emphasizes the dynamic and changing character of many groups and is responsive to the potential for creating new cultural combinations. Pluralism sees in cosmopolitanism a threat to identity, while cosmopolitanism sees in pluralism a provincial unwillingness to engage the complex dilemmas and opportunities actually presented by modern life.

Can cosmopolitanism be refashioned to serve a new purpose for the United States of America in the twenty-first century? Clearly the idea of pluralism or multiculturalism leading to an incoherence of purpose, a loss of moral certainties, a 'disuniting of America', has gripped the minds of public intellectuals and politicians. Though drawing sympathetically on Hollinger, Aleinikoff (1998: 80–6), a leading academic lawyer who has also worked in the US Department of Justice and the Carnegie Endowment, is wary of using the word 'cosmopolitanism'. He wants to reconcile a 'transnational reality' with, as he sees it, a 'strong justification for the nation-state'. For him, the idea of an American nation is still worth defending *against* multicultural and cosmopolitan attack. He advances *mutuality* (recognition rather than the mere tolerance of group differences) and *permeability* (the acceptance of group boundaries, but also the freedom and ability to cross them). His final formula, perhaps just short of being an oxymoron, is the idea of 'multicultural nationalism'.

Meditations and Conclusions

In discussing *Zeno's moment*, we said we would come back to the idea of belonging, which was posed probably for the first time in a recognizably contemporary form by the stoics and cynics. The narrowest version of a political community, the city-state (the *polis*), is contrasted with the notion of a more diverse cosmopolitan state and most ambitiously, a spaceless cosmopolitanism of the mind—a rather transcendent notion of belonging. Probably the most persistent attack on cosmopolitanism has been the idea that it provides the opportunity of *not belonging*—for a selfish individualism, a freedom from social bonds that most people cannot/should not dispense with. Such attacks are legion. For example, in a rather unbecoming style for a contributor to the rather sober *Encyclopaedia of the Social Sciences*, Boehm (1953: 458) suggested that the obligations that cosmopolitanism lays upon its adherents are 'comparatively negligible'. Cosmopolites seldom go beyond 'demonstration, sentimentality, propaganda and sectarian fanaticism'. The people who believe in it are often those 'whom fortune has relieved from the immediate struggle for existence . . . and who can afford to indulge their fads and enthusiasms'.

The US commentator, Lasch (1995), in his posthumous collection of essays, echoed this attack. He talks there of 'the darker side of cosmopolitanism'.

The loosely defined 'privileged classes' or 'elites' are said to be in revolt against the nation-state. This is because they no longer identify with it. 'In the borderless global economy, money has lost its links to nationality. . . . The privileged classes in Los Angeles feel more kinship with their counterparts in Japan, Singapore and Korea than with most of their countrymen' (Lasch 1995: 46). This detachment from the state means they regard themselves as 'world citizens' without any of the normal obligations of national citizenship. They no longer pay their share of taxes or contribute to democratic life.

Such attacks on the self-indulgence or selfishness of cosmopolites are paralleled and often accompanied by the somewhat contradictory argument that Zeno and his spiritual descendants are attempting the impossible. This is Berlin's position. It had been a mistake of Kant, he thought, to suppose that people could live through abstract principles, cosmopolitan values or 'idealistic but hollow doctrinaire internationalism'. The rejection of 'natural ties' was 'noble but misguided' (Ignatieff 2000: 292). But this proposition is far from tested, particularly under contemporary conditions. 'Supposing', says Waldron (1992: 762) 'that a freewheeling cosmopolitan life, lived in a kaleidoscope of cultures, is both possible and fulfilling'. Suppose further that this life is rich and creative and creates no more unhappiness than other life choices. Surely, he continues, it can no longer be said that 'all people *need* their rootedness in a particular culture in which they and their ancestors were reared in the way that they need food, shelter and clothing'. Clearly this is an empirical question, but one can reasonably surmise that Waldron is right.[11] Probably for the first time, the historical conditions for the realization of Zeno's most ambitious notion are now present.

Let us now turn to *Kant's moment*, where we can ruminate on three related problems:

The problem with Kant's philosophy of history is that it offers the consolation of philosophy for the violence and suffering of the existing world. It says in effect: 'We know terrible violence is taking place but the good news is that the laws of history are drawing it to a close. Keep your eyes on the future, for the future is beautiful. Let us reconcile ourselves to the violence of the present in the knowledge that perpetual peace will be the final end'. By its own curious dialectic, unspeakable horror converts itself into the triumph of perpetual peace. Every barbarity is justified by the redemptive future and optimism is achieved at the expense of looking horror in the face. When the worst that can happen is that some people are killed in war, perhaps this makes a certain sense; but when what is at issue is the very future of humankind, as it was in the phenomena of totalitarian terror such as the holocaust, what good can be distilled from this evil?

---

[11] One lucid defence of the problems and possibilities of travelling with 'a wardrobe of selves' comes from Pico Iyer (1997, 2000).

The problem with Kant's metaphysics of justice is that it instructs people and rulers in what they must do, without involving them in the process of deciding what must or must not be done. Its idea of reason is based on spurious deductions, and takes the form of legislative prescriptions that pay no heed to the lessons of experience or the consequences of following a certain course of action. It takes it as read that the primary evil is that of war and that the primary goal is that of perpetual peace, but there are other moral issues at stake in people's lives—questions of justice, poverty and famine—which also excite the cosmopolitan sensibility to identify with those who suffer at a distance. The identification of cosmopolitanism with peace offers a restrictive view of what is involved in the development of a cosmopolitan consciousness. It tells people that perpetual peace must be their highest priority and treats those who disagree simply as lacking in reason. This is no way to start a dialogue at a cosmopolitan level.

The problem with trying to attach the philosophy of history to the metaphysics of justice lies not only in the assimilation of what is right to the movement of history and in the assimilation of history to the self-realization of right, but in the conviction that the idea of a cosmopolitan order is a resolution of all prior antagonisms. If it takes the form of a world state, then it becomes like any other state except that it has no competition from other states and is all the more dangerous as a result. If it takes the form of a federation of free and independent states, then it faces the old problem of those nations putting national interest before the interests of the whole. All this is to say that cosmopolitan right is like any right a form of coercion and the character of that coercion is not something outside politics. Cosmopolitanism contains its own equivocations, its own difficult judgements and its own conflicts of interest and outlook. The translation of the cosmopolitan idea into a pure idea of reason or into the end of history takes it out of the realm of human contestation—as if it were not a social relation at all but the embodiment of something divine here on earth.

This sense of disembodiment also appears in *Arendt's moment*. As she herself realized, cosmopolitan law, like all law, remains a form of coercion; it cannot 'jump out' of political life; it presupposes a certain exercise of power. In relation to it, the great powers have a cautious and equivocal attitude. For many years they largely ignored it. Now, in the post-cold war world, they are once again using it, seeking to put it into the service of their own interests, to restrict its sphere of operation, to forestall its capacity for independent initiative, to appropriate its means of enforcement. This is certainly not a reason to dismiss cosmopolitan law, but it *is* a reason to advance the critical cosmopolitanism which Arendt did much to initiate.

Today, crimes against humanity (in the forms of ethnic cleansing and genocide) are again at the front of our minds. We also see the resurrection of cosmopolitan law, based on the precedent of Nuremberg and actualized in the *ad hoc* tribunals for the prosecution of war criminals in the former Yugoslavia,

as arguably the most hopeful aspect of current endeavours to address the problem. As Rousseau said, the worst and the best of humanity arise together. In the
face of these developments, the difficulties of understanding have not diminished. On the one hand, the concept of crimes against humanity must be justified in universalistic terms if it is not to be seen as a mere tool of power politics.
On the other hand, its universal potential puts it in danger of becoming over-
extended, meaningless, banal—a moralistic catch-all for everything of which
we disapprove in which all specificity is lost.

Arendt does not resolve this conflict between generality and specificity, but
she teaches us how to live with it: without the cynicism of those who say that
homo homini lupus (man is a wolf to man) and nothing can be done to change it;
without the scepticism of those who say that cosmopolitan law is merely
victor's justice and possesses no transcendent validity; without over-determined
images of the totalitarian propensities of modernity; without an illusion that
waits to be disillusioned—that if only it could be fully completed, cosmopolitan
law provides the absolute key to perpetual peace and universal freedom. Arendt
enjoins us to recognize the difficulties of understanding but not to turn them into
an excuse for inaction. As she put it, 'Many people say that one cannot fight
totalitarianism without understanding it. Fortunately this is not true; if it were,
our case would be hopeless' (Arendt 1994: 308). The 'incompletion' of the concept of crimes against humanity is at once a prescription for making judgements, and taking decisions with the tools we have at hand.

Finally, we can recognize in *Nussbaum's moment* the central paradox facing
states that once used strong ideologies of assimilation and integration to absorb
immigrants. It is hardly a revelation that the resultant societies were more a salad
bowl than a melting pot. But assimilatory ideologies functioned as powerful
myths, closely tied to myths of social mobility. Now Pandora's box is seen to
be open. The nation-state is going to have to adapt to a more complex and
more recalcitrant mosaic of cultures, religions, languages and citizenships.
Transnationalism and nationalism will have to coexist. In the United States of
America, they will have to do so in a virtually oxymoronic way—as in Franklin's
'cosmopolitan nationhood' or Aleinikoff's 'multicultural nationalism'.

What the US debate notably has not transcended is its insistence on place, on
land, on territory. Remember Guthrie's song 'This land is your land, this land is my
land, from California to the New York Island, from the redwood forest to the Gulf
Stream waters'. The transnational, diasporic, communities that now populate
many US cities do not, and cannot, have this intimate tie to the land; it was, after
all, derived from the 'pioneers', farmers and early settlers—Hispanic and anglo-
phonic. They are sojourners, transients, multiply located: their identities cannot
be constituted by reference to the land. The formulae that worked for so long in the
United States of America no longer work and whether Nussbaum's critics like it or
not, some version of cosmopolitanism will have to occupy centre stage.

Cosmopolitanism as a placeless meeting of minds, cosmopolitanism as perpetual peace, cosmopolitanism as justice, cosmopolitanism as an answer to social fragmentation, extreme nationalism or ethnic hostility. No one notion will carry all this weight and the other burdens placed upon it. But those who advocate cosmopolitan solutions can no longer escape the burden of social responsibility for their ideas. Far from being a selfish, idiosyncratic or indulgent choice, to advocate, delimit and develop cosmopolitanism in the global age has become an urgent moral necessity—even if the pessimism of the intellect dictates an orange rather than a green light forward.

III

Contexts of Cosmopolitanism

10

Colonial Cosmopolitanism

PETER VAN DER VEER

Is cosmopolitanism a view from nowhere? Is its locus the enlightened individual whose allegiance transcends the boundedness of the traditions in which he or she is socialized? *Sapere aude* ('have the courage to use your own intelligence instead of following traditional authority') is the slogan of the Enlightenment, according to Kant. The boundaries of traditional authority, of belonging to one's nationhood, ethnicity and religion, have to be transcended if one wants to be cosmopolitan and feel allegiance only to a worldwide community of mankind. In other words, one has to be an enlightened individual. At least this is the way I understand the notion of cosmopolitanism and already it is clear that I do not see it as a view from nowhere, but as a view from somewhere and from sometime, namely from the European Enlightenment of the eighteenth century. It is an inextricable part of European modernity and of the claim that its Reason is universally applicable. Universalism and cosmopolitanism go together. Some thinkers in the Enlightenment, especially Hegel, would not deny that Reason is a view from somewhere, that it is located in some periods, in some societies, but would also assert that there is the promise of universalization and, in fact, that universalization is inescapable.

At first glance anthropology's cosmopolitanism seems less Eurocentric, since it takes its concept of culture from the Romantic tradition in which besides the universality of Culture also the diversity of particular cultures is asserted. Ulf Hannerz has suggested that 'genuine cosmopolitanism is first of all an orientation, a willingness to engage with the other. It entails an intellectual and aesthetic openness toward divergent cultural experiences, a search for contrasts rather than uniformity' (Hannerz 1996: 103). The picture of the attitude that is required for cosmopolitanism, drawn by Hannerz, refers to enlightened intellectuals and foremost to the anthropologist. It is a very flattering image, an ideal to aspire to. The counter-image is that of the parochial person, tied down by the narrow confines of 'local' life, and therefore simply not interested in different people and different customs. Cosmopolitanism is often seen as a liberating alternative to ethnic and nationalist chauvinism. However, one does want to ask what intellectual and aesthetic openness entails and on what terms one engages the other. When one turns one's attention to the colonial period—something unavoidable for anthropologists—one cannot deny missionaries or colonial officers a willingness to engage with the other. In that connection I have always understood Johannes Fabian's *Time and the Other* (1983) with its emphasis on the 'coevalness' of the other as a profoundly missionary book, theologically interpreting the grounds of misrecognition between the missionary and the missionized. Anthropologists are not that different from missionaries and colonial officers, since they all share an enabling condition of engagement, namely Western imperialism.

The anthropological search for contrasts is different from the Hegelian urge to homogenize, but both are versions of colonial cosmopolitanism and I would like to draw attention to some of the contradictions inherent in them. I want to examine colonial cosmopolitanism as a form of translation and conversion of the local into the universal. Second, I want to examine the secularity of colonial cosmopolitanism. Third, I want to look at an alternative to enlightened, secular cosmopolitanism, which can be found in the discourse around the concept of 'spirituality'.[1]

Translation and Conversion

The cosmopolitan as an intellectual, who is not limited by the local culture of his place of upbringing, is a trope of secular modernity. In gender terms the cosmopolitan is more usually conceived as a man, an individual who has the ability to live anywhere and the capacity to tolerate and understand the barbarism of others. The trope comes up in English language in the early nineteenth century, a period marked by the simultaneous expansion of imperialism and nationalism. These two historical formations belong together, since the nation-state emerges within an expanding world-system (see van der Veer and Lehmann 1999). Their intimate connection is already expressed very well in Adam Smith's thinking about the tension between the fiscality of the state and global free trade. It is in the context of his writing on political economy that in 1848 John Stuart Mill referred to capital as becoming more and more 'cosmopolitan'. Cosmopolitanism is the Western engagement with the rest of the world and that engagement is a colonial one, which simultaneously transcends the national boundaries and is tied to them. Instead of perceiving cosmopolitanism and nationalism as alternatives, one should perhaps recognize them as the poles in a dialectical relationship. The importance of imperial migration for nationalism is perhaps clearest in the 'pioneer' nationalisms of the Americas and some of the later nationalist movements in Europe, Asia and Africa (Anderson 1991; van der Veer 1995a).

---

[1] Some of the arguments in this chapter can be found in greater detail in van der Veer (2001).

But more generally, it is important to consider the development of cultural nationalism in Western Europe in the context of empire building (Said 1993). National culture in Britain, for instance, nationalizes the imperial encounter and reflects upon the mission of the nation in the empire, while cosmopolitanism is based upon the possibilities of encounter as given in the empire (Baucom 1999).

In Daniel Lerner's classical statement of modernization theory *The Passing of Traditional Society*, published in 1958, one finds the argument that Western modernity has depended principally on 'the mobile personality'—that is, on a type of person eager to move, to change and to invent. Lerner argued that empathy defined the mobile personality, and he glossed 'empathy' as 'the capacity to see oneself in the other fellow's situation'. As Talal Asad argues in his discussion of Lerner's text, the basis of empathy is the power to get into the life world of the other and transform it. Such power is neither good nor bad, but it is also never completely disinterested.[2]

Colonizing modernity disclaims its roots in a European past and claims a cosmopolitan openness to other civilizations. However, this is an openness to understanding with a desire to bring progress and improvement, a cosmopolitanism with a moral mission. This is quite explicit in such projects as British utilitarianism, French *mission civilisatrice*, and Dutch *Ethische Politiek*. There is the desire to spread the morality of the modern nation-state, the cosmopolitanism of the colonial empire.

A further understanding of that quality of 'empathy' and 'improvization' that the cosmopolitan as a mobile personality possesses is perhaps reached if we look at the problem of cultural translation. Translation is the activity in which the cosmopolitan in his open engagement with the other has to excel and it shows exactly that some languages are weaker than others. Talal Asad has argued that, 'because the languages of Third World societies are seen as weaker in relation to Western languages (and today, especially English), they are more likely to submit to forcible transformation in the translation process than the other way around. The reason for this is, first, that in their political–economic relations with the Third World countries, the Western nations have the greater ability to manipulate the latter. And, second, the Western languages produce and deploy desired knowledge more readily than the Third World languages do' (Asad 1993: 190).

If we speak of translation we, of course, understand that this implies a conversion of a conceptual framework into another that is more powerful and thus more universal. Difficulties of this sort have been discussed at length in Rodney Needham's book on *Belief, Language, and Experience* (1972). Needham points out that most languages do not have an equivalent for the English 'belief' and

---

[2] The references to Lerner and Greenblatt are taken from Asad (1993: 11–12).

that for missionaries and anthropologists to say that the X believe such and such has already major conceptual implications. In a fascinating book on translation and conversion in the Tagalog society in the Philippines in the late sixteenth century, Vicente Rafael (1988) has argued that conversion (changing one thing into something else) is synonymous with translation (changing one language into another). The language of the other had to be converted into a language that could carry the holy message. The indeterminacy of translation creates a field of interaction that is riddled with anxiety.

The issue of translation and conversion not only raises the question of the power of languages, but also that of differences in colonial trajectories and languages of conquest. There are considerable differences between being colonized by the Spanish, the Portuguese, the French, the British, or the Dutch. By having Spanish as the colonial language, one enters into colonial cosmopolitanism in a quite different way than one that is conquered by the British. A colonial language, like Spanish, can be used as a medium of resistance against the American hegemony in Latin America, while it becomes at the same time a significant rival in the heartland of global English, the United States of America.

The cosmopolitan person is not only a translator, but also a spy who commands more languages than the people he spies upon, as well as the ability to translate their languages into the language of the rulers. It is the ultimate cosmopolitan fantasy, well expressed in Kipling's writings, that the colonial hero has a perfect grasp of the language and the customs of the 'natives', the 'locals', but still in his crossing over remains true to himself and returns to his own world where he uses his acquired knowledge for the improvement of colonial rule. Interestingly enough, Westernized natives in the colonized areas were not considered to have the ability to cross over, but were ridiculed as impostors, as wogs.

Undoubtedly, the best Dutch realization of the cosmopolitan as a spy has been Christiaan Snouck Hurgronje (1857–1936), one of the greatest orientalist students of Muslim law. In 1884 he went to Jeddah to study the Haj and in 1885 he converted to Islam to be able to enter Mecca. He was financially supported by the Dutch colonial ministry, which needed information about Muslims from the Dutch Indies who stayed in Mecca. Not only the Dutch, but also all colonial governments had a theory that Muslims all over the world might unite in a 'panislamism' that would be a serious threat to colonial rule. Mecca would play a crucial role in that worldwide conspiracy. Snouck's expert knowledge on the Aceh Muslims in Mecca later made him a perfect political advisor for Muslim affairs in the Dutch Indies. His policy advice became crucial in the military campaign of the Dutch to repress a Muslim rebellion in Aceh, the bloodiest episode in Dutch colonial history. The question of whether Snouck had been converted to Islam and had secretly married in the Dutch Indies with one or two Muslim wives is still hotly debated in Holland. I recently heard from an historian in Leiden, where Snouck is revered as the patron saint of Oriental Studies, that people were considering opening Snouck's grave to see whether he had been buried in the direction of Mecca. Whatever the results might be of this far-going empiricism, to all parties in this debate it is clear that Snouck had been a truly cosmopolitan man (see van der Veer 1995*b*).

Cosmopolitanism is, thus, not only a trope of modernity but also, and very specifically, of colonial modernity. It is therefore ironic to see the celebration of cosmopolitanism in some post-colonial writing without any critical reflection on the genealogy of the concept. For instance, the literary critic Homi Bhabha is quite exuberant in his description of the possibilities of migrant populations, of subjects 'formed-in-between'. 'Such cultures of a post-colonial contra-modernity may be contingent to modernity, discontinuous or in contention with it, resistant to its oppressive, assimilationist technologies; but they also deploy the cultural hybridity of their borderline conditions to "translate", and therefore reinscribe, the social imagery of both metropolis and modernity' (Bhabha 1993: 6). In my view, however, Bhabha does not find a contra-modernity, but precisely a modernity that invites intellectuals from the post-colony not only to receive and imbibe it as in the Macaulayan project of educating the natives, but to become agents in its reproduction after the demise of the colony-metropole divide. The racial distinction between natives and metropolitans has become obsolete and is replaced with the notion that anyone can be cosmopolitan, as long as one remains open, mobile, and improvising, and forgets about one's traditions.

The celebration of hybridity, syncretism and multiculturalism in post-colonial studies needs to be critically examined (see van der Veer 1997: 90–105). Bhabha's claim that one can bring newness into the world, that one can reinvent oneself when one is writing literature from the cultural interstices, is a conceit of the literature-producing and consuming world. Literary texts are the very sites of self-fashioning in modern, bourgeois culture. Literature has replaced religious texts as a source of elevated reflection about the nature of the self. Salman Rushdie's literary work, which Bhabha takes as a prime example of cosmopolitan writing, takes part precisely in this replacement of the religious by literary secularity. What is remarkable in Rushdie's work is the extent to which it feeds on Indian culture and Muslim and Hindu religious traditions. It translates these materials for a Western audience.

My argument, so far, has been that cosmopolitanism is best understood as a form of improvization and translation that characterized colonial modernity and that has insinuated itself in the multicultural hybridity celebrated in post-colonial literary studies. My suggestion is that the cosmopolitanism of the nineteenth and early twentieth centuries can be 'provincialized', that is can be shown to be a 'view from somewhere' that is universalized through colonialism.

The Secularity of Colonial Cosmopolitanism

It is quite striking that in recent discussions of the concept of cosmopolitanism there is hardly any systematic attention to religion (see, for instance, Cheah and Robbins 1998). Perhaps the enlightened assumption is that a cosmopolitan person has to transcend religious tradition and thus be secular. Kant's view on the matter seems to have been that there is, in fact, a universal, enlightened religion that is the source of morality and thus of cosmopolitanism, but that universal religion is located in the interior life of the individual and not in social institutions, such as the church. Organized religion is also seen by John Stuart Mill as a threat to the liberty required in a peaceful exchange of views in the modern world. In his essay *On Liberty* (1993) Mill depicts both the Roman Catholic Church ('the most intolerant of churches') and Calvinist churches as intolerant institutions, which only when they cannot convert others to their opinion by force or persuasion reluctantly accept a difference of opinion (Mill 1993: 76). It is of great concern to Mill to defend the right of atheists and blasphemers to express their opinion and he defends that right by arguing that Christ was put to death as a blasphemer (Mill 1993: 93). The persecution of Christians as heretics is his main historical example in his argument for liberty. He rejects firmly the idea that the Christian doctrine provides a complete morality, while at the same time arguing that the recorded teachings of Christ contain nothing that contradicts what a comprehensive morality requires (Mill 1993: 118).

Mill's examples from comparative religion are as remarkable as his defence of unbelief and blasphemy and his attacks on Calvinism. He cites the Muslim prohibition of the eating of pork and the tendency that in a society in which the majority is Muslim the eating of pork is prohibited. He compares that with the Puritanical prohibition of dancing and music in regions where they have the majority and to Sabbatarian regulations. Mill's conclusion is unequivocal. Individuals and minorities have to be protected against the religious sentiments of the majority. This line of argument has a history in the persecution of dissenters by the state and the established church in the seventeenth and eighteenth centuries and the response to that in America by Jefferson (as well as Madison and other 'founding fathers') with the separation of the Church and the State.

Mill argues for a complete liberty of opinion and the expression thereof and thus advocates a free exchange of ideas, close to what Jurgen Habermas has called '*burgerliche Oeffentlichkeit*' or 'bourgeois public sphere'. Critics of this view have generally objected to the fact that the liberal public sphere excludes certain groups of people. It is interesting in this connection to read the motto of Mill's famous essay, taken from Wilhelm von Humboldt's *Sphere and Duties of Government* (1792): 'The grand, leading principle, towards which every argument unfolded in these pages directly converges, is the absolute and essential importance of human development in its richest diversity' (Mill 1993: 69). This, in fact, contains the principle of exclusion in Mill's views on liberty below (Mill 1993: 78–9):

It is perhaps unnecessary to say that this doctrine is meant to apply only to human beings in the maturity of their faculties. We are not speaking of children, or of young persons below that age which the law may fix as that of manhood or womanhood. Those who are still in a state to require being taken care of by others, must be protected against their own actions as well as against external injury. For the same reason, we may leave out of consideration those backward states of society in which the race itself may be considered in its nonage. The early difficulties in the way of spontaneous progress are so great, that there is seldom any choice of means for overcoming them; and a ruler full of spirit of improvement is warranted in the use of any expedients that will attain an end, perhaps otherwise unattainable. Despotism is a legitimate mode of government in dealing with barbarians, provided the end be their improvement, and the means justified by actually effecting that end. Liberty, as a principle, has no application to any state of things anterior to the time when mankind have become capable of being improved by free and equal discussion. Until then, there is nothing for them but implicit obedience to an Akbar or Charlemagne, if they are so fortunate as to find one. But as soon as mankind have attained the capacity of being guided to their own improvement by conviction or persuasion (a period long reached in all nations with whom we need here concern ourselves), compulsion, either in the direct form or in that of pains of penalties for non-compliance, is no longer admissible as a means to their own good, and justifiable only for the security of others.

I have reproduced this long quotation from Mill's essay because it lays out so clearly that his concern is with liberty in the service of progress. It depends on the notion that some societies are at a lower stage of evolution. Such a notion of evolutionary stages had already been developed in the Scottish Enlightenment and is the basis of all historical thought in the nineteenth century. Societies at lower stages of evolution have to be educated like children to make them capable of enjoying freedom. Mill is not in any simple way prejudiced in racial or religious terms, as his position in the controversy over the behaviour of Governor Eyre in Jamaica and in his response to the Indian Mutiny shows. His position allows for the tolerance of diverse religious opinions, but only if they already belong to modern civilization and thus contribute to the moral principle of progress. One has to be free to be able to express oneself freely; that is the idea. Mill's view allows himself to be at the same time a radical advocate of freedom and a supporter of enlightened (progressive) imperialism. It is not insignificant to remember here that it is not only the evolutionary theory that leads him to claim freedom at home and support despotism in the colony, but also his lifelong employment in the service of the East India Company where, at the end of his career, he held the highest administrative position, a post previously held by his father, James Mill. The evolutionary theory is therefore not just a grand narrative of progress and modernity, but belongs to the joint predicament of nationalism and imperialism.

The idea that it is especially organized religion that is a threat to freedom of thought and expression has thus a history in the Enlightenment, is firmly established in the liberal tradition, and indeed is expressed till the present day. Of course, religious people can be cosmopolitans, but they have to become modern Christians, modern Hindus, or modern Muslims, that is to say progressive liberals with private, religious world-views.

Ironically, the Age of the Enlightenment is also the Age of Evangelicalism. Moreover, the nineteenth century can be characterized not only by nationalism and imperialism, but also by an expansionist Christianity both in the national and in the imperial spheres. The world religions like Christianity and Islam had always, in principle, shown allegiance to humankind and enlightened, secular notions of progress, and cosmopolitanism can well be seen as a transformation of the religious notion of salvation and catholicity. Nevertheless, it is only in the nineteenth century that modern forms of government make it possible to target both the national and the world population in missionizing projects.

The evangelical revival starts conventionally with John Wesley in the first half of the eighteenth century, but there was an important second wave in the 1790s, which lasted into the nineteenth century (Wolffe 1994: 22). The growth of evangelical movements in the first half of the nineteenth century is spectacular, but more significant than these numbers is the considerable impact evangelicalism had on religious groups and individuals of every kind. Evangelicalism aimed at inward conversion, but also at an outward activity in converting others. Itinerant preachers and later bible societies and missionary societies reached far and deep. What one has here is a strong civilizing and educational effort aimed at transforming people's personal lives. There can be little doubt about the importance of evangelicalism in producing modern, civil and hard working individuals.

At the same time evangelicalism had a very significant political impact. The term 'evangelicalism' obviously covers a broad range of ideas and attitudes, but its campaign for the abolition of slavery in the first decades of the nineteenth century shows how evangelicalism despite its diversity could have a strong political message. Here, we see also how evangelicalism at home was connected to the empire, as exemplified in the words of William Wilberforce, one of the leaders of the evangelical Clapham sect (quoted in Hilton 1988*a*: 209–10):

I consider it my duty to endeavour to deliver these poor creatures from their present darkness and degradation, not merely out of a direct regard for their wellbeing ... but also from a direct persuasion that both the colonists and we ourselves shall be otherwise the sufferers. The judicial and penal visitations of Providence occur commonly in the way of natural consequence and it is in that way I should expect the evils to occur.

David Brion Davis suggests that the abolition of the slave trade in 1807 and of slavery in 1833 were 'genuine rituals', evoking fantasies of death and rebirth, and 'designed to revitalize Christianity and atone for national guilt' (quoted in Hilton 1998*b*: 210).

These attitudes towards the rest of the world were new, thoroughly modern and decidedly cosmopolitan. Until the 1790s there was hardly any interest in missionization abroad. Missions such as the Society for the Propagation of the Gospel, which was founded in 1701, employed chaplains, but their task was mainly to minister to the trading company's men (Thorne 1990: 67).[3] The 1790s proved a turning point, however, which is perhaps best captured in the title of William Carey's book *An Enquiry into the Obligation of Christians, to Use Means for the Conversion of the Heathens* (1792). A great number of missionary societies were founded, including the well-known London Missionary Society (LMS) and the Christian Missionary Society (CMS). All these societies saw themselves engaged in a battle against idolatry and an endeavour to save heathen souls. Not only were these souls thought to go to hell if not saved, but also it came to be seen as a Christian duty to save them. One can only wonder about the extent to which the Christian imagination in Britain was fuelled by the imagery of the poor Hindus, Muslims and other beings lost for eternity. What we do know is that one out of two missionary speakers at provincial anniversary meetings of missionary societies in 1838–73 came from India (Stanley 1983: 278). There can be little doubt that the simultaneous evangelical activities of bible societies, missionary societies, and Sunday schools created a public awareness of a particular kind of world and of an imperial duty of British Christians in the empire.

Liberal cosmopolitanism and evangelical cosmopolitanism had much in common in the colonial era. Their commonality can be well expressed in the phrase 'the white man's burden'. The terms of engagement with the religious and civilizational other were given in the imperial state. Both the nation-state and the empire were taken as given by secular liberals and religious evangelicals alike.

Spirituality: An Anti-Colonial Cosmopolitanism

A radical alternative for colonial cosmopolitanism can be found in what Weber sees as the 'non-modern', that is the 'non-worldly', 'world-renouncing', 'mystical', 'non-rational' and thus 'non-mystical' aspect of religion that is captured in the term 'spirituality'. In the British Empire one turns to Hindu India for anti-colonial cosmopolitanism as much as one does for colonial cosmopolitanism. More than anything else the metaphysical ruminations, collected in the

---

[3] The situation was similar in the Netherlands. See van Rooden (1996: 65–89).

Vedanta (the Upanishads and the philosophies built around them) are thought to capture the essence of Hinduism in both the European and the Indian imagination. This is a complex story connecting Immanuel Kant, Madame Blavatsky and Swami Vivekananda in a variety of ways, and which show global connections that are different from world capitalism or modernity as usually conceived.

Nietzsche, the great polemicist against Christian morality in the German-speaking world, clearly expresses his admiration for the Vedanta in *Jenseits von Gut und Bose* (Nietzsche 1960: 616):

The newer philosophy, as a form of epistemological scepticism, is, hidden or openly, antichristian; however, for more subtle ears, by no means antireligious. . . . Kant wanted essentially to show that one could not prove the subject on the basis of the subject—nor indeed the object; the possibility of an illusionary existence of the subject, or the 'soul', will not have been alien to him, since it is an idea that has been present on earth already with tremendous power as Vedanta-philosophy.

Nietzsche (following Schopenhauer) argues that Kant's modern philosophy, which he sees as antichristian but not antireligious, was prefigured in Indian Vedanta. This is, obviously, not literally true, since Kant was much less influenced by Indian philosophy than the great philosophers of German Romanticism, Schlegel, Schopenhauer and Schelling, but still Nietzsche has an intuition here, which is worth pursuing. As Peter van Rooden has pointed out, Kant's view of a universal, enlightened religion, which is the source of morality, locates religion in the interior life of the individual and not in social institutions, such as the church. This makes it possible for the German Romantics to interpret Kant's enlightenment not as a secular rationalism, but in a somewhat perverse way as a mystical enlightenment. It should perhaps not surprise us that Kant's *Kritik der Reinen Vernunft* was translated into English by the greatest interpreter of Indian traditions in nineteenth-century Britain, the Indologist Friedrich Max Muller, also the translator of the Rig Veda. As the founder of *Religionswissenschaft*, the science of religion, the cosmopolitan Muller argued in Kantian fashion that there is religion, transcendental truth, and that there are historical religions (in the plural), including Christianity, which all contain some elements of religion as truth. The science of religion enables one to discover religion by studying religions. For Muller it was quite clear that the Vedanta expressed this universal truth. That Max Muller could put Christianity at the same level as other historical religions in his science of religion (much more explicit and daring than Kant), while teaching in an academic institution like Oxford, which was part of the clerical establishment, is an important sign of the shifting location of religion in nineteenth-century Britain. Muller could make such a radical argument without losing touch with the political elites, among whom he was in general very popular, or even without having to fear that his argument would be taken as an attack of the state. Where Kant constantly affirms his support of institutional religion and of the state and narrowly defines the limits of enlightened debate, Muller can make similar arguments a century later without all these precautions.

Madame Blavatsky, another cosmopolitan of the nineteenth century, stood in a tradition of popular beliefs and practices that seems to be the opposite of Kantian enlightenment. Nevertheless, there is some common ground in the rejection of the established church as the site of true religion, although with very different political consequences. While Kant and his latter-day follower Muller continue to see the state as guaranteeing reason and progress, Blavatsky's position leads her in the opposite direction of attacking the state and its support of established religion. Blavatsky was a mysterious woman who had left her husband, a vice-governor of Yerevan in the Caucasus to travel on her own around the world. On a visit to Vermont in 1874 to see the Eddy family, who were remarkably successful in spiritualism (communication with spirits), she met Olcott who had been a colonel in the Union Army in the American Civil War. Spiritualism was highly popular in the United States of America, especially after the war (as indeed it was after the First World War in Europe) and had spread to Britain. Together they founded the Theosophical Society of the Arya Samaj of India on 22 May 1878, with Swami Dayananda as its head because the Arya Samaj claimed to go back to the original sources of Hindu tradition, the Vedas and Vedanta. In 1879 the couple went to India to meet Dayanand, but this was not a success and the relation between Theosophy and the Arya Samaj was broken off. Theosophy became highly popular for a period in India and had a significant impact on early nationalism, especially thanks to Annie Besant, Madame Blavatsky's successor as leader of the Theosophical Society.

The experiments of Olcott and Blavatsky had very little to do with Hinduism as Dayananda knew it, but Blavatsky made the brilliant move to connect spiritualism, the communication with spirits, with spirituality, the mystical search for transcendent truth. According to her, both the major spirits ('the Masters of the Universe') and spiritual thought originated in 'the East' and since Tibet could not be visited, Hindu India and Buddhist Sri Lanka replaced it for all practical purposes. Theosophy came to play a significant role in the development of radical, anti-colonial politics, both in Britain and in India. It could do so because it enunciated a strong opposition against established Christianity by advocating a morality based upon scientific rationality and the experience of a higher spirituality. Theosophists claimed on the one hand a universal spirituality and on the other hand located it in the mixture of Root-Races that came about through worldwide migration. This view was decidedly cosmopolitan and not Eurocentric, since it saw Hindu India as the spiritual teacher of the world. At the same time, however, it contained a racial evolutionism and racial hierarchy that made for a quite peculiar mix of cosmopolitanism and racism. The career of Annie Besant, which I describe elsewhere, exemplifies these features and their political consequences in India and Britain (see van der Veer 2001).

Perhaps the most important expounder of the doctrine of 'Hindu spirituality' has been the founder of the Ramakrishna Mission, Vivekananda (1863–1902) (see van der Veer 1994). Narendranath Datta, who adopted the name Vivekananda when he took his ascetic vows, was an extremely talented student who had been thoroughly educated in contemporary Western thought and was influenced by the rational religion of the Brahmo Samaj. As Tapan Raychaudhuri emphasizes, Vivekananda was 'more than anything else a mystic in quest of the Ultimate Reality within a specific Indian tradition' (Raychaudhuri 1988). It is this tradition that was vividly presented to Vivekananda not by learned discourse in which he himself was a master, but by the charismatic presence of a guru, Ramakrishna, whose trances had first been treated as 'insanity', but which later came to be regarded as possession by the goddess. What I want to argue is that the articulation of Brahmo 'rational religion' with the religious discourse of Ramakrishna produced the specific brand of 'Hindu spirituality' that Vivekananda came to propagate.

Western discourse on 'Eastern spirituality' is reappropriated by the Indian religious movements of this period. I would not quite know how to translate 'spirituality' into Sanskrit, but it is a fact that Hindu religious discourses are now captured under the term 'spirituality'. Spirituality is a comparative, polemical term used against Christian colonialism. As in Britain itself, it contests the very colonial domination of scientific knowledge by showing that there are either earlier or alternative forms of science available in Hinduism.

Vivekananda's translation of Ramakrishna's message in terms of 'spirituality' was literally transferred to the West during his trip to the United States of America after Ramakrishna's death. He visited the World Parliament of Religions in Chicago in 1893, a side-show of the Columbian Exposition, celebrating the four-hundredth anniversary of Columbus's voyage to the New World, but perhaps more importantly Chicago's recovery from the Great Fire of 1871. Religions represented in this show of religious universalism included Hinduism, Buddhism, Judaism, Roman Catholicism, Eastern Orthodoxy, Protestantism, Islam, Shinto, Confucianism, Taoism, Jainism and various others (Ziolkowski 1993). But the representative of Hinduism, Swami Vivekananda, stole the show. In his speech to the Parliament, Vivekananda claimed that 'he was proud to belong to a religion which had taught the world both tolerance and universal acceptance' (Mullick 1993: 221). Vivekananda's spirituality was neither modest nor meek; it was forceful, polemical and proud. As the response in the Parliament and in his further lecture tours in the United States of America indicates, this was a message that resonated powerfully among American audiences. His writings in English often compare the lack of spirituality in the West with the abundance of it in India. Vivekananda is probably the first major Indian advocate of a 'Hindu spirituality', feeding on Indian discourses on Brahman, on Western discourses on Geist and on the anti-Christian and anti-colonial rhetoric of spiritualist circles in Britain (van der Veer 1994).

A major achievement was Vivekananda's creation of yoga as the Indian science of supraconsciousness. Yoga, which has a complex history with a number of disparate traditions, was now made into the unifying sign of the Indian nation, not only for national consumption, but also for the entire world to consume The body exercises of hatha yoga, underpinned by a metaphysics of mind–body unity, continue to be a major article of the health industry, especially in the United States of America. What I find important in Vivekananda's construction of yoga as the core of Hindu 'spirituality' is that it is devoid of any specific devotional content that would involve, for example, temple worship and thus a theological and ritual position in sectarian debates. Vivekananda is first and foremost interested in Hindu Unity. At a lecture entitled 'Common Bases of Hinduism' (quoted in Basu 1997: 76), he said:

Here am I, not to find difference that exists among us, but to find where we agree. Here I am trying to understand on what ground we may always remain brothers, upon what foundations the voice that has spoken from eternity may become stronger and stronger as it grows. . . . National union in India must be a gathering up of its scattered spiritual forces. A nation in India must be a union of those whose hearts beat to the same spiritual tune. There have been sects in this country. There are sects enough in the future, because this has been the peculiarity of our religion that in abstract principles so much latitude has been given that, although afterwards so much detail has been worked out, all these details are the working out of principles, broad as the skies above our heads, eternal as nature itself. Sects must exist here, but what need not exist is sectarian quarrel. Sects must be but sectarianism need not.

This lack of religious specificity together with the claim to be scientific is crucial for the nationalist appeal of Vivekananda's message. From Vivekananda's viewpoint, religion is based upon reason, not belief. Yoga is legitimized as a scientific tradition in terms of rational criteria. An offshoot of this is that health issues could be addressed in terms of a national science of yoga. I would suggest that Vivekananda has developed a translation of Hindu traditions in terms that are remarkably similar to what is cobbled together in theosophy and its later offshoot, Steiner's anthroposophy. Hindu nationalism and spiritual cosmopolitanism go very well together and their political message is anti-colonial.

It is Vivekananda's social reformism and anti-colonial, anti-Christian radicalism that connects him to the spiritualists in Britain. Although the same word 'spirituality' was used in English, the unifying language of the empire, very different things were meant with it in the metropole, where it stood in relation to Christian traditions and in the colony, where it stood in relation to Hindu traditions. The point here is that these divergences did not stand in the way of a shared antinomian radicalism against the state in Britain and the colonial state in India.

Conclusion

What does this tale of Kant, Madame Blavatsky and Swami Vivekananda tell us in terms of a history of cosmopolitanism? It may tell us that a history of cosmopolitanism can perhaps be written if we avoid both centre–periphery models and the identification of originary moments, but try to describe historical entanglements. There is no reason to equate capitalism and modernity and search for independent modernities in a variety of societies outside Europe before the last quarter of the eighteenth century. The writing of a history of modernity as a political project since 1800 involves European societies as much as it does the societies with which they interact, although the latter has been neglected.[4] This political project is the formation of the nation-state, but always in relation to significant others in the great game. Cosmopolitanism is the engagement with the other in the colonial context.

The story of 'religion' is significant especially because religion is precisely the site of difference between modernity and what is not modernity. The genealogy of such a category in the context of historical interactions between Britain and India shows an intricate interplay of rationalism and spirituality, universalism and nationalism, material science and spiritualism. Evangelical Christianity of the nineteenth century is clearly cosmopolitan in its aims and engagements. It is much less anti-liberty than John Stuart Mill thinks—as is shown by its leadership in the anti-slavery movement in Britain. The contradictions inherent in universalism and cosmopolitanism are theologically interpreted in Christian debates about religion as a universal category and Christianity as a superior form of religion. This could be inversed by Hindu spokesmen like Swami Vivekananda who saw Hinduism as the pinnacle of universal spirituality and was supported in that claim by the Theosophists.

There is no opposition between cosmopolitanism and nationalism. They emerged together and they belong together in the context of an emerging capitalist world-system. It is useful to distinguish a number of cosmopolitan projects

---

[4] See, for attempts to find modernity everywhere in every period, ' "Modernity" and its Contents in the Economic and Social History of the Orient', Special Fortieth Anniversary Issue, *Journal of the Economic and Social History of the Orient*, 40 (4) 1997, my invited response (van der Veer 1998: 285–95) and David Washbrook's reply to that in the same issue.

that have different political consequences. Historically, the empire has been the context of many such projects. In the post-colonial world, new patterns of migration and political and economic interdependence have emerged and, thus, new forms of cosmopolitanism have merged. But, again and again, it is shown in discussions of these new developments that many of the older patterns of thought are still dominant and thus require historical scrutiny.

11

Media Corporatism and Cosmopolitanism

AYSE CAGLAR

Recent literature on cosmopolitanism (Clifford 1998; Robbins 1998*a*) tries to go beyond defining cosmopolitanism in opposition to locality. Beck (chapter 6, in this volume) urges us to 'think about the cosmopolitan disposition as something that does not have to exclude the perspective of the local'. Instead of approaching cosmopolitanism with a universalist nostalgia in the idiom of a complete detachment (Clifford 1998), we could consider it a reality of (re)attachment with multiple affiliations. In cosmopolitanism there is definitely a concern to go beyond the locality. However, it can still be conceived of as a mode of attachment, which, by entailing multiple, uneven and non-exclusive affiliations, challenges the conventional notions of locality as well as of belonging. It is not their presence or absence, but the *nature* of attachments that is decisive for cosmopolitanism. Cosmopolitan ties are multiple, not necessarily ethnic, and most importantly weak or loose, so that they enable cosmopolitans to participate in many worlds without framing a community with fixed boundaries. Once cosmopolitanism is conceptualized in this way it can be extended to transnational experiences that are particular (Robbins 1998*a*). However, transnationalism and cosmopolitanization can by no means be equated. Transnationalism can foster cosmopolitanism but it can also hinder the development of cosmopolitanism if the attachments forged within transnationalism fail to go beyond the topos of the ethno-cultural.

Although the relationship between states and transnationalization processes is dealt with in the literature (Schein 1998*a*; Leavitt 2000), the entanglements that exist between states, transnational groups, business interests and cosmopolitanism do not receive due attention. In this chapter, on the basis of the emergent media and advertising agencies targeting the German Turks in Germany, I will explore the role of these new media developments in the establishment of new transnational cultural spaces in Germany and Turkey and their consequences for forging cosmopolitanism there.

Nowadays in Berlin, Turkish is in the air. After almost 40 years of a Turkish immigrant presence in the city, suddenly the Turkish language became respectable in big companies like the *Deutsche Telekom*, *Bundespost* and

Mercedes. Plastic bags containing 'Turkish bread' are covered with *Telekom* ads in Turkish and the *Döner Kebabs* are also wrapped in paper covered with Telekom ads in Turkish. The German Turks receive mail in Turkish from *Bundespost* informing them about what services they offer in Turkish. Similarly, the *Telekom* distributes postcards with pictures of famous Turkish pop or *arabesk* singers in Turkey to Turks, along with information (in Turkish) about *Telekom* facilities that give access to private Turkish channels through cable operators like the *Kanal D* or *Aktif Television (ATV)*—broadcast from Turkey.

The *Deutsche Commerzbank's* new service, the 'Investmentfund Alsukoor European Equity Fund' is another example of such differentiated services aimed at the German Turks. It is designed to function according to Shariat rules and explicitly aims to target the German Turks.

Since the mid-1990s, there has been an increased interest in the Turkish media in Germany in public, popular as well as scholarly debates (Becker 1996; Kosnick 2000). This interest parallels the increased presence of Turkish-speaking media broadcast from Turkey or received through satellite. Around 70 per cent of German Turks have satellite dishes with which to receive the numerous commercial channels from Turkey—like the *ATV, Kanal D* and *Star*—and more than 85 per cent of all Turkish households in Germany can receive the Turkish state broadcasting channel TRT–INT, which has already gone transnational (IP Arbo 1998/1999). Furthermore, over the last few years, the media (print, radio and TV broadcasters) have been targeting the German Turkish consumers in German (*Etap, Türkis*), in a mixed language of German and Turkish (*Merhaba, TD1*) and in Turkish (Metropol FM), showing a remarkable proliferation.

The impact of these media on the relationship of the German Turks to German society and to its institutions has been of a common concern to the public and the subject of numerous scholarly debates. Often, these media are accused of impoverishing the German Turks' competency in German. Surprisingly, however, more Turkish-speaking media (radio and TV channels) based in Germany and financed by German institutions are being planned. Interestingly, not only is the language of these media predominantly Turkish, but the social, economic, political and cultural news from Turkey also forms a crucial part of their projects. The new radio station in Nord Rhein Westfahlen (in German and Turkish languages mixed) and the *Gazete* published in Berlin by Grune & Jahr are a couple of examples of very recent developments in this area. Given the proliferation of complaints about the German Turks' enduring ties with Turkey, their Turkish orientation, the negative impact of these ties on their 'integration' into German society and the above-mentioned alleged negative effects of the Turkish media on the German Turks' competency in German, these developments require an explanation.

Why did different institutions start to focus on the question of providing Turkish-speaking services to the German Turks? How do the Turkish-speaking media play a role in shaping new cultural spaces for the German Turks in Germany and Turkey? And what effects do these new media developments have on sustaining the German Turks' multiple cross-border affiliations? On these questions, I will deal first with the factors that lie behind the increased interest of the Turkish-speaking media in targeting the German Turks before going on to disentangle the cultural agendas and business interests inherent in these developments. After focusing on the processes that lie behind the discovery of the German Turks as a consumer group in Germany, I will explore the consequences of this discovery for public spheres in Germany and Turkey.

A New Consumer Group is Born: 'The German Turks'

Two surveys on German Turks played a crucial role in bringing this group, as an important but long neglected consumer group, to the forefront. The first survey, 'Turks in Germany', conducted by Nürnberger Gesellschaft für Konsumforschung (GfK) for the company IP Arbo (which markets advertising space and time for the Radio Tele Luxembourg (RTL) but also for TRT–INT) found that the annual net income of 1.85 million German Turks in 1996 reached DM 18 billion, and that 97 per cent of this amount was spent in Germany. Contrary to the popular belief that the German Turks wanted to make cheap purchases, this survey documented that the German Turks were ready to spend more on quality products, for example on designer goods (20 per cent of all German Turkish car owners drove Mercedes compared with 7.6 per cent of Germans). They were designated as loyal and conscious consumers who believed in advertisements more than Germans. Moreover, they spent more hours than Germans did watching television.

The Turkish population in Germany is demographically very young in comparison with the Germans (82 per cent of the German Turks fall into the 14–49 age group compared with 56 per cent of the German population). This is the most important age group for the advertising market. Consequently, the German Turks were defined as a highly interesting and unexploited consumer group with which to promote the commercial interests of diverse sectors. The repeat of the survey in 1997 with similar results strengthened the profile of the German Turks. Their demographic properties, wages (salaries) and consumer desires all indicated a need for marketing strategies to target this group, namely ethno-marketing.

The next major problem for firms targeting Turkish consumers was how to gain access to this group, which was solved when another survey conducted by ZfT in 1997 on the media consumption behaviour of Turks in Germany provided the answers. The most crucial finding of this survey was that 55.7 per cent of the German Turks informed themselves only through Turkish newspapers, while 38 per cent did so through both the German and Turkish newspapers.[1] In terms of television, the findings paralleled the printed media and it was found that the German Turks informed themselves through the Turkish-speaking television broadcasts, especially through TRT–INT. Once these two findings were put together, a new target group for marketing and advertising agencies was born.[2]

The outcome, Turkish-oriented and Turkish-speaking marketing, was quick and significant. After an intensive advertising campaign in Turkish, aimed at the German Turks with their differentiated services, the telephone company *Otelo* was able to persuade 190 000 Turkish customers of *Deutsche Telekom* to switch to *Otelo*. Given that the average telephone bill of a Turkish household was twice as high as the average of that of a German household, losing 190 000 customers meant a substantial loss for *Telekom*. To counter *Otelo's* success, *Telekom*, which had until recently enjoyed a monopoly in telecommunications in Germany, like *Otelo*, introduced an information call centre in Turkish. It started to offer Turkish-speaking services that were thought to suit the German Turks' 'needs' and launched a heavy advertising campaign in the Turkish media—both printed and in radio and television broadcasting. The outcome was an advertising battle between *Telekom* and *Otelo*, which in turn proved to be extremely profitable for the Turkish-speaking media in terms of advertising revenues.

In addition to these telephone companies, *Deutsche Bundespost*, various banks, insurance companies, some pharmaceutical companies (like *Bayer*) and Mercedes[3] all directed their attentions to the new consumer group. Some advertising agencies established branches to specialize in directing marketing to the Turks in Germany; some—like Do It in Düsseldorf—devoted as much as 25 per cent of their budgets to this group, while others increased their budgets for marketing their products for the German Turks. For example, Mercedes increased its budget for Turkish-oriented advertisements to 25 per cent in the last year (interview with *Beys*, *WMF* December 1999).

The phenomenon of ethno-marketing is not new and Germany is in fact a latecomer in this area. However, the important thing about the 'discovery' of the German Turks as a lucrative consumer group is the consequences of these

---

[1] There are nine daily Turkish newspapers available in Germany. They are basically the dailies based in Turkey that have Europe editions. *Hurriyet* is the most important of these with an overall circulation of 160 000 in Europe, of which 110 000 are circulated in Germany.

[2] These survey results were quoted (without exception) in all the portfolios of advertising agencies marketing Turkish products to the media in Berlin.

[3] Mercedes belongs to the first of such corporations targeting the German Turkish market. It started its advertising campaigns aimed at Turks in 1993. However, in this early awareness of the market some personal factors played a role.

developments for the German Turks' incorporation into wider public spheres, both in Turkey and Germany, for until then they had been incorporated in a particularly restricted way.

Advertising revenues are important for all commercial media, and the Turkish media in Germany are no exception. For example, *TD1* in Berlin— a private local channel in Turkish that has been operating since 1985—is financed wholly by advertisements. Although in the beginning it was mainly Turkish firms that placed advertisements with them, its owner claims that now they could not survive without the input of advertisements from German companies (interview, January 2000).[4] The situation for AYPA—another local television broadcaster (in German), with a sole focus on the German Turks and Turkey, is similar.[5] Sales of advertising space and time are also important sources of income for the Turkish state broadcaster TRT–INT, with 98 per cent of its advertisements coming from German business. The TMM (a branch that specializes in Turkish media marketing within IP Arbo) also markets advertising time and space for TRT–INT. By 1994, the income IP Arbo (then called IP Plus) received from TRT–INT for mediating services between the advertisers and the TRT–INT had reached DM 25 million.

The printed media that target the German Turks (in either Turkish or German) are even more significant. In fact, *Hürriyet* has the lion's share in this market. Not only the dailies but also the monthly and bi-weekly journals that are distributed free, like the *TD1*, *Merhaba* and *Türkis*, are all financed by their income from advertisements. For *Etap*, a monthly journal that appeared in the autumn of 1999 (and disappeared in the spring of 2000), advertising revenues covered a substantial portion of its costs (interview, November 1999).

The situation is similar in radio broadcasting. Metropol FM, which went on air in June 1999 and is already a huge success among the German Turks, is also financed by advertisements. In fact, this broadcaster sees itself—unlike Radio Multikulti—as a '*Werbeträger*' (cf. Vertovec 1996). Its director formulates this very clearly. 'Our broadcasts do not want to imitate a Multikulti programme; instead we sell advertisements' (interview, March 2000). The use of space in Metropol FM reflects this priority. The largest part of its 300-square-metre office is reserved for its advertising section. However, despite this straight emphasis on business, it is worth focusing on Metropol FM to explore the entanglements between the advertising sector, media and the public sphere.

---

[4] According to a recent study in 2000 by Ausländerbeauftragte on the German Turks' media consumption in Berlin, *TD1*, with a 70.1 per cent rating, is the most popular television station among the German Turks, followed by the TRT–INT with a 34.6 per cent rating.

[5] AYPA is the only television broadcasting in German with a focus on Turkey and the German Turks. Only 0.6 per cent of the German Turks in Berlin seem to watch AYPA regularly (Ausländerbeauftragte 2000: 29).

Metropol FM and Cosmopolitanism

Metropol FM is the first radio broadcaster in Turkish outside Turkey that is on air twenty-four hours a day. It has twenty-seven employees who speak German and Turkish[6] and who are familiar with Berlin, the German Turks in Berlin, and Germany (interview, March 2000).[7] Metropol FM provides its audiences with non-stop Turkish music, entertainment, news and some programmes about the difficulties the German Turks face in their daily lives in Berlin. However, it is basically a Turkish music channel and it quickly became popular among the German Turks. According to a recent study, 71 per cent of the German Turkish radio audiences in Berlin listen to Metropol FM regularly (compared with 2.1 per cent who listen to SFB (Radio Multikulti). Although it sees itself as a commercial broadcaster selling advertising time and space, Metropol FM helps mediate and sustain complex affiliations and multiple attachments among the German Turks. Metropol FM presents itself as a German Turkish enterprise broadcasting for German Turks.[8] All its programmes are produced in Berlin and a familiarity with Turkish life in Berlin, as well as with German and Turkish society, are crucial to its employment policy (interview, March 2000). It not only recognizes that German Turks as a group are different from the Turks in Turkey and the Germans in Germany, but it also fosters their numerous connections with other places in Europe, including Turkey. The broadcasting is in Turkish, but there is a playful and creative approach to Turkish (and to German), which gives rise to a crossover between German and Turkish (which is already widespread among the German Turks). Most importantly, Metropol FM serves as a medium to institutionalize this new language.[9]

Metropol FM audiences are acquainted with different places. News from Turkey is an integral part of its hourly news service, but more significant than news from Turkey is the Turkish weather forecast (integrated into the weather forecast it provides for Berlin and Germany). Both the news and the weather forecast help to orient Metropol FM's audience to Turkey. In addition to such built-in synchronizations, Metropol FM observes events in Turkey and Turkish religious holidays. After the earthquake in August 1999, Metropol FM, like Turkish radio broadcasters in Turkey, joined in the mourning by adjusting its programmes.[10]

---

[6] Though their language skills differ considerably.

[7] Its owners are Moira Rundfunk GmbH, H. Schnaudt (president) and H.W. Ehlgen.

[8] Apart from the manager and bookkeeper, all its employees are German Turkish.

[9] The cartoon *Kanakman* in *Etap* is also an example of this new language.

[10] The Turkish discos in Berlin also observed a period of mourning and were closed for that reason.

Metropol FM and the journals *Etap* and *Türkis* provide sites in which to forge a kind of vernacular or localized cosmopolitanism. Metropol FM adopts the perspective of the local. However, the 'local' here entails multiple, uneven, and non-exclusive affiliations. Thus, it represents an attachment with multi-affiliations.

The city is the location for the kind of cosmopolitanism that Metropol FM could be conceived to forge. Belonging to the city is not the same as belonging to a community with fixed boundaries. The fragmented nature of urban culture and its inherent openness play a crucial role in bringing a sense of belonging to the city to the forefront. There is, for example, an identification with Berlin, but not necessarily with Germany. Different kinds of belonging are reflectively challenged and negotiated around the image of the city.

The emphasis on the city in Metropol FM is apparent in its programmes, in its staffing policy and even in the sequence in which it presents the news. Its news programmes open with local news from Berlin, followed by news from Germany, then from Turkey, and then finally, to round up, the international news. This city emphasis is not unique to Metropol FM (though it is very strong there). Radio Multikulti does not have a particular Berlin focus but it integrates news programmes like City Spots that cover the other European cities in which the Turkish immigrants are settled. As I showed elsewhere (Caglar 1998), the references to Turkey in German-Turkish youth discourse, all refer to the metropoles and urban spaces in Turkey. The spatial references and attachments are not to Turkey as a cultural space but to urban spaces in Turkey, which are seen to be connected to all sorts of other cities and for this reason could hardly stand in a metonymical relation to Turkey as a homogeneous cultural space. As the person in a Turkish café-bar in Berlin put it, 'here we turn towards Istanbul and Izmir, but in fact we are catching up with New York via Istanbul. Here we are part of all these places. At 1001 [the name of the café] I feel like I am in Istanbul, Berlin, Europe and in New York at the same time' (Caglar 1998). In the emergent discourses centred on these spaces, heterogeneity and being cosmopolitan seem to have replaced the ethnic closure of the common representations of Turkey and Turkishness that conflate the public and scholarly discourses on the German Turks in Germany. Consequently, the sense of belonging is not envisaged as being to nations but to urban spaces. The relationship between the nation and the city is uncoupled. The urban spaces become the strategic arena for the development and reformulation of emergent forms of belonging. Here we have, to use Sassen's (1996) term, the 'unmooring of identities' from what have been the traditional sources of identity. Reattachments entailing multiple affiliations that are loose or weak are 'unbound' attachments (Anderson 1998) and urban spaces are the locality of these unbound—cosmopolitan—ties.

It is possible to observe the construction of the new communicational cultural spaces in and across Europe through urban sites. The Turkish journals targeting German Turkish youth[11] foster a kind of multi-connectedness by means of an urban attachment. They cover the European metropoles and Turkish life in these places, as well as metropoles in Turkey. Hence, they contribute to the formation of a space in which transnational imaginaries are forged and a new language or repertoire of a loose, unbound 'community' whose boundaries are not drawn on ethnic lines is negotiated. These new media whose dynamics are set in motion by commercial interests and advertising agencies contribute to the transnationalization of German Turks as well as to the development of a 'vernacular cosmopolitanism' among them.

Incorporation into the Public Sphere

The emergent media had implications and consequences for the transformations taking place in the public spheres both in Germany and in Turkey. The discovery of German Turks as a lucrative market contributed not only to the development and proliferation of the Turkish media in Germany, which in turn gave impetus to the establishment of a kind of a 'diasporic' public sphere, but also had consequences in terms of the German Turks' incorporation into the wider public sphere both in Germany and Turkey.[12] These new developments in the media simply expand the discursive space. However, more is at stake here than the formation of multiple publics.

One of the consequences of the popularity and 'commercial success' of Turkish media was that the German Turks and Turkish as a medium became attractive to the established German media. In March 2000, one of Germany's biggest publishing companies, Grüne and Jahr, started an advertising newspaper, *Gazete*, in Turkish in Berlin. In addition to advertisements, it carries news from the Turkish community in Berlin. Another established newspaper in Germany—*Die Tageszeitung*—started a weekly supplement in Turkish (*Persembe*) in September 2000.[13] It carries political, social and cultural news from Turkey, news from Germany, and commentaries from German Turkish perspectives. Although the desire to break the monopoly of some of the conservative and nationalist Turkish dailies is very strong behind this initiative, the attractiveness of the flourishing advertising market targeting the German Turks is definitely as strong as the former.[14]

[11] Here it has to be noted that the substantial portion of *Türkis* is devoted to the programmes of Turkish channels that can be received in Germany.

[12] The designation of 'diasporic' should be used cautiously here. Although this sphere might seem to be built on the ethnic axis of homelands and abroad, it entails attachments and references that lie beyond the limiting dominion of ethnically informed arrangements, transactions and senses of belonging. For the limitations of the concept of diaspora, see Soysal (2000).

[13] In fact it is basically in Turkish with a small section in German.

[14] See the internal reports of *Persembe*.

These developments set in motion by market forces did not remain without an impact at the state level. In October 1999, the Institute for Foreign Relations organized a workshop with representatives from the German and Turkish media, political parties and several German Turkish associations to discuss the modalities of intervening in the Turkish media landscape in Germany. This German Turkish media dialogue, which was at the initiative of the federal press office, aimed to break the monopoly of Turkish dailies, to establish a German Turkish media advisory board composed of German and Turkish journalists and publishers, to publish a weekly report in German on the Turkish media for the benefit of German journalists, to provide know-how and support to local Turkish media and to establish a bilingual TV channel that could also be received in Turkey.

These developments cannot be read simply as efforts to give an expression to differences within the framework of a particularistic multiculturalism. They do not simply refer to a mere increase or growth of a secluded public sphere and to the arrangements taking place there. If we do not limit participation to an activity that is only possible in a narrowly defined political realm, but see it as an activity that can be realized in the social and cultural spheres as well (Benhabib 1992), these media networks and developments can be seen as challenges to the spaces offered to the German Turks for participation in Germany and to an extent in Turkey. These new spaces mean more than the constitution of an ethnically bounded public sphere. As seen in the new bilingual television project, the minority spaces are being opened up to transnational European spaces.[15] What are at stake here are the transformations taking place within the wider public sphere. This means creating new openings for imaginings of what 'community', 'membership' or 'belonging' might mean both for the German Turks and, most importantly, for Germans. Benhabib argues that 'the public' is a term of inclusion as well as exclusion and it is based on defining the 'we' and the 'they'. Thus, every group in the public—by entering the public—not only refashions itself as a presence in the public, but also brings transformations to the nature of the public because their inclusion brings a reconfiguration of the self-definition of the collectivity, namely of the 'we' and the 'they' (Benhabib 1992). Incorporation of Turkish into the public sphere beyond the terms and mission of multiculturalism is already a critical change in a polity in which language plays a central role in construing the 'imagined community'. This is a process that makes the German state more and more polyglot. And it is ironic that the dynamics of the inclusion of Turkish into the wider public sphere are largely set in motion by commercial concerns. Though motivated by economic

---

[15] The second stage of the planned bilingual television project is to establish a new European television financed by private foundations, and by the local federal and European sources that would be attractive to all 'world open' audiences.

concerns, these developments alter the opportunities and the terms of German Turks' participation in the life of the society at large, as well as the nature of the public sphere itself.

Bauböck argues that the overlapping forms of political community the transnational groups generate 'may pave the way for a greater responsiveness of state-based policies towards the multiple political identities of their citizens' (Bauböck chapter 8, this volume). In its efforts to accommodate them, the receiving society and its conception of political community may be durably changed (Ibid.). 'If these minorities can become catalysts for a cosmopolitan transformation of democracy,' says Bauböck, 'this is neither due to their ambiguous citizenship nor to their political consciousness. What may bring about such a change is an endogenous change in the conception of the national community in domestic as well as international arenas that can pave the road for cosmopolitan projects' (Ibid.). The emergent Turkish-speaking media could be seen as a catalyst for such an endogenous change.

The flourishing Turkish media in Germany also had consequences for the recognition of the German Turks as a distinct group with different (diasporic) interests and identities in Turkey. In Turkey too we see some attempts to incorporate the German Turks into the wider public sphere. One recent attempt came from *Cumhuriyet*—a left-wing established daily in Turkey. *Cumhuriyet* is being opened up to German Turks (as shareholders) to start a *Cumhuriyet TV* that would also be broadcast to Germany and change the nature of the already existing weekly published in Europe[16] (interview, February 2000). Here again, the phenomenon of discovering the German Turks not only as a lucrative consumer group but also as a group whose savings can be mobilized in different kinds of investments is in play.[17]

However, whatever the motivations are, the different Turkish television broadcasters try to broadcast programmes produced in Germany. Although these channels differ in their political orientations, they all agree that the German Turks' distinct needs, interests and concerns need to be recognized and incorporated into the programmes. Here a similar kind of fragmentation of the public sphere, as the one I referred to in Germany, is in play. Even the incorporation of a different kind of Turkish—a kind of a creolized and for that reason 'impure' Turkish—into this sphere, is itself important to break some of the structures of the public sphere in Turkey. A series of developments triggered by commercial interests end up contributing to the incorporation of the German Turks into the wider social sphere both in Turkey and in Germany.

---

[16] *Cumhuriyet* is obviously seeking a solution to the economic crisis in which it finds itself. The attractiveness of the Turkish media for advertising revenues is economically tempting for *Cumhuriyet*.

[17] In this project the fact that some companies—like *Jet Pa* and *Kombassan*—succeeded in mobilizing the German Turks' investments played an important role.

Concluding Remarks

The topography of the German Turks' inclusion and exclusion landscape in Germany is going through a transformation, which is the result of the entanglements between state policies and business interests. Consumption is an arena for sociality that is itself subject to societal mechanisms of regulation. Thus, with their consumption practices, the German Turks construe and negotiate their sociality and participation in both Turkish and German society. In doing so, they forge a localized and vernacular cosmopolitanism with an unbound belonging. A series of developments in the Turkish media landscape in Germany, set in motion by the advertising industry, contribute to cosmopolitan openings in the public spheres in Germany as well as in Turkey.

12

Both Sides, Now: Culture Contact, Hybridization, and Cosmopolitanism

CHAN KWOK-BUN

Ssu-ma Niu grieved, saying, everyone else has brothers; I alone have none. Tsu-hsia said, I have heard this saying, '... if [a gentleman] behaves with courtesy to others and observes the rules of ritual, then all within the Four Seas are his brothers.' How can any true gentleman grieve that he is without brothers?

Jan Jung asked about goodness. The Master said 'Behave when away from home as though you were in the presence of an important guest. Deal with the common people as though you were officiating at an important sacrifice. Do not do to others what you would not like yourself.'

—The Analects of Confucius (Waley 1936: 162–3)

Cosmopolitanism arises through the interrelated processes of increased connectivity and cultural contact. In this chapter I will consider five possible theoretical processes and outcomes of cultural contact. However, following Femminella (1980), I will lay particular emphasis on the process. Three examples of how cosmopolitanism arose in Chinese settings are considered before concluding with some reflections on how humanity at large might rediscover what it shares as well as how it differs. Rather than address the question of cosmopolitanism purely abstractly, I look to the unspectacular, practical, every-day life activities that allow movement beyond group identities to the business of simply living together and solving practical problems collectively.

Though discussions of increased connectivity have been linked to globalization since the 1980s, the phenomenon itself is certainly not new. Discourses on its economic aspect are as old as the world system theory of Wallerstein (1974), while the technological revolution and innovation associated with post-industrialism have

This chapter is extracted from a considerably longer essay available from the author. I would like to thank Anthony Richmond, John Rex, Meena Alexander, William Liu, Huang Chih Lien, Caroline Pluss, Gerard Postiglione, Francis Femminella, Rose Liang and Tan Bin-ky for their critical reading of my essay and their useful suggestions.

been examined by sociologists since the 1960s (see, for example, Richmond 1969). Globalization refers to a compression of time and space, of the world, and to the intensification of the consciousness of the world as a whole, which in itself is rooted in the colossal spread of various new forms of capitalism made possible by the superhighways of global communication and transportation.

Central to this sudden awareness of the multi-layered 'complex connectivity' of humans is a keen sense of consciousness of the other—the immigrant, the foreign labourer, the expatriate, the tourist or the vagabond—who is in our midst for short or long periods, with whatever motives and desires. In global cities like Hong Kong, Tokyo, New York, London, Paris, and, may I now add, Shanghai, encounters with strangeness and differences have now been built into the very fabric of everyday life, simultaneously evoking feelings of curiosity and hostility. Empirical works on transnationalism in the past ten years, which narrate a dual structure of feelings attached both to where one is at ('destination') and where one is from ('origin'), begin to show a person can be at more than one place at one time—simultaneity being the defining characteristic of transnationalism.

The magnitude of transnationalism in the midst of the greatest global cities all over the world sensitizes us to an inevitable question: While here, do 'strangers' also have meaningful ties and feelings that lie elsewhere? A more interesting question for the pragmatists is whether this deep duality of structure of feelings is also functional. Can this 'doubleness', or even multiplicity, of ethnicity be put to good use, not only in economic terms, but also in terms of its potential to facilitate cross-cultural and cross-national understanding? The clashes of cultures or even civilizations, if any, can be located in social relations, but also inside the minds of the immigrants now transformed. Seen in this way, the immigrants next door are not all that 'foreign' because they must adapt their transplanted culture to the daily, practical exigencies of living here and now, thus transforming themselves and the milieu with which they are entangled. Ironically, a sociological gaze at foreignness can lead to a sense of our shared sameness. Are we all that different? 'Foreignness' may turn out to be a smoke-screen, a label, a rhetoric, a mental trick, an artefact of the mind, a mask, an exaggeration that blinds us to the common hybridity we have long shared but exorcized because of the politics of living together. In a very important way, foreign populations remain foreign only because they are seen as groups, as categories; they cease to be seen as individuals, as persons.

Dialectics of Culture Contact

What then happens to one's identity, ethnicity, and culture as a consequence of migration or, more precisely, of transnationalism? There are many possibilities, at least conceptually speaking.[1] Let us designate the culture of the place of 'departure' as A and the culture of the place of 'arrival' as B. It may be better to talk in terms of 'departure and arrival', following the language of international airports or railway terminals, rather than 'origin and destination'. The former expression conjures up an image of a serial ongoing mobility within one's life-span, which in the end blurs and absolves the origin/destination distinction of its solidity, its hardness and its absoluteness. I shall suggest five possible processes as well as outcomes of encounters between A and B, giving each a label in its verb rather than noun form, thereby emphasizing the processual and the ongoing rather than the 'done with', the completed.[2]

Essentializing: $A \leftrightarrow B = A/B$

Both A and B essentialize and ossify upon their 'encounters with difference or strangeness', retreating to their respective 'unchanging same'. This possibility is particularly real when it happens at the group level—the group acting as a breeding ground of prejudice, discrimination and racism because groups in contact manufacture and exaggerate differences, while stereotypes of the group and thus its members are constructed and put to destructive use.

Alternating: $A \leftrightarrow = A+B$

B is internalized by the person through socialization but will coexist, side by side, with A formerly residing inside the mind of the person, both now suffi-ciently compartmentalized, divided, kept separate. Individuals will retrieve A or B depending on the occasion and the presence of others. They alternate their identities, oscillate, practise internal mental migration, engage in what socio-logists call 'passing', putting one mask on at this moment and another mask at the next (Tong and Chan 2002). They are identity jugglers though the perpetual fear of dropping a ball or two is real. Identity is thus a matter of positioning—a view explored in *Alternate Identities: The Chinese of Contemporary Thailand* (Tong and Chan 2001).

Converting: $A \leftrightarrow B = B$

This option is perhaps the most widely discussed, historically. Many terms have been invented for narrative purposes, for example: assimilation, acculturation, Anglo-conformity, and conversion. The image here suggests a replacement or,

---

[1] In my discussion of the dialectics of culture contact in this section, I follow but also freely interpret an incisive essay by Femminella (1980).

[2] I thank Caroline Pluss for her suggestion that I should name these five possibilities. The actual names used are mine.

more accurately, a displacement of A by B, usually because of an alleged loss or negation of one culture by another because the person is by now uprooted and has buried his 'old self', so to speak. Yet, these processes are by no means assured. For example, Skinner's prediction or, more precisely, prescription that by the fifth generation all the Chinese in Thailand would have been assimilated and have become, for all intents and purposes, Thai is strongly contested in Tong and Chan (2001).

Hybridizing: $A \leftrightarrow B = AB$ or Ab or Ba

In this option, the air-tight compartmentalization, which incidentally is another sociological concept as in 'the compartmentalization of roles', is removed intentionally, as well as unconsciously, if people can culturally 'let go' and be less 'uptight' about their 'cultures of origin' and, at the same time, strive not to be overly critical about the culture of the place of 'arrival'. This kind of mental agility and tolerance can open up many fascinating, exciting possibilities. Hybridization is a shorthand description of the processes that transpire. Immigrants live out their daily existence in the midst of neighbours who are initially unlike them in many fundamental ways. But a process of mutual entanglement of the self and other, of a collision of different cultures is inevitable, as, having been for years co-residents of a common public place that engenders in them a shared sense of history, the foreigners and the locals must learn to work out and work through their sense of belonging and neighbourliness, a flowing together of everyday life activities (see Hiebert, Chapter 13, in this volume for examples).

Innovating: $A \leftrightarrow B = AB$ or Ab or $Ba \rightarrow C$

In this possibility, the entanglement and collision of cultures within the mind of the person may take the form of a trauma, an existential pain, a dialectic of opposites, which may sometimes degenerate into pathologies of various kinds. But the good news is C, a new product, a new culture, a novelty. At this moment, the cosmopolitan star is born. My foregoing analysis is, of course, constructed in purely abstract theoretical terms, knowing full well such an analysis is by necessity complicated or corrupted by the politics of difference and power between A and B. For example, when B signifies the majority culture and A is the minority culture, the carriers of A must learn strategies to work themselves into the institutional landscapes of B—oftentimes expecting denigration, disapproval, discrimination or even outright rejection, thus being pushed out while trying to ease themselves in. Acute feelings of ambivalence are often the result.

Femminella's Processual Analysis of Impact-Integration

Several theoretical elements can be teased out from Femminella's (1980) processual analysis of what transpires when two different cultures, two sides,

A and B, are in contact with each other (see Postiglione 1983, for an appreciation of Femminella's work).

In the first stage of this culture encounter, dialectics would predict that, man
being a territorial animal, B's anxiety over defending one's own space and
resources would create the absolute, polar opposite in A—in the form of the
'estranged intruder', the stranger. This is a stage of 'boundary crisis'. The
dialectical character of human nature is such that we see and experience in our
psyche the different other as the stranger, keeping us apart, at a distance. In the
second stage, A enters into conflict and competition with B over resources in the
market place, with B demanding A to submit but A displaying a stubborn resistance to submission. The conflicts, contradictions and paradoxes thus generated
during this stage of collision of cultures and mutual entanglement of A and B
can only be resolved through a synthesis in the third stage called, appropriately,
'impact-integration' or 'emergent culture' by Femminella. He claims that it is
out of 'this impacting' that new syntheses evolve. The conflict is in a cultural
integration that changes not only the persons involved, or even their groups, but
also the whole society itself (Femminella 1980: 170). The society is depicted as
being bi-directional, moving towards the core culture and then back to the
ethnic subculture (Femminella 1980: 172).

Meanwhile, ethnicity and ethnic communities persist, in a form of voluntary
segregation because A does not want to totally assimilate into B. People have a
need to be both a part of and simultaneously apart from others; to have order
without inexorability; to value non-conformity and individuality, but also con-
formity with concern for others; to be both ruled and freed. It is out of the dialectics of these positive and negative forces, out of this tension, that culture and
community evolve. And this tension of contradictions is synthesized in a new
form. Something very new, a new ethnicity, is born each time and every time.

Humankind is not merely territorial; it is also migratory so as to find a new life
in a new or renewed, reinvigorated society—thus the numerous massive migrations of human histories everywhere. People are not merely tension-ridden
animals, they also seek tension-reduction through the tension-synthesizing function of the dialectic, which continuously creates and invents new social forms.
And this cycle repeats itself biographically in each individual. It is herein that one
can locate Femminella's theory of human nature, personality and character.

One detects in Femminella's writings a particular style, a logic that privileges
the mixing of things that are different, the confrontational encounters of individuals, groups and cultures—a tense and intense triangulation only temporarily resolved by synthesis, by unification. A dialectical process articulated as
such can be a rather brutal, violent one because conflicts and competitions are
an inevitability, indeed a given. This is a theoretical throwback to Robert E.
Park's cycle of race relations (Park and Burgess 1921; Park 1937). As
Femminella (1973: 8) maintains, 'the coexistence of these conflicting values

and ideas in the United Statesian cultural system can be accounted for by virtue of their origins in the intergroup processes of evolving human nature, including the processes of cooperation, competition, conflict, accommodation and assimilation'.

The third stage of the impact-integration process is similar to Park's idea of assimilation, the social process whereby people of different races and cultures are drawn into 'the ever narrow circle of common life'. To Femminella, 'It referred to the erasing of external differences, the development of superficial uniformities particularly in manners and fashion but also in language that enables newcomers to participate in the new life, in a "practical working arrangement", so that like-mindedness in individual opinions, sentiments and beliefs may eventually accrue' (Femminella 1973: 11).

What perhaps sets Femminella apart from the other social theorists on culture contact is that he forces a rethink of the straight-line, one-way, linear theories of assimilation by solving the problem of unification through dialectics. But a dialectic that unites, changes, but does not homogenize the groups concerned. Unlike others, Femminella's logic of thinking always keeps both sides, A and B, in full view, trying to figure out what is on the minds of both, their respective perspectives, not either/or. But, again, dialectically, even a resolution will in time generate its opposite, thus the tension again, one more time. Femminella places A and B at opposite poles; they approach each other on a continuum but never intersect. Equilibrium is never reached, nor is it a desired state. Tension is therefore a constant. Postiglione (1983: 164) makes this interpretation of Femminella explicit, alluding to 'a point of intersection, although always focused upon by both groups, is never reached. A group may move in the direction of another but never merge. This is similar to the idea of walking toward a wall by continually cutting the distance in half. One never reaches the wall'.

Conceptually and empirically, one can in fact display the parallel entanglements of industrialism, modernism and migration—and their triangulation—within the hub of the modern-day global city. To study how such entanglements resolve themselves, which invariably change the societies/cities, the immigrants and the local residents themselves, one is in fact studying human nature, the dialectics of its very character. So the early theoretical as well as practical concerns of the Chicago urbanists are now reinvoked when we cast our gaze on cosmopolitanism. Can these insights, derived often from European or American examples, translate to other cultural settings, such as that of China?

Dialectics of Chinese Culture

In a short but thought-provoking essay (the original text is in Chinese), the Chinese philosopher Tang (1990), now teaching at Beijing University, interrogates classical Confucian texts to read Chinese history and culture. He invokes the idea of 'harmony/integration in difference', or *he'erbutang*, from a series of dialectical exchanges in the Confucian texts.

One must first begin to be principally cognizant of an intrinsic difference that marks and separates the two sides, A and B, when they encounter each other; it is only on this basis of explicit cognition of differentness when different matters can proceed to interact and produce the growth of each and both sides. Also, the interactions between A and B are necessarily dialectical—and mutual and reciprocal—A, during the process of interaction with B, changes itself and changes B. By integration, Confucius did not mean B totally assimilating or obliterating A, or vice versa, but rather a process of A and B finding a point of confluence during interactions, thus benefiting from change and growth in a reciprocal/mutual fashion.

When two cultures, two sides, A and B, encounter each other, Tang reasons, there are at least four possible benign processes that can emerge.

First, A and B, upon 'dialoguing' with each other, discover that they are not all that different and that they share some common concepts. Cultures communicate with each other to discover shared commonness; discovery in the process of and as a result of communication. One finds variants of the concept of love in Christianity, Buddhism, Confucianism and Moism (not to be mistaken as Maoism). On a generalized, abstract level, all these concepts of 'love' provide a common foreground and background to find and discover a shared discourse, yet, equally importantly, each preserves its own uniqueness or differentness. Second, A interacts with B and discovers something new in B which is not, upon deep self-reflection, antagonistic to A; upon adaptation, it is 'worked into' A, thus enriching, invigorating and reinventing A. One should note the social psychological principle of selective attention and inattention in this discovery process. Tang cites the example of the non-existence of the concept of supreme realization or intuition of the Dao in China, which was later imported into Chinese systems of thinking by Cheng-Zhu and Lu-Wang during the Sung and Ming dynasties.

Third, A interacts with B and discovers a new concept in B, which is oppositional to another essential concept in A. To work the new concept from B in, the old concept in A must go. This process is similar to that of displacement or replacement in culture contacts. Tang cites the example of the transplantation of the concept of democracy, which required the abandonment of the old *San Gang* idea in China that articulates three principles of duties: on the part of the official to the emperor, of the son to his father and of the wife to her husband. Fourth, A interacts with B and both discover new concepts that are non-existent in both, sort of inventing new things upon a collision of the minds, for example: peaceful coexistence, critical pluralism or what we would now call multiculturalism.

When a foreign (in the sense of being 'new') idea from A is transported into B, it either adds something new in its originality to B or the newness assumes an adapted, transformed form because it must take the B culture into account in its transformation, a sort of adaptational prerequisite. This new idea from A, when imported into B, may help facilitate the full expression and realization of something in A that would otherwise remain dormant because it is not adequately 'released'. This idea of release is like a sudden bursting of sense on the hearing of an utterance.[3] I heard you. I now see what I did not see before. This is yet another form of cultural change, following the principle of being 'harmonious but not the same'. Tang articulates this most elegantly: Harmony in diversity engenders growth, while sameness results in degeneration. It is a matter of encounters with difference leading to or resulting in 'deference', of yielding to others, of postponing, of delaying until a later, much later time until communication brings forth something beneficial to both sides. Following Hall (1990), the verb 'defer' thus has a double sense: I defer my conduct till a later time because I must act with due deference to you, and it is hoped, vice versa. This is expressly acting against ethnocentrism and prejudice—that blindness that William James (1977) wrote so eloquently about. It is a matter of etiquette, a mannerism of conduct that requires a certain capacity not to be impulsive, not to act on the spur of the moment, literally to arrest one's body from acting, from saying, from doing anything. Philosophically, it is about listening, understanding and feeling—in one word, 'waiting' for one's turn, which is crucial to a new time of reconciliation.

First Narrative of Impact-Integration: Buddhism in China

As Tang (1999*a*: 191–8) argues, when Buddhism was first imported from India into China during the late Western Han and Eastern Jin, it sort of 'rode on the back of' Han's 'magical arts', using the local pre-existing systems of ideas and beliefs as a carrier or medium of transfusion. Through Wei and Jin, Buddhism was grafted onto the Wei-Jin Metaphysics. The then Buddhist discourse on the non-destruction of the spirit, soul and 'ghost' found its resonance in the local Chinese belief that the body can vanish but the spirit continues to thrive, and that humans turn into ghosts upon death and can cause harm to the living. The Buddhist discourse in causality also resonated with the Chinese belief in the beneficial consequences of altruism—merit making—and its reverse. On the conceptual, cognitive level, measures were invented to interpret, and sometimes misinterpret, Buddhism.

Any culture has its conservative, stubborn side, resisting the intrusion, the penetration, of outside culture. Outside culture would then sometimes endeavour to

---

[3] Personal communication with Meena Alexander.

recognize and meet the psychological needs of self-maintenance and self-defence, thus grafting itself onto the local culture, sort of a 'cultural piggy-backing', to avoid a brutal frontal collision of cultures at the very outset—all in an attempt to facilitate its own eventual diffusion and integration.

Yet, the widespread and broad-scale diffusion of Buddhism during the Eastern Jin in China resulted, inevitably, in the surfacing of contradictions and clashes of the two cultures, which dialectically led to change in the Chinese culture as a whole. There emerged contradictions between the Chinese this-worldliness and the Buddhist other-worldliness, as well as between debates on loyalty to the emperor and filial piety. The two emperors Northern Wei Taiwudi and Northern Zhouwudi both adopted radical measures to exterminate Buddhism, but both met with failure. It was out of the dialectics of a mutual entanglement between the two cultures that both deeply transformed and regenerated themselves.

By the time of the Sui and the Tang dynasties, Indian Buddhism, then sufficiently sinicized, was generally integrated into Chinese culture. By the Sung dynasty, Buddhism had become so much a part of the Chinese culture that it led to the birth of Sung-Ming Neo-Confucianism. Buddhism reached the zenith of its growth, its golden age, during the Tsui and Tang periods. Buddhism had differentiated into several highly influential sects and spread to Korea and Japan. In China, Buddhism had become more this-worldly and more fully integrated into, rather than separated from, the everyday living of all Chinese, monks or not monks. One could practise self-cultivation and reach self-perfection by serving the emperor and the father in this world.

It took close to one millennium for Buddhism to complete its history of impact-integration, following a dialectical process consisting of three distinct stages: grafting, contradictions and collisions, and impact-integration. During this process, both cultures changed and transformed themselves, each finding new forms of identity.

Indian Buddhism requires a surreal world of ecstasy. This idea had been greatly transformed in China such that this surreal world could be dispensed with—one can be a Buddha by doing simple and practical chores like fetching water and chopping firewood. As such, one does not worship the Buddha, neither does he read the scripture; one is to strive for self-cultivation. I 'know', therefore I am Buddha—or, 'I put down the butcher's chopper, I become Buddha instantly, on the spot' (Tang 1999b: 226–41). A young monk finished eating and asked an elder, 'What should I do next?' He was thinking to himself that he should be reading scripture or doing something serious. The elder replied abruptly, 'You don't know what to do after dinner? Go do the dishes!' (Tang 1999b: 235) This idea of practical this-worldliness had found its way into the Confucianism of the Sung dynasty. The most celebrated writers during the Tang dynasty like Wang Wei, Bai Juyi and Lui Zongyuan, as well as Su Shi in the Sung dynasty, were all Buddhists. Indian Buddhism has been thoroughly worked into the Chinese cultural core; Buddhism has thus changed both itself and China. It is in this sense that we intend the principle of reciprocal (two-way) and mutual influence in culture change to be understood at both the theoretical and empirical levels.

Second Narrative of Impact-Integration: China's Migration Saga

In an outstanding essay (text in Chinese), which attempts to re-read and reinter-pret Chinese history, An and Wang (1992) take the rare position among Chinese historians that focuses its analytical gaze on the representative historical occa-sions of 'booming collision' and mutual entanglement of the myriad cultural systems in China. During the two Han dynasties, the Yellow River culture 'collided' with the Mongolian culture from the north as well as with the Qiang culture from the west. The Han agriculture-based culture met with a 'foreign' nomadic culture from the north and the west, resulting in the importation into China of, for example, cattle-breeding techniques and an entire culture based on such knowledge and technology. The Great Wall proved to be a mere mili-tary barrier; it did not stop interaction between the agricultural and the nomadic cultures.

One important way to read Chinese history is to assess the overall impact of the massive internal migrations throughout Chinese history on China's cultural development. The sociologist of history would need to tie migration with cul-ture change, but view this tie with a long historical eyepiece. An and Wang note that during the Han and Wei dynasties, tribes north and west of the Yellow River region were beginning to move in, resulting in mixed dwellings and entangled everyday living among these ethnic minorities amid the Han people. By the end of the West Cheng Dynasty, political corruption among the government offi-cials resulted in sharp social contradictions within the Han society, a period called 'Five Barbarians and Sixteen Kingdoms'. To An and Wang, what appeared from the outside to be a monumental ethnic chaos among tribes was in fact an 'internal culture wrestling' among the plural communities them-selves. What classical historians called 'Five Barbarians Throwing the Han into Chaos' was in fact a 'booming collision' between the Han and the 'barbarian' cultures. The consequence was that the Han culture had incorporated from the 'barbarians', among others, an emphasis on athletics and martial arts, a forward-looking, adventuresome spirit, a sense of mutual aid in interpersonal relations and of equality among nationalities, as well as strivings for frugality and modesty—while slowly banishing from its culture core things such as cronyism, life styles of decadent materialism and prejudice against ethnic minorities. The famous Chinese historian Chen Yingue described this transformative process as the injection of a vigorous alien blood into a sickly Han body, shedding old habits and rebuilding new living forms. Chen (1996) and An and Wang (1992) attribute the cultural brilliance of the Tang dynasty to such a transformation as a result of the booming collision, an aftermath of 'blood transfusion'.

The massive internal migrations from the north and the west into the Yellow River region that began in the Early Qin and Qin-Han continued throughout the Sung, Yuen, Ming and Ching dynasties. The Mongolians and the Qiang tribes moved and spread themselves wide, residing in mixed neighbourhoods with the Han people.

On the other hand, during the Eastern Jin period, celebrated families like the Wangs, Xies, Lins and Chens moved from the Yellow River region down south. Due to wars, natural calamities and severe food shortages, tens of thousands of refugees headed south, and in turn provided the much needed labour and production technology for the development of what was south of the Yellow River, the Jiangnan. These massive southward migrations took place periodically after the Invasion of the Year of Jiangkang. It was also at this time that the famous poets from Shangtung like Li Qingzhao and Xen Qiji undertook their southward movements. In the subsequent 500 years of the Yuen, Ming and Ching dynasties, such population mobility led to a structural merging of the Yellow River culture of the north and the Yangtze River culture of the south. According to An and Wang, generations of Chinese historians believed that all these large-scale migrations throughout Chinese history led to the mixing and matching, interaction, competition, conflict and accommodation of peoples and cultures—while wishing and pushing for an eventual unification, a sort of synthesis. An and Wang insist that such a reading and fashioning of Chinese history has penetrated into the Chinese soul and the Chinese consciousness—thus, the distinct Chinese way of thinking and their conduct.

As three major cultural systems, the Pasture, Yellow River, and Yangtze River cultures engaged in thousands of years of interactions and exchange with each other, exerting a deep and massive influence that was necessarily reciprocal, two-way and mutual. As An and Wang so elegantly put it, the end result was such that 'I find myself in you, and you find yourself in me'—because one was continually interrogating, 'messing' the other up. Culture change is thus a long historical process of forgetting—and remembering—this or that part of oneself; it is of pick and choose, of mutating, transforming together simultaneously.

Third Narrative of Impact-Integration: Ethnic Chinese Rituals in Thailand

There is another site to empirically observe the process of encounters with difference, in this case in terms of what happens to the Chinese and the Thais in

Thai society. I shall examine the anthropology of two types of rituals, wedding and death, observed by the Chinese of Thailand. Amid a collection of essays I co-edited in *Alternate Identities*, Bao (2001) puts forth the thesis that the Sino-Thai ethnic identity is a function of how their choices of wedding symbols adapt from an eclectic juxtaposition of apparently unrelated symbols embedded in Thai Buddhism, Chinese Confucianism and Western consumerism. For the middle and upper class Sino-Thai, the wedding ceremony, as Bao points out, is the most important ritual in a person's life because it often involves a transfer of rights to a family business. The Sino-Thai make the tea ceremony, a Confucian practice, intelligible to the Thai though it also represents differences that set the Sino-Thai and Thai apart. When a Sino-Thai switches from a Thai Buddhist ritual to a Confucian tea ceremony, the two 'seemingly unrelated rituals' are integrated into a larger hierarchical structure in which the Thai male-dominated norm is complementary, not opposed, to the patrilineal family structure that the Sino-Thai have transplanted from China. This culture switching is made possible by the value complementarity of a gender-embedded hierarchical order shared by the Chinese and Thai cultures. A Sino-Thai, as Bao puts it, is a 'married daughter' of China, China being her natal home; she is also the 'daughter-in-law' of Thailand, her 'husband's home'. By reworking and remaking Chinese Confucianism and Thai Buddhism, the Sino-Thais reconstruct their own images and 'attempt to cultivate a *new generation* (my emphasis) according to their understanding of themselves and the world around them'. The Sino-Chinese are thus neither completely Chinese nor completely Thai. Their identity project has also been affected by a 'new modernity' in Thailand associated with consumerism, higher education and advanced technology (Blanc 1997).

In her essay on religious eclecticism among the Chinese descendents in Thailand, Hill (2001) stresses the syncretic tendencies inherent in the traditions of Chinese popular religion brought by Chinese immigrants into Thailand. She makes references to Welch (1967), a formidable scholar of Buddhism in China, who comments on Buddhist sects being 'closely interlocked' with Confucianism and Daoism—Chinese popular religion's trademark syncretism in its combination of elements from three discrete religions. Hill also cites Thompson (1993) who notes Chinese popular religion's propensity to absorb deities from diverse sources, including the 'canonization' of historical persons, personifications of natural phenomena and figures in Buddhist and Daoist narratives.

Based on her fieldwork in Chiang Mai in 1990, Hill (2001) comments on the incorporation of Thai Buddhist monks and some local Northern Thai death practices in the local Chinese funerals, hence the tendency of the Chinese popular religion in China and in immigrant Thailand to take on local colouring and local traditions. More significantly, Hill observes the lack of concern with ideological consistency among Chinese religion practitioners, at moments of adoption of Thai rituals, such as Thai merit making, into Chinese ones.

The Way Out

Can we reconcile such traditions with the discourses of modern philosophy and the social sciences? One common starting point is to look to how shifts in consciousness arising from cultural contact can allow emotional transference. The term sympathy refers to 'the capacity to apprehend the pain, suffering, or signs of negative emotions in man or animals and to respond to these with appropriate negative feelings' (Wispe 1968: 441). Sympathy is the apprehending of suffering—I try to feel your pain. As Wispe continues, 'the sorrow of the other person is grasped as his sorrow, and the sympathizer's sorrow is directed toward this fact' (Wispe 1968: 445). To feel sympathy is to experience real pain, which, to Cooley, connotes 'the sharing of any mental state that can be communicated'; it refers to a kind of communion, 'an entering into and sharing the mind of someone else' (Cooley 1902/1956: 102). Since society, as Cooley sees it, exists in the minds of men, sympathy, or what Cooley calls sympathetic understanding, or what Mead (1934) calls 'role taking', is the means by which one enters into another's mind, consciousness and, thus, eventually, society. Love provides one of the motives to do so.

The very antithesis of sympathy as conceptualized above is what William James (1977: 4) called 'a certain blindness in human beings', 'the blindness with which we are afflicted in regard to the feelings of creatures and people different from ourselves'. The others are too absorbed in their own 'vital secrets' to take an interest in ours—and so are we. This blindness is the walls we build, the blinds we hang in between two rooms, the veiled partitions to ensure we do not see into each other's heart; the nature of your conduct, including your pain, your suffering, is absolutely excluded from my apprehension and comprehension. The secret is 'vital' and is something each of us is deeply conscious of because it is the stuff of one's own self-consciousness, one's inner identity, but it is also where one seeks in vain for sympathy and an understanding of others (Park 1966). It is thus, as social psychology has taught us, an important source of collectivistic, pluralistic ignorance—no one in the end knows anybody else except oneself in total solitude. Everybody is busy building and rebuilding the walls of one's own imprisonment.

What is the way out? How does one cure oneself of this blindness? To make sure blinds don't blind. We all live in two worlds: the world of birth and the world of the sun—the little world of family in which the predominant order is intimate, personal and moral, and the great world of commerce and politics in which competition in the more sublimated form of conflict and rivalry prevails (Park 1966: 167–70). Under the modern conditions of life, we would want to escape from the warmth, security and isolation of the little world to participate more actively in the social life of the great world. They, thus, often necessarily encounter each other as strangers, painfully aware of the social distance that separates one from the other, which makes the struggle for existence all the more difficult. In the larger world, human relationships are symbiotic rather than social, but yet, ironically, to Park, conflicts because of different interests of the self and the other heighten self-consciousness in all during moments of interaction. Park the optimist has some kind things to say about the implications and consequences of such encounters in the great world. As he wrote, 'anything that intensifies self-consciousness and stimulates introspection inevitably brings to the surface and into clear consciousness, sentiments and attitudes that would otherwise escape rational criticism and interpretation. Otherwise they would probably, as the psychoanalysts tell us, continue in the "dark backgrounds of consciousness" (Park 1966: 175–6). Or, in what James calls 'vital secrets', the blindness of being human. Conflicts in encounters with difference sharpen consciousness and thus increase knowledge of the self and the other 'since the attitudes and sentiments which we find in ourselves we are able to appreciate and understand, no matter how indirectly expressed, when we find them in the minds of others' (Park 1966: 176). The deep human paradox is that it is as a result of the dialectics of conflict and contradiction that the understanding of both the self and the other is achieved. The authenticity of what I have discovered about myself is strengthened because I have found affirmation of a bit of myself in you, and you, in me—because of the interpenetration of minds and bodies through intentional scrutiny and imagination.

We have begun with an occasion of encounter with difference and, in the course of it, through competition and conflict, rediscovered our shared humanity. Living in this great world, which is my choice and intention, I must examine myself every day to discover the sources of my anger, humiliation and shame at the hands of others, knowing I can be the source of other's suffering and pain also.

Ancient Chinese philosophy is rather explicit, clear and insistent about what constitutes an ideal cosmic order in which humans locate themselves, which is embodied in the concept of *taihe*, or cosmic harmony. As an ideal cosmic order, *taihe* is realizable processually in four stages: Confucianists believe that the first moment begins with moral self-cultivation to achieve peace with oneself, which leads to the second moment of peace between the self and the others, followed by the third moment of harmony between humans and nature, and, finally, nature's own harmony and peace. Such a processual view of an ideal cosmic order stresses the importance of moral self-cultivation and acquisition of knowledge as the starting point, achievable by discipline and diligence.

However, in encounters with difference or differentness, interestingly, the first behavioural imperative, for Confucius, is explicitly to recognize and respect the difference between the self and the other, not to make one become the other through coercion or assimilation. Again, looking back to the thoughts of the ancient Chinese sages, the necessary discourse that will lead to self-knowledge is one that stresses the fact that 'turtles are without hair and rabbits have no horns'—as opposed to animals that have hair or horns. This juxtaposition of the self and the other by contrast, contributes to a strategic realization of what marks the self off, and peace with and in oneself. It is also the first moral injunction against the violence of hegemony, of making the other the same as the self, of 'sameing'. The Chinese word *he* in ancient usage could function as a verb—as in reconciling and reconciliating things or people that are different in order to achieve an order of harmony and peace, but never striving to make things become similar and one. To *he* is to allow for all things different to coexist, to be side by side with each other, to find ways to achieve an order in which things that are different interact, live and let live. Such interactions contribute to growth, new happenings, and development. '*He* leads to growth and newness; sameness, to decay and nothingness'. The ideal of the '*taihe* of tens of thousands of things' stresses diversity, coexistence, non-coercion, the absence of injury or harm to others, naturalness, spontaneity. The spirit is a spirit of things in their multiplicity, not oneness or unity. Metal, wood, water, fire and earth are five different elements, which, when combined and fused, engender the birth and growth of all matter and people. So Confucius states the point most succinctly, 'The gentleman strives for a peaceful order among things different; the petty man, a disharmonious, conflictual order among things similar'.

Among the motives of self-cultivation is an acquired personal capacity for understanding and thus sympathizing with things that are different. The modern Chinese philosopher is most explicit about such an attitude and competence when he thinks of ways for contemporary students of philosophy to attempt to read ancient Chinese texts—another exercise in dealing with difference. To read these texts, one must approach them like an artist would while attending to ancient Chinese watercolours. Truly to understand, one must let one's mind go wild and loose, to meditate, ponder and imagine that the reader and the author are in the same imagined context, such that one feels sympathy and empathy for the author, imagines what the author feels—arguably the only condition in which one should do one's reading and criticism of the texts. Or, in one expression, 'understand (the different) to feel sympathy (by imagination)' (Chen 1996)—a form of sympathy or sympathetic understanding that relies on a powerful imagination to cross the barriers of time and space as a breeding ground of difference and misunderstanding as well as dis-understanding. It is perhaps in the same way that such an imaginary conduct is imperative for us to make sense of ancient thoughts, and one strives to understand other forms of difference, be they ethnic, racial or sexual.

Conclusion

In this chapter I have alluded to the rather psychically and existentially threatening idea of difference as personified in the sociologist's imagination of the stranger, as well as their discriminatory treatment by the other in the city. In the mind of the sociologist and of the stranger, the city was and continues to be a public place that is hostile and alienating and sometimes indeed violent to things and beings that are strange. In the city, as in the modern-day shopping centre, The Festival Walk, in Kowloon Tong, Hong Kong, where multiple floors of long elongated pedestrian corridors dominate as the distinguishing architectural feature, (potential) consumers are eternally mobile objects who pass each other by, never converging, never connecting, never stopping. The city-state of Singapore feels like one huge shopping centre in which people, objects, images, messages, meanings, even waste, are moving at a frightening speed (see Urry 2000*a* on hypermobility). The city is alienation institutionalized, immortalized, fixed. At the individual, psychological level, the stranger experiences the torment of his denial by others in his mind, when cultures, civilizations, differences encounter each other outside him, 'objectively'—thus the dark side of cosmopolitan encounters. The cosmopolitan is in a seemingly unchanging condition of boundless loneliness, tentative about himself, frightened, afraid, nervous, stressed, self-conscious and intense. The Chicago School sociologists portrayed such personalities and their psyches with a visual and graphic intensity—and with the compassion and understanding of a poet—a feat rarely equalled in the history of sociological writing. However, competent social historians and social theorists are not content merely to stay at the level of the individual and of the mind, no matter how fascinating it promises to be. There is another side to these cosmopolitan encounters—at the historical and structural levels. Again, the Chicago School brand of urban sociology on the subject of ethnic or racial encounters, be it Park's race relations cycle and assimilation process, or Shibutani and Kwan's (1965) subsequent rendition of Park's ideas, give sociology a freshness, an optimism, a sparkle that found its re-expression in Femminella's eloquent and elegant ethnic dialectics. The analysis here is now focused on the mutual entanglement, the blooming collision, of two different cultures—a dialectics that eventually changes both groups, or at least the possibilities are all there.

In this chapter I have articulated three narratives of such mutual entanglement: the introduction of Buddhism from India into China; China's social history when read as moments and sites of culture contact because of the massive migration and population dispersal; and, in the contemporary era, the syncretism of wedding and burial rituals witnessed among the Chinese of Thailand. In all three narratives, the analytical gaze is on the unspectacular, practical, usual, everyday life fusion and hybridization that happens when groups share a neighbourhood, a history and memory based on simply living together and solving the practical problems of living that require a certain transcendence of group identities, important as they too are. As it happens, one culture sort of 'slips into' another culture, half forgetting itself and half changing the other;

'one is allowing oneself to be inhabited by the other while still recognizing the other' (Segato quoted in Canclini 2000). Anybody can be a cosmopolitan, anyone (van der Veer, Chapter 10, in this volume). Dialectically, one is no less than one, but more than a sum total of two.

In narratives of such cosmopolitan encounters, it is also important to stress the continuing salience of group difference itself. Difference or strangeness or unfamiliarity attracts because it offers something new; it makes the dialectics possible in the first place. Strangeness arouses and excites, not only in a sensual sense. Cosmopolitanism thus does not, and should not, absolve local attachments based on locality or region, because such attachments provide the individual, however cosmopolitan, with a spiritual anchor, thus the seemingly self-contradictory ideas of 'rooted cosmopolitanism' or the 'cosmopolitan patriot' (Appiah 1998), the local cosmopolitan, the Chinese cosmopolitan (Chan 1997) and so on. The global does not exclude the local. As James reminds us, the blindness in being human is a fountainhead of one's 'vital secrets' that energize, excite and motivate. Difference matters because it makes the person feel important and passionate. Or, as Hall (Chapter 2, this volume) puts it, family cultures support you as you leave them and you know it. That may well be the reason why we keep coming back to the family, at least in a metaphorical sense. Most people want both roots and routes, tunnels to the past and corridors to the future as a sensible articulation of the present—the past fused with the future as the eternal present, always receding to the background of the past, which stifles but comforts and consoles, but yet also pushing forward into the unknown future, which frightens but fascinates and excites.

A discourse on cosmopolitanism does not dispense with diversity and difference. Difference will and should stay. Difference must stay because it reminds us, as all good sociologists would know and insist, that there are many ways of doing one thing, or what is done in one way can be done in another way—the kind of artificiality that underlines Berger's (1963) fascinating, almost magical, world of makeability. Things can be done and redone, made, unmade and remade in a world of continuing enchantment and magic. The social world is a world of many turn-ons. Of course, diversity, difference or pluralism, as several writers in this volume insist, is not the same as cosmopolitanism or hybridization, though, I insist, thinking dialectically, the former *can* lead to the latter, a miraculous product of newness, of novelty born and reborn.

The humanities and the social sciences are forging forward to look for a language, a vocabulary, an imagery to conceive cosmopolitanism. As Calhoun (Chapter 7, in this volume) argues, our social imaginary of cosmopolitanism suffers a deficit, too thin and casual. My own earlier portrayal of the Chinese cosmopolitan provides such an alternative imaginary (Chan 1997). I sense a tinge of pessimism, a dark cloud, behind such a discursive search. But this search must go on because the future for a Kantian notion of a 'perpetual peace order' depends on it, singularly. As argued in this chapter, the cosmopolitanism idea is nothing new; it is found in the classical Chinese texts, in the many historical encounters of China's Han people with other ethnic groups from the north and the west, in the many everyday life strategies of generations of Chinese immigrants overseas coping with living with others culturally, in the social psychology and urban sociology of America in the 1920s, and onwards.

Yet as Nussbaum (1997a), the University of Chicago philosopher, reminds us, a cosmopolitan attitude is not a given; rather one must labour against the habits of 'mental blindness'. Indeed it is a lifelong, relentless labour at mental alertness. Thus Seneca asked himself at the end of every day why he was angry with being slighted—with being seated too low at a table and so forth (Nussbaum 1997a: 45). The Confucianist must be self-reflexive, three times a day. Confucius asks himself, 'Do I do to others what I don't want to be done to myself'? Would I exchange my condition with that of the stranger whom I have mistreated? How else does sympathy, empathy, role-taking come about if not through self-cultivation (Nussbaum 1997b; and Beck, Chapter 6, in this volume) and continuing moral education? The stoic philosophers, the Confucianists, the American sociologists and social psychologists in Chicago, as well as the contemporary philosophers, sociologists, anthropologists and poets, east and west, pose the same question and seem to advocate the same recipe in various guises, but without a guarantee: educating the mind by a language yet to be found, but which must be found or we shall remain speechless. Yet the task is an urgent one: to think about, design and put in place a cosmopolitan curriculum such that we will not mis-teach or dis-teach our children. Or should we say we should let our children teach us a thing or two?

The parent and child, man and woman, foreign and native, Chinese and non-Chinese, east and west, self and other, A and B, must come together, engage in dialogue and seek mutual understanding—both sides, now.[4] Not later, but now. The Classical Chinese philosopher would admonish us to 'know *and* act, now'—the two realms of being would thus become one. Is it utopian to join the poet Meena Alexander (1996): 'To be at home everywhere/in this moving world/as the Buddha taught'?

---

[4] Joni Mitchell's title of a 1974 popular ballad in America: 'I've looked at clouds from both sides now/from up and down, /I've looked at love from both sides now,/from give and take'.

13

Cosmopolitanism at the Local Level: The Development of Transnational Neighbourhoods

DANIEL HIEBERT

To set the scene for this chapter, I would like to begin at the micro-geography scale of the street I live on in Vancouver's Eastside (or, more precisely, the lane behind my street). My street is situated in a neighbourhood called Cedar Cottage, which for around 100 years has been an area of active immigrant reception, at first of new arrivals from the United Kingdom, then central, southern and Eastern Europe and, most recently, the Asian side of the Pacific Rim. According to the latest census (1996), 72 per cent of the residents of my part of Cedar Cottage are immigrants, 20 per cent having arrived in the last ten years. A large variety of national backgrounds are represented, including remnants of the earlier European migrations and, of course, many Asian-Canadians. In fact, just below 60 per cent are classified by the census as 'visible minorities', meaning that they are of non-Aboriginal, non-European descent. Of these, the bulk is of Chinese origin, from a number of countries that include China, Hong Kong, Singapore, Taiwan and Indonesia. Beyond the Chinese-Canadian population, there are still many, mainly older, Europeans, and new immigrants from various countries.

How does this diversity work in practice? This is a theme I wish to explore in detail below, but here I offer one vignette of neighbourhood life that speaks to the growing body of transnational literature, one that also reflects my personal background as a geographer. I shall call this 'towards a cosmopolitan ecology'. I mean ecology here in the straightforward sense of a particular regime of plant communities. On my lane, a great deal of neighbourly communication is focused around gardening (including, of course, the perennial subject of the weather). Members of the different cultural groups in the neighbourhood tend to grow the garden plants they grew up with in former countries, to, in effect, recreate familiar landscapes in their new residential setting.[1] Two particularly

---

[1] A number of researchers have noted this tendency, such as Gerda Wekerle in Canada and Susan Thompson in Australia (Thompson *et al.* 1999). Wekerle has collaborated with others to mount an exhibit on immigrant groups and their gardening practices in Toronto ('Growing cultures'), which opened in May 2000 at the Royal Ontario Museum (see: http://*www.rom.on.ca/news/releases/ public.php3?mediakey=bej80w3358*).

interesting things happen in this respect. First, in keeping with the literature on transnationalism, much of this activity contravenes the surveillance of the nation-state. To everyone outside the bureaucracy of Agriculture Canada, this will seem a rather paltry example of black marketeering, but several of my neighbours have told me that they routinely bring seeds from their homeland, secreted in their pockets as they pass through Canadian customs. Thus, there are non-sanctioned varieties of tomatoes on my lane that come from Calabria, varieties of mint from Vietnam, *bok choi* from China, and broad beans from Portugal. Second, gardeners from these different cultures exchange their seeds with one-another. For example, my neighbour who came to Canada from Italy has become a connoisseur of *bok choi*, and eagerly shares his tomatoes and basil with people who come from Asia. The end result is a new ecology on my lane, where plants from different corners of the world are brought into juxtaposition and (I am told by my biogeography colleague) selectively hybridize. Thus, a new micro-ecology, unlike any other on earth, is being created, one that has escaped the attention of the Canadian agricultural ministry—which would be horrified to learn of it—and that only exists because of a combination of frequent to-and-fro transnational movements and the everyday cosmopolitan behaviour of neighbours. I could, of course, build on this example by speaking of the recipes that are exchanged along with the seeds and garden produce, how another of my neighbours sells 'grey market' salmon that he catches on the Fraser River, and so on.

However, aside from adding yet another example—in this case ecological—to the vast literature on transnationalism, I use this vignette, together with more 'formal' research, to pose several questions about the lived experience of transnationalism and cosmopolitanism. First, what is the relationship between transnational lifestyles and cosmopolitan behaviour? How does cosmopolitanism arise at the micro-geographical scale of the neighbourhood? Who participates (and who does not) in cosmopolitan interaction? Finally, what does it mean to grow up in a cosmopolitan setting? Tentatively, I find that transnationalism and cosmopolitan behaviour are both uneven, differing between groups by gender and across generations. Further, while the evidence I can bring to bear on this question is limited, it appears that transnationalism and cosmopolitanism—two processes routinely celebrated by researchers and others who champion the effects of globalization—may not be complementary. In fact, in certain cases transnational lifestyles may actually inhibit cosmopolitanism.

Conceptual Beginnings

Before exploring these issues, two background comments are necessary. First, the bulk of the material I discuss in this chapter has emerged out of a large ongoing

research project, which is focused on understanding how the processes of immigrant settlement and integration differ in five distinct neighbourhood settings in
Greater Vancouver. The neighbourhoods in question range from East Vancouver,
a traditional settlement area, to distant suburbs that are playing a role in immigrant settlement for the first time. Seven researchers are conducting this community studies project,[2] and we are using a combination of methods to acquire
information. In this chapter, I explore material gathered from two phases of
the project, a series of fifteen focus groups, between two and four in each of the
neighbourhoods mentioned above, plus a set of detailed interviews that were conducted with families in East Vancouver (a large area of the city that includes
Cedar Cottage). The families in question are from several different cultural
groups, and we are interviewing them approximately every eighteen months over
the 1996–2002 period. There is a similar, though larger, project under way by
researchers in Montreal, concentrating on the development of multi-ethnic
neighbourhoods. I will also draw upon their work in the pages that follow.

Second, given the varied meanings associated with the increasingly popular
concepts of transnationalism and cosmopolitanism, I begin with a comment on
my use of these terms. By transnationalism, I refer to individuals who experience, and are attached to, two or more places simultaneously (Glick-Schiller
et al. 1992; Appadurai 1996). As a geographer, my training has always emphasized the long-term relationship between people and place that is sedimented
into distinctive, local landscapes. The process of hyper-mobility that lies behind
transnationalism undermines this traditional way of understanding the peo-
ple/place nexus. Instead, immigrant communities should be conceptualized as
'dense fields consisting of people, money, goods, and information that are constituted and maintained by migrants over time, across space, and through cir-
cuitry, which repeatedly cross borders' (Goldberg, quoted in Hyndman and
Walton-Roberts 1999: 6). According to this logic, national borders are 'spaces
of possibility' as well as spaces of control, and diasporic groups develop identities based on *movement* and connection across space (Ong 1999), rather than
intimate associations with specific places.

The term cosmopolitanism has been used more variably. In everyday language, the term is generally applied to places with a marked cultural diversity
(for example, 'x is a more cosmopolitan city than y'). Among researchers, cosmopolitanism is often equated with political internationalization, whether in

[2] The research team is comprised of Gillian Creese (Sociology, University of British Columbia),
Isabel Lowe Dyck (Medical Rehabilitation Sciences, University of British Columbia), Daniel Hiebert,
Audrey Kobayashi (Geography, Queens' University), David Ley (Geography, University of British
Columbia), Arlene Tigar McLaren (Sociology, Simon Fraser University) and Geraldine Pratt
(Geography, University of British Columbia). While I have written this chapter, we framed the research
project, collected information, and discussed our findings together. This chapter, therefore, represents a
joint effort despite its apparent single authorship.

the form of institutions such as the UN, or global protest movements (Kaldor 1996; Wainwright *et al.* 2000). Alternatively, many use cosmopolitan as an adjective to describe individuals who are well travelled and have learned to be comfortable in many cultural settings (Hannerz 1996; Robbins 1998*a*; Ong 1999). Ghassan Hage (1998) follows this line of thought, and portrays 'cosmopolites' as elites who pursue refined consumption and are 'open to all forms of otherness': just as important as his or her urban[e] nature, the cosmopolite is a *class* figure and a *white* person, capable of appreciating and consuming 'high quality' commodities and cultures, including 'ethnic' culture (Hage 1998: 201).

Their sense of citizenship is 'beyond' affiliations with local places or nation-states (Van Hear 1998; Cohen 1999; Urry 2000*b*). Craig Calhoun (Chapter 7, in this volume) makes a similar point, noting that this type of cosmopolitanism is frequently achieved by elites but rarely by others. Christopher Lasch (1995: 6) takes this argument furthest, asserting that cosmopolites feel no loyalty to particular places or polities, and live lives in which 'no commitments [are] required' (see also Rainer Bauböck's characterization, Chapter 8, in this volume, of the elite cosmopolitan as a 'nowhere man'). From this perspective, cosmopolites have much in common with transnationals, since both make use of the interstices between places.

I wish to retain aspects of these views, but emphasize a different dimension of cosmopolitanism. In particular, I think of cosmopolitanism as a way of living based on an 'openness to all forms of otherness', associated with an appreciation of, and interaction with, people from other cultural backgrounds. This lifestyle is exemplified in the vignette of my back lane, where men and women from different origins create a society where diversity is accepted and is rendered ordinary. I use the term not in the sense of an uncaring, disconnected elite, but as the capacity to interact across cultural lines. This perspective bears some resemblance to Leonie Sandercock's (1998) utopian view of *cosmopolis* as a place of a civic culture based on 'multiple publics', where people build 'bridges of cooperation across difference' (Sandercock 1998: 218), and also to Stuart Hall's concept of 'vernacular cosmopolitanism' and Steven Vertovec's characterization of cosmopolitanism as a 'practice' or 'habitus' (Chapter 1 and 2, in this volume). Using this logic, I prefer to equate cosmopolitanism with cultural 'outreach', with the everyday practices of hospitality (see Germain and Gagnon 2000) between people of different cultural backgrounds.

Cosmopolitanism, in this sense, can occur in several facets of everyday life, as I try to show in a rough way in Figure 13.1. Each row is related to a basic context of social life: the home and neighbourhood, work, consumption, and social interaction. The columns indicate the type and degree of cross-cultural interaction in each of these domains. For example, an individual might be of British origin, live in a neighbourhood dominated by British people, have only British friends and shop in British markets, consuming products associated with

FIGURE 13.1. Conceptualizing cosmopolitanism

setting	Interaction		
	Mono-cultural		Multicultural
	Dominant	Minority	
Neighbourhood production (work)			
Consumption			
Social interaction			

British culture. Similarly, an Indo-Canadian person might confine all of his or her interactions within a co-ethnic context. In contrast, some people live in multicultural neighbourhoods, spend their days in mixed-culture workplaces, interact socially with a variety of people, and consume a multicultural menu of products. Of course many people are not so easily classified, and interact in mono-cultural contexts in certain aspects of their lives (e.g. friendship networks) and cosmopolitan ones in other aspects (e.g. at work).

Individuals who fall into the first column, which in Canada would be those of European ancestry who keep to their own culture, are outside the frame of cosmopolitan behaviour and may in fact be constructing exclusionary barriers. Individuals in the second column are equally non-cosmopolitan, which may be the result of discrimination, choice or a combination of both. Most, though not all, people in this category suffer from a diminished opportunity. Those in the third column, especially those who consume multicultural products and services and who interact across cultures, are actively cosmopolitan.

Most theories of globalization and multiculturalism imply a sense of process, assuming that the dominant and minority cultures will become 'integrated', and that this process will be impeded if individuals live out their lives exclusively within the bounds of their cultural communities. At the individual scale, this means that people gradually move from the left or centre column of the table toward the right column, increasingly adopting cosmopolitan ways of life. Furthermore, we tend to assume that this is both a one-way process and that it is desirable: once individuals become cosmopolitan they do not return to mono-cultural patterns of interaction, and their lives are enriched by their experience of alternate cultures. As I will explain in more detail later, we should be wary of this logic.

Generally, transnationalism and cosmopolitanism are depicted as complimentary aspects of globalization, as twin outcomes of the movement of people from around the world into closer quarters, particularly in world cities. In fact, they

FIGURE 13.2. Examples of transnationalism and cosmopolitanism

Melting pot	Cedar Cottage
Gated suburb	Sojourners

appear to be used interchangeably by some writers. Yet, according to the definitions used in this chapter, the two terms refer to separate states/processes, as
seen in Figure 13.2.

Transnationalism and cosmopolitanism converge in certain kinds of multicultural settings (as in the vignette of everyday life in my back lane), but not in
all of them. We can find examples where neither occurs, such as in homogeneous societies with little inward or outward movement (for example
Newfoundland in Canada), or in exclusive residential subdivisions where
minorities are absent. But there are also many instances where only one or the
other exists. Labour migration, or sojourning, is a classic case where individuals move around the world in search of economic opportunity but do not interact much with the societies they enter. At the opposite end of the spectrum, the
American 'melting pot' ideology, where immigrants from many places settle
and interact but, critically, *become American* by embracing their new society
and detaching themselves from their old one, is an example of cosmopolitanism
without transnationalism.

Summarizing these general remarks, I emphasize these points: the experiences of transnationalism and cosmopolitanism are both uneven—they are
more fully realized in some places, and among some groups, than others;
transnationalism and cosmopolitanism do not necessarily occur together; and
we should adopt a critical stance to the frequently assumed belief that people
become increasingly cosmopolitan over time.

Transnationalism and Cosmopolitanism in Vancouver

Nearly 400 000 immigrants settled in metropolitan Vancouver during the
1990s, accounting for the lion's share of population growth over the decade. The
1996 census captured a snapshot view of the changing nature of Vancouver at a
particularly opportune time, the peak of Asian migration to the city (Hiebert
1999; Ley 1999). The census revealed a complex emerging social geography of
immigrant settlement, with several inner-city neighbourhoods populated
almost exclusively by immigrants (most of whom are non-European minorities), as well as a number of immigrant concentrations in the suburbs. These are
relatively new on the Vancouver scene and are challenging the long-held
assumptions about the difference between inner-city and suburban communities. The growing immigrant presence in suburbs is becoming widely reported

in the local media, and there is a strong tendency to associate particular groups and neighbourhoods (e.g., the suburban municipalities of Richmond with Chinese-Canadians; Surrey with Indo-Canadians; and North Vancouver with immigrants who have recently arrived from Iran). Significantly, however, nearly all parts of Vancouver—including the areas just mentioned—are characterized by ethnic diversity. The proportion of ESL (English as a second language) students in schools in mid-city and even some outer suburbs, for example, is frequently over half. Typically, one cultural group predominates in these areas, but there are always a number of other groups present. Many of Vancouver's neighbourhoods, then, both inner-city and suburb, are characterized by multicultural diversity. Most also house a mixture of recent immigrants and individuals born in Canada. The potential is high, therefore, for both transnational linkages and cosmopolitan systems of social interaction.

In the initial phase of immigrant settlement, the social interaction between immigrants and people outside their cultural community is minimal, and is mainly confined to the mechanics of finding work and shelter. Most immigrants to Vancouver are not fluent English speakers and this creates major obstacles inhibiting everyday interaction. In focus groups and family interviews, immigrants emphasized, repeatedly, the stress associated with this period of isolation from mainstream society. Few have sufficient experience of the 'host' society and the luxury of time needed to evaluate the reception they receive. Most rely on local in-group social institutions, and many are also nurtured by extensive transnational networks. Cosmopolitanism, in an active sense, occurs rarely given the struggle for survival and communication barriers.

Systems of in-group support become institutionalized into social, economic and political enclaves, especially for larger cultural groups. In Vancouver, the Chinese-origin population of nearly 300 000 is the extreme case, and individuals can live their entire lives in a Chinese milieu if they so choose. Similar, though not quite as extensive, enclaves have been developed by Vancouver's Indian and Persian communities (though, significantly, not by a number of other groups, notably from the Philippines, Latin America and African countries). Many of the immigrants surveyed for this chapter noted the double-sided nature of these enclaves, how they both help immigrants cope but also hinder their integration with mainstream society or, using different terms, impede their capacity for intercultural communication. For this reason, critics have charged that institutions such as the Richmond Chinese soccer league, or the separate Chinese commercial district that has emerged in Richmond (with around 50 'Asian theme malls'), fragment society.

However, there is also abundant evidence that immigrants are engaged in a process of integration. A South Asian woman living in Surrey, for example, speaks of the 'confidence of language' she has attained since coming to Canada, and how she feels increasingly comfortable with her new neighbours. A Latin

American teenager in East Vancouver noted that, while there is definite ethnic fragmentation in ESL classes, once students join the regular school system they mix readily with their classmates of different cultures. In fact, there was a general feeling throughout the focus groups and family interviews that children integrate quickly and build friendship networks that span cultural boundaries. When asked about her experience of integration, a Ugandan-born woman mused that she used to feel that Canadians were distant and obsessed with performing their jobs and other activities; however, as the pace of her life has increased, she realizes she has fallen into the same behavioural patterns and no longer feels culturally isolated. On the contrary, her family who come to visit from Uganda have begun to comment on *her* obsession with time.

Reflecting the classic predictions of 'assimilation' made nearly a century ago by sociologists at the University of Chicago, a large number of immigrants make deliberate choices to leave their cultural enclaves behind and embrace multicultural lifestyles. In general, when recent immigrants were asked in interviews where they would prefer to live in Greater Vancouver, they favoured multicultural neighbourhoods. Many have already exercised this choice. A woman born in Bolivia, for example, spoke of her decision to leave the major concentration of Hispanic people in Vancouver because she craved a quieter environment; another woman from El Salvador moved from the same area to ensure that her children would grow up in an English-speaking neighbourhood, believing that their long-term opportunities might be compromised if she stayed in her cultural enclave. My colleagues and I heard, over and over, criticisms from Chinese-origin immigrants that there are 'too many Chinese' in Richmond. Finally, a young Punjabi-origin woman commented unfavourably on the level of surveillance and corresponding lack of freedom in an ethnic enclave. As a female Indo-Canadian participant in the Surrey focus group put it:

That was a conscious effort to move into a multicultural neighbourhood and not just an Indo-Canadian neighbourhood, because there would have been a lot of other things being monitored in our neighbourhood: what time we left the house, came home and all that kind of stuff would have been a concern had we been living in an Indo-Canadian dominated neighbourhood.

How does the shift from in-group to cosmopolitan interaction—indeed cosmopolitan preference—occur? Almost everyone who was asked to consider this question gave some variation of the same answer: active multiculturalism depends, fundamentally, on the attitudes and behaviour of the 'host' society. As mentioned, immigrants spend little time thinking about the culture of reception when they first arrive, but reflect on this question more and more as time passes. They endorse many aspects of Canadian society, especially the substantial effort made by settlement NGOs on their behalf. They also appreciate the adjustments many institutions have made to introduce multilingual services (e.g., libraries, hospitals and the provision of counsellors to explain the workings of the educational system). A few of the families interviewed in the community studies project participated in the host programme (newly arrived families are matched with volunteers who are well established in Canada), for which they are grateful. Finally, some—certainly not all—speak of a welcoming environment, of day-to-day acts of hospitality offered by their new neighbours, of efforts to provide a sense of belonging.

The issues of reception and the sociability of multicultural neighbourhoods have been studied extensively in Montreal (Rose 1997; Archambault *et al.* 1999). Like Vancouver, immigrants there typically settle in multicultural areas, though the degree of suburbanization has been more modest in Montreal. Researchers have paid close attention to the types of social networks that emerge in these settings and, based on the ideas of Granovetter, distinguish between 'strong' (family, kin and friends) and 'weak' (acquaintances and neighbours who are not close friends) ties. They have found that immigrants who rely mainly on strong ties—those who have extensive in-group networks that often cross international boundaries—generally form closely-knit but isolated communities. In contrast, those with the most developed weak ties are more fully integrated (Chicoine *et al.* 1997). Groups with a combination of both types of social networks appear to adjust most readily to their new circumstances (Rose *et al.* 1998; Carrasco *et al.* 1999). Moreover, they have found that intergroup contact is self-perpetuating, that the more individuals from different cultural backgrounds interact, the more they develop an appreciation of other cultures and a tolerance for diversity (Joly 1996). In the light of these findings, Germain *et al.* (1995) and Germain and Gagnon (2000) highlight the importance of public space and municipal governments in facilitating local-scale 'cultures of hospitality' that reach out to immigrants, especially when the invitation for participation comes from the 'host' society in non-coercive ways. This type of hospitality fosters cosmopolitanism.

While, as mentioned, immigrants have made many complimentary remarks about their reception in Vancouver, and we can identify certain aspects of the hospitality that Germain and Gagnon advocate, they also voice a long list of concerns and criticisms. Above all, they express dismay over the way that credentials and experience obtained in their home countries are routinely disregarded when they attempt to find work in the Canadian labour market. The disappointment associated with finding work was raised in almost every focus group and family interview conducted as part of the community studies project. Nothing does more to foster a sense of Canada as a closed society. Moreover, the difficulty of finding appropriate work in Canada forces many immigrants to rely on their ethnic community and transnational networks for economic support; one immigrant stated, when speaking on this issue 'I'll have to keep coming and going and coming and going'. As Ley (2000) has discovered, it also lies behind the 'astronaut' phenomenon, where adults commute across the Pacific Ocean for work while their children stay in Vancouver.

There were other complaints, but none were as universally made. Many believe 'Canadians' are aloof, and think that immigrants who come from the global south are ill-equipped to thrive in an industrialized environment (e.g., we were told that immigrants from India are often asked if they had ever seen a computer before coming to Canada). Canadians are also criticized as uncaring in general, and oblivious to the immigrants living within their society. Some speak of subtle discrimination in everyday events, such as store clerks who smile politely at whites but treat minorities perfunctorily. A few told us that they experienced incidents of overt racism. As a man from Bangladesh put it, 'the general people, the people who are living in this country, apart from [those who administer] the immigration Canada are not very much happy about people like us coming in'. Immigrants living in areas with high numbers of minorities (Richmond and Surrey) are convinced that there is widespread white flight, and that this exodus creates more homogeneous residential spaces—and, of course, fewer opportunities for cosmopolitan engagement. A focus group was held with European-origin residents of the Kerrisdale-Oakridge neighbourhood, an upper middle-class area that has seen a rapid population turnover during the past 15–20 years. Unfortunately, some of these concerns appear to be well founded, as a few (though by no means all) participants noted that they feel increasingly isolated as the number of Chinese-origin residents increases, and that they see immigrants as 'pushy'. In this context at least, a degree of aloofness, of cultural distance, was expressed.

But one of the most consistent findings of both focus groups and family interviews was that immigrants reserve their most bitter criticisms for members of *other minority groups*. When asked about her experience of racism in public schools, a young woman from Guatemala living in East Vancouver commented that she felt little hostility from whites—there were almost none in her school—but that children who had already adjusted to Canada were dismissive, or worse, to those in ESL programmes. Another Latina complained that her recently arrived Polish co-workers treated non-whites with disdain. A Filipina, asked about relations between cultural groups in her office, said 'There's racism in our office. Yeah. Chinese against any culture'. While few made such categorical statements, many immigrants from groups with small numbers expressed resentment against the Chinese-origin community, who are perceived as receiving special accommodations in Vancouver due to their large population base and growing level of political participation.[3] Within the Chinese community, too, there is a notable degree of competition, sometimes friction, between the

---

[3] For example, pamphlets from the major political parties, City Hall, and many other institutions are routinely translated into Chinese but not Tagalog, Punjabi, Vietnamese, and so on.

Cantonese and Mandarin speakers. Finally, a number of immigrants did not raise specific criticisms of other groups, but questioned the legitimacy of the Canadian multicultural project, seeing little in common between their group and others. The man previously quoted, from Bangladesh (an East Vancouver focus group participant), stated this view the most forcefully: 'So that's basically my opinion, you know, not to have too many races all together side by side. You cannot mix them up, you know. It is very difficult, probably it is very, very, very difficult. It takes quite a while, you know. The children of children, you know, probably they'll be able to mix, not me, base generation'.

These comments raise a number of sensitive and important issues about the meaning of racism, and demonstrate that it is far more complex than simply the subordination of one undifferentiated group of 'others' by an equally homogeneous dominant population. In particular, they challenge the idea that we can draw a sharp boundary between 'hosts' and 'newcomers' in a society that receives large numbers of immigrants. In total, one out of every three residents of greater Vancouver was born outside Canada; in some neighbourhoods, the ratio is much higher, in a few cases virtually 100 per cent. In these places, the 'host society' is made up of immigrants who have been in Canada a little longer than those who have just arrived. Therefore, immigrants themselves are critical to the development of—or lack of—a culture of hospitality and cosmopolitan engagement.

Learning, and Unlearning, Cosmopolitanism

How do individuals shape their sense of identity in an increasingly diverse society? Returning to the conceptualization of cosmopolitanism introduced at the outset of this chapter, do individuals move steadily from in-group to cosmopolitan forms of interaction? What of second-generation immigrants raised in multicultural Vancouver, who have little experience of their parents' home countries? The evidence on these points reveals widely divergent patterns, with some appreciating culturally diverse workplaces, neighbourhoods and the general ethos of multiculturalism, and—as already noted—others expressing discomfort with diversity. In this final section of the chapter, I turn to examine statements made by young adults who either came to Canada as children or who were born in Canada shortly after their parents arrived in the country. So far, all of the young adults interviewed are from Indo-Canadian and Chinese-Canadian backgrounds, both relatively large groups characterized by a high degree of transnationalism and active immigrant settlement. In focus groups dedicated to exploring the experience of these young adults, they were asked to reminisce about their childhood. Most, nearly all in fact, grew up in neighbourhoods where they were part of small minority populations. In most cases, they adjusted to the dominant culture, which, twenty or so years ago, was European. In effect, they adopted the dominant culture, though this process was often fraught with anxiety and, inevitably, partial. Here are a few sample statements:

During the mid-1980s, ... between the ages of 7 and 12, I went through this big emotional backlash—this identity crisis about being Chinese. ... I seriously hated being Chinese. I would look at the television and quite honestly say, 'man, I wish I were white' (a) (Kerrisdale-Oakridge focus group participant, female, Chinese-Canadian).

I lived in Port Coquitlam from kindergarten to grade one. But I mean, when you are radically different, when you are the only person who is Chinese, I didn't think about myself as a Chinese person actually. You sort of look how everybody else is Caucasian and you don't even realize your own ethnicity is different until you look in the mirror (b) (Kerrisdale-Oakridge focus group participant, male, Chinese-Canadian).

All my friends were white and I thought of myself as white except when I got home I was Chinese (c) (Kerrisdale-Oakridge focus group participant, male, Chinese-Canadian).

When I grew up I had Caucasian friends, and you just never talked about Chinese things because they were Caucasian, obviously (d) (Richmond focus group participant, female, Chinese-Canadian).

During my elementary and high school I could say that I almost about never spoke Chinese other than inside of my home and I could almost say that I didn't have any Chinese friends (e) (Kerrisdale-Oakridge focus group participant, male, Chinese-Canadian).

The last three quotations indicate something almost universally stated by the Chinese-Canadians and Indo-Canadians who grew up a decade or two ago, as well as the children of the families in small cultural groups that we are currently interviewing. In these cases, children develop hybrid (at times confused) identities and intercultural friendship networks, though these processes can be unsettling. A young Latina woman was the most animated on this question, insisting that she should not be seen as one cultural type or another (in her terms, Spanish versus Canadian)—she saw both labels as simplifying a much more complex reality.

   Yet, just as the either/or approach to identity is unrealistic, so is the assumption that individuals who become cosmopolitan remain that way, that the development of a multicultural mode of behaviour is linear and irreversible. These experiences, for example, reveal that different outcomes are possible:

In elementary school I noticed that they had friends of all religions and ethnic[ities] but then as they matured they, like most adults, like to be with their own kinds and so they just sort of filter off and they're more attracted to whoever they have more in common with, I guess (Kerrisdale-Oakridge focus group participant, female, European origin).

Before I was totally into listening to Caucasian music—white music or whatever. Not involved in my culture at all. I wasn't participating in anything really. And then I guess, as my cousins came, the next—like you said—the new wave of immigrants, all they did was speak Punjabi language all the time. I picked up on a lot more words and they just totally got us involved into our own culture a lot, I think (Surrey focus group participant, male, Indo-Canadian).

I can speak Chinese. I can understand it all and yet, when I went to work I actually thought I wasn't Chinese. . . . The only time I'm reminded that I'm Chinese is when I got older and into Richmond now, and here there's all Chinese people, and then the reminder, of course, is that you really are Chinese (Richmond focus group participant, male, Chinese-Canadian).

These last two speakers indicate that their identity shifted in response to the large influx of new immigrants to Vancouver during the past few years. Actually, all the five individuals I quoted earlier went on to make similar points:

After that period the benefits were that there was a heightened awareness of my own sense of self and my sense in the community. I think of that entire growth of population, the biggest thing that I got out of it was that I identified myself as being Chinese, as a Chinese-Canadian. I no longer felt this hatred of being Chinese. I seriously hated being Chinese (a) (Kerrisdale-Oakridge focus group participant, female, Chinese-Canadian).

When I grew up I had Caucasian friends, and you just never talked about Chinese things because they were Caucasian, obviously. And the older I got, the closer I became with my Chinese background. . . . Friends from your own background become more important (d) (Richmond focus group participant, female, Chinese-Canadian).

During my elementary and high school, I could say that I almost about never spoke Chinese other than inside of my home and I could almost say that I didn't have any Chinese friends. But I notice that besides myself, I see a lot of Chinese people as they reach adulthood or when they are going through university there's a big change in their life. They start to look for their roots. That happened with me. Even first-year university I spoke all English, but now if you look at my friends, most of my friends are Chinese now. A lot of times I speak Chinese now (e) (Kerrisdale-Oakridge focus group participant, male, Chinese-Canadian).

These statements suggest a retreat from cosmopolitanism, or at least a different version of it. All of them—and they are representative of a much larger number—came to value their cultural background in new ways as they entered adulthood. A crucial phase in the life cycle became registered in a new mode of cultural interaction. This process of cultural reflection and re-evaluation occurred in conjunction with the entry of new immigrants, as stated, and a deepening degree of transnationalism. In fact, many spoke of a growing desire to visit, in some cases even to relocate to, Hong Kong. Several who had lost their Chinese or Punjabi language in an effort to conform, are relearning it. They are, in the process, challenging a view of cosmopolitanism as an end state, and also as the most desirable state.

Qualifications and Conclusions

It is tempting to end here, questioning the logic of globalization and the interpretation of multiculturalism as a unidirectional process. However, significant qualifications are in order in the light of the methodology behind this study. First, while the interviews and focus groups that form the background of this paper included some 150 immigrants and 1000 pages of transcripts, there are over 600 000 immigrants living in Greater Vancouver, and perhaps that number again are second-generation immigrants. Therefore, despite the fact that the methods of recruitment for this study were comprehensive, I can hardly claim that the material presented here is representative.

Second, I have reported everything in this chapter as a series of straightforward texts, with little thought to the many subtleties and potential difficulties involved in collecting and representing these 'data'. It is difficult to judge the effects of the particular structure of the focus groups and interviews reported here. Most of these sessions were comprised of white researchers and non-white participants. Bilingual and multilingual research assistants were frequently involved, but this was logistically possible only for the Chinese, Punjabi and Hispanic groups. Meetings between the researchers and subjects are inevitably performative events, where each side assumes certain roles. No doubt the uneven power relations involved in this project, between the academic researchers and recently arrived minority immigrants, had an impact on what we were, and were not, told. I vividly recall, for example, an interview in the living room of a couple who had come to Vancouver from Hong Kong. I conducted the meeting with the help of a Cantonese interpreter. At the end, as usual, I asked if the interviewees had anything else they would like to say. They turned to the translator and initiated, in Cantonese, an animated conversation about their experience of discrimination and its effect on their lives. They had said none of this to me, even though I had asked several questions related to the issue of prejudice. Also, the dynamics of focus groups with first- versus second-generation immigrants were completely different. In the former case, individuals treated the events formally, had to grope for words to make their points, and, in some cases, participants seemed uncomfortable. In the latter, conversation flowed freely and no one seemed to mind discussing sensitive issues of identity or their experiences as minorities. Clearly, there are important limitations to the chapter and the material lying behind it.

With these considerable caveats in mind, I was surprised in this research by the flux of identity and patterns of communication within and between immigrant communities, by how some immigrants become cosmopolitan, some stay within the boundaries of their group and some shift—back and forth—between these options. At times, as in my back lane, everyday hospitality extends between groups that each are linked into extensive transnational networks. In other cases, there appears to be a contradiction between the development of transnationalism and the intensity of intercultural communication. In a society that, at least officially, espouses multiculturalism, should we worry about the potential for transnational networks to fragment individuals into distinct, bounded cultural worlds? I am afraid the answer is, yes and no.

I take my cue here from Iris Marion Young's (1990, 1999) thoughtful work on the politics of difference, where she attempts to balance a commitment to diversity with a concern for exclusion. In advocating 'differentiated solidarity', Young maintains that societies must, on the one hand, allow groups the freedom to form residential concentrations and build in-group cultural institutions. Above all, she believes the dominant culture should keep a respectful distance from minorities, that it should exercise 'an openness to unassimilated otherness' (Young 1999) and allow multiple identities and hybridities to flourish. The flux of identity described in this chapter—especially the return to in-group social networks—therefore carries no negative connotations. On the other hand though, Young reminds us that ethnic solidarity, in all its forms, can yield exclusionary barriers. For example, if the Chinese-Canadians who spoke about the comfort of interacting with people from the same background begin to show a preference for Chinese-origin workers when they are in charge of hiring, or Chinese-origin tenants in their buildings, at some point a significant line is crossed. It makes little difference to a Filipina or Vietnamese immigrant, for example, if white or Chinese-origin employers or landlords exclude her—the end result is the same. From this point of view, it is important to maximize the frequency and intensity of interaction between groups, as Richard Sennett advocates (Chapter 4, in this volume), and to ensure that neighbourhoods in multicultural cities become 'spaces of shared responsibility' where no groups suffer exclusion.

The trick, as Young argues, is to reach a point where group solidarity can develop without the corollary of exclusion. In the Canadian context, the dominant population has not managed to achieve this state of affairs and, through time, has marginalized minorities. Arguably, though, the degree of openness is gradually increasing, especially as legal and institutional frameworks are being created to address discrimination and racism. Significantly, as minorities increasingly become hosts, with all of the power relations that such a turn of events implies, they take on the same responsibilities to extend fairness and hospitality, to newcomers—in effect, to be cosmopolitan. It is hoped that they will exercise these responsibilities more conscientiously than the dominant group has done!

IV

Practices of Cosmopolitanism

14

Not Universalists, Not Pluralists: The New Cosmopolitans Find Their Own Way

DAVID A. HOLLINGER

Within the past five years, a host of initiatives in critical and democratic theory have been launched under the old sign of cosmopolitanism. The symposium, 'Cosmopolitanism Then and Now' published in a recent issue of *Constellations* (March 2000) is but one of a flurry of relevant happenings in the quarterlies. *The Partisan Review* and *Dissent* printed ringing cosmopolitan manifestos from two continental theorists, Pascal Bruckner (1996: 242–4) and Ulrich Beck (Beck 1999a: 53–5), and the *American Literary History* published a state-of-the-art essay on cultural theory declaring that cosmopolitanism was the concept now replacing multiculturalism in the work of the most methodologically up to date and ideologically self-aware of literary scholars (Pattell 1999: 166–86). *Public Culture* has devoted an entire issue to cosmopolitanism (see Pollock *et al.* 2000). The movement has found strong voices in a number of disciplinary communities, as represented, for example, by Bruce Ackerman and Alexander Aleinikoff in law, Ross Posnock and Tobin Siebers in English, James Clifford and Paul Rabinow in anthropology, Seyla Benhabib and Mitchell Cohen in political science, Samuel Scheffler and Jeremy Waldron in philosophy, Prasenjit Duara and Malachai Hacohen in history and Amartya Sen in economics. On campuses, major cross-disciplinary conferences on the new cosmopolitanism have been held at Wisconsin, Stanford, Harvard and Illinois. Timothy Brennan's (1997) book, *At Home in the World*: *Cosmopolitanism Now*, is a sign of the times, as is G. Pascal Zachary's (2000b) *The Global Me: New Cosmopolitans and the Competitive Edge.* Among the most representative

This chapter was previously published in *Constellations* 8, 236–48 (2001). © Blackwell Publishers Ltd. Reproduced by kind permission.

I would like to acknowledge the stimulation provided by the students and faculty of the Department of Philosophy at The New School for Social Research, to whom an early version of this chapter was presented orally on 13 April, 2000. This chapter also reflects the influence of conversations during the last few years with my Berkeley colleagues Carol J. Clover, Robert C. Post, Samuel Scheffler and Yuri Slezkine.

artefacts of the movement are two collections, *Cosmopolitics*, edited by Pheng Cheah and Bruce Robbins (1998), and *For Love of Country*, in which 16 prominent intellectuals respond to a manifesto by the philosopher Martha Nussbaum (Cohen 1996).

Exactly why the new cosmopolitanism emerged with such force in the second half of the 1990s is an interesting question I will not try to answer here.[1] Instead, I want to attempt an analysis that seems to me is more urgently needed. I want to indicate the most prominent features of the new cosmopolitanism, and, at the risk of rendering the movement more unified than it is, to explain how it is marking out a distinctive doctrinal position between what I believe is best called the 'universalism' of Nussbaum and the 'pluralism' of Will Kymlicka. In so doing, I will call attention to the relevance of the case of the United States of America to the development of a cosmopolitanism that is responsive to contemporary global conditions.

One prominent feature of the new movement is the reticence of most of the discussants about the label, cosmopolitanism. This reticence is displayed in the frequency and earnestness with which its apparent adherents modify the naming noun with one or more of a remarkable string of adjectives. On my desk at one time recently, I had books and articles espousing vernacular cosmopolitanism, rooted cosmopolitanism, critical cosmopolitanism, comparative cosmopolitanism, national cosmopolitanism, discrepant cosmopolitanism, situated cosmopolitanism and actually existing cosmopolitanism. And that does not even count the highly significant use of the adjectival form of cosmopolitanism to modify other ideologically salient nouns in the same domain: one can find tracts for cosmopolitan patriotism, cosmopolitan nationalism, cosmopolitan democracy and cosmopolitan post-colonialism. The point of all this modifying is not to draw sharp distinctions between the contemporary wings of the movement. The different adjectives do not denote different schools, but different attempts to say pretty much the same thing in relation to the one, huge shadow over the new cosmopolitanism: the image of the old cosmopolitanism, or to put the point more sharply, the image of the cosmopolitanism associated with the Enlightenment.

The latter, it is often alleged, was insufficiently responsive to diversity, particularity, history, the masses of humankind, the realities of power and the need for politically viable solidarities.[2] And it is in response to this cluster of images

---

[1] Among the historical circumstances that have the most obviously helped to call forth this movement, to be sure, are (a) the dead ends reached by identity politics within the United States of America, (b) the destruction caused abroad by the ethno-religious nationalism in the wake of the end of the cold war and (c) the challenges to provincial orientations presented by the economic and technological processes that get called 'globalization'.

[2] I do not mean to endorse this view of the cosmopolitanism of the Enlightenment, or to accept the belief—so widespread today—that the cosmopolitanism of Enlightenment was monolithic. For a helpful corrective, see Pauline Kleingeld (1999: 505–24).

that the new cosmopolitans generate their modifying adjectives: the point of a rooted, situated, national, vernacular, critical, and so on, cosmopolitanism is to bring cosmopolitanism down to earth, to indicate that cosmopolitanism can deliver some of the goods ostensibly provided only by patriots, provincials, parochials, populists, tribalists and above all nationalists.

Nussbaum's exchange with her critics in *For Love of Country* is worth dwelling upon because it displays several of the tensions and uncertainties within the movement. The book opens with Nussbaum's sweeping call for an empathic identification with humanity as a whole. Concerned that the patriot-ism endorsed by Richard Rorty and Sheldon Hackney will give itself to jingo-ism, Nussbaum recommends the world-citizenship prophesied by the ancient stoic philosophers, by Kant and by the great Bengali savant, Rabindranath Tagore. Insisting that moral obligations know no borders, Nussbaum calls on everyone to embrace the worldwide community of human beings. Although she enters some modest caveats along the way to the effect that of course we will allocate our energies so that our children, our families and those close to us will get more of our own attention than will the species as a whole, it is the generally unmodified character of her cosmopolitanism that animates almost everything said by all of her sixteen critics. Indeed, Nussbaum is not among those who use any of the modifying adjectives to which I have referred. She is for cosmopol-itanism, unmodified, although, as I will argue below, her position is best repres-ented as 'universalist' (Nussbaum 1996: 3–17).

The subtitle of the Nussbaum-centred book, *Debating the Limits of Patriotism*, is misleading. On the contrary, what Nussbaum's critics debate are the limits of cosmopolitanism, and their chief tools are the various versions of patriotism. I believe it is fair to say that only two of Nussbaum's critics—the conservative historian Gertrude Himmelfarb and the Chicago legal scholar Michael McConnell—dissent significantly from what I will describe in a moment as the core position of the new cosmopolitanism, but these fourteen 'new cos-mopolitans'—including Robert Pinsky, Elaine Scarry, Amy Gutman, Benjamin Barber and Sissela Bok, among others—end up presenting themselves as crit-ics of cosmopolitanism because the latter has been defined, for the purposes of *For Love of Country*, by the polemically unmodified Nussbaum.

This truth about Nussbaum's critics—that they themselves are new cosmopolitans—becomes unavoidably clear when *For Love of Country* is read alongside the Cheah and Robbins collection, *Cosmopolitics*.[3] In the latter, the

---

[3] This volume is the most important single artefact of the movement. It contains a combination of new and reprinted essays by sixteen contributors, including Amanda Anderson, Benedict Anderson, Etienne Balibar, Bonnie Honig, Scott Malcolmson, Jonathan Ree and Richard Rorty. The two introductory essays by Robbins and Cheah are among the most helpful discussions of the new cosmopolitanism now in print. But see also Robbins's own collection (1999), and the lucid essay by Samuel Scheffler

modifiers hold sway, and the cosmopolitanism the modifiers espouse can easily accommodate Nussbaum's critics, one of whose contributions to *For Love of Country*, in a link both symbolic and substantive, is reprinted in *Cosmopolitics*. This is Appiah's much-discussed 'Cosmopolitan Patriots', perhaps the closest thing to a classic text yet generated by the new cosmopolitanism (Appiah 1996: 21–9; a much expanded version of this essay appears in Cheah and Robbins 1998: 617–39). What Appiah and the other cosmopoliticians, in the Cheah and Robbins collection and elsewhere, try to do is to connect the notion of a species-wide community to actual politics, to the complex of possibilities and restraints found on the ground.

What this means, among other things, is respecting the instincts to give a special treatment to those with whom one is intimately connected and by whom one is socially sustained, and respecting, further, the honest difficulties that even virtuous people have in achieving solidarity with persons they perceive as very different from themselves. It is out of respect for these instincts and honest difficulties that the new cosmopolitanism looks towards nation-states, as well as towards transnational organizations, as potential instruments for the support of the basic welfare and human rights of as wide a circle of humanity as can be reached. What makes the new cosmopolitanism cosmopolitan is its determination to maximize species-consciousness, to fashion tools for understanding and acting upon problems of a global scale, to diminish suffering regardless of colour, class, religion, sex and tribe. Yet, what makes the new cosmopolitanism new is its demurrer, if not its dissent, from Tagore's compelling aphorism, 'The gods of humanity shall appear in the ruins of the temple of the tribe'.

The claims of tribe and nation are not always products of hate, insist the new cosmopolitans. These claims are sometimes advanced as instrumental reactions to the inequities of the global capitalist economy and to the cultural hegemony of the North Atlantic West. The human need for solidarities smaller than the species, moreover, is primal. The drive for belonging is more than an atavism to be renounced by all mature selves, and it is not easily detached from politics. The challenge is to take a realistic account of the ethnos as well as of the species, and to assess existing and potential solidarities according to their capacity as viable instruments of democratic-egalitarian values.

The new cosmopolitanism begins by trying to keep in single focus at all times both a universalist insight that nationalists tend to deny, and a nationalist insight that universalists tend to deny. The universalist insight, which drives Nussbaum and her non-modified comrades, is that even the least blood-intensive and least

(1999: 255–76). Of particular value is Scheffler's distinction between cosmopolitanism 'about justice' and cosmopolitanism 'about culture and the self'. I have not employed that distinction here, but I believe it does illuminate different emphases within the movement. Harvey (2000) appeared too late for me to engage in this chapter.

chauvinistic of national solidarities threaten to inhibit any transnational project strong enough to serve the interests of a wider human population. The national-ist insight, which communitarians grasp better than some liberals do, is that the primal need for belonging is poorly satisfied by solidarities large enough to act effectively on challenges that are global in scope. This is the contradiction—the contradiction between the needs of the ethnos and the needs of the species—that the new cosmopolitanism faces, rather than ignores. This disposition to confront honestly the tragic contradiction at the heart of efforts to expand the circle of the we leads to all the modifying, to all the historicizing, the particu-larizing, the situating, to the engagements with states, constitutions and rules of law. This disposition also leads the new cosmopolitans, virtually, to abandon the term, 'universalist', which I just now invoked in relation to Nussbaum. For Nussbaum, universalism and cosmopolitanism are synonyms, but for most of the new cosmopolitans there is an important difference.

We can distinguish between a universalist will to find common ground and a cosmopolitan will to engage human diversity. For cosmopolitans, the diversity of humankind is a fact; for universalists it is a problem. Cosmopolitanism shares with universalism a suspicion of enclosures, but the cosmopolitan under-stands the necessity of enclosures in their capacity as contingent and provision-ally bounded domains in which people can form intimate and sustaining relationships, and can indeed create diversity. With a bow to Gayatri Spivak, we might call this 'strategic communitarianism'. Cosmopolitanism urges each individual and collective unit to absorb as much varied experience as it can, while retaining its capacity to achieve self-definition and to advance its own aims effectively. In this view, cosmopolitanism and universalism, while often united against common enemies are now best distinguished.

Another term the new cosmopolitans tend to avoid is pluralism. Cosmopolitanism and pluralism have often been united in the common cause of promoting tolerance and diversity. But cosmopolitanism is more liberal in style: it is more oriented to the individual, and expects individuals to be simul-taneously and importantly affiliated with a number of groups, including civic and religious communities, as well as with communities of descent. Pluralism is more conservative in style: it is oriented to the pre-existing group, and is likely to ascribe to each individual a primary identity within a single commun-ity of descent. Both the cosmopolitans and pluralists are advocates of diversity, but pluralists are more concerned to protect and perpetuate the cultures of groups that are already well established at whatever time the ideal of pluralism is invoked, while cosmopolitans are more inclined to encourage the voluntary formation of new communities of wider scope made possible by changing the historical circumstances and demographic mixtures. Cosmopolitans are spe-cialists in the creating of the new, while cautious about destroying the old; pluralists are specialists in the conservation of the old while cautious about creating the new. It is only by, thus, separating out cosmopolitanism from what we might call its universalist left and its pluralist right—limited as may be the utility of a left–right spectrum in this context—that the new cosmopolitanism comes into view.[4] 'A cosmopolitan perspective', as the French philosopher Michel Feher has put it succinctly, 'calls for a dynamic of mutual transformation, not for a static respect for each other's integrity or for a pledge to a universal notion of humanity' (Feher 1994: 276).[5]

If Nussbaum has emerged as the most visible voice to the 'universalist left' of new cosmopolitanism, the Canadian philosopher Will Kymlicka has emerged as the most visible voice to its 'pluralist right'. Kymlicka challenges the new cosmopolitans to engage strong claims for group rights within the frame of the civic solidarities generally favoured by the new cosmopolitans. Kymlicka's 'American Multiculturalism in the International Arena', an essay of 1998 published in *Dissent*, is worth scrutinizing here because it challenges the new cosmopolitanism on what is potentially its weakest ground: what does it have to say about nations other than the United States of America? That particular nation, which has been the primary focus of the new cosmopolitans, possesses both a highly individualistic constitutional tradition and a highly immigration-intensive demographic tradition. Kymlicka worries that the example of the United States of America, especially when understood in the cosmopolitan frame of reference of which he generously takes my book, *Postethnic America*, as 'the most sophisticated defence', is having a pernicious influence in the debates going on in countries that have 'national minorities' rather than simply 'immigrant groups' (Kymlicka 1998b: 74; see also Kymlicka 1995).

Kymlicka distinguishes sharply between these two types of groups. What Kymlicka calls a 'national minority' is a people 'involuntarily incorporated into a larger state, as a result of colonization, conquest or the ceding of territory from one imperial power to another'. His examples within the Western democracies include the Catalans and Basques in Spain, the Scots and the Welsh in the United Kingdom and the Quebecois and indigenous peoples in Canada. These national minorities, and others found in CEE often 'seek control over the language and curriculum of schooling in their region', and sometimes not only adopt an ideology of nationhood but demand some form of political autonomy short of secession, which is also a goal for some. Kymlicka complains that

---

[4] These paragraphs distinguishing between cosmopolitanism, universalism and pluralism draw upon earlier efforts I have made to sharpen these distinctions, especially in Hollinger (1995: 84–6; 1998: 92–4).

[5] Feher (1994: 276) adds that cosmopolitanism is not 'colour-blind or colour-bound', but 'colour-curious'. Feher's sense of cosmopolitanism is almost precisely that enunciated in 1916 by the American critic, Randolph Bourne (1916: 86–97).

nation-states trying to work out fair accommodations with these national minorities are not helped by American slogans such as 'individual rights, not group rights'. Indeed the ideology of civic as opposed to ethnic nationality has become a tool in the hands of majority nationalists who 'crush minority nationalism' and 'strip national minorities of their separate public institutions and rights of self-government'. He cites examples of the latter in Slovakia, Romania, Serbia and Russia. When it comes to countries dealing with immigrant groups, however, Kymlicka endorses 'Hollinger's account of a post-ethnic America' as 'a good model', from which 'countries like Austria and Belgium could learn a great deal' (Kymlicka 1998*b*: 74–75, 79).

Kymlicka is surely correct that the nation-states of CEE, and many of those in other parts of the world that fall outside the scope of Kymlicka's North-Atlantic focus, require a politics more complicated than a banning of group rights in the interests of an American-style individualism. Yet, on basic human rights grounds I worry more than Kymlicka does about the repression that can take place within the national minorities of which he is so protective. Territories dominated by Kymlicka's 'national minorities' often include other minorities, as is true in much of Balkan Europe. I do not doubt that a limited autonomy for territorially concentrated and culturally homogeneous minority groups in some nation-states will prove to be a better solution than forced assimilation or secession, but the less territorially concentrated and the less culturally homogeneous the group, the less justification for dismissing the experience of the United States of America as an irrelevant distraction. And in the great calculus of atrocities, the depredations committed in the name of civic nationality should not be considered in isolation from those committed in the name of ethnic integrity. The civic-inspired violence to which Kymlicka refers may have less to do with the ideal of civic nationality than with the lack of democratic political culture. The particular circumstances of each country will of course put practical limits on whatever balance emerges between the civic and ethnic principles for political community; here, as so often, Kymlicka's concerns are congruent with those of the new cosmopolitanism. But I am less willing than Kymlicka to relax the tension between the claims of the tribe and the claims of the human, and to carve out a political space in which the tribe simply rules. And I am less confident that the national minorities in democratic and non-democratic states fall into a class sufficiently unified to be theorized about in the same terms.

It is only when addressing cases within the democratic states of the North Atlantic west that Kymlicka develops his most pointed argument for group rights for national minorities. He declares that the minority nationalisms of Quebec, Scotland and Catalonia are all 'post-ethnic in Hollinger's sense'. He concedes that the Basque and Flemish nationalism, by contrast, are more racial in orientation. Kymlicka's evidence that Quebec displays 'just the sort of fluid hybridic multiculturalism . . . that Hollinger endorses' is worth quoting because it displays a turn in his argument on which I want to comment (Kymlicka 1998*b*: 77):

Quebec accepts immigrants from all over the world: it has roughly the same per capita rate of immigration as the United States.... The province administers its own immigration program, actively recruiting immigrants, most of whom are nonwhite. These immigrants are not only granted citizenship under relatively easy terms, but are encouraged by Quebec's own 'interculturalism' policy to interact with the members of other ethnic groups, to share their cultural heritage, and to participate in common public institutions.... Far from trying to preserve some sort of racial purity, Quebec nationalists are actively seeking people of other races, cultures, and faiths to join them, integrate with them, intermarry with them, and jointly help build a modern, pluralist, distinct (French-speaking) society in Quebec.

What I find remarkable about this account is its implication that Quebec is potentially a civic nation virtually identical to the United States of America, except that the official language is French instead of English. What, other than linguistic particularism, makes Quebec by Kymlicka's description here any more a national minority in Canada than New Jersey or Colorado is a national minority in the United States of America? Kymlicka is right to complain that I grouped Quebec unfairly with a number of other nationalist movements that are most ethno-racially exclusive. But the more we are asked to see Quebec as a proto-nation of immigrants, the less claim Quebec has, by Kymlicka's own standards, to standing as a national minority, and less salience his key example has to the general argument he seeks to advance.

Kymlicka comes close to recognizing this dilemma when he questions that the United States of America, Canada and Spain have any stronger claim to nationhood on liberal principles than do Catalonia, Puerto Rico and Quebec (Kymlicka 1998*b*: 78). The latter three entities are just as post-ethnic, just as liberal, as the first three. Whatever the truth in this claim, the posing of the question effectively transfers the location of the problem Kymlicka is addressing from the realm of 'national minorities' (on the destiny of which a post-ethnic perspective is ostensibly pernicious) to that of civic nations or proto-nations with immigrant populations (where a post-ethnic perspective is ostensibly sound). Hence, Kymlicka's case for group rights for national minorities as a matter of general liberal theory proves to be, here, largely a defence of Quebec as an exception to the pattern of illiberal traits that render minority nationalism problematic for liberals. Kymlicka tries to neutralize the liberal suspicion of the nationalism of national minorities by presenting this nationalism as an example of liberal nationalism, not of illiberal nationalism.

Yet, Kymlicka's representation of Quebec's nationalism as liberal and generous to non-French ethnics is somewhat undercut by the recent political events. An effort to change the name of a bridge to honour an Italian immigrant whose contributions to the province had rendered him a respected and much appreciated figure, was thwarted by crude ethnic chauvinism. The bridge carried the name of two French families. Although one of these families was honoured by 106 named streets, parks and other public places, and although the other of these families was honoured by 179 such named locations and arte- facts, the protests against the loss of this one French label were so ferocious that officials were obliged to drop the plan to change the bridge's name in honour of the Italian immigrant. Not a trace of the glorious French past can be erased to make room for anything new.[6]

Even if Kymlicka's representation of Quebec were to be accepted without qualification, his pivotal distinction, however, between national minorities and immigrant groups does not carry us very far once we leave Canada. Kymlicka admits with admirable candour that this distinction is of no help in understand- ing the situation of the blacks in the United States of America, but neither does this distinction precisely take account of the historical situation of the Mexican- Americans. This huge community of descent is overwhelmingly immigrant on Kymlicka's terms, but lives to a significant extent on land taken from Mexico by conquest in 1848. Kymlicka's terms are of limited value even in addressing the actual, demographic and social circumstances of Indians, who reported an out- marriage rate of about 60 per cent in the 1990 census.[7] Even in Europe, Kymlicka's distinction appears not to do as much analytic work as Kymlicka asks it to. Do the Tyrol Germans really have a better claim to group rights in Italy than do Turkish immigrants in Belgium or mixed-descent East Indians in the Netherlands? Are claims for group rights that might be advanced on behalf of the Muslim 'guest workers' of some western European nations, marginalized as they often are from the full benefits of citizenship, so much weaker than those advanced on behalf of the Scots in the United Kingdom, who have obtained considerable benefit from three centuries of union with England?

The Quebec question is the key to Kymlicka's perspective. Kymlicka's argu- ments are the strongest at every point when the needs and dilemmas of the peo- ples of Canada, not those of Europe or of Asia or even of the United States of America, are at issue. If Kymlicka is correct to warn against an uncritical appli- cation to the world of my analysis of the United States of America, I hope it is fair to warn against the taking of Quebec-preoccupied Canada as a basis for

---

[6] See 'On Ethnic Battlefield, the French Retake a Bridge', *New York Times*, 23 February 2000, A4.

[7] Although Kymlicka's approach to multiculturalism and nationalism offers little to the study of the United States of America, Kymlicka is right to complain that *Postethnic America* has almost nothing to say about the groups he calls 'national minorities' within the United States of America: Puerto Rico, Guam and the Indian tribes. He is also right to suppose that I neglected these cases because 'they are relat- ively peripheral, both geographically and numerically, in the American context'. He is right, further, to fear that a failure of Americans to recognize these anomalous cases within the United States of America might lead to a failure to appreciate that other civic nations, such as Canada, confront challenges more akin to dealing with the limited sovereignty of the Indian tribes than to dealing with the immigrant groups. For a helpful, informed discussion of the American Indian case, see Velie (1999: 191–205).

a liberal theory of group rights applicable to the world. Kymlicka's principles for political organization make the most sense in an ethno-racially and linguistically diverse polity in which there is a minimum of mixing and mingling. But to the extent that the species experiences more of the migrating, mixing and multiple identities taken by Zachary (2000*b*) and other observers of global change to be a major part of the global future, it follows that the demographically unruly case of the United States of America is worthy of the world's scrutiny.

The unruly character of the American demographic history is most visible in the extraordinary amount of ethno-racial mixing found in the United States of America. Descendants of the immigrant groups of the great European migration of 1880–1924 intermarried extensively with one another and with the descendants of old-stock Anglo-Protestants. Marriage and reproduction across the line dividing these European-Americans from non-European groups of Americans has sharply increased in recent years. The 1990 census revealed an out-marriage rate of about 35 per cent for Hispanics and of about 50 per cent for Asian Americans.[8] Yet more striking, when the United States of America is contrasted with most other national societies with a high rate of immigration, is how rapidly the descent communities are regarded as standard change. As recently as the Second World War, the Jews were widely regarded as a separate 'race' and out-married at single-digit rates, but less than fifty years later they out-married at about 50 per cent and had disappeared, for the purposes of most discussions of public policy, into a 'white' or 'European-American' group contrasted with four 'non-white' groups (African-Americans, Indians, Hispanics and Asian-Americans), one of which, the Hispanic, had extensive Indian as well as European genetic sources and was traditionally understood as a 'white' ethnic group.

This demographic experience of the United States of America suggests the relevance for liberal theory of a distinction quite different from the one drawn by Kymlicka between national minorities and immigrant groups. We might distinguish between two kinds of communities of descent within a polity: those that are *historically continuous and remain sharply separate from one another*, and those that are *temporary and overlapping*. This is a behavioural distinction, while Kymlicka's distinction between national minorities and immigrant groups is an abstract one based on the legal circumstances of the group's origin within a constitutional regime. The Flemish and the Walloons of Belgium fall clearly on one side of the behavioural distinction I have just drawn, as do the various ethno-linguistic groups of Switzerland and the numerous ethno-religious and ethno-linguistic groups of India and Indonesia. Most of the ethno-racial groups in the United States of America fall on the other side. I say 'most' because the African-American group has been more continuous and more sharply separate from other groups than have other communities of descent

---

[8] For an extensive study of the 1990 census, see Farley (1998: 85–128).

within the United States of America. African-Americans reported an out-marriage rate of only about 6 per cent in 1990, despite the obvious genetic fact that most of the 'black' people in the United States of America have a substantial white ancestry.

Yet, this somewhat special situation of the African-American group suggests the need for another distinction, within those descent communities that are historically continuous and largely separate. Some descent communities of that type maintain their continuity and their measure of separation *voluntarily*, while others do so because other groups force them to. No doubt many individual black people would continue to affirm the African-American identity even if given a chance to do otherwise, but the continuity and degree of separation of the black people as a group have been heavily influenced, historically, by the manifest refusal of the whites to accept black people as equals, by the outlawing of black–white marriages in many states until 1967, and by the 'one-drop rule' developed by the white slaveholders and segregationists. This distinction in agency, like the distinction in behaviour, can be pushed too far. A Quebecois can cease to speak French and assimilate into Anglo-Canada by intermarriage more easily than an Indian Tamil can become an Indian Sikh or an Israeli Jew can become an Israeli Arab; but Anglo-Canadian prejudice has made its exit from the Quebecois community of descent rather more complicated than a simple act of will. The blacks within the United States of America have had virtually no right of exit, while in other cases within the United States of America and beyond, opportunities to exit vary considerably from case to case.

This variation suggests that what I have been calling a distinction between the voluntary and the forced continuity of a descent community is best seen as a spectrum. So, too, might we get more out of the distinction between the temporary and overlapping, on the one hand, and the historically continuous and largely separate, on the other, if we view it, also, as a spectrum along which are distributed a number of different cases. Even Kymlicka's distinction between immigrant groups and national minorities is of the most value to liberal theory if construed, as Kymlicka himself sometimes does, as a spectrum of circumstances of a minority group's origin within a polity, ranging from voluntary immigration to involuntary incorporation. Here, Kymlicka's loaded adjective 'national' is best dropped because it carries the presumption that circumstances of origin confer proto-national status.[9] One might make a stronger case for group rights in the case of the blacks in the United States of America, who are not, according to Kymlicka, a 'national minority', than for the Scots in the United Kingdom, who are.

In assessing claims for group rights for a community of descent within a democratic society, then, theorists might want to consider how a given case is

---

[9] On the portentous consequences of characterizing a solidarity as 'national', see the classic analysis of David Potter (1962: 924–50).

positioned on three spectra. One is a spectrum of circumstances of origin within a polity, ranging from voluntary immigration to involuntary incorporation. A second is a spectrum of group behaviour over time, ranging from the historically continuous and largely separate to the temporary and overlapping. A third is a spectrum with greatest relevance to the historically continuous and largely separate descent communities; this third spectrum runs from the voluntary to the forced. These three American-inspired spectra do not encompass all of the issues, but, taken together, they carry us farther toward a framework for liberal theorizing about group rights around the world than does the Kymlickian, Quebec-inspired distinction between the national minorities and immigrant groups.

This is, emphatically, not to say that the United States of America should be construed as a model for the world. The historical particularity of each nation militates strongly against so arrogant a notion as a model to be followed, especially when the candidate for model status is the globe's most formidable military and economic power, and one whose record of interaction with the rest of the world is filled with an ignorant disregard of the histories of other peoples. But the case of the United States of America is of special interest because it is a world-historical domain in which one can observe the interaction of a great variety of communities of descent, and on terms that provide a modicum of hope for cosmopolitans.

The scrutiny of the United States of America is often cut off prematurely by the valid, but imperfectly contextualized complaint that the black–white colour line continues to mock the American ideals of ethno-racial equality, and that the European and Asian ethnic groups have got ahead in American society partly by defining themselves as 'not black'. The missing context is that many countries of the world experience ferocious antagonism, prejudice and discrimination *within* populations that are entirely white or entirely black. This is so, for example, in Northern Ireland and in Israel. The same is true in Rwanda, Nigeria and Kenya. To confront this context—and thereby to recognize the fact that the United States of America has been a historic engine of ethno-racial change— does not require falling into the trap of a mystical 'American exceptionalism', nor need it push one to banal and distracting debates over whether the moral 'glass' of the United States of America is 'half-empty or half-full', and whether anti-black racism is 'anomalous' or 'structural' to the public culture of the United States of America. The degree of mixing found in the United States of America is all the more important *because* it is so evidently and deeply marked by racism. If it were not, the ethno-racial mixing found there would be of less interest to societies that share racism with the United States of America. The United States of America has not fulfilled a cosmopolitan programme, but its history since the 1960s is at least a standing rebuke to those who would throw in the towel, and accept the conflicts between descent communities as inevitable and virtually eternal even within democratic nation-states organized on a civic principle of nationality.[10] The case of the United States of America can serve humbly to remind a heavily racialized world that even a society with a deeply racist past can incorporate individuals from a great variety of communities of descent on terms of considerable intimacy within a civic solidarity.[11]

This reminder is being carried to the world by the new cosmopolitan in a variety of voices, and in relation to a variety of different analyses of the 'globalization'. Some new cosmopolitans are much more suspicious than others of the world capitalist economy. The point about the new cosmopolitanism is not that its adherents have figured everything out, or that they are agreed upon everything. But in the twenty-first century the new cosmopolitans may be more positioned than universalists and pluralists to find and exploit whatever capacities historically situated human beings may have to form sustaining communities, while engaging problems that affect a human population larger than that embraced by those communities.

[10] 'Before proceeding too far down the path [Kymlicka recommends] toward the entrenchment of difference', notes Richard Wolin wisely, 'one should give the potential of a democratic public culture another try'. See Wolin's trenchant critique of Kymlicka in Wolin (1997: 135–41, especially 141).

[11] In this paragraph I draw on the language I have used in two other papers, Hollinger (1997: 559–69; 1999).

15

Interests and Identities in Cosmopolitan Politics

JOHN TOMLINSON

Cosmopolitanism is still largely a speculative discourse. The massive social and technological shifts that separate our world from that of the great cosmopolitan thinkers of the eighteenth and nineteenth centuries have not—in the crucial area of the cultural-political organization—increased our confidence a great deal. Writing about these issues can thus be a disconcerting business, as what begin as apparently plausible deductions and arguments soon seem to peter out into possibilities and conditionals, and the subjunctive mood comes to dominate. Part of the problem is in coming to terms with the political implications of the sheer complexity of globalization. David Aaronovitch (2000: 14) puts this with admirable journalistic clarity:

Paradoxically, we have lots more government than we had a hundred years ago. But it is less able to command the turning of the globe than once it was. Large corporations, the demands of electorates, the movements of money and markets and the trillions of individual decisions taken by the world's citizens every hour constrain our representatives who follow behind events, attempting to construct a political framework appropriate to the new circumstances.

This context at least is clear, but how to think beyond it, how to formulate plausible regulatory regimes for globalization in all its manifestations seems to defeat political theorists as much as politicians. This is more than simply the difficulty and risks of large-scale social speculation—what Anthony Giddens once called the 'perils of punditry'. There is a broader cultural uncertainty in the air surrounding our collective ability to control events. Not pessimism, but, it appears to me, a genuine *ambivalence*. In the end, as Aaronovitch says, it seems to come down to that most banal of speculatory reduction: 'Heads we manage it, tails we do not'.

It is within this context of radical uncertainty that we have to consider interventions like that of Charter 99's 'Charter for Global Democracy'. This initiative, launched on 24 October 1999—United Nations Day—set out a radical agenda for democratic global political and economic governance, which it aimed to lay before the September 2000 UN Millennium Assembly and Summit.

The Charter begins from the well-founded premise that a *de facto* 'world government' already exists in the form of powerful and exclusive elite institutions— 'G8 [Group of Eight leading industrial nations], OECD [Organization for Economic Cooperation and Development], the Bank of International Settlements, the World Bank, the IMF, the World Trade Organization'. Reinforced by high-level informal networks of government officials and alliances like NATO or the EU, and always open to influence from transnational capital, this web of unaccountable institutions forms the real regulatory framework for our current stage of global modernity. The Charter's most immediate call is therefore to make these agencies accountable to their effective 'constituency'—'the peoples of the world'. Addressing the representatives of the UN Millennium Assembly, it continues:

We call on you, therefore, to start the new century by initiating the process of democratic global governance following three fundamental principles:

- openness and accountability;
- environmental sustainability; and
- justice.

The first aim is to make the already existing processes of world administration and governance accountable. We want to know what decisions are being taken and why. We want the decision takers to know they are answerable to the public in every country that feels the breath of international bodies.

Then we want all decisions to be compatible with public criteria of environmental sustainability.

Finally, if most ambitiously, we want them to be compatible with the principles of human rights and justice, including social and economic justice. [1]

This is followed by a more detailed 12-point agenda based on reforming and expanding the scope and power of the UN as the core of a new institutional framework of democratic global governance. For instance, there are calls to reform the Security Council and to phase out the single country veto, to create mechanisms for the regulation of transnational corporations and financial institutions and to bring the WTO into the UN system, to create an annual Forum of Civil Society, to establish a permanent and directly recruited UN Rapid Reaction force to 'police gross violations of human rights', to 'accept compulsory jurisdiction of the International Court of Justice, the International Criminal Court and the UN Human Rights Committee', to establish a UN institution for Economic and Environmental Security and an International Environmental Court, to cancel Third World debt and to 'secure universal access to safe

---

[1] *www.Charter99.org* p. 2. All the following quotations from the Charter for Global Democracy are from this website.

drinking water, health care, housing, education, family planning, gender equality, sustainable development and economic opportunities'.

On any reckoning this is a hugely, many would say unrealistically, ambitious agenda. Its sponsors admit all the potential difficulties in its realization and even anticipate a sceptical reaction: 'If only we could work as one world, then we could solve the world's problems together. If only! Sometimes with a sigh, sometimes with contempt, these calls have been dismissed as impractical' (p. 1). Yet the charter stands as a deliberate political intervention, insisting on its practicality, couched within sober formulations, accompanied by action plans and timescales, advertised in the heavyweight broadsheet press and supported by serious-minded people—members of parliament, directors of international commissions, senior academics. It adduces a context of related initiatives—the Commission on Global Governance, the Rio Earth Summit, the Hague Agenda for Peace, along with a growing academic interest in policy in relation to globalization—as evidence of an international tide of opinion favourable to its radicalism. In short, despite all the obvious objections, it displays an apparently judicious confidence in the possibility of success.

Probing this confidence a little, we might decide that it is grounded rather more in faith than in calculation. An interesting piece of apparent web-site untidiness perhaps betrays this: 'The creation of democratic global governance may be complicated. But [it will be achieved because] the need for it is simple and urgent' (p. 3). The phrase in square brackets (omitted from the newspaper version) may simply be an accidentally overlooked editorial marking, but the parenthesis speaks eloquently of the ambivalence that must accompany such rhetorical deductions. And this brings us back to the context of ambivalence with which I began. For, can we genuinely, wholeheartedly react to this intervention in the same spirit that its rhetoric demands? However much we may approve and applaud its aims, however grim the prospect of a political culture in which such ambition does not find voice, still my guess is that a typical late-modern response will be equivocal, at best one of hope tempered by experience. Not necessarily pessimistic, but ambivalent, in two minds—heads or tails.

There are of course plenty of good reasons for a straightforward scepticism. These are generally well known, but it is worth picking out the most significant ones.

First, the intrinsic problems of reform of a body like the UN that has always existed as an international rather than a cosmopolitan institution—it has always been trapped within an uneasy and frequently disabling constitutional compromise between protecting national sovereignty and enabling collective security. And this is not to mention the vested interests of the internal hierarchy that maintains the Security Council, or the chronic crisis over funding, which reflects low levels of commitment from member states. Second, the increasing number of conflicts and human rights abuses arising as a consequence of the fragmentation of nation-states brought about by the globalization process—what Mary Kaldor (1999) calls 'new wars'—and the doubts one must have over the capacity of even a reformed UN to deal with these, given its intrinsic constitutional features, constraining intervention. Third, the undiminished power and structural embeddedness of the interests of global capital, seemingly inextricably meshed with the geopolitical interests of nation-states, and increasingly forming the backdrop to local cultural experience in which the agency is defined and exercised primarily within the sphere of consumption. Finally, and perhaps most intractably, is the problem of cultural, moral and political 'distance'. By this I mean the enduring pull of locality as a focus of cultural, moral and political solidarities in the face of the complex structural connectivity of globalization. 'Distance' here refers both to a gap, in certain cases, between the objective interests of local communities and the global commonweal, and more broadly to the remoteness, in terms of cultural experience and perception, of global issues and cosmopolitan outlook from the everyday life world of ordinary people. The problem can be rather glibly summarized in the implausibility of a regime of global as distinct from national and local taxation. But this instantiation scarcely does justice to the depth of the problem of the intersection of political interests with local cultural identities and moral horizons. Indeed, it could be argued that this cultural-phenomenological problem underpins many of the structural-institutional obstacles to the achievement of a progressive democratic cosmopolitanism.

Cultural Distance and Cultural Difference

This is the problem I want to probe in what follows. But to do so I am going to frame the problem in quite a different way, in the process taking some critical distance from the broadly liberal-democratic (albeit within this context, radical) cosmopolitanism of Charter 99. The approach I am going to consider involves the interpretation of cultural distance as cultural *difference*, and takes the defence of this difference as its orienting principle. Within this critical perspective cosmopolitanism appears as a more problematic project, and localism is seen as a virtue rather than an obstacle, 'parochial' not as inevitably a pejorative term.

From this vantage point, Charter 99's project might appear misconceived in principle. The key suspicion is over the issue of 'universalism', detectable, for example, in the address of the Charter to 'the peoples of the world' as a single undifferentiated constituency—at least implicitly so, since nowhere is the Charter's cosmopolitan rhetoric disturbed by the claims of a radical cultural pluralism. Equally suspicious, from this perspective, is the key concern with the assertion and protection of 'human rights', showing nowhere acknowledgement of the various cultural inflections of the idea (for instance as between Western liberal and Islamic versions).

Challenges to the universal pretensions of cosmopolitanism come, in fact, from a variety of sources generating greater and lesser degrees of persuasion. Least persuasive, perhaps, is the simple, formal relativism, often associated with postmodern positions, in which universal propositions are *automatically* rejected as contravening some supposed law of ineluctable and irreconcilable cultural plurality. Such thinking, erected around formal, quasi-philosophical categories of universality and difference, and curiously blind to the ubiquitous commerce between real cultural formations, seems to me to pose, on its own account, merely a weak scholastic challenge to cosmopolitan projects. It can also be, as Terry Eagleton argues, rather rigidly un-pluralist in its critical strategy (Eagleton 1996: 25–6):

Postmodern theory often operates with quite rigid binary oppositions, with 'difference', 'plurality' and allied terms lined up bravely on one side of the theoretical fence as unequivocally positive, and whatever their antitheses might be (unity, identity, totality, universality) ranged balefully on the other. Before battle has been joined, these more disreputable-looking conceptual warriors have usually been subtly got at—tampered with, disabled or travestied in some way, so that the victory of the angelic forces is well-nigh assured.

Beyond this formalist and inherently censorious theoretical sensibility, however, a range of more convincing critical positions associates the particular claims to the universality of Western culture with the West's political-economic dominance and cultural hegemony.

A key theme here is the legacy of the European Enlightenment and its claims to universal rationality, a hubris the political philosopher John Gray (1997: 158, 160), for example, counts as, 'one of the . . . most dangerous aspects of the western intellectual tradition' and which leads him to reject in principle, 'the left project of universal emancipation in a cosmopolitan civilization'. Gray, along with other critics of the Enlightenment legacy, tends to associate universalist thinking particularly with the West, and thus to find intrinsic fault in the idea itself. But of course other cultures have been equally prone to universalizing thought. It is the West's vigorous assertion of its *particular* universalizing projects—for instance in the claims of liberalism as an all-embracing political philosophy—that is the problem. As Clifford Geertz (quoted in Rorty 1999: 271) argues, this

has brought it into open conflict with other universalisms with similar intent, most notably with that set forth by a revenant Islam, and with a large number of alternative versions of the good, the right and the indubitable, Japanese, Indian, African, Singaporean, to which it looks like just one more attempt to impose Western views on the rest of the world—the continuation of colonialism by other means.

The prime objection is therefore not to universalism in principle (which it can be argued is a feature of the many diverse cultures that the difference theory speaks in the name of) but of a vicious form of universalizing discourse, circulating in hegemonic cultures, in which a power play *disguises* itself as a valid ethical-political principle—universalism as a sort of 'masquerade' (Tomlinson 1999).

Critique along this line can move beyond a generalized suspicion of Western cultures, and the ritual parading of their past colonial guilt, to the identification of specific contemporary instances relevant to the sort of cosmopolitan project we are considering. Ulrich Beck, for instance, in his 'Cosmopolitan Manifesto' (1998) points out the risks that, 'a "cosmopolitan façade" arises which legitimises western military intervention. . . . Subordination of weak states to the institutions of "global governance" opens up space for power strategies disguised as humanitarian intervention' (Beck 1998: 29).

The most obvious recent instance that suggests itself here—the case of the NATO intervention in Kosovo in 1999—is instructive in its moral complexity. For this was an action that was, throughout, presented within the liberal-democratic consensus of the West as a clear-cut humanitarian intervention on behalf of the beleaguered Kosovo Albanians. Though clearly quite a different case from, for example, the Gulf War, in which the material and strategic interests of the NATO members were manifest, nevertheless many—presumably including the supporters of Charter 99—questioned the nature of the intervention. For it was clear that NATO's action was not the outcome of a democratically achieved resolution of all the world powers, much less of all the world's peoples. The suspicion of a Western power play was thus not so much a suspicion of some concealed deep-strategic motivation, as a sense that 'the West' (and here read, particularly, the United States of America) once again was assuming and asserting its self-appointed role of the independent guardian of human rights.

The case of Kosovo is a prime example of the sort of conflict that Charter 99 would seek to bring within the domain of governance of a reformed and empowered UN. But now we can see that the attitude of ambivalence towards the *practical* prospects of cosmopolitanism that I described earlier is here matched with a *moral* ambivalence. This is because, even were its proposed institutional reforms able to free a project of global governance from any blemish of concealed power strategies, moral doubt would remain over its universalizing, regulatory (in particular, interventionist) thrust. On the one hand, the case for intervention in Kosovo seemed compelling, judged on the universalizing criteria of the defence of the human rights of the Albanians; on the other, the claims of 'difference' (in embedded local interests, in cultural assumptions), respect for local autonomy on both sides, and a sense of the sheer historical complexity of the situation combined to create qualms about interference.

This at any rate is how the issue struck me, and many of those I spoke to at the time: ambivalence—vacillating between two sets of convictions. For, we simply do not have a way of hierarchizing the claims of a universalizing moral-ity and a respect for localism. And this, of course is the dilemma. We seem to have sets of strong rational principles pulling in different directions—human rights or cultural difference? We do not really know which flag to go and stand beside because in most cases there seem good reasons to stand beside both. At the heart of the cultural-political problems posed by cosmopolitan projects, then, lies what Amanda Anderson has nicely described as the 'divided legacies of modernity'—the problem of 'how we might best combine the critique of par-tial or false universals with the pursuit of those emancipatory ideals associated with traditional universalism' (Anderson 1998: 265).

This same moral ambivalence surrounds many issues brought to us as a result of the cultural compression of globalizing forces. Should we be morally out-raged at the denial of fundamental rights (e.g., the right to education or to pro-fessional occupation outside the home) to women in Afghanistan under the Taliban regime? Or is this to mistake, as Geertz warns, one set of (Western, liberal) moral priorities for universal ones? More seriously, is it to slip towards sheer anti-Islamic prejudice? These are familiar and, perhaps, exasperating moral dilemmas. However our response to them is, I think, crucial for any viable cosmopolitan project. We cannot, practically, let them simply remain as perplexing, disabling double binds; but nor should we be tempted simply to opt, out of moral intuition or weight of sympathy, for one principle. If we insist that there is no clear moral higher ground to occupy here, that there is right in both positions, we have to find modes of moral and practical-political response that preserve both.

What this might mean, for example, in the case of attitudes towards the Taliban regime, is respect for the interpretation of Islamic principles that the regime represents, alongside an equal respect and concern for the culture—the lived experience—of the educated, professional urban women of Kabul who have been, apparently, accidentally trapped within the political dispensa-tion of this community. The 'clash of cultures' that this represents is thus not best seen as one of a philosophical principle between an enlightened West (which somehow 'adopts' the Kabul women as nominal citizens of global modernity) and an anachronistic, pre-modern, Islamic fundamentalism. Rather, it should be seen as a clash in real social time–space between two sorts of localism, in which differences between, for example, rural and urban cultural experience figure as much as religious interpretations of how life should be lived. Seen in this way, the rights of the women of Kabul do not have to be argued for in terms of universal human rights (likely to be rejected as a Western cultural imposition) but, in a certain sense, as *local* cultural rights: the right to live their lives according to (however historically recently) established practice. These clashes between different localisms need ultimately to be negotiated and resolved at the local level. In order to be effective, cosmopolitanism cannot stand upon universal abstractions but always needs a mode of local articulation. The question remains whether any regime of global governance can be constructed so as to allow this.

Universalism or Difference

One way of pursuing this question is to think in more depth about the general compatibility of positions that maintain the importance of locality/difference in moral/political terms with the regulatory, 'interventionist' stance of projects of global governance. There is a favourable theoretical context for this in what may be regarded as a certain recent discovery of common ground between (at least some) defenders of universalism and of 'difference' (Anderson 1998; Appiah 1998).

For example, Mary Kaldor's recent work (1999) in some senses exemplifies the humanist, ethical interventionism of what might be called 'universalizing cosmopolitanism', close in spirit to the project of Charter 99. She is on the side of 'those who support cosmopolitan civic values, who favour openness, toleration and participation' as against 'those who are tied to particularist, exclusivist, often collectivist political positions' (Kaldor 1999: 147). What this comes down to in direct policy terms is the advocacy of international intervention—'cosmopolitan peacekeeping'—in wars like those fought in the Balkans. Kaldor sees such intervention, directed specifically towards, and legitimated by, the protection of universal human rights, as the responsibility of a global community— perhaps organized along the sort of federal lines envisaged in Kant's famous cosmopolitan politics (Kant 1991). However, Kaldor is also sensitive to the claims of locality and difference. She not only accepts as legitimate the defence of local cultural rights, but also goes on to define cosmopolitanism as involving 'a celebration of the diversity of global identities, acceptance and indeed enthusiasm for multiple overlapping identities' (Kaldor 1999: 88). If pressed in terms of her specific policy commitments, Kaldor might well declare herself of the universalizing camp; nevertheless, the recognition of the claims of pluralism is clear. A discourse of balance and accommodation of principles, rather than of sharp antitheses is established.

A parallel shift can be detected, as it were, from the other pole of cosmopolitan thinking—what we might call its 'pluralizing' branch. Here Richard Rorty's pragmatism can be seen as in some ways the epitome of a philosophically consistent pluralism. Yet, Rorty has famously declared himself to be a subscriber to the idea of a culture of human rights (Rorty 1998), albeit a culture that he denies has any foundation in abstract transcultural universals such as the notion of a universal human nature (Geras 1995). In his most recent writing, Rorty (1999) takes his distance, at least as emphatically as Eagleton, from 'a mindless and stupid cultural relativism' that some postmodernists feel drawn to by the combination of the rejection of 'grand narratives' and a formulaic partisanship towards *any* non-hegemonic culture: 'the idea that any fool thing that calls itself culture is worthy of respect' (Rorty 1999: 276). The implication is that a rigorous pluralism, while rejecting ahistorical abstract universalist notions of Enlightenment 'reason' can, none the less, find rational means to distinguish between better and worse cultural/political developments. As Rorty (1999: 275) puts it:

We have learned quite a lot, in the course of the past two centuries, about how races and religions can live in comity with one another. If we forget these lessons we can reasonably be called irrational. It makes good pragmatic and pluralist sense to say that the nations of the world are being irrational in not creating a world government to which they should surrender their sovereignty and their nuclear warheads, that the Germans were being irrational in accepting Hitler's suggestion that they expropriate their Jewish neighbours, and that Serbian peasants were being irrational in accepting Milosevic's suggestion that they loot and rape neighbours with whom they had been living peacefully for 50 years.

Whatever the problems with his philosophical pragmatism overall—problems that might be summarized in his rhetorical use of the term 'we'—Rorty, it seems to me, makes a significant pragmatic point here. This is that a rejection of abstract universalism need not fetch up in a disabling stance of ethical-political abstention; that we indeed have a responsibility, in certain cases, to judge and, where (a culturally and historically sensitive) rationality compels, even to 'intervene'. The distance between Rorty's pragmatist pluralism and Kaldor's ethical interventionism does not then seem quite so large—maybe more a question about the conditions, forms and limits of intervention than matters of absolute principle.

As a third example of accommodation across the theoretical terrain of cosmopolitanism I would cite Zygmunt Bauman's (1999) reflections on 'recalling universalism from exile'. Bauman's sociology has generally been associated with postmodernism—certainly pluralist in spirit—though always with a hermeneutically sensitive 'ethical-humanist' strand that retains a sense of the 'universal' as at least an honourable aspiration, abused in practice and overwhelmed by the sheer contingent impact of globalizing forces (Bauman 1995: 24). His recent recuperation of the idea, explicitly denies that 'universality is the enemy of difference' or that its pursuit involves 'the smothering of cultural polyvalence or the pressure to reach cultural consensus'. For Bauman, universality represents a species-wide communicational capacity to achieve mutual understanding, in Wittgenstein's sense of ' "knowing how to go on"—to cope with the task of sorting out right, adequate or passable responses to each other's moves'. The virtue of universality is thus the essentially pragmatic one of allowing a 'conversation' across domains of cultural difference—between cultures 'that have a right to go on differently' and thus 'without recourse to already shared meanings and agreed interpretation'. This sort of cosmopolitan conversation is, Bauman argues, 'the sole alternative to blind, elemental, erratic, uncontrolled, divisive and polarizing forces of globalization' (Bauman 1999: 202).

Each of these examples demonstrates, in different ways, attempts to think beyond the stark opposition between universalism and difference. None offers, so far as I can see, any miraculous theoretical transcendence of these two sets of moral/political claims. But what they do suggest is a climate of thought in which neither claim is dismissed out of hand, and some attempt is made—however tentative or problematic—to reconcile them. It is within this context that I want to approach my final theoretical example, the recent work of Michael Walzer.

Reconciling Universalism and Difference

Difference is, as Walzer says, his 'major theme and abiding interest'. And yet his book *Thick and Thin* is an attempt to 'endorse the politics of difference and at the same time, to describe and defend a certain sort of universalism' (Walzer 1994*a*: x). What motivates this is Walzer's view of 'the necessary character of any human society: universal because it is human, particular because it is a society' (Walzer 1994*a*: 8).

He approaches this task, I think elegantly, by deploying the metaphor of cultural 'thickness' derived from Geertz (1973) to represent the local, context-laden, particular provenance of *all* moral outlooks and principles: 'morality is thick from the beginning, culturally integrated, fully resonant' (Walzer 1994*a*: 4). This anthropological insight is, however, as Walzer says, quite at odds with the dominant philosophical (and also commonplace) idea that cultures somehow arrive at different moral outlooks by a process of adaptation or elaboration of a few core common precepts: 'They start thin as it were and thicken with age, as if in accordance with our deepest intuition about what it means to develop and mature'. But this common intuition is wrong: difference in moral discourse runs, like the words in Blackpool rock, all the way through.

What this pluralist account of morality suggests is that universalism, as a sort of moral foundationalism, must be mistaken. However, it does not mean that there can be no sort of 'universal' moral discourse whatever. Walzer's point is that universal positions must be *derived* from difference—from local, culturally thick moral narratives—as, as it were, 'thin' distillates. Universal propositions are therefore like glimpses of recognition across cultural difference: they are 'morally minimalist' in the sense that we can recognize—in terms like 'truth' and 'justice'—a thin, stripped down version of the local, context-determined 'moral maximalist' version proper to our own culture. The hope of solidarity comes, for Walzer, in instances of this 'minimalist' recognition of our own moral convictions in the moral claims of others. In the image of a protest march in Prague that runs through his account, we recognize minimalist moral terms like 'truth' and 'justice' inscribed on the banners of the marchers and, 'imaginatively join the march' (Walzer 1994a: 7). But the point is that we can never do more than vicariously participate: we are not discovering solidarity in some core abstract values here; we are always catching 'thin and intense' references to our own maximalist context which remains, in all its peculiarity and complexity, the only substantive morality that we have available as a reference.

This of course radically restricts the critical force of universalism. Moral minimalism is not derived from abstract universals, but neither, Walzer insists, can it be made to be morally or politically foundational. Minimalist moral recognition cannot be 'built upon' to establish a cross-cultural edifice of binding universal judgement. It provides, at best, a temporary structure of solidarity: 'It is a jerry-built, ramshackle affair, as hastily put together as the signs for the Prague march' (Walzer 1994a: 17).

Walzer, it might be argued, reconciles the claims of universalism and of difference by giving the barest of attention to the former—this indeed seems implicit in the logic of moral minimalism. And so, we might ask, what sort of a universalism is it that cannot ever be foundational, that is only to be achieved, *ad hoc*, in fleeting moments of contingent outline agreement, that constantly collapses back into the thickness of parochial context, that cannot ever be pressed into any lasting regulatory framework? For there seems little prospect of Walzer's thin morality generating anything like the regulatory institutions envisaged in Charter 99's project. Indeed, Walzer is clear that 'thin or minimalist reasons . . . can't be made to generate an alternative totality—the empire of reason, say. . . . Moral minimalism, while reasonable enough and universal enough, has no imperial tendencies; it doesn't aspire to global rule' (Walzer 1994a: 64). Not even when 'global rule' is conceived, within the liberal-democratic voice that eschews imperialism but clings to the idea of rational regulation, as 'global governance'.

Against a politics of universal regulation (implying a degree of cultural convergence) institutionalized as global governance, Walzer offers a politics of divergent coexistence, predicted on the thin principle of self-determination (Walzer 1994a: 67 ff.) and the development of appropriate regimes of toleration (Walzer 1997). And, if pressed by more ambitious cosmopolitans, my guess is that he would defend this modest politics as the more practical. For example, to take again the case of Kosovo, Walzer might well argue that the present situation there illustrates perfectly the impossible ambitions of global governance. As the UN forces struggle desperately to enforce a mandate promoting multi-ethnic territorial cohabitation between the deeply hostile Serb and Albanian populations, both apparently wanting only separatism, no one could describe this as a practical 'solution'. Walzer might point to this as evidence of his claim that the attempt to enforce a multicultural solution to contemporary 'tribalism' is 'neither morally permissible nor politically effective'. He compares this strategy—an intuitive response, he argues, particularly of Enlightenment-inspired leftist internationalism—with the policy advocated by a seventeenth-century Puritan minister resisting the new doctrine of divorce: 'If they might be separated for discord, some would make a commodity of strife; but now they are not best to be contentious, for the law will hold their noses together 'til weariness make them leave off struggling' (quoted in Walzer 1994*a*: 67). The 'law' could equally refer to the Yugoslav communism that bound the Serbs and the ethnic Albanians (and the Croats and the Bosnians) temporarily together within a constructed—enforced—national identity, and to the current UN mandate, repeating, perhaps for want of any better ideas, the same sort of mistake.

Walzer's moral minimalism can therefore be interpreted to imply a broad scepticism over the prospects for global governance. This, of course, is driven by his underlying commitment to the claims of pluralism but not, importantly, as a doctrinaire anti-universalizing stance. Rather, it is a *practical* as much as a moral scepticism. Is it one that we should share? Well, I think this all depends on how irrevocable we regard the condition of cultural locality in today's world as a generator of difference.

Pluralism, Location and Locality

The great virtue, it seems to me, of a pluralism such as Walzer's is that it connects moral principle firmly with cultural situation. This is why its implicit reservations over the ambitions of projects of global governance are at once moral and practical. The claims—and indeed the prospects—of human solidarity are never dismissed, but they are always contextualized in terms of particular instantiations of the human condition in particular cultural locations. But it is in this view of the *ineluctable* particularity of the way in which life is lived that the problems of imagining a functioning system of broad global regulation arise.

One response may be to decide that the regulatory ambitions of projects like Charter 99 simply have to accommodate this cultural reality. We might then be led to consider reformulating the grand institutional designs of global governance in terms of more modest proposals: perhaps of aiming to create an institutionalized space of open cultural-political encounter and dialogue *prior* to any project of binding global regulation. This would almost certainly slow dramatically the pace of cosmopolitan reform. But then a slower paced process of hermeneutic encounter is probably implicit in the practicalities that lie behind the rhetoric of projects like Charter 99. For example, the notion that nation-states or cultural communities will 'accept compulsory jurisdiction' by global bodies across a broad front surely realistically supposes something other than a once-and-for-all binding undertaking. In practice, it supposes a process of painstaking, ongoing dialogue, matched to the present realities of cultural difference.

But we might also look at things another way. Walzer and pluralists like him, we might decide, are actually being *insufficiently ambitious* in their assumptions of the limits imposed by the inevitability of locally derived difference. The clue to this way of thinking is to treat *locality*, rather than difference, as the key concept. We should not mistake the particularities that arise from the location of cultures for some innate principle of 'difference' that is at the core of all cultural practices. This a mistake that John Gray, for example, makes in his opposition to cosmopolitan projects. Gray believes that 'the disposition to constitute for itself different cultures or ways of life appears to be universal and primordial in the human animal' (Gray 1997: 177) and that universalizing political projects are bound to fail since they fly in the face of this innate cultural order—this 'natural' pluralism of ways of life.

But this, it seems to me, is to confuse the difference that arises contingently from the historical, material and spatial *location* of cultural practices with some obscure human tendency towards diversity. (A supposed tendency, moreover, that is congruent with the sort of neo-conservative view of social imperfectability that Gray represents.) Cultural practices provide resources of meaning through collective symbolization woven into a set of material practices that sustain a viable way of life. The business of culture then is surely *primarily* the constitution of meaning within a community rather than the constitution of distinctions between communities. This is not to deny, of course, the cultural force of such distinctions once established, but it is to place the horse in the appropriate position to the cart. Seeing culture as local, particular, tied to and expressive of place, and thereby as generative of difference is very different from seeing difference as, somehow, the telos of culture.

Location and locality, then, rather than difference itself, could be seen as the primary terms in the pluralist case. And this opens up a question that is entirely missing from Walzer's account—the idea that the nature of cultural location is *itself* being transformed under the conditions of globalization: by the very conditions of connectivity and compression that simultaneously reveal the political schisms deriving from historically constituted cultural differences.

What I am thinking of here is the cluster of processes—grasped in terms like 'disembedding' or 'deterritorialization' (Giddens 1990; Canclini 1995)—by which localities become increasingly penetrated by globalizing forces. The consequent weakening of the ties of cultural experience to geographical locality across a range of mundane activity—from food culture to electronically mediated communications—is a complex and ambiguous condition, which I have tried to describe elsewhere (Tomlinson 1999). The point for the present discussion is that this transformation in the lived experience of locality (most notable in developed Western cultures, but certainly not restricted to them) has clear implications for the pluralist case.

For 'globally-penetrated' modern localities cannot be assumed to be generators of difference in quite the same way as what Marc Augé (1995: 94) refers to as the 'anthropological spaces of the organically social'. Modern localities, it might be argued, integrate local and distant (global) cultural experiences within the same phenomenological space. Knowledge, mediated cultural influences, consumer practices, senses of closer and more distant relationships and belongings, glimpses even of wider horizons of solidarity and ethical commitments combine here in ways radically different from anything in the historical record. This fact must be counted to qualify the assumption made by Walzer and others (e.g., Smith 1995) that the required human solidarity of cosmopolitanism has no foundations in common cultural experience. 'Humanity, by contrast [with particular societies] has members but no memory, and so it has no history and no culture, no customary practices, no familiar life ways, no festivals, no shared understanding of social goods' (Walzer 1994*a*: 8). But consideration of the transformed localities of globalization might make us begin to question this. 'No familiar life ways? No shared understanding of social goods'? Is it not precisely such cultural commonalities that critics of globalization so frequently point to as features of an encroaching cultural homogenization? To be sure, these features of a globalized consumer culture are, arguably, for the most part morally shallow, in themselves unpromising, for any broader solidarities. And yet, integrated as they are with local attachments in the individual life world, and woven into lifestyle narratives, it is hard to argue that they constitute a cultural experience any less thick and resonant than that of a supposed undisturbed localism.

Deterritorialized localities therefore may be seen as cultural spaces 'opened up to the world' in some regards. It does not, of course, follow that this openness, as presently constituted, is morally edifying or politically progressive. But what it does suggest is that common everyday experience—the ultimate substance of moral agency and political engagement—is no longer irrevocably confined within the parochial. The challenge of cosmopolitan cultural politics—perhaps more urgent than projects of institutional reform—may thus be to begin to build and shape this nascent openness in the direction of consensually emergent global solidarities.

16

Cosmopolitan Harm Conventions

ANDREW LINKLATER

Cosmopolitanism seemed to fall on hard times in the 1980s and 1990s in large part because of a major development within social and political theory in which every moral and political universal and all grand historical narratives were treated with suspicion. It is arguable that those who challenged universal doctrines and ideals—postmodern or post-structural writers—assumed a moral universal in their own work when they defended the rights of the culturally different. It is clear too that many who challenged universalism were not opposed to all its forms but rather to particular varieties in the West, which rested on pernicious distinctions between the advanced and backward peoples. They were concerned about the forms of power that had been created by certain forms of universalistic thinking. But their own universalistic commitments are evident in arguments for a universal speech community and for a new international citizenry (for further discussion, see Linklater 1998).

Cosmopolitanism has enjoyed something of a revival in recent years. We can see this in Nussbaum's defence of cosmopolitanism and cosmopolitan education in the United States of America, and in arguments for cosmopolitan democracy and cosmopolitan citizenship in the United Kingdom (Nussbaum *et al.* 1994; Held 1995*a*; Hutchings and Danreuther 1999). None of these developments pass without criticism, as recent publications by Zolo (1997) and Miller (1999*a*) reveal. The purpose of this chapter is to defend the cosmopolitan turn in recent political theory and the theory of international relations, by focusing on the concept of harm and by supporting the further development of what I shall call cosmopolitan harm conventions (hereafter CHCs). The first task of this paper is to define the concept of harm, harm conventions and their cosmopolitan varieties. A second is to identify the different types of harm and their principal sources and to comment on some harm-reducing measures in international relations. A third is to consider how the study of CHCs contributes to recent efforts to defend the ideal of world citizenship.

What is Harm?

What is harm? For the purposes of this chapter, harm is regarded as 'evil (physical or otherwise) as done to or suffered by some person or thing: hurt, injury, damage, mischief' (OED). Its effects include 'grief, sorrow, pain, trouble, distress, affliction'. The concept of harm is fundamental to everyday social life and moral codes. We can see this in phenomena as diverse as the Hippocratic oath, the Declaration of the Rights of Man and the Citizen in France in 1789, and modern international legal conventions on the environment, torture and genocide. The notion of harm or its equivalent may be said to be universal since it is hard to imagine a society without some notion of harm or injury; but, of course, notions of what constitutes harm vary from culture to culture. What I shall call the harm conventions in any society give harm its public meaning. Harm conventions also set out what is permissible in relations with other human beings, what is obligatory and what is officially proscribed. Harm conventions are an essential part of the social regulation of human behaviour within bounded communities, and they are no less necessary for regulating relations with other societies. In addition, harm conventions define how human beings should treat non-human species and the physical environment (Thomas 1984).

Although all societies have harm conventions, not all have the CHCs or support them to the same degree. The dominant harm conventions in Nazi Germany legitimated terrible acts of violence to insiders and outsiders alike. Over several centuries, European colonial powers claimed the right to deprive indigenous peoples of their land. The harm conventions have legitimated or prescribed the murder and extermination of other peoples, and some have horrified the members of other groups. It is possible to imagine an international system in which there are no CHCs and the citizens of each state are literally enemies of the rest of the human race, but this is not the historical norm. Most forms of world political organization have developed at least some CHCs, and few societies have taken the view that their members are free to do exactly as they please in relations with outsiders.

There are many reasons for this including the desire to comply with religious prohibitions against violence, a common interest with other societies in regulating the use of force and the fear that internal order may suffer in the long term if members are at liberty to ignore the normal constraints on violence in relations with other groups. What makes a harm convention cosmopolitan is the fact that it does not privilege the interests of insiders over outsiders. Eglantyne Jebb, the founder of the Save the Children Fund, captured its spirit in a statement in 1919 that there is no such thing as an enemy child (Chabbot 1999).

A related sentiment is evident in the moral conviction that noncombatants should be spared unnecessary injury in war because they do no harm, that prisoners of war are entitled to lead as decent a life as possible during their period of confinement and that the captured also have their obligations: since they must not treat their captors as enemies even though they may find it impossible to embrace them as friends (Walzer 1970). In these cases, cosmopolitanism does not mean freedom from 'national limitations or attachments' (OED) or suggest that loyalty to the whole of humankind should always come before duties to particular communities, but it does require a notion of respect for persons or its equivalent, and a belief that one of the elementary principles of international morality is the duty of each society to avoid unnecessary harm and to do whatever good it can (Jackson 1995).

The CHCs are anchored in the belief then that the differences between insiders and outsiders are not always morally relevant. They state that insiders do not have the moral right to promote their security and welfare by imposing fear or insecurity on the members of other societies, and they do not have the right to treat outsiders in ways that are widely regarded as reprehensible within their own group. The existence of the CHCs means that group members believe the boundaries of the moral community are not coextensive with the boundaries of the political community but are wider and more inclusive than them. Of course, obligations to these different moral constituencies clash from time to time, and all societies with a commitment to the CHCs have to make decisions about the relative importance of obligations to distant strangers and obligations to kith and kin. How they conceptualize and deal with moral conflicts of this kind is an important question for the student of the CHCs. A related issue is that societies demonstrate different levels of reflectiveness about the ultimate foundations of their ethical duties to insiders and outsiders. What Hobhouse (1906) called 'the rationalization of the moral code' is pronounced in Western societies that have produced professional philosophers who are concerned with the foundations of ethics, with the reasons for and against regarding obligations to co-nationals as special, and with the particular question of how to resolve conflicts between the duties to the state and duties to persons elsewhere.

This is not the place to consider ways in which they have dealt with such questions. Suffice it to note that in many international systems cosmopolitan perspectives have developed that hold that separate communities are governed by moral principles that are in some sense higher than their concrete social moralities, or that should not be overridden by them. In the case of the humanitarian law of war, for example, modern political communities have agreed that there are cosmopolitan duties that can override duties to co-nationals and the obligation to obey military orders. The Nuremberg conventions codified these international responsibilities and, in so doing, inaugurated a new era in the development of a world or cosmopolitan law. Important debates have arisen between the communitarians, who believe that society is the source of moral sentiments and understandings, and the cosmopolitans who believe that human reason can comprehend ethical principles that should apply everywhere. One argument against cosmopolitans is that they claim to enjoy an Archimedean perspective, whereas the reality is that the language of all universalistic moralities reveals their national or cultural origins (for further discussion, see Linklater 1998).

The contention is that cosmopolitan principles can be used to oppress culturally different peoples in the name of allegedly universal truths and ideals. In short, cosmopolitanism may be a source of, rather than the remedy for, transnational harm—harm that flows across the boundaries separating independent political communities. Debates about whether or not there is an Archimedean perspective, or 'a view from nowhere', should not obscure the plain sociological fact that for cosmopolitans a shared capacity for pain and suffering, and a general recognition of common human frailty, personal vulnerability to mental or physical harm and to social or natural disaster, is more important than the social differences between us and them (Rorty 1989; Turner 1993). The desire not to be cruel, and feelings of obligation to those who are vulnerable to our actions, whether or not they stand in any special relationship to us as family, friends or co-nationals, have long been the central motives for developing the CHCs (Goodin 1985). A desire to avoid cruelty to others is fundamental, but no less important is the question of whether societies are prepared to enter into dialogue with past or potential victims, to compensate them for earlier injuries and to consult them about decisions that may cause future injury. Societies do not always need to engage in dialogue with outsiders to discover whether or not they have harmed them. The torturer who specializes in causing harm does not have to consult the victim to discover whether or not certain actions are painful. But it is not always possible to understand how our actions harm others, and relations between colonial and aboriginal Australia illustrate the point. Government departments and missionary groups often moved indigenous peoples off their land for what were good intentions. Missionaries thought they were saving souls, protecting the 'natives' from encroaching settlers with murderous intent and ensuring adequate food supplies in times of severe drought. They did not always know that removal from land that was thought to have been created by ancestral beings, and for which there was a fundamental duty of care, would have disastrous consequences for indigenous populations (Rowse 1998). In this case, the pain and suffering that resulted from the creation of missions could not necessarily have been foretold in the absence of forms of dialogue and understanding that delivered insights into the very different social world of the other (Shapcott 1994). Relations between colonial and aboriginal Australia are a reminder that globalization, or the greater interconnectedness of the human species, creates new opportunities for transnational harm but that this may not be accompanied by legal and political frameworks that give vulnerable groups any guarantees against harm. The greater global reach of some societies should therefore be accompanied by the development of the CHCs—since the absence of a sense of global community makes it easier to cause harm or to neglect its existence. During the Enlightenment, the lengthening chains of cause and effect associated with globalization produced changes in the moral imagination as the strong considered how their actions affected the weak (Tronto 1993). But the logic of these moral changes should not simply be to pity others or to make unilateral decisions about how others should be protected, but rather to support the creation of what have been called 'speech communities' or 'universal communication communities', which allow the members of other communities the right to protest against injuries inflicted on them (see Linklater 1998). Recent studies of cosmopolitan democracy that defend the creation of transnational democratic institutions in the context of globalization address this important theme, as do enquiries into the notion of 'cosmopolitan conversations', which deal with the question of justice in relations between radically different peoples (Held 1995a; Shapcott, forthcoming).

Many moral philosophers have argued that the duty not to harm another is the bedrock of ethics on which relations of beneficence can be built in time (Ross 1930: 22). Some have argued that this duty—otherwise known as the harm principle—makes too few demands of moral subjects. Macaulay (1880) argued that it is 'desirable that (human beings) should not merely abstain from doing harm to their neighbours, but should render active service to their neighbours' (see also Geras 1998: 58). Similar sentiments frequently arise in response to humanitarian emergencies. On this argument, states should act for humanity and citizen/soldiers should be prepared to die for desperate strangers who are the victims of genocide and ethnic cleansing (Kaldor 1999). An additional point made in this context is that the failure to assist the desperate constitutes harm in its own right. Put differently, harm can be caused by acts of omission as well as by acts of commission. Large issues arise here, however the argument that the harm principle should have a central place in international ethics can be built around the following observations. First, independent political communities have been primarily concerned with promoting the interests of their citizens rather than with enhancing the welfare of peoples elsewhere. Desirable though it is that higher levels of beneficence should develop in international relations, the fact remains that only limited amounts of altruism have existed in the relations between separate states. Moreover, international politics have been greatly influenced by what Bauman (1989: 192ff.) has called the production of social distance—the practice of increasing the sense of distance between the self and the other, and of reducing the sense of responsibility for other societies. For these reasons, one of the central problems in international relations has been how to reduce the amount of harm that self-interested actors have been prepared to do to one another, especially in times of war. Second, the fact is that there is no conception of the good society or the good life, and no notion of a world common good, on which peoples everywhere agree. Consequently, when states do act to promote their vision of the good, others often protest against what they regard as the harm caused by efforts to impose alien values. NATO's 'humanitarian war' against Serbia in 1999 was criticized on related grounds, namely that it proceeded without the consent of the UN Security Council and caused more harm than good. Third, because there is so little moral consensus in international relations, there is much to be said for the argument that the project of building an international community should concentrate on certain minimalist ethical aspirations. Defending such an approach, Vincent (1986: 126) argued that the sensible way to proceed would be to 'seek to put a floor under the societies of the world and not a ceiling over them'. The floor in question would consist of an international agreement to protect the most vulnerable 40 per cent of the world's population from the permanent emergency of starvation and malnutrition. Vincent argued that such a minimalist ethic should be able to command the consent of all states, and from its implementation more radical advances might in time develop. One such development might be the willingness to accept responsibility for actions that compound the problems faced by the most vulnerable sections of the world's population. The CHCs can be defended on similar grounds. What the project of creating such conventions seeks to accomplish is a generalized understanding that states, which are obligated to promote the welfare of their citizens and which do not subscribe to some universalizable conception of the good, have fundamental duties not to cause harm to their respective populations. This is not to support an ethic that is concerned only with the avoidance of harm and that has no place for altruism and charity. But it is to suggest, returning to Ross's point, that major progress in that direction may be difficult to make or to sustain without agreements about the harm that societies must not do to each other.

International Relations and the Study of Harm

The study of international relations has a long history of studying harm; indeed its very existence was a result of the new levels of violence and suffering caused by the First World War. A new academic discipline was created to study the possibility of world peace and to promote the cause of internationalism. Some approaches to international relations have been especially concerned with harm reduction; these include peace research and conflict studies. Realism and neorealism—the dominant perspectives in the field since the Second World War—have argued that harm is inevitable in an anarchic system in which sovereign states are responsible for maintaining their own security and often use military force to settle their disputes. Other approaches such as the English School maintain that states belong to an international society, and they argue that states have had some success in regulating force but it has been easier for them to agree on how to prevent harm to states than on how to prevent harm to individuals considered in their own right. States have developed laws of war that limit the harm they do to each other and to their respective populations, but they have not had the same success in creating a system of cosmopolitan law that protects the rights of persons everywhere. Difficulties in the latter domain have arisen because rival conceptions of human rights exist in international society and because new states in particular have been anxious to ensure that support for the international protection of human rights does not become a pretext for intervening in their internal affairs.

The English School is useful for framing an analysis of the development of CHCs in the modern society of states and for reflecting on future possibilities and desirable directions. As is to be expected of a mainstream approach to international relations, it has been especially concerned with the harm that some groups have inflicted on others in conquest or war—which is unsurprising since war and conquest have been dominant features of international politics for more than five millennia. Members of the English School have been largely concerned with what I shall call concrete harm: the harm that particular agents intentionally inflict on other groups and which they justify on the grounds of self-interest or because of their assumed cultural or racial superiority. Measures for dealing with concrete harm in war include the development of the humanitarian law of war. Measures for dealing with concrete harm associated with conquest have included notions of international trusteeship first developed in the period of the Spanish conquest of the Americas and incorporated in more recent times in the League of Nations mandates system and the UN trusteeship system. Eventually, of course, these latter measures were thought insufficient and the European colonies, assisted by the anti-imperial powers, the United States of America and the Soviet Union, laid claim to complete independence as a means of reducing harm. Measures for dealing with concrete harm that is anchored in hierarchical conceptions of racial or cultural differences range from the abolition of slavery and the slave trade to more recent international legal conventions that outlaw genocide and apartheid. War, conquest and notions of cultural and racial superiority are three interrelated phenomena that have caused high levels of concrete harm in international relations and that have led the victims and their sympathizers to work for the establishment of CHCs. It is arguable that the core industrial areas of the world political system are making progress in abolishing forms of concrete harm anchored in hierarchically arranged social differences. War and conquest are virtually inconceivable in relations between the core states, although force has not been eradicated from the relations between core and periphery, and many would argue that informal empire has survived the dismantlement of the overt instruments of colonial administration.

The observation that more deaths have occurred since the Second World War because of civil as opposed to interstate war brings us to a further reason for developing the new CHCs, namely as a response to the violent effects of pathological forms of nation-building and state-formation, which include ethnic cleansing or the expulsion of peoples (see Rae, forthcoming). Especially since the end of the Second World War, states have been concerned with introducing new cosmopolitan conventions in reaction to the forms of concrete harm that some governments have inflicted on sections of their own population. Several international conventions make explicit mention of harm and are clearly designed to eradicate concrete harm as defined above. Article II of the 1973 International Convention on the Suppression and Punishment of the Crime of Apartheid maintains that the crime of apartheid includes efforts to maintain racial domination 'by the infliction upon the members of a racial group or groups of serious bodily or mental harm, by the infringement of their freedom or dignity, or by subjecting them to torture or to cruel, inhuman or degrading treatment or punishment' (Evans 1994: 218). Other articles of international law that outlaw 'serious bodily or mental harm' to 'national, ethnical, racial or religious groups' are contained in the 1948 Convention on the Prevention and Punishment of the Crime of Genocide, and in the 1993 statute that established the tribunal authorized to prosecute persons responsible for violations of international humanitarian law in the former Yugoslavia (Evans 1994: 37, 393). Progress in incorporating the CHCs into modern international law is illustrated by these conventions.

Traditionally, the idea of sovereignty has stood in the way of efforts to punish governments for human rights violations. We do not yet know how far this principle will be eroded and how far the international community will be prepared to intervene in the internal affairs of states where human rights violations occur. The creation of safe havens and no-fly zones in Iraq and Bosnia, the further development of international criminal law following acts of genocide in Bosnia and Rwanda, NATO's action against Serbia over Kosovo and the Australian-led force in East Timor, and the challenge to the principle of sovereign immunity in the recent effort to secure the extradition of Pinochet, suggest that the international community is developing new CHCs that are designed to protect citizens from their own governments. Critics argue that humanitarian wars are highly selective and that the great powers are prepared to punish non-compliant regimes such as Iraq or Serbia but unwilling to take action against allies such as Turkey, which is in a virtual state of war with the Kurds (Chomsky 1999). Even so, a strong case can be made for the proposition that the modern society of states has been slowly redefining the boundary between matters that properly fall within the sovereign jurisdiction of the state and matters that rightly concern the international community at large. Sovereign prerogatives have already shrunk with the growth of the human rights culture (Vincent 1990). Despite divisions between its members, the society of states is not simply concerned with the harm that different societies do to each other in times of war; it is increasingly concerned with the forms of concrete harm that national governments and ethnic groups do to individuals and groups within their national boundaries. The strengthening of international criminal law in recent years marks a new stage in the development of the CHCs.

Three other reasons for introducing CHCs have grown in importance in the most recent phase of world politics. The first reason is economic globalization, and especially the global patterns of trade and investment, which create insecurity and immiseration for large sections of the world's population. The second is global industrialization with its harmful consequences for the physical environment and for its inhabitants (an example being the Bhopal catastrophe). The third is the structure of the world order itself, including the insecurities that have resulted for peoples in the Third World as a result of the global commitments to neo-liberal conceptions of economy and society, and because of structural readjustment policies promoted by global economic institutions such as the IMF and the World Bank (Cornia *et al*. 1987).

In each case, possibilities exist for introducing harm conventions that will increase human as opposed to national security. The inequalities and insecurities that result from global patterns of trade and investment have led the international nongovernmental organizations (INGOs) in particular, to proclaim ethical principles such as fair trade, socially responsible investment and ethical tourism. Concerns about forms of trade (and about the arms trade in particular) and patterns of investment that shore up regimes that violate human rights are leading themes in the politics of the INGOs. A related concern is the multinational exploitation of foreign labour, including child labour and 'sweatshops' (Cavanagh 1997).

Environmental degradation has produced a new language that is concerned with protecting current populations and future generations from obvious forms of risk and from less tangible dangers (see Beck 1992: 21ff.). Support for the precautionary principle within environmental movements and in international law, and declarations—as in the Convention on Biological Diversity—that the possession of sovereignty does not entitle a state to cause environmental harm to its neighbours and to the global commons are important means of dealing with the growing importance of the phenomenon of abstract harm. This is harm that is not exported from one society to another as in war, but that is transmitted across national boundaries by global capital markets and industrial systems of production. As for the structure of world order and the operating principles of global financial institutions, the assumption that they should be responsible for improving national economic efficiency while national governments would deal with domestic social inequalities has been challenged by the idea of 'adjustment with a human face'. This is in response to the evidence of growing inequalities within the societies involved, the increasing poverty of women and children, and inadequate responses by the 'responsible' national governments (Cornia *et al*. 1987).

Modern international society is changing with the development of cosmopolitan as opposed to international law, and with the introduction of conventions that are designed to prevent harm to individuals, minority nations and indigenous peoples as opposed to harm to states. As Hurrell (1995: 139) has observed, there 'has indeed been a most important shift in emphasis away from the individual rights of states and towards an acceptance of common duties. We have seen a very important change in the character and goals of international society: away from the minimalist goals of coexistence towards the creation of rules and institutions that embody notions of shared responsibilities, that impinge heavily on the domestic organization of states, that invest individuals and groups within states with rights and duties, and that seek to embody some notion of the planetary good.' He adds that despite the recent reawakening of a sense of membership of the *magna societas generis communis*, the greater human society, which is more inclusive than an international society in which states rather than individuals are regarded as the ultimate members, old tensions remain about how the planetary good is to be interpreted and realized in the face of conflicting political interests and moral preferences. Further, the INGOs that form the environmental movement are important initiators of global change, but there is still a great deal of work to be done on how far states, which are often seen as part of the problem of world order, can become part of the solution (Hurrell 1995: 165). Finally, progress in the area of global environmental management is more likely to take place through the reform rather than through the (highly improbable) supersession of the international states-system. Progress is most likely to occur in the way that Kant envisaged, that is through efforts to make a society of sovereign states increasingly answerable to cosmopolitan law and to the ideals of world citizenship that are expressed by the progressive elements in a transnational civil society.

Implications for World Citizenship

What does all this mean for the notion of world citizenship? Citizenship is a term used to describe the rights and duties that unite citizens in a bounded political community. Citizenship has been national; according to this line of reasoning, world citizenship is a misnomer (Walzer 1994*b*; Miller 1999*a*). Yet, the idea of world citizenship has a long and distinguished pedigree that can be traced back to the Stoics and analysed in its many reincarnations including the cosmopolitanism of the Enlightenment and the various appeals to planetary citizenship that abound today. The question that arises, given that many believe that citizenship loses all meaning when it is separated from the state, is what cosmopolitan citizenship means in the absence of a world state that specifies the rights and duties of citizens. What does world citizenship mean in an international system of sovereign states where each claims to be the vehicle for promoting the ideal of national citizenship?

There are three main answers to this question. Each is linked with the project of moving beyond traditional international law, which is concerned with the rights and duties of states, to world law, which is concerned with the rights and duties of individuals; and each is linked with the project of creating CHCs. The first is concerned with the realm of cosmopolitan duty; the second with the sphere of cosmopolitan rights; the third with the process and project of creating a democratic worldwide public sphere. Each of these levels will now be considered in turn. The oldest notions of cosmopolitan citizenship stressed moral duties to the rest of humankind. Cicero's claim that all human beings 'are subject to a single law of nature' and are, accordingly, 'bound not to harm anyone' (see Nussbaum 1997a: 31), and Kant's claim that each person has a duty of hospitality to other human beings entering sovereign or strange lands, illustrate the general point (Kant 1970: 214). The claim that the citizens of one state should be concerned about the welfare of other human beings, and about humanity at large, has acquired new support given the development of increasingly destructive instruments of war ranging from nuclear weapons to chemical and biological weapons and anti-personnel landmines. Support for world citizenship has grown with rising levels of environmental harm and associated forms of transnational, or cross-boundary, harm in the most recent stage of economic globalization. The notion of world citizenship stresses the individual's duty to act with consideration for the environment, for distant strangers and for unborn generations. Those who believe that citizenship cannot be used sensibly outside the national political sphere have argued that world citizenship lacks any conception of participation in politics. This is largely true, but the notion of world citizenship now as in the Enlightenment defends the ideal that there are obligations to avoid acting in ways that result in the domination and exploitation of other peoples (Vogel 2000).

Cosmopolitan citizenship is an important weapon in the critique of exclusionary forms of political community and in the development of global harm conventions, which reject the assumption that the welfare of co-nationals inevitably matters more than the welfare of other members of the human race. Judged by these criteria, many nongovernmental organizations can be regarded as the latter-day custodians of the ideal of world citizenship. One of the problems of world citizenship, understood as duties to human beings elsewhere, is that obligations are imperfect rather than perfect: their non-performance may be the cause of personal guilt or shame but inaction does not lead to official public sanctions. For this reason, it is important to consider a second definition of cosmopolitan citizenship, one that is concerned with what may be called the rights of world citizens. Major developments in the sphere of cosmopolitan rights include the Nuremberg conventions, which maintained that the duty to obey superior orders does not entitle military personnel to commit crimes against humanity. A 'constitution formed by the laws of world citizenship' is emerging with the development of the humanitarian law of war. It has been created through numerous international conventions such as the 1948 Convention on the Prevention and Punishment of the Crime of Genocide, the 1948 Universal Declaration of Human Rights, the 1966 International Covenant on Social and Political Rights and the 1984 Convention Against Torture and other Cruel, Inhuman or Degrading Treatment or Punishment. Other manifestations of an emerging international constitution, which sets out the rights of world citizens, include conventions and declarations on the rights of the child, the rights of indigenous peoples and minority nations and duties towards the global commons.

As noted earlier, such conventions are evidence of efforts to develop world law that is concerned with the rights and duties of individuals rather than states. Miller (1999*a*: 74), who strongly defends the republican ideal of active citizenship with its stress on the civic virtue of promoting the public good, argues that the idea that 'individual people can invoke international law against their own state does bring us closer to a recognizable ideal of citizenship' although this 'is at most a thin version of liberal citizenship' since the 'citizen is not a lawmaker' in any meaningful sense. With cosmopolitan rights, the stress is on personal rights rather than on public virtue and political participation. The upshot of Miller's argument is that world citizenship is in important respects inferior to the republican conceptions of citizenship, which can only be developed within bounded political communities where citizens are united by a common nationality and culture. It is important to add that states remain the most important agents in the area of enforcing international law, although there is some evidence that this is changing in important respects. Despite this dependence on states, and despite the absence of participation and representation within a worldwide public sphere, the second notion of world citizenship captures the respects in which the differences between citizen and alien are no more morally relevant than distinctions based on class, ethnicity, gender, religion or race. It is a means of advancing the claim that individuals, as well as states, have an international legal personality and of promoting the argument that robust CHCs that protect individuals everywhere should be enshrined in international law.

In what sense can world citizens be said to participate in a democratic public sphere: in a worldwide sphere since many citizens are already at a liberty to try to promote matters of global concern within their respective national societies? The INGOs may be said to be key players in the development of a worldwide public sphere. Their involvement in global public domains is intermittent and is often linked with the major international UN conferences such as those held in Beijing and Rio de Janeiro in recent years. Demands for access to actually existing permanent international institutions are increasing, as the claims made by many NGOs at the meeting of the WTO in Seattle in 1999 illustrate. The defence of a more democratic world polity is evident in the recent theories of cosmopolitan democracy (Held 1995*a*). At this stage, world citizenship as a democratic involvement in major international institutions is an aspiration rather than a reality; it may nevertheless be possible to speak of a process and a project of the democratic reform of these institutions in which many NGOs are key actors. The idea of world citizenship can be used to describe the politics of creating a worldwide public sphere and the politics of promoting cosmopolitan concerns within actually existing national public spheres (Bohman 1997: 191). It can be used to describe the politics of creating new forms of domestic and international political community in which the most vulnerable members of world society can protest against actual and potential forms of injury. The notions of cosmopolitan duty and cosmopolitan right are incomplete without this politics of transforming political community. The ultimate purpose of more democratic international institutions is to ensure that the rights and duties of world citizens are negotiated and created from below rather than imposed from above.

The CHCs, properly so-called, have to be determined in an open dialogue within a worldwide public sphere. This is one of the central themes in the recent theories of world citizenship.

Conclusion

In this chapter I have tried to contribute to the current reawakening of interest in cosmopolitanism by arguing for CHCs that are concerned with protecting vulnerable individuals and non-state human communities from the harms caused by conquest and war, pathological forms of nation-building and state-formation, global patterns of trade and investment, environmental damage and the current world order. The argument has suggested that avoiding harm may seem less ambitious than promoting good, but it is nevertheless a central element in any international ethic and an important objective for a humane system of international law. The development of world as opposed to international law is largely about protecting the vulnerable from the kinds of harm mentioned above. It has to be noted, however, that conventions that deal with the problem of war and conquest, and with abuses of state power, are more evident in the current cosmopolitan law than measures to deal with vulnerability to the harmful effects of global economic processes or environmental damage. Unsurprisingly, the CHCs tend to reflect the values of the dominant powers and to avoid clashes with their most cherished interests. This raises complex questions about the extent to which states can be in the vanguard of the politics of creating CHCs that deal with problems caused by global capitalism and industrialization, and about the relationship between the international states-system and transnational civil society, but these are not matters that can be discussed here.

Various links between cosmopolitan citizenship and CHCs have been suggested above. Against those who argue that citizenship is only found in any meaningful sense within the nation-state, and who suggest that cosmopolitan citizenship could only really be said to exist if all human beings belonged to a world state, three points may be made: first, that the idea of national citizenship is losing its monopoly as regionalization and globalization encourage the development of post-national conceptions of citizenship that defend duties to human beings elsewhere; second, that world citizenship is an important means of advancing claims in support of the international legal personality of the individual; third, that world citizenship is an important vehicle for recapturing for the modern world the Stoic conception of a dual membership—membership of particular cities or states and membership of the wider community of humankind. World citizenship can be used to refer to the process of creating CHCs and of democratizing the ways in which they are created within an international society, which respects the rights of every human being. Alongside other concepts such as human security, universal human rights and the global commons, cosmopolitan citizenship and CHCs are important terms in the politics of remaking national and international political communities. They deserve an important place, if not pride of place, in the emerging 'cosmopolitan manifesto' (Beck 1998).

17

Cosmopolitanism and Organized Violence

MARY KALDOR

In this chapter, I argue for a cosmopolitan political project as a way of responding to the spread of what I call 'new wars'. And I suggest that this argument can be treated as a way of deducing the more general case for a cosmopolitan political project for three reasons.

First, the rupture with classical modernity that is associated with the process of globalization is perhaps most decisively illustrated by the changes in the pattern of organized violence. The twentieth century can be described as the period in which the nation-state system reached its apogee, and this period will probably be best remembered for the terrible barbarity of totalitarianism and war. But the twentieth century was also the moment when the nation-state system exhausted itself and when these statist phenomena (totalitarianism and interstate war) were abolished, like slavery in an earlier period.

Second, what I call 'new wars' is an extreme manifestation of the erosion of the autonomy of the nation-state under the impact of globalization. Indeed, in contrast to the wars of modernity, in which states were able to mobilize resources and extend administrative capacities, these wars could be described as implosions of the state. The general case for cosmopolitan democracy is based on the argument that democracy at a national level is weakened by the erosion of the autonomy of the state and the undermining of the state's capacity to respond to democratic demands (Held 1995a). In the specific case of war-torn societies, it is the collapse not just of democracy but of the consensus on which state rule is based under the impact of globalization.

Third, the legitimacy of political institutions is intimately linked to the physical protection of citizens. New wars can be viewed as 'protection-failures' (Jones 1999). How and whether this protection is provided will shape the future of political institutions. The extent to which it is possible to echo Diogenes's claim to be a world citizen (*Kosmou polités*) may depend on whether protection (at least against threats to physical security) can be guaranteed at a global level.

I will develop this argument in a schematic way. I will sketch my own definitions of the relations between civil society and war within the states system. Then I will give a brief summary of what I mean by new wars. I will propose a way of classifying the different tendencies of global politics and will elaborate what is meant by a cosmopolitan political project. And in the final section, I will show how a cosmopolitan project can apply to the new wars.

War, Civil Society, and the States System

The seventeenth-century theorists of civil society based their argument on the concept of a social contract. For them, a civil society (*societas civilis*) was a rule of law in which citizens gave up the freedom of the state of nature in exchange for the guarantee of certain rights—security for Hobbes plus liberty and property for Locke. The later definitions of a civil society included the idea of an active citizenry checking violations of the social contract by the state.

I define civil society as the medium through which a social contract between the governing institutions and the governed is negotiated and reproduced. This includes defining moments—constitutional conventions and round tables, for example—as well as everyday public pressure through the media, political parties, churches, NGOs and so on. Thus, civil society is inextricably linked to individual rights.

The emergence of the civil society in the West was bound up with the construction of modern states and with interstate wars. What Norbert Elias called the 'civilizing process'—the removal of violence from everyday life within the boundaries of the state—was based on the establishment of public monopolies of violence and taxation. As Elias (1982: 104) states:

The society of what we call the modern age is characterized, above all in the West, by a certain level of monopolization. Free use of weapons is denied the individual and reserved to a central authority of whatever kind, and likewise, the taxation of property or income of individuals is concentrated in the hands of a central social authority. The financial means thus flowing into this central authority maintain its monopoly of force, while this, in turn maintains the monopoly of taxation. Neither has in any sense precedence over the other; they are two sides of the same monopoly.

A crucial point about this monopoly process was the balance between the interests of the ruler (private) and the interests of the members of what Elias called 'state-regulated society' (public). The shift from a private to a public monopoly, from absolutism to the nation-state, was part of the process of state-building and of concentrating the means of violence and of taxation; for it required a complex and specialized administrative apparatus and social interdependence, which, in turn, restricted the power of the ruler.

The construction of these public monopolies was, as Tilly (1990) has shown, intimately bound up with war against other states. Interstate war became the only legitimate form of organized violence and, moreover, was sharply distinguished from peace. In the place of more or less continuous warfare, war became a discrete episode that was reserved for use against other states and was excluded from internal relations. Domestic pacification (the elimination of private armies, the reduction of corruption, violent crime, piracy and brigandage), the growth of taxation and public borrowing, the regularization of armed forces and police forces, the development of nationalist sentiment, were all mutually reinforcing in wartime. Essentially, the social contract associated with the construction of the nation-state could be said to have taken the following form; civil and political rights were guaranteed in exchange for paying taxes and fighting in wars. The individual rights that citizens enjoyed in peacetime were exchanged for the abrogation of those rights in wartime. In wartime, the citizens became part of a collectivity, the nation, and had to be ready to die for the state. In exchange for civil and political rights in peacetime, the individual citizen accepted a kind of unlimited liability in wartime. Hence, Elias, writing just before the Second World War, feared that the civilizing process would be engulfed by the barbarity of war.

Interstate war is sometimes described as Clausewitzean war. The wars of classical modernity had a kind of extremist logic that is well analysed by Clausewitz. As war became more extreme and terrible, so the social contract was extended, reaching its logical end point during the cold war period. Essentially, during this period, there were unprecedented gains in economic and social rights. But the risks were also dramatically extended. The price of these gains, during this period, was the readiness to risk a nuclear war.

This was the essence of the political compromises made in the late 1940s between the Democrats and the Republicans in the United States of America (the Democrats retained big government in exchange for an anti-communist crusade) and between Europe and America (the Social Democrats could come to power in exchange for agreeing to NATO) (Kaldor 1995*a*). It should be stressed, as Gellner does, that civil society was a Western phenomenon (Gellner 1994). The 'civilizing process' hardly extended beyond a small urban elite in either the colonial or the eastern empires. It would be wrong, however, to treat these empires or their post-colonial and/or communist successors as traditional states. Rather, they were modern states based on a mixture of consent and coercion but consent was, for the most part, mobilized through populist communitarian ideologies such as nationalism or socialism of the statist variety rather than through a rights-based social contract. In these societies, the distinction between war and peace was less acute since collective forms of social organization predominated, rules were imposed from above rather than through a process of negotiation. Or, to put it another way, in these societies the collective organization for war was also the salient element of state-building, but in these societies the balance between consent and coercion was tilted towards the latter and the forms of social organization that predominated in war-time tended to be sustained in peace-time.

The changes in the states system, on this analysis, can be explained by two phenomena. First of all, the social contract of the cold-war period was called into question. On the one hand, after Vietnam, the readiness to risk life in war was no longer automatic. And indeed, by the 1980s, mass movements against nuclear war had developed. On the other hand, the growing neo-liberal consensus and the spread of globalization eroded the guarantee of economic and social rights. Secondly, under the impact of globalization, the distinction between the Western and non-Western societies is collapsing. On the one hand, the capacity of non-Western states to sustain populist projects within closed societies is undermined. On the other hand, the increasing interconnectedness at a political as well as a cultural level provides some protection for disaffected individuals and allows them to demand extensions of political and civil rights, which, in turn, contributes to a speeding up of globalization. As Beck (chapter 6, this volume) puts it, 'the categories framing world society—the distinction between highly developed and under developed countries, between tradition and modernity—are collapsing. In the cosmopolitan paradigm of the second modernity, the non-Western societies share the same space and time horizon with the West'.

Globalization and New Wars

Globalization is a wild process involving interconnectedness and exclusion, integration and fragmentation, homogenization and diversity. The fundamental source of the new wars is the crisis of the state authority, a profound loss of legitimacy that became apparent in the post-colonial states in the 1970s and 1980s and in the post-communist states only after 1989. Part of the story of that crisis is the failure or exhaustion of populist emancipatory projects such as socialism or national liberation, especially those that were implemented within an authoritarian communitarian framework. But this failure cannot be disentangled from the impact of globalization.

What is new about the crisis of state authority in the 1980s and 1990s is not simply the uncompleted character of the 'civilizing process' in non-Western societies but, rather, something that could be described as its opposite—the unravelling of the process. The monopoly of violence and taxation is being eroded and the balance between public and private and internal and external has shifted. On the one hand, in those areas prone to conflict, the balance between the public and private has shifted as a consequence of the legacy of authoritarianism, the longevity of ruling groups or the failure of populist projects. In particular, the centralized economic systems often tend to generate shortages of resources, which are rationed according to privileged and personalistic networks. On the other hand, the balance between the internal and external has also shifted as a consequence of the growing interconnectedness at a political, economic and social level.

The combination of privatization and globalization can give rise to a process that is almost the reverse of the process through which modern states were constructed. Corruption and clientilism lead to an erosion of the tax revenue base because of declining legitimacy and the growing incapacity to collect tax and because of declining investment (both public and private) and, consequently, production. The declining tax revenue leads to a growing dependence both on external and on private sources, through, for example, rent seeking or criminal activities. The reductions in public expenditure as a result of the shrinking fiscal base, as well as pressures from the external donors for macro-economic stabilization and liberalization (which also may reduce export revenues), further erode legitimacy. A growing informal economy associated with increased inequalities, unemployment and rural–urban migration, combined with the loss of legitimacy, weakens the rule of law and may lead to the re-emergence of privatized forms of violence—organized crime and the substitution of 'protection' for taxation, vigilantes, private security guards protecting economic facilities, especially international companies, and paramilitary groups associated with particular political factions. In particular, the reductions in security expenditure, often encouraged by external donors for the best of motives, may lead to breakaway groups of redundant soldiers and policemen seeking alternative employment.

It should be stressed that the impact of privatization and globalization is, of course, Janus-faced. Privatization breaks down authoritarian tendencies. Globalization can bring positive external pressures for reform, particularly democratization. On the one hand, external donors and outside powers have pressured governments to introduce political reform as a precondition of economic reform, to reduce corruption, increase respect for human rights and introduce democratic institutions. On the other hand, support from the outside powers and international NGOs for civil society has helped to strengthen domestic pressures for democratization. It can be argued that it is in those situations where domestic pressures for reform are weak and where civil society is least developed that the opening up of the state both to the outside world and to increased participation through the democratization process is most dangerous. In a number of countries, the process of democratization is largely confined to elections. Many of the essential prerequisites of democratic procedures—rule of law, separation of powers, freedom of association and of expression—are not in place. And even where procedures are more or less in place, decades of authoritarianism may have left the political culture vulnerable to populist ideologies based on the appeal to various forms of exclusive prejudices. Terms like virtual democracy, semi-democracy, or choiceless democracy have been used to describe societies characterized by elected authoritarian leaders.

These are the circumstances that give rise to the 'new wars'. It is the lack of authority of the state, the weakness of representation, the loss of confidence that the state is able or willing to respond to public concerns, the inability to control the privatization and informalization of violence that give rise to violent conflicts. Moreover, this 'uncivilizing process' tends to be reinforced by the dynamics of the conflicts, which have the effect of further reordering political, economic and social relationships in a negative spiral of incivility.

I call the conflicts 'wars' because of their political character although they could also be described as massive violations of human rights (repression against civilians) and organized crime (violence for private gain). They are about access to state power. They are violent struggles to gain access to or to control the state. As the state becomes privatized, that is to say, it shifts from being the main organization for societal regulation towards an instrument for the extraction of resources by the ruler and his (and it is almost always 'his') privileged networks, so access to state power becomes a matter of inclusion or exclusion, even, in the latter case, of survival.

In the majority of cases, these wars are fought in the name of identity—a claim to power on the basis of labels. These are wars in which political identity is defined in terms of exclusive labels—ethnic, linguistic or religious—and the wars themselves give meaning to the labels. The labels are mobilized for political purposes; they offer a new sense of security in a context where the political and economic certainties of previous decades have evaporated. They provide a new populist form of communitarian ideology, a way to maintain or capture power that uses the language and forms of an earlier period. Undoubtedly, these ideologies make use of pre-existing cleavages and the legacies of past wars. It is also the case that the appeal to tradition and the nostalgia for some mythical or semi-mythical history gains strength in the social upheavals associated with the opening up to global pressures. But, nevertheless, it is the deliberate manipulation of these sentiments, often assisted by diaspora funding and techniques and speeded up through the electronic media, that is the immediate cause of conflict.

In these wars, violence is itself a form of political mobilization. Violence is mainly directed against civilians and not another army. The aim is to capture territory through political control rather than military success. And political control is maintained through terror, through expulsion or elimination of those who challenge political control, especially those with a different label. Population displacements, massacres, widespread atrocities are not just the side effects of war; they are a deliberate strategy for political control. The tactic is to sow the 'fear and hate' on which exclusive identity claims rest.

These are also globalized wars in another sense. Unlike interstate wars, which were highly regulated and which indeed provided a model for statist forms of planning, these wars could almost be described as the model for the contemporary informal economy, in which privatized violence and unregulated social relations feed on each other. In these wars, physical destruction is very high, tax revenues plummet further and unemployment is very high. The various parties finance themselves through loot and plunder and various forms of illegal trading; thus, they are closely linked to and help to generate organized crime networks. They also depend on support from neighbouring states, diaspora groups and humanitarian assistance.

The 'new wars' are no longer discrete in time and space. The various actors—the states, remnants of states, paramilitary groups and liberation movements—depend on continued violence for both political and economic reasons. Cease-fires and agreements are truces, breathing spaces that do not address the underlying social relations—the social conditions of war and peace are not much different. The networks of politicians, security forces, legal and illegal trading groups, which are often transnational, constitute a new distorted social formation, which has a tendency to spread through refugees and displaced persons, identity based networks often crossing continents, as well as criminal links. Moreover, the conditions that give rise to the 'new wars' and that are exacerbated by them, exist in weaker forms in most of the urban conglomerations in the world and indeed often have direct links with the most violent regions.

All the same, social formations that depend on violence are always vulnerable, fragile and close to exhaustion. As Hannah Arendt pointed out, power depends on legitimacy not on violence—it is very difficult to sustain forms of political mobilization that depend on violence. Herein lies the possibility for a cosmopolitan, namely non-exclusive, alternative.

The Configuration of Global Politics

I am among those who have argued that the division between the so-called realists and cosmopolitans has come to supplant the traditional division between left and right (see Giddens 1994). Yet observing events in Seattle and Washington, it is clear that those traditional divisions still exist. I want to propose a somewhat more differentiated categorization of contemporary politics as outlined in Figure 17.1. The rows show the difference between the left and right (I have included the Greens as left). And the columns show the difference between the parochialists or realists, those who see society bounded by the state, and the globalists. These distinctions could be said to correspond to a communitarian/individualist distinction, although it is possible to imagine a global communitarian—someone who favours a world state and homogenous global society.

Those in the lower left box, I would argue, have no future. Globalization cannot be reversed. The collapse of communism demonstrated that it is no longer possible to sustain closed societies and to insulate large parts of the world from growing global interconnectedness. 'Socialism in one country' is no longer an option, if it ever was. Of course, fundamentalists and de-globalizers

FIGURE 17.1. Divisions in global politics

	Parochialist/communitarian	Globalist/individualist
Neo-liberal	New Right, for example Thatcher, Haider, Northern Leaguers, and Putin?	New Centre, for example MNCs, Gore
Distributionist (and environmentally concerned)	Old Left	Cosmopolitans

may succeed in establishing temporarily closed states, for example Iraq or Serbia, but these cannot be sustained and have to be understood as an ongoing reaction to rather than a reversal of globalization.

Those in the top right box, who favour globalization, are here to stay. But they need alliances with those who offer some form of political regulation. The two possible alliances that can be made suggest two possible directions for global-ization. The New Right favours an unregulated economy, but strong and even authoritarian political states. They favour the movements of trade and capital but they are against the free movement of people. They want to restrict asylum seekers and maintain ethnic purity. An alliance with the New Right suggests a world of wild globalization, managed or contained through authoritarian nationalism and coercion. The realist view that 'stability' is more important than democracy—that, for example, favours Putin or negotiates with Milosevic—is also in line with this approach, even though its proponents might express themselves in more moderate terms.

The alternative is an alliance with the cosmopolitans—the people often described as a global civil society, the new transnational NGOs, the human rights community, those who support multiculturalism, and so on. I have put the cosmopolitans in the lower right box because I do consider that cosmopoli-tanism involves a commitment to human rights, and I also take the view that civil, political and social rights are indivisible. Jones (1999) defines the cosmo-politan standpoint as 'impartial, universal, individualist and egalitarian' and argues for a system of global justice based on a cosmopolitan moral position.

What then makes cosmopolitanism any different from a human rights perspec-tive? Appiah suggests that cosmopolitanism is different from humanism in that it celebrates multicultural diversity and the free movement of people. He argues for the notion of a rooted cosmopolitan—someone who is attached to a particular place or home with its cultural particularities 'but takes pleasure from the pre-sence of other, different places that are home to other different people' (Appiah 1996: 22) and also is able to choose his or her home. Of course, it could be argued that a human rights perspective must include respect for different cultures—the right to worship freely or to use one's language, for example. Appiah suggests that a humanist position is compatible with a world government, whereas a cosmopolitan perspective implies a variety of polities. I am not convinced of this point since a world government implies such a concentration of power that guarantees of individual liberty would be hard to sustain.

However, the utility of the term 'cosmopolitan' as opposed to humanist does seem to lie in its presumed emphasis on cultural and political diversity. This is partly explained by its colloquial usage. A cosmopolitan tends to be someone who is familiar with different cultures and languages—although it does have an urban, elitist connotation. More importantly, it derives from the original Kantian use of the term. Kant envisaged a global system divided into states in which cosmopolitan right overrides the claims of sovereignty. This is usually interpreted as human rights. But an interesting aspect of the original Kantian position is the way in which he insisted that, as a condition for perpetual peace, cosmopolitan right could be confined to the right of hospitality. This can be interpreted as a plea for multiple identities. Strangers need to be treated as guests—politely but not as members of the family. Hospitality, surely, requires respect for human rights, but this is not the same as integration.

Thus, an alliance between the new globalist centre and the cosmopolitans implies a global 'civilizing process'. The aim is a rights-based system of global governance. And this implies a global social contract—a global civil society. Cosmopolitanism is often treated as a sentiment or moral standpoint. I want to suggest that it is, in fact, a political project, which is best elucidated in relation to 'new wars'.

A Cosmopolitan Approach to New Wars

It follows from the argument about the character of 'new wars' that efforts aimed at conflict prevention or management focus on a reversal of the 'uncivilizing process', on the reconstruction of relations based on agreed rules and public authority. Above all, the centrepiece of any peace strategy has to be the restoration of legitimate authority. It has to counterpoise the strategy of 'fear and hate' with a strategy of 'hearts and minds'. This kind of restoration of legitimate authority cannot mean a reversion to statist politics; it must imply multi-layered authority—global, regional and local as well as national. It is impossible to revert to a bounded 'civilizing process'.

First and foremost such an approach has to start by building a new form of cosmopolitan politics to counter the politics of exclusion. At a local level, cosmopolitan politics can include both political movements and parties that are secular and non-nationalist or religious, as well as moderate identity-based parties that respect and cherish different identities. Cosmopolitan or democratic politics is usually associated with a civil society, in particular with the NGOs and independent media, but it may also have political representation in parliaments or even governments. What is needed is a transnational alliance that includes both the local actors and those engaged in a variety of international activities committed to a cosmopolitan approach.

In nearly all conflict zones, it is possible to identify individuals, groups or even local communities that try to act in inclusive democratic ways. Precisely because these are wars that are not total and in which participation is low, in which the distinction between war and peace is eroding, there are often what might be called 'zones of civility' that struggle to escape the polarization imposed by the logic of war and provide space for cosmopolitan politics. Examples include Tuzla in Bosnia-Herzegovina, northwest Somaliland as well as many other places (Kaldor 1999). Pro-democracy groups are not, moreover, confined to non-violent resistance. Self-defence groups or reformist forces like the Rwanda People's Front (RPF) in Rwanda or even elements in the Kosovo Liberation Army (KLA) may be counted among these cosmopolitan or democratic political groupings.

Strengthening cosmopolitan politics is much more important than trying to reconcile opposing exclusivist groups, even though conflict resolution efforts at a societal level may be important in changing political perspectives. The negotiations among warring parties help to legitimize those who support exclusive approaches to politics and may result in impossible compromises involving various types of partition and power sharing that entrench identity politics. There may be a case for negotiations to stabilize violence and create a space for alternative cosmopolitan groupings, but how this is done and with what aim should be understood as part of a common cosmopolitan strategy.

Second, a cosmopolitan approach requires respect for cosmopolitan law. This is international law that applies to individuals and not to states. The two main components of cosmopolitan law are the Laws of War and Human Rights Law. The strategies adopted in new wars directly violate cosmopolitan law. The lacuna in cosmopolitan law is enforcement. I have argued for a reconceptualization of humanitarian intervention as cosmopolitan law enforcement. Understood in this way, humanitarian intervention has to involve the direct protection of civilians and the arrest of individual war criminals. Typically, the techniques of humanitarian intervention have to be defensive—the creation of safe zones, safe havens, no-fly zones, and humanitarian corridors—and cannot be confused with traditional war fighting. The aim is not to engage an enemy but to defend civilians, not to destroy or weaken enemy soldiers and infrastructure but to save lives.

Third, a cosmopolitan approach requires global justice, namely respect for economic and social rights even in conflict zones. Indeed, if cosmopolitan politics is to counter the populist appeal of exclusive identity politics, it has to be able to address everyday concerns. But this is not just a matter of global distribution, of, for example, the provision of humanitarian assistance, which in any case helps to feed the forces of violence. It is a matter of building legitimate sources of employment and of providing a way of living that is consistent with human dignity, so that young men and women have a real alternative to becoming a criminal or living off humanitarian aid. In other words, it means the construction or reconstruction of a regulated market economy and this is inextricably linked to the rebuilding of legitimate authority with legitimate sources of revenue.

A cosmopolitan approach of this kind implies a new global social contract—it is the beginnings of a global civilizing process. The elements of a global civil society already exist. There have been defining moments—the founding of the UN, the Helsinki Agreements, even though the actors were states. The contract established in these defining moments is revised, reproduced and extended through public pressure from the media, NGOs and some international officials. But although human rights have been codified, the capacity or the willingness of the national and global institutions to implement those rights is still quite inadequate.

Can there be a global social contract that would guarantee the implementation of fundamental social rights? Does this imply that the individual has to be prepared to pay global taxes or, more importantly, does the individual have to be prepared to die for humanity? I think the individual has to be prepared to risk life for humanity but not in an unlimited way (as was the case with statist wars) since he or she is part of humanity. Humanitarian intervention is less risky than war fighting although more risky than the kind of risk-free war (at least from the point of view of the soldiers) that the United States of America and NATO are promoting as a form of humanitarian intervention. Indeed, the human rights activists and aid workers already risk their lives for humanity. It is sometimes said that this notion is ridiculously utopian—dying for hearth and home is quite different from risking one's life for something as grand and abstract as humanity. But risking one's life for one's nation is in fact a relatively recent invention. The notion that there is some higher good beyond the secular notions of the nation and state long preceded this invention.

In her reply to those who criticized her plea for cosmopolitanism, Martha Nussbaum refers to the 1172 trees in Jerusalem that commemorate the 'righteous goyim'—individuals, couples or families who risked their lives in the Second World War to save Jewish lives. As Nussbaum (1996: 132) put it:

The terror which persists is the terror of the question they pose. Would one, in similar circumstances, have the moral courage to risk one's life to save a human being simply because he or she is human. More generally, would one, in similar circumstances, have the moral courage to recognize humanity and respond to its claim, even if the powers that be denied its presence?

In the new wars, it is possible to find cosmopolitans who risk their lives to save others. Can their experience offer a moral basis for future forms of cosmopolitan governance?

REFERENCES

Aaronovitch, David (2000). 'The New Millennium: Society'. *The Independent*, 1 January.

Adam, B. (1998). *Timescapes of Modernity*. London: Routledge.

Adorno, Theodor W. (1974). *Minima Moralia*. London: Verso.

Albright, Madeline (1998). 'Menschenrechte und Außenpolitik'. *Amerika-Dienst*, 35.

Albrow, Martin (1996). *The Global Age*. Cambridge: Polity Press.

Aleinikoff, T. Alexander (1998). 'A Multicultural Nationalism?'. *The American Prospect*, 36, 80–6.

Alexander, Meena (1996). *River and Bridge*. Toronto: Toronto Review Press.

Althusius, Johannes (1965). *Politica: Politics Methodically Set Forth and Illustrated with Sacred and Profane Examples*. Frederick S. Carney (ed.). Indianapolis: Liberty Fund. [First published in 1603].

An Zuozhang and Wang Keqi (1992). 'The Yellow River Culture and The Chinese Civilization [Huanghe wenhua yu zhinghuo wen ming]'. *Journal of Literature, History and Philosophy* [*Wen Shi Zhe*], 4, 3–13.

Anaya, S. James (1996). *Indigenous Peoples in International Law*. New York: Oxford University Press.

Anderson, Amanda (1998). 'Cosmopolitanism, Universalism, and the Divided Legacies of Modernity'. In P. Cheah and B. Robbins (eds) *Cosmopolitics: Thinking and Feeling Beyond the Nation*, pp. 265–89. Minneapolis: University of Minnesota Press.

Anderson, Benedict (1983). *Imagined Communities: Reflections on the Origins and Spread of Nationalism*. London: Verso.

——(1991). *Imagined Communities*. London: Verso.

——(1998). 'Nationalism, Identity, and the World-in-Motion: On the Logics of Seriality'. In P. Cheah and B. Robbins (eds) *Cosmopolitics: Thinking and Feeling Beyond the Nation*, pp. 117–33. Minneapolis: Minnesota University Press.

Appadurai, Arjun (1990). 'Disjuncture and Difference in the Global Cultural Economy'. In M. Featherstone (ed.), *Global Culture*, pp. 295–310. London: Sage.

——(1996). *Modernity at Large: Cultural Dimensions of Globalization*. Minneapolis: University of Minnesota Press.

——and Carol Breckenridge (1988). 'Why Public Culture?'. *Public Culture*, 1, 5–9.

Appiah, Kwame Anthony (1996). 'Cosmopolitan Patriots'. In J. Cohen (ed.), *For Love of Country: Debating the Limits of Patriotism: Martha C. Nussbaum and Respondents* pp. 21–9. Cambridge, MA: Beacon.

——(1998). 'Cosmopolitan Patriots'. In P. Cheah and B. Robbins (eds), *Cosmopolitics: Thinking and Feeling Beyond the Nation*, pp. 91–114. Minneapolis: University of Minnesota Press.

Archambault, J., B. Ray, D. Rose, and A.-M. Séguin (1999). *Atlas de l'Immigration à Montréal*. Immigration et Métropoles. (http://im.metropolis.net/research-policy/research_content/atlas/index.html).

Archibugi, Daniele (1998). 'Principles of Cosmopolitan Democracy'. In D. Archibugi, D. Held, and M. Köhler (eds), *Re-imagining Political Community*, pp. 198–228. Cambridge: Polity.

——(2000). 'Cosmopolitical Democracy'. *New Left Review*, 4 (July–August), 137–50.

——and David Held (eds) (1995). *Cosmopolitan Democracy: An Agenda for a New World Order*. Cambridge: Polity Press.

——David Held, and Martin Köhler (eds) (1998). *Re-imagining Political Community: Studies in Cosmopolitan Democracy*. Cambridge: Polity Press and Stanford, CA: Stanford University Press.

Arendt, Hannah (1958). *The Human Condition*. Chicago: University of Chicago Press.

——(1970). *Men in Dark Times*. San Diego: Harvest Books.

——(1978). *The Life of the Mind*. New York: Harcourt Brace Jovanovich.

——(1983). *Men in Dark Times*. New York: Harcourt Brace Jovanovich.

——(1994). *Essays in Understanding*. New York: Harcourt Brace.

——and Jaspers, Karl (1992). *Correspondence: 1926–1969*. New York: Harcourt Brace.

Asad, Talal (1993). *Genealogies of Religion*. Baltimore: Johns Hopkins University Press.

Augé, Marc (1995). *Non-Places: Introduction to the Anthropology of Supermodernity*. London: Verso.

Ausländerbeauftragte des Senates von Berlin, Die (2000). *Repräsentativumfrage zur Lebenssituation Türkischer Berlinerinnen und Berliner*. Berlin: Senatsverwaltung für Arbeit, Socialer und Franen.

Bao, Jiemin (2001). 'Sino-Thai Ethnic Identity: Married Daughters of China and Daughters-in-law of Thailand'. In Chee Kiong and Chan Kwok Bun (eds), *Alternate Identities: The Chinese of Contemporary Thailand*, pp. 271–98. Singapore: Times Academic Press and Leiden: Brill Academic Publishers.

Barber, Benjamin (1995). *Jihad vs. McWorld*. New York: Times Books.

Barry, Brian (1998). 'The Limits of Cultural Politics'. *Review of International Studies*, 24 (3), pp. 307–19.

——(1999). 'Statism and Nationalism: A Cosmopolitan Critique'. In I. Shapiro and L. Brilmayer (eds), *Global Justice*. New York: New York University Press.

——(2000). *Culture and Equality*. Cambridge: Polity.

Basch, Linda, Nina Glick Schiller, and Cristina Szanton Blanc (1994). *Nations Unbound: Transnational Projects, Postcolonial Predicaments and Deterritorialized Nation-states*. New York: Gordon & Breach.

Basu, Shamita (1997). *Religious Revivalism as Nationalist Discourse: Swami Vivekananda and the Nineteenth Century Neo Hindu Movement in Bengal*. Doctoral dissertation, Roskile University.

Bauböck, Rainer (1994). *Transnational Citizenship: Membership and Rights in International Migration*. Cheltenham: Edward Elgar.

——(1998). 'Sharing History and Future? Time Horizons of Democratic Membership in an Age of Migration'. *Constellations*, 4 (3), 320–45.

——(1999). 'Liberal Justifications for Ethnic Group Rights'. In C. Joppke and S. Lukes (eds), *Multicultural Questions*, pp.133–57. Oxford: Oxford University Press.

——(2000). 'Political Community Beyond the Sovereign State: Supranational Federalism and Transnational Minorities'. Paper presented to the Conference on *Conceiving Cosmopolitanism*, University of Warwick, 27–9 April.

Baucom, Ian (1999). *Out of Place: Englishness, Empire and the Locations of Identity*. Princeton: Princeton University Press.

Bauer, Otto (1907). *Die Nationalitätenfrage und die Sozialdemokratie*. Wien: Verlag Ignaz Brand.

Bauman, Zygmunt (1989). *Modernity and the Holocaust*. Cambridge: Polity.

——(1995). *Life in Fragments*. Oxford: Blackwell.

——(1999). *In Search of Politics*. Cambridge: Polity.

Baumann, Gerd (1996). *Contesting Culture: Discourses of Identity in Multi-ethnic London*. Cambridge: Cambridge University Press.

——(1999). *The Multicultural Riddle: Rethinking National, Ethnic and Religious Identities*. London: Routledge.

Beck, Ulrich (1992). *Risk Society: Towards a New Modernity*. London: Sage.

——(1996*a*). 'World Risk Society as Cosmopolitan Society?' *Theory, Culture and Society*, 13 (4), 1–32.

——(1996*b*). *Ecological Politics in an Age of Risk*. Cambridge: Polity Press.

——(1998). 'The Cosmopolitan Manifesto'. *New Statesman*, 20 (March), 28–30.

——(1999*a*). 'Democracy Beyond the Nation-State: A Cosmopolitan Manifesto'. *Dissent* (Winter), 53–5.

——(1999*b*). *World Risk Society*. London: Sage.

——(2000*a*). *What is Globalization?* Cambridge: Polity Press.

——(2000*b*). *Brave New World of Work*. Cambridge: Polity Press.

——(2000*c*). 'The Cosmopolitan Perspective: Sociology of the Second Age of Modernity'. *British Journal of Sociology*, 51 (1), 79–105.

——(2001). 'The Cosmopolitan Society and its Enemies'. *Theory, Culture and Society*, 18 (6), pp. 17–44.

——and E. Beck-Gernsheim (1995). *The Normal Chaos of Love*. Cambridge: Polity Press.

——and W. Bonß (eds) (1999). *Reflexive Modernisierung*. Frankfurt/M: Suhrkamp.

——Anthony Giddens, and S. Lash (1994). *Reflexive Modernization*. Cambridge: Polity Press.

Beck-Gernsheim, E. (1999). *Schwarze gibt es in allen Hautfarben*. Frankfurt/M: Suhrkamp.

Becker, Jörg (1996). 'Zwischen Integration und Dissoziation: Türkische Medienkultur in Deutschland'. *Politik und Zeitgeschichte*, 44/45, 39–47.

Beetham, David (1998). 'Human Rights as a Model for Cosmopolitan Democracy'. In D. Archibugi, D. Held, and M. Köhler (eds), *Re-imagining Political Community: Studies in Cosmopolitan Democracy*, pp. 58–71. Cambridge: Polity.

Beisheim, M., S. Dreher, G. Walter, B. Zangl, and M. Zürn (1999). *Zeitalter der Globalisierung?* Baden-Baden: Nomos.

Bellah, Robert *et al.* (1984). *Habits of the Heart*. Berkeley: University of California Press.

Bellamy, Richard and Dario Castiglione (1998). 'Between Cosmopolis and Community: Three Models of Rights and Democracy within the European Union'. In D. Archibugi, D. Held and M. Köhler (eds), *Re-imagining Political Community*, pp. 152–78. Cambridge: Polity.

Benhabib, Seyla (1992). *Situating the Self: Gender, Community and Postmodernism in Contemporary Ethics*. Cornwall: Polity.

Berger, Peter (1963). *Invitation to Sociology*. Harmondsworth: Penguin.

Bernstein, Richard J. (1996). *Hannah Arendt and the Jewish Question*. Cambridge: Polity.

Bhabha, Homi (1993). *The Location of Culture*. London: Routledge.

Bienen, Derk, Volder Rittberger, and Wolfgang Wagner (1998). 'Democracy in the United Nations System: Cosmopolitan and Communitarian Practices'. In D. Archibugi, D. Held and M. Köhler (eds), *Re-imagining Political Community: Studies in Cosmopolitan Democracy*, pp. 287–308. Cambridge: Polity.

Biersteker, T. and C. Weber (eds) (1996). *State Sovereignty as Social Construct*. Cambridge: Cambridge University Press.

Blanc, Christina Szanton (1997). 'The Thoroughly Modern 'Asian': Capital, Culture, and the Nation in Thailand and the Philippines'. In Aihwa Ong and Donald M. Nonini (eds), *Ungrounded Empires*, pp. 261–86. New York: Routledge.

Bobbio, Noberto (1989). *Democracy and Dictatorship*. Cambridge: Polity.

Boehm, Max Hildebert (1953). 'Cosmopolitanism'. In E. Seligman and A. Johnson (eds), *Encyclopaedia of the Social Sciences* (Vol. 3, pp. 457–61). New York: Macmillan.

Bohman, James (1997). 'The Public Spheres of the World Citizen'. In J. Bohman and M. Lutz-Bachmann (eds), *Perpetual Peace: Essays on Kant's Cosmopolitan Ideal*. Cambridge, MA: MIT Press.

——(1998). 'The Globalization of the Public Sphere'. *Philosophy and Social Criticism*, 24 (2/3), 199–216.

——and Matthias Lutz-Bachmann (eds) (1997). *Perpetual Peace: Essays on Kant's Cosmopolitan Ideal*. Cambridge, MA: MIT Press.

Bosniak, Linda (2000). 'Citizenship Denationalized'. *Indiana Journal of Global Legal Studies*, 7, pp. 447–510.

Bourdieu, Pierre (1999). *Acts of Resistance*. New York: New Press.

——(2001). *Contre-feux II*. Paris: Raisons d'Agir.

Bourne, Randolph (1916). 'Transnational America'. *Atlantic Monthly*, CXVIII, 86–97.

Bozeman, A. B. (1984). 'The International Order in a Multicultural World'. In H. Bull and A. Watson (eds), *The Expansion of International Society*. Oxford: Oxford University Press. pp. 387–406.

Brennan, Timothy (1997). *At Home in the World: Cosmopolitanism Now*. Cambridge, MA: Harvard University Press.

——(2001). 'Cosmopolitanism and Internationalism'. *New Left Review*, 7 (January–February), 75–85.

Breuilly, J. (1992). *Nationalism and the State*. Manchester: Manchester University Press.

Brown, C. (1995). 'International Political Theory and the Idea of World Community'. In K. Booth and S. Smith (eds), *International Relations Theory Today*. Cambridge: Polity. pp. 90–109.

Brubaker, Roger (1996). *Reframing Nationalism: Nationhood and the National Question in the New Europe*. Cambridge: Cambridge University Press.

Bruckner, Pascal (1996). 'The Edge of Babel'. *Partisan Review*, (Spring), 242–54.

Buchanan, Allen (1991). *Secession: The Morality of Political Divorce from Fort Sumter to Lithuania and Quebec*. Boulder, CO: Westview Press.

Bull, Hedley (1977). *The Anarchical Society*. Basingstoke: Macmillan.

Caglar, Ayse (1998). 'Popular Culture, Marginality and Institutional Incorporation'. *Cultural Dynamics*, 10 (3), 243–61.

Calhoun, Craig (1997). *Nationalism*. Buckingham and Minneapolis: Open University Press and Minnesota Press.

——(1999). 'Nationalism, Political Community, and the Representation of Society: Or, Why Feeling at Home Is Not a Substitute for Public Space'. *European Journal of Social Theory*, 2 (2), 217–31.

——(2002). 'Constitutional Patriotism and the Public Sphere: Interests, Identity, and Solidarity in the Integration of Europe'. In Pablo DeGreiff and Ciaran Cronin (eds), *Global Ethics and Transnational Politics*, pp. 275–312. Cambridge, MA: MIT Press.

Canclini, N. Garcia (1995). *Hybrid Cultures: Strategies for Entering and Leaving Modernity*. Minneapolis: University of Minnesota Press.

——(2000). 'The State of War and the State of Hybridization'. In Paul Gilroy, Lawrence Grossberg, and Angela McRobbie (eds), *Without Guarantees: In Honour of Stuart Hall*, pp. 38–52. London: Verso.

Carew Hunt, R. N. (1957). *A Guide to Communist Jargon*. London: Geoffrey Bles.

Carey, William (1792). *An Enquiry into the Obligations of Christians to Use Means for the Conversion of the Heathens*. Leicester: Ann Ireland.

Carlyle, Thomas (1888). *Critical and Miscellaneous Essays*, Vol. 1. London: Chapman and Hall.

Carrasco, P., Damaris Rose, and J. Charbonneau (1999). 'La constitution de liens faibles: une passerelle pour l'adaptation des immigrantes Centro-Américaines mères de jeunes enfants à Montréal'. *Études ethniques au Canada/Canadian Ethnic Studies*, 30, 73–91.

Cassese, Antonio (1995). *Self-Determination of Peoples: A Legal Reappraisal*. Cambridge: Cambridge University Press.

Castells, Manuel (1997). *The Power of Identity*. Oxford: Blackwell Publishers.

Cavanagh, J. (1997). 'The Global Resistance to Sweatshops'. In A. Ross (ed.), *No Sweat: Fashion, Free Trade and the Rights of Garment Workers*, pp. 39–50. London: Verso.

Chabbot, C. (1999). 'Development INGOs'. In J. Boli and G. Thomas (eds), *Constructing World Culture: International Non-Governmental Organizations since 1875*. Stanford: Stanford University Press, pp. 222–48.

Chan Kwok-bun (1997). 'A Family Affair: Migration, Dispersal, and the Emergent Identity of the Chinese Cosmopolitan'. *Diaspora*, 6 (2), 195–214.

Cheah, Pheng and Bruce Robbins (eds) (1998). *Cosmopolitics: Thinking and Feeling Beyond the Nation*. Minneapolis: University of Minnesota Press.

Chen Yinke (1996). Liu Guisheng and Zhang Buzhou (eds), *Chen Yinke's Scholarly and Cultural Works*. Beijing: Zhongguo Qingnian Chubanshe.

Chicoine, N. and J. Charbonneau (with the collaboration of D. Rose and B. Ray) (1997). 'Le processus de reconstruction des réseaux sociaux des femmes immigrantes dans l'espace Montréalais'. *Recherches féministes*, 10 (2), 27–48.

Childers, Erskin and Brian Urquhart (1994). *Renewing the United Nations System*. Uppsala: Dag Hammerskjöld Foundation.

Chomsky, Noam (1999). *The New Military Humanism: Lessons from Kosovo*. Monroe: Common Courage Press.

Clifford, James (1992). 'Travelling Cultures'. In L. Grossberg, C. Nelson and P. Treichler (eds), *Cultural Studies*, pp. 96–116. London: Routledge.

——(1998). 'Mixed Feelings'. In Peng Cheah and Bruce Robbins (eds) *Cosmopolitics: Thinking and Feeling Beyond the Nation*, pp. 362–70. Minneapolis: University of Minnesota Press.

Clifford, Ronald (1937). 'The Nature of the Firm'. *Economica*, 4, 386–405.

Cohen, Joshua (ed.) (1996). *For Love of Country: Debating the Limits of Patriotism: Martha C. Nussbaum and Respondents*. Cambridge: Beacon Press.

Cohen, Mitchell (1992). 'Rooted Cosmopolitanism: Thoughts on the Left, Nationalism and Multiculturalism'. *Dissent* (Fall), 478–83.

Cohen, Robin (1997). *Global Diasporas: An Introduction*. Seattle: University of Washington Press.

——(1999). 'Back to the Future: From Metropolis to Cosmopolis'. In J. Hjarnø (ed.), *From Metropolis to Cosmopolis*, pp. 9–26. Esbjerg: South Jutland University Press.

——and Shirin Rai (eds) (2000). *Global Social Movements*. London: Athlone.

Cooley, Charles H. (1902/1956). 'Human Nature and the Social Order'. In Charles H. Cooley (ed., revised edition) *Two Major Works: Social Organization and Human Nature and The Social Order*. Glencoe, IL: Free Press.

Cornia, G. A., R. Jolly, and F. Stewart (eds) (1987). *Adjustment with a Human Face: Protecting the Vulnerable and Promoting Growth* (Vol. 1). Oxford: Clarendon Press.

Delanty, Gerard (2000). *Citizenship in a Global Age*. Buckingham: Open University Press.

——(2001). 'Cosmopolitanism and Violence: The Limits of Global Civil Society'. *European Journal of Social Theory*, 4 (1), 41–52.

Dostoevsky, Fyodor (1981). *The Brothers Karamazov*. New York: Bantam. [First published in 1880].

Dunn, John (1990). *Interpreting Political Responsibility*. Cambridge: Polity.

Durrell, Lawrence (1962). *The Alexandria Quartet*. London: Faber.

Eade, John (ed) (1997). *Living the Global City*. London: Routledge.

Eagleton, Terry (1996). *The Illusions of Postmodernism*. Oxford: Blackwell.

Elazar, Daniel (1987). *Exploring Federalism*. Tuscaloosa: University of Alabama Press.

Elias, Norbert (1982). *The Civilising Process: State Formation and Civilisation*. Oxford: Blackwell. [Originally published in German in 1939].

Elkins, David J. (1995). *Beyond Sovereignty: Territory and Political Economy in the Twenty-first Century*. Toronto: University of Toronto Press.

Elster, Jon (1992). *Local Justice: How Institutions Allocate Scarce Goods and Necessary Burdens*. Cambridge: Cambridge University Press.

Evans, M. D. (1994). *International Law Documents*. London: Blackstone.

Eze, Emmanuel Chukwudi (1967). *Race and the Enlightenment: A Reader*. Oxford: Blackwell.

Fabian, Johannes (1983). *Time and the Other: How Anthropology Makes its Object*. New York: Columbia University Press.

Falk, Richard (1998). The United Nations and Cosmopolitan Democracy. In D. Archibugi, D. Held and M. Köhler (eds), *Re-imagining Political Community*, pp. 309–31. Cambridge: Polity Press.

———(2000). *Human Rights Horizons: The Pursuit of Justice in a Globalizing World*. New York: Routledge.

Farley, Reynolds (1998). 'Racial Issues: Trends in Residential Patterns and Intermarriage'. In Neil Smelser and Jeffrey Alexander (eds), *Diversity and its Discontents: Cultural Conflict and Common Ground in Contemporary American Society*, pp. 85–128. Princeton: Princeton University Press.

Featherstone, Mike (ed.) (1990). *Global Culture: Nationalism, Globalization and Modernity*. London: Sage.

Feher, Michel (1994). 'The Schisms of '67: On Certain Restructurings of the American Left, from the Civil Rights Movement to the Multiculturalist Constellation'. In Paul Berman (ed.), *Blacks and Jews: Alliances and Arguments*. New York: Delacorte Press, pp. 263–85.

Femminella, Francis X. (1973). 'The Emigrant and Urban Melting Pot'. In M. Urofsky (ed.), *Perspectives on Urban America*. New York: Doubleday Publishing Co.

———(1980). 'Societal Ramifications of Ethnicity in the Suburbs'. In S. La Gumina (ed.), *Ethnicity and Suburbia: The Long Island Experience*, pp. 9–14. Garden City, NY: Nassau Community College.

Fine, Robert (1998). 'Equivocations of Arendt's Politics'. In *The Finnish Yearbook of Political Thought* (Vol. 2, Political Judgement), pp. 90–111. Jyväskylä: University of Jyväskylä.

Finkielkraut, Alain (1989). *Remembering in Vain: The Klaus Barbie Trial and Crimes against Humanity*. New York: Columbia University Press.

Freeman, Gary P., and James Jupp (eds) (1992). *Nations of Immigrants: Australia, the United States, and International Migration*. Melbourne: Oxford University Press.

Friedman, Jonathan (1994). *Cultural Identity and Global Process*. London: Sage.

Frith, Simon (2000). 'The Discourse of World Music'. In G. Born and D. Hesmondhalgh (eds) *Western Music and its Others*, pp. 305–22. Berkeley: University of California Press.

Gadamer, G.-H. (1975). *Truth and Method*. London: Sheed & Ward.

Geertz, Clifford (1973). *The Interpretation of Cultures*. New York: Basic Books.

———(1986). 'The Uses of Diversity'. *Michigan Quarterly Review*, 25, 105–23.

Gellner, Ernest (1965). *Thought and Change*. London: Weidenfeld & Nicolson.

———(1983). *Nations and Nationalism*. Oxford: Basil Blackwell.

———(1994). *The Conditions of Liberty: Civil Society and its Rivals*. London: Hamish Hamilton.

Geras, Norman (1995). *Solidarity in the Conversation of Mankind: The Ungroundable Liberalism of Richard Rorty*. London: Verso.

———(1998). *The Contract of Mutual Indifference*. London: Verso.

Germain, Annick and Julie E. Gagnon (2000). 'Constructing Cultures of Hospitality: Municipalities and the Management of Cultural Diversity'. Paper presented to the *Fourth National Metropolis Conference*, Toronto, March.

Germain, A., J. Archambault, B. Blanc, J. Charbonneau, F. Dansereau, and D. Rose (1995). *Cohabitation interethnique et vie de quartier*. Ministère des Affaires internationales, de l'immigration et des communautés culturelles, collection Études et recherches, no. 12. Québec: Gouvernement du Québec.

Giddens, Anthony (1985). *The Nation-State and Violence* (Vol. 2). *A Contemporary Critique of Historical Materialism*. Cambridge: Polity.

——(1990). *The Consequences of Modernity*. Cambridge: Polity Press.

——(1991). *Modernity and Self-Identity*. Cambridge: Polity Press.

——(1994). *Beyond Left and Right*. Cambridge: Polity Press.

——(1996). *Beyond Left and Right*. Cambridge: Polity Press.

——(1999*a*). *The Third Way*. Cambridge: Polity Press.

——(1999*b*). *Runaway World*. London: Profile Books.

——and C. Pierson (1998). *Conversations with Anthony Giddens*. Cambridge: Polity Press.

Glick-Schiller, Nina, Linda Basch, and Christina Blanc-Szanton (eds) (1992). *Towards a Transnational Perspective on Migration: Race, Class, Ethnicity, and Nationalism Reconsidered*. New York: The New York Academy of Sciences.

Goodin, Robert (1985). *Protecting the Vulnerable: A Reanalysis of our Social Responsibilities*. London: University of Chicago Press.

——(1986). 'What is so Special about our Fellow Countrymen?' *Ethics*, 98 (July), 663–86.

Gottlieb, Gidon (1994). 'Nations Without States'. *Foreign Affairs*, 73 (3), 100–12.

Gray, Alexander (1963). *The Socialist Tradition: Moses to Lenin*. London: Longman.

Gray, John (1997). *Endgames: Questions in Late Modern Political Thought*. Cambridge: Polity.

Guéhenno, Jean-Marie (1994). *Das Ende der Demokratie*. München: Artemis & Winkler.

Gutman, Amy (ed.) (1994). *Multiculturalism: Examining the Politics of Recognition*. Princeton: Princeton University Press.

Habermas, Jurgen (1989). *Structural Transformation of the Public Sphere*. Cambridge, MA: MIT Press.

——(1994). 'Struggles for Recognition in the Democratic Constitutional State'. In Amy Gutman (ed.), *Multiculturalism: Examining the Politics of Recognition*. Princeton: Princeton University Press.

——(1998*a*). C. Cronin and P. De Greiff (eds), *The Inclusion of the Other*. Cambridge, MA: MIT Press.

——(1998*b*). *Die postnationale Konstellation*. Frankfurt/M: Suhrkamp.

——(1999). 'Bestialität und Humanität'. *Die Zeit*, 18 (April), 6–8.

Hage, Ghassan (1998). *White Nation: Fantasies of White Supremacy in a Multicultural Society*. Sydney: Pluto Press.

Hall, Stuart (1990). 'Cultural Identity and Diaspora'. In Jonathan Rutherford (ed.), *Identity: Community, Culture and Difference*, pp. 222–37. London: Lawrence & Wishart.

——(1992). 'The Question of Cultural Identity'. In S. Hall, D. Held, and A. McGrew (eds) *Modernity and its Futures*, pp. 273–326. Cambridge: Polity.

Hammar, Tomas (1990). *Democracy and the Nation State: Aliens, Denizens and Citizens in a World of International Migration*. Aldershot: Avebury.

Hannerz, Ulf (1990). 'Cosmopolitans and Locals in World Culture'. In M. Featherstone (ed.) *Global Culture: Nationalism, Globalization and Modernity*, pp. 237–51. London: Sage.

——(1996). *Transnational Connections: Culture, People, Places*. London: Routledge.

Harvey, David (1989). *The Conditions of Postmodernity*. Oxford: Blackwell.

——(2000). 'Cosmopolitanism and the Banality of Geographical Evils'. *Public Culture*, 12 (2), 529–64.

Heater, Derek B. (1996). *World Citizenship and Government: Cosmopolitan Ideas in the History of Political Thought*. London: Macmillan.

Held, David (1995*a*). *Democracy and the Global Order: From the Modern State to Cosmopolitan Governance*. Cambridge: Polity.

——(1995*b*). 'Democracy and the International Order'. In D. Archibugi and D. Held (eds) *Cosmopolitan Democracy: An Agenda for a New World Order*, pp. 96–120. Cambridge: Polity.

——(1996). *Models of Democracy* (2nd edition). Cambridge: Polity.

——and A. McGrew (eds) (2000). *The Global Transformation Reader*. Cambridge: Polity.

——A. McGrew, D. Goldblatt, and J. Perraton (1999). *Global Transformations: Politics, Economics and Culture*. Cambridge: Polity Press.

Herder, Johann Gottfried (1872) *Zur Philosophie und Geschichte*. Stuttgart: J. G. Cotta.

Hiebert, Daniel (1999). 'Immigration and the Changing Social Geography of Greater Vancouver'. *BC Studies*, 121, 35–82.

Hill, Ann Maxwell (2001). 'Tradition, Identity and Religious Eclecticism among Chinese in Thailand'. In Tong Chee Kiong and Chan Kwok Bun (eds), *Alternate Identities: The Chinese of Contemporary Thailand*, pp. 299–317. Singapore: Times Academic Press and Leiden: Brill Academic Publishers.

Hilton, Boyd (1988*a*). *The Birth of Methodism in England: The Influence of Evangelicalism on Social and Economic Thought, 1795–1865*. Oxford: Clarendon Press.

——(1988*b*). *The Age of Atonement: The Influence of Evangelicalism on Social and Economic Thought, 1795–1965*. Oxford: Clarendon Press.

Hirsch, Fred (1976). *Social Limits to Growth*. Cambridge, MA: Harvard University Press.

Hirst, Paul (1994). *Associative Democracy: New Forms of Economic and Social Governance*. Cambridge: Polity.

——and G. Thompson (1996). *Globalization in Question: The International Economy and the Possibilities of Governance*. Cambridge: Polity.

Hobhouse, L. T. (1906). *Morals in Evolution*. New York: Henry Holt & Company.

Hobsbawm, Eric (1990). *Nations and Nationalism since 1780: Programme, Myth, Reality*. Cambridge: Cambridge University Press.

Höffe, Otmar (1999). *Demokratie im Zeitalter der Globalisierung*. München: Beck.

Hollinger, David A. (1995). *Postethnic America: Beyond Multiculturalism*. New York: Basic Books.

——(1997). 'National Solidarity at the End of the Twentieth Century: Reflections on the United States and Liberal Nationalism'. *Journal of American History*, LXXXIV, 559–69.

——(1998). 'Nationalism, Cosmopolitanism, and the United States'. In Noah Pickus (ed.), *Immigration and Citizenship in the 21st Century*, pp. 92–4. New York: Rowman & Littlefield.

——(1999). 'Authority, Solidarity, and the Political Economy of Identity: The Case of the United States'. *Diacritics*, 29, pp. 116–27.

Hourani, Albert (1983). *Arabic Thought in the Liberal Age, 1798–1939*. Cambridge: Cambridge University Press. [First published in 1962].

Huntington, Samuel P. (1996). *The Clash of Civilizations and the Remaking of World Order*. New York: Simon & Schuster.

Hurrell, A. (1995). 'International Political Theory and the Global Environment'. In K. Booth and S. Smith (eds), *International Relations Theory Today*. Cambridge: Polity.

Hutchings, Kimberly (1999). 'Political Theory and Cosmopolitan Citizenship'. In K. Hutchings and R. Dannreuther (eds), *Cosmopolitan Citizenship*, pp. 3–32. Basingstoke: Macmillan.

——and Roland Dannreuther (eds), (1999). *Cosmopolitan Citizenship*. Basingstoke: Macmillan.

Hyndman, Jennifer and Margaret Walton-Roberts (1999). *Transnational Migration and Nation: Burmese Refugees in Vancouver*, Working Paper 99-07. Vancouver: Vancouver Centre of Excellence for Research on Immigration and Integration in the Metropolis (RIIM).

Ignatieff, Michael (1999). 'Benign Nationalism? The Possibilities of the Civic Ideal'. In E. Mortimer and R. Fine (eds), *People, Nation and State*, pp. 141–7. London: I.B.Tauris.

——(2000). *Isaiah Berlin: A Life*. London: Vintage.

IP Arbo (1998/1999). *International Magazine Yearbook*. München: IP Arbo.

Iyer, Pico (1997). 'The Nowhere Man'. *Prospect*, February, 30–3.

——(2000). *The Global Soul: Jet Lag, Shopping Malls and the Search for Home*. New York: Knopf.

Jackson, R. (1995). 'The Political Theory of International Society'. In K. Booth and S. Smith (eds), *International Relations Theory Today*. Cambridge: Polity.

Jacobson, David (1996). *Rights Across Borders: Immigration and the Decline of Citizenship*. Baltimore: Johns Hopkins University Press.

James, William (1977). *On a Certain Blindness in Human Beings*. Philadelphia: R. West [First published in 1899].

Jameson, F. and M. Miyoshi (eds) (1998). *The Cultures of Globalization*. Durham: Duke University Press.

Jaspers, Karl (1961). *The Question of German Guilt*. New York: Capricorn Books [First published in 1945].

Joly, J. (1996). *Sondage d'opinion publique québécoise sur l'immigration et les relations interculturelles*. Québec: Ministère des Relations avec les Citoyens et de l'Immigration, Études et recherches collection, No. 15.

Jones, Charles (1999). *Global Justice: Defending Cosmopolitanism*. Oxford: Oxford University Press.

Kaldor, Mary (1995a). *The Imaginary War: Understanding the East–West Conflict*. Oxford: Basil Blackwell.

——(1995b). 'European Institutions, Nation-States and Nationalism'. In D. Archibugi and D. Held (eds), *Cosmopolitan Democracy. An Agenda for a New World Order*, pp. 68–95. Cambridge: Polity.

——(1996). 'Cosmopolitanism versus Nationalism: The New Divide?' In R. Caplan and J. Feffer (eds), *Europe's New Nationalism*, pp. 42–58. Oxford: Oxford University Press.

——(1999). *New and Old Wars: Organised Violence in a Global Era*. Cambridge: Polity.

——(2002). 'Beyond Militarism, Arms Races and Arms Control'. In Craig Calhoun, P. Price and A. Timmer (eds) *Understanding September 11*. New York: New Press.

Kant, Immanuel (1795/1995). 'Zum ewigen Frieden'. In Horstman, Rolf-Peter (ed) *Immanuel Kant Werke* (Vol. 6) pp. 279–333. Köln: Könemann.

——(1970). 'Perpetual Peace'. In M. Forsyth *et al* (eds) *Theories of International Relations: Selected Texts from Gentili to Treitschke*. London: Unwin.

——(1991). 'Perpetual Peace: A Philosophical Sketch'. In H. Reiss (eds), *Kant: Political Writings*, pp. 93–130. Cambridge: Cambridge University Press.

——(1999). *Geographie (Physische Geographie)*. Paris: Bibliotheque Philosophique.

Keck, Margaret and Kathryn Sikkink (1998). *Activists Beyond Borders*. Ithaca: Cornell University Press.

Keddie, Nikki (1968/1983). *An Islamic Response to Imperialism*. Berkeley: University of California Press.

Kedourie, Elie (1966/1997). *Afghani and Abduh: An Essay on Religious Unbelief and Political Activism in Modern Islam*. London: Frank Cass.

Kieserling, A. (1998). *Massenmedien*. Unpublished manuscript.

Kirwan-Taylor, Helen (2000). 'The Cosmocrats'. *Harpers and Queen*, October, 188–91.

Kleingeld, Pauline (1999). 'Six Varieties of Cosmopolitanism in Late Eighteenth-Century Germany'. *Journal of the History of Ideas*, 60 (July), 505–24.

Köhler, Martin (1998). 'From the National to the Cosmopolitan Public Sphere'. In D. Archibugi, D. Held, and M. Köhler (eds), *Re-imagining Political Community*, pp. 231–51. Cambridge: Polity.

Kosnick, Kira (2000). 'Building Bridges: Media for Migrants and the Public-Service Mission in Germany'. *European Journal of Cultural Studies*, 3.

Kraus, Peter (1998). 'Kultureller Pluralismus und politische Integration: Die Sprachenfrage in der Europäischen Union'. *Österreichische Zeitschrift für Politikwissenschaft*, 27 (4), 443–58.

Kristeva, Julia (1991). *Strangers to Ourselves*. New York: Columbia University Press.

Kymlicka, Will (1989). *Liberalism, Community, and Culture*. Oxford: Clarendon Press.

——(1990). *Contemporary Political Philosophy: An Introduction*. Oxford: Oxford University Press.

——(1995). *Multicultural Citizenship: A Liberal Theory of Minority Rights*. Oxford: Oxford University Press.

——(1998a). *Finding Our Way: Rethinking Ethnocultural Relations in Canada*. Toronto: Oxford University Press.

——(1998b). 'American Multiculturalism in the International Arena'. *Dissent*, Fall.

——and Wayne Norman (2000). 'Citizenship in Culturally Diverse Societies: Issues, Context, Concepts'. In W. Kymlicka and W. Norman (eds), *Citizenship in Diverse Societies*, pp. 1–41. Oxford: Oxford University Press.

Lapid, Y. and F. Kratochwil (eds) (1997). *The Return of Culture and Identity in IR-Theory*. Colorado: Boulder.

Lasch, Christopher (1995). *The Revolt of the Elites and the Betrayal of Democracy*. New York: W. W. Norton.

Lash, Christopher and John Urry (1994). *Economics of Sign and Space*. London: Sage.

Latour, B. (1999). *Politiques de la nature*. Paris: Edition La Decouverte.

Lerner, Daniel (1958). *The Passing of Traditional Society: Modernizing the Middle East*. Glenco, IL: Free Press.

Levitt, Peggy (2000). 'They Prayed in Brazil and it Rained in Boston: Dominican and Brazilian Transnational Religious Life'. Paper presented to the Symposium *German-American Frontiers of the Social and Behavioural Sciences*, Atlanta, 23–26 March.

Ley, David (1999). 'Myths and Meanings of Immigration and the Metropolis'. *The Canadian Geographer*, 43, 2–19.

——(2000). *Seeking Homo Economicus: The Strange Story of Canada's Business Immigration Program*. Working Paper 00-02. Vancouver: RIIM.

Liebes, T. and E. Katz (1993). *The Export of Meaning: Cross-Cultural Readings of Dallas*. Cambridge: Polity.

Linklater, Andrew (1998). *The Transformation of Political Community: Ethical Foundations of the Post-Westphalian Era*. Cambridge: Polity and London: Verso.

Luhmann, N. (1975). 'Weltgesellschaft'. In *Soziologische Aufklärung* (also in Luhmann 1995). Opladen: Westdeutscher Verlag.

——(1997). *Die Gesellschaft der Gesellschaft*. Frankfurt/M: Suhrkamp.

Lyons, G. and M. Mastanduno (eds) (1995). *Beyond Westphalia? State Sovereignty and International Intervention*. Baltimore: Johns Hopkins Press.

Macaulay, Lord (1880). 'Notes on Penal Reform in India'. In Lord Macaulay (ed.), *Miscellaneous Works of Lord Macaulay*. New York: Harper.

MacIntyre, Alistair (1981). *After Virtue*. London: Duckworth.

——(1988). *Whose Justice? Which Rationality?* London: Duckworth.

McNeill, William H. (1986). *Polyethnicity and National Unity in World History*. Toronto: University of Toronto Press.

Mann, Michael (1986). '*The Sources of Social Power*' (Vol. 1) of *A History of Power from the Beginning to AD 1760*. Cambridge: Cambridge University Press.

——(1987). 'Ruling Strategies and Citizenship'. *Sociology*, 21 (3), pp. 339–54.

Mannheim, Karl (1936/1960). *Ideology and Utopia*. London: Routledge & Kegan Paul.

Mardin, Serif (1962). *The Genesis of Young Ottoman Thought*. Princeton: Princeton University Press.

Margalit, Avishai and Joseph Raz (1994). 'National Self-Determination'. In Joseph Raz (ed.), *Ethics in the Public Domain: Essays in the Morality of Law and Politics*, pp. 125–45. Oxford: Clarendon Press.

Marrus, Michael (1997). *The Nuremberg War Crimes Trial 1945–46: A Documentary History*. Boston: Bedford Books.

Marx, Karl and Friedrich Engels (1976). 'Manifesto of the Communist Party'. In Karl Marx and Friedrich Engels (eds) *Collected Works*, pp. 477–519. London: Lawrence & Wishart.

Mason, Ian Garrick (1999). 'Cosmopolitanism: Then and Now'. www.stlawrenceinstitute.org/vol14mas.html.

Mayall, J. (ed.) (1996). *The New Interventionism 1991–1994: United Nations Experience in Cambodia, Former Yugoslavia and Somalia*. Cambridge: Cambridge University Press.

Mead, George Herbert (1934). *Mind, Self and Society* (edited and with an introduction by Charles W. Morris). Chicago: University of Chicago Press.

Meijer, Roiel (ed.) (1999). *Cosmopolitanism, Identity and Authenticity in the Middle East*. London: Curzon.

Meyer, B. and P. Geschiere (eds) (1999). *Globalization and Identity*. Oxford: Blackwell.

Meyer, J. W., J. Boli, G. M. Thomas, and F. O. Ramirez (1997). 'World Society and the Nation State'. *American Journal of Sociology*, 103 (1), 144–81.

Micklethwait, John and Adrian Wooldridge (2000). *A Future Perfect: The Challenge and Hidden Promise of Globalization*. London: Heinemann.

Mill, John Stuart (1965). *Principles of Political Economy with Some Application to Social Philosophy*. London: Routledge and Kegan Paul.

Mill, John Stuart (1972). 'Considerations on Representative Government'. In H. B. Acton (ed.), *Utilitarianism, Liberty, Representative Government*. London: Everyman's Library [First published 1861].

——(1993). *Utilitarianism, On Liberty, Considerations on Representative Government* (edited by Geraint Williams). London: J.M. Dent [First published 1859].

Millar, F. *et al.* (1967). *The Roman Empire and its Neighbours*. London: Weidenfeld & Nicholson.

Miller, Daniel (1992). 'The Young and the Restless in Trinidad: A Case of the Local and the Global in Mass Consumption'. In R. Silverstone and E. Hirsch (eds), *Consuming Technology*. London: Routledge, pp. 163–82.

Miller, David (1988). 'The Ethical Significance of Nationality'. *Ethics*, 98. pp. 647–62.

——(1995*a*). *On Nationality*. Oxford: Oxford University Press.

——(ed.) (1995*b*). *Worlds Apart: Modernity Through the Prism of the Local*. London: Routledge.

——(1999*a*). 'Bounded Citizenship'. In K. Hutchings and R. Dannreuther (eds), *Cosmopolitan Citizenship*, pp. 60–80. London: Macmillan.

——(1999*b*). 'Justice and Inequality'. In A. Hurrell and N. Woods (eds), *Inequality, Globalization and World Politics*, pp. 147–210. Oxford: Oxford University Press.

Mitchell, Tim (1988). *Colonizing Egypt*. Cambridge: Cambridge University Press.

Modood, Tariq and Pnina Werbner (eds) (1997). *The Politics of Multiculturalism in the New Europe*. London: Zed Books.

Monaci, Massimiliano, Mauro Magatti, and Marco Caselli (2001). 'Network, Exposure and Rhetoric: Italian Occupational Fields and Heterogeneity in Constructing the Globalized Self'. Paper presented to conference of the *Global Studies Association*, Manchester.

Montesquieu, Charles de (1748/1949). *The Spirit of the Laws*. New York: Hafner Press and Macmillan.

Mullick, Sunrit (1993). 'Protap Chandra Majumdar and Swami Vivekananda at the Parliament of Religions: Two Interpretations of Hinduism and Universal Religion'.

In Eric Ziolkowski (ed.) *A Museum of Faiths: Histories and Legacies of the 1893 World's Parliament of Religions*. Atlanta: Scolars Press.

Nagel, Thomas (1986). *The View from Nowhere*. Oxford: Oxford University Press.

Nairn, Tom (1997). *Faces of Nationalism: Janus Revisited*. London: Verso.

Nandy, Ashis (1993). *Traditions, Tyranny and Utopias*. Oxford: Oxford University Press.

——(1998). *Exiled at Home*. Oxford: Oxford University Press.

Nassehi, Armin (1998). 'Die "Welt"—Fremdheit der Globalisierungsdebatte: Ein phänomenologischer versuch'. *Soziale Welt*, Heft 2, 151–66.

Needham, Rodney (1972). *Belief, Language, and Experience*. Oxford: Blackwell.

Nietzsche, Friedrich (1960). 'Jenseits von Gut und Bose'. In Kark Schlechta (ed.) *Werke in Drei Banden: Zweiter Band*, pp. 563–761. Munich: Carl Hanser Verlag.

Nussbaum, Martha (1994). 'Patriotism and Cosmopolitanism'. *Boston Review*, 19 (5), 3–34.

——(1996). 'Patriotism and Cosmopolitanism'. In Martha C. Nussbaum and J. Cohen (eds), *For Love of Country: Debating the Limits of Patriotism*, pp. 3–17. Cambridge, MA: Beacon Press.

——(1997a). 'Kant and Cosmopolitanism'. In James Bohman and Mattias Lutz-Bachmann (eds), *Perpetual Peace: Essays on Kant's Cosmopolitan Ideal*, pp. 25–58. Cambridge, MA: MIT Press.

——(1997b). *Cultivating Humanity: A Classical Defense of Reform in Liberal Education*. Cambridge, MA: Harvard University Press.

——(2000). *Women and Human Development: The Capabilities Approach*. Cambridge: Cambridge University Press.

Nussbaum, Martha *et al.* (1994). 'Patriotism and Cosmopolitanism'. http://www.phil.uga.edu/faculty/wolf/nussbaum1.htm. [Published with replies in 1994 *Boston Review* 19 (5), 3–34].

O'Neill, O. (1991). 'Transnational Justice'. In D. Held (ed.), *Political Theory Today*, pp. 276–304. Cambridge: Polity.

OECD (1997). *Communications Outlook*. Paris: Organization for Economic Cooperation and Development.

Ong, Aihwa (1999). *Flexible Citizenship: The Cultural Logic of Transnationality*. Durham, NC: Duke University Press.

Parekh, Bhikhu (2000). *Rethinking Multiculturalism: Cultural Diversity and Political Theory*. Cambridge, MA: Harvard University Press.

Park, Robert E. (1937). 'Introduction'. In E. V. Stonequist (ed.), *The Marginal Man*, pp. xiii–xviii. New York: Charles Scribner's Sons.

——(1966). 'Reflections on Communication and Culture'. In Bernard Berelson and Morris Janowitz (eds), *Reader in Public Opinion and Communication*, pp. 167–77. New York: The Free Press.

——and Ernest W. Burgess (1921). *Introduction to the Science of Sociology* (3rd edition, revised with an introduction by Morris Janowitz). Chicago: University of Chicago Press.

Pattell, Cyrus R. K. (1999). 'Comparative American Studies: Hybridity and Beyond'. *American Literary History*, 11 (Spring), 166–86.

Pogge, Thomas W. (1992). 'Cosmopolitanism and Sovereignty'. *Ethics*, 103, 48–75.

Pollock, Sheldon, Homi K. Bhabha, Carol A. Breckenridge and Dipesh Chakrabarty (2000). 'Cosmopolitanisms'. *Public Culture*, 12 (3), 577–89.

Poole, Ross (1999). *Nation and Identity*. London: Routledge.

Postiglione, Gerard A. (1983). *Ethnicity and American Social History: Toward Critical Pluralism*. Lanham: University Press of America.

Potter, David (1962). 'The Historian's Use of Nationalism and Vice Versa'. *American Historical Review*, LXVII, 924–50.

Putnam, Robert (2000). *Bowling Alone*. New York: Simon & Schuster.

Radhakrishnan, R. (1995). 'Toward an Eccentric Cosmopolitanism'. *Positions*, 3, 814–21.

Rae, Heather (2002). *State identies and the Homogenisation of Peoples*. Cambridge: Cambridge University Press.

Rafael, Vincente (1988). *Contracting Colonialism: Translation and Christian Conversion in Tagalog Society Under Early Spanish Rule*. Ithaca: Cornell University Press.

Randeria, S. (1998). *Against the Self-sufficiency of Western Social Sciences*. Unpublished manuscript.

Rawls, John (1971). *A Theory of Justice*. Cambridge, MA: Harvard University Press.

——(1993). *Political Liberalism*. New York: Columbia University Press.

——(1999). *The Law of Peoples* with *The Idea of Public Reason Revisited*. Cambridge, MA: Harvard University Press.

Raychaudhuri, Tapan (1988). *Europe Reconsidered*. Delhi: Oxford University Press.

Reiss, H. (ed.) (1970). *Kant's Political Writings*. Cambridge: Cambridge University Press.

Richmond, Anthony (1969). 'Sociology of Migration in Industrial and Postindustrial Societies'. In J. A. Jackson (ed.) *Migration*, pp. 238–81. Cambridge: Cambridge University Press.

Robbins, Bruce (1993). *Secular Vocations: Intellectuals, Professionalism, Culture*. London: Verso.

——(1998a). 'Introduction Part I: Actually Existing Cosmopolitanism'. In Peng Cheah and Bruce Robbins (eds) *Cosmopolitics: Thinking and Feeling Beyond the Nation*, pp. 1–19. Minneapolis: University of Minnesota Press.

——(1998b). 'Comparative Cosmopolitanisms'. In P. Cheah and B. Robbins (eds), *Cosmopolitics: Thinking and Feeling Beyond the Nation*, pp. 246–64. Minneapolis: University of Minnesota Press.

——(1999). *Feeling Global: Internationalism in Distress*. New York: New York University Press.

——(2001). 'The Village of the Liberal Managerial Class'. In Vinay Dharwadker (ed.) *Cosmopolitan Geographies: New Locations in Literature and Culture*, pp. 15–32. New York: Routledge.

Robertson, Roland (1992). *Globalization: Social Theory and Global Culture*. London: Sage.

Rogers, Alisdair, Robin Cohen and Steven Vertovec (2001). 'Editorial Statement'. *Global Networks*, 1 (1), 1–3.

Rorty, Richard (1989). 'Solidarity'. In Richard Rorty (ed.), *Contingency, Irony and Solidarity*. Cambridge: Cambridge University Press.

——(1998). 'Human Rights, Rationality and Sentimentality'. In *Truth and Progress, Philosophical Papers Volume 3*, pp. 167–85. Cambridge: Cambridge University Press.

——(1999). 'Pragmatism, Pluralism and Postmodernism'. In Richard Rorty (ed.), *Philosophy and Social Hope*, pp. 262–77. London: Penguin.

Rose, Damaris (1997). 'State Policy, Immigrant Women's Social Support Networks and the Question of Integration in Montréal'. In J. Fairhurst, I. Booysens and P. Hattingh (eds), *Migration and Gender: Place, Time and People Specific*, pp 403–24. Pretoria: University of Pretoria, Department of Geography, on behalf of International Geographical Union, Commission on Gender and Geography and Commission on Population Geography.

——Pia Carrasco, and Johanne Charboneau (1998). *The Role of 'Weak Ties' in the Settlement Experience of Immigrants with Young Children: The Case of Central Americans in Montreal*. Joint CERIS Working Paper, Toronto.

Rose, Gillian (1996). 'Beginnings of the Day: Fascism and Representation'. In Gillian Rose (ed.) *Mourning Becomes the Law*, pp. 41–62. Cambridge: Cambridge University Press.

Rosenau, James N. (1998). 'Governance and Democracy in a Globalizing World'. In D. Archibugi, D. Held, and M. Köhler (eds), *Re-imagining Political Community: Studies in Cosmopolitan Democracy*, pp. 28–57. Polity: Cambridge.

——and E. O. Czempiel (eds) (1992). *Governance without Government*. Cambridge: Cambridge University Press.

Ross, W. D. (1930). *The Right and the Good*. Oxford: Clarendon Press.

Rowse, T. (1998). *White Flour, White Power: From Rations to Citizenship in Central Australia*. Cambridge: Cambridge University Press.

Rushdie, Salman (1988). *The Satanic Verses*. London: Viking.

——(2000). *The Ground Beneath her Feet*. London: Vintage

Sabine, George H. (1961). *A History of Political Theory*. New York: Holt, Rinehart & Winston.

Said, Edward (1993). *Culture and Imperialism*. New York: Knopf.

Sandercock, Leonie (1998). *Towards Cosmopolis: Planning for Multicultural Cities*. Chichester, NY: John Wiley.

Sassen, Saskia (1996). *Losing Control? Sovereignty in an Age of Globalization*. New York: Columbia University Press.

Scheffler, Samuel (1999). 'Conceptions of Cosmopolitanism'. *Utilitas*, 11 (3), 255–76.

Schein, Louisa (1998a). 'Forged Transnationality and Oppositional Cosmopolitanism'. In M. P. Smith and L. E. Guarnizo (eds) *Transnationalism from Below*, pp. 291–313. New Brunswick: Transaction.

——(1998b). 'Importing Miao Brethren to Hmong America: A Not-So State-less Transnationalism'. In P. Cheah and B. Robbins (eds) *Cosmopolitics: Thinking and Feeling Beyond the Nation*, pp. 163–91. Minneapolis: University of Minnesota Press.

Schlereth, Thomas J. (1977). *The Cosmopolitan Ideal in Enlightenment Thought: Its Form and Function in the Ideas of Franklin, Hume and Voltaire, 1694–1790*. Notre Dame, IN: University of Notre Dame Press.

Schulte-Tenckhoff, Isabelle (1998). 'Reassessing the Paradigm of Domestication: The Problematic of Indigenous Treaties'. *Review of Constitutional Studies*, 4 (2), 239–89.

Sen, Amartya (1999a). *Development as Freedom*. New York: Anchor Books.

—— (1999*b*). 'Global Justice. Beyond International Equity'. In I. Kaul, I. Grunberg, and M. Stern (eds), *Global Public Goods. International Cooperation in the 21ˢᵗ Century,* pp. 117–25. New York: Oxford University Press.

Sennett, Richard (1977). *The Fall of Public Man.* New York: Knopf.

Shapcott, R. (1994). 'Conversation and Coexistence: Gadamer and the Interpretation of International Society'. *Millennium,* 23, 57–83.

—— (2001). *Justice, Community and Dialogue in International Relations.* Cambridge: Cambridge University Press.

Shaw, Josephine (1997). 'Citizenship of the Union: Towards Post-National Membership?' *Jean Monnet.* Working Paper No. 6/97. www.law.harvard.edu/Programs/JeanMonnet.

Shibutani, Tamotsu and Kian M. Kwan (1965). *Ethnic Stratification: A Comparative Approach.* New York: Macmillan.

Singer, Peter and Renata Singer (1988). 'The Ethics of Refugee Policy'. In Marc Gibney (ed.), *Open Borders? Closed Societies?* pp. 111–30. New York: Greenwood Press.

Sklair, Leslie (2000). *The Transnational Capitalist Class.* Oxford: Blackwell.

Smith, Anthony (1986). *The Ethnic Origins of Nations.* Oxford: Blackwell.

—— (1990). 'Towards a Global Culture?' In M. Featherstone (ed.), *Global Culture: Nationalism, Globalization and Modernity,* 171–92. London: Sage.

—— (1995). *Nations and Nationalism in a Global Era.* Cambridge: Polity Press.

Smith, Jackie (1998). 'Global Civil Society? Transnational Social Movement Organizations and Social Capital'. *American Behavioral Scientist,* 42 (1), 25–42.

——Charles Chatfield, and Ron Pagnucco (eds) (1997). *Transnational Social Movements and Global Politics.* Syracuse, NY: Syracuse University Press.

Smith, M. G. (1969). 'Institutional and Political Conditions of Pluralism'. In Leo Kuper and M. G. Smith (eds), *Pluralism in Africa.* Berkeley: University of California Press, pp. 27–66.

Soysal, Yasemin Nuhoglu (1994). *Limits of Citizenship: Migrants and Postnational Membership in Europe.* Chicago: University of Chicago.

—— (2000). 'Citizenship and Identity: Living in Diasporas in Post-War Europe?' *Ethnic and Racial Studies,* 23 (1), 1–15.

Stanley, Brian (1983). 'Christian Responses to the Indian Mutiny of 1857'. In W. J. Sheils (ed.), *Studies in Church History,* The Church and War (Vol. 20). Oxford: Blackwell, pp. 277–89.

St. John de Crevecoeur, J. Hector (1968). *Letters from an American Farmer.* Gloucester, MA: P. Smith.

Sznaider, Nathan (1999). 'Über nationale Identitäten und ob man sie konsumieren kann'. Unpublished manuscript.

Taguieff, Pierre-André (1990). 'The New Cultural Racism in France'. *Telos,* 83, 109–22.

Tamir, Y. (1993). *Liberal Nationalism.* Princeton: Princeton University Press.

Tang Yijie (1990). 'The Principle of Harmony in Difference and its Value Origins'. In *Not Full, Not Empty* ('He'erbutang de jiazhi ziyuan', *Feishi feixuji*), pp. 249–55. Beijing: Huawen Chubanshe.

—— (1999*a*). 'Culture's Two-way Choice: A Study of Transmission of Indian Buddhism into China' [Wenhua de Shuangxiang xuanze: Yindu fojiao shuru zhong-guo de kaocha]. In *Not Full, Not Empty* [*Feishi feixu ji*], pp. 191–8. Beijing: Huawen Chubanshe.

——(1999*b*). 'Reflections on Culture's Historical Process' [Wenhua Licheng de fansi yu zhan wang]. In *Not Full, Not Empty* [*Feishi feixu ji*], pp. 226–41. Beijing: Huawen Chubanshe.

Taylor, Charles (1994). 'The Politics of Recognition'. In Amy Gutman (ed.) *Multiculturalism: Examining the Politics of Recognition*. Princeton: Princeton University Press, pp. 25–74.

——(2002). 'Modern Social Imaginaries'. *Public Culture*, 14 (February).

——Amy Gutman, and Jürgen Habermas (1994). *Multiculturalism: Examining the Politics of Recognition*. Princeton: Princeton University Press.

Taylor, Paul (1999). 'The United Nations in the 1990s: Proactive Cosmopolitanism and The Issue of Sovereignty'. *Political Studies*, 47: 538–65.

Therborn, Goran (1977). 'The Rule of Capital and the Rise of Democracy'. *New Left Review*, 13.

Thomas, Keith (1984). *Man and the Natural World: Changing Attitudes in England, 1500–1800*. Harmondsworth: Penguin Books.

Thompson, E. P. (1971). 'The Moral Economy of the English Crowd in the Eighteenth Century'. *Past and Present*, 50, 76–136.

Thompson, Janna (1998). 'Community Identity and World Citizenship'. In D. Archibugi, D. Held and M. Köhler (eds) *Re-imagining Political Community: Studies in Cosmopolitan Democracy*, pp. 179–97. Cambridge: Polity.

Thompson, J. B. (1995). *The Media and Modernity*. Cambridge: Polity.

Thompson, Laurence G. (1993). *Chinese Religion: An Introduction*. Belmont, CA: Wadsworth.

Thompson, Susan, *et al.* (1999). 'Urban Governance and Citizenship: The Sydney Case'. Paper presented to the workshop on *Immigration, Integration, and Social Cohesion: Sydney and Vancouver in Comparative Perspective*, June.

Thorne, Susan (1990). *Protestant Ethics and the Spirit of Imperialism: British Congregationalists and the London Missionary Society, 1795–1925*. Dissertation defended at the University of Michigan, Ann Arbor.

Tilly, Charles (1990). *Coercion, Capital and European States AD 990–1990*. Oxford: Basil Blackwell.

Tomlinson, John (1999). *Globalization and Culture*. Cambridge: Polity.

Tong Chee Kiong and Chan Kwok-bun (2001). *Alternate Identities: The Chinese of Contemporary Thailand*. Singapore: Times Academic Press and Leiden: Brill Academic Publishers.

——(2002). 'One Face, Many Masks: The Singularity and Plurality of Chinese Identity'. *Diaspora* (forthcoming)

Toulmin, Stephen (1990). *Cosmopolis: The Hidden Agenda of Modernity*. New York: Free Press.

Tronto, J. (1993). *Moral Boundaries: A Political Argument for an Ethic of Care*. London: Routledge.

Turner, Bryan (1986). *Citizenship and Capitalism: The Debate over Reform*. London: Allen & Unwin.

——(1993). 'Outline of a Theory of Human Rights'. *Sociology* (3), 489–512.

UNESCO (1950). *World Communications Report*. Paris: United Nations Educational, Scientific and Cultural Organization.

UNESCO (1986). *International Flows of Selected Cultural Goods*. Paris: United Nations Educational, Scientific and Cultural Organization.

UNESCO (1989). *World Communications Report*. Paris: United Nations Educational, Scientific and Cultural Organization.

Urry, John (1995). 'Tourism, Europe and Identity'. In J. Urry (ed.), *Consuming Places*, pp. 263–70. London: Routledge.

——(2000*a*). 'Mobile Sociology' *The British Journal of Sociology*, 51 (1), 79–106.

——(2000*b*). *Sociology Beyond Societies: Mobilities for the Twenty-First Century*. London: Routledge.

Van der Veer, Peter (1994). *Religious Nationalism: Hindus and Muslims in India*. Berkeley: University of California Press.

——(ed.) (1995*a*). *Nation and Migration*. Philadelphia: University of Pennsylvania Press.

——(1995*b*). *Modern Orientalism* (in Dutch). Amsterdam: Meulenhoff.

——(1997). 'The Enigma of Arrival: Hybridity and Authenticity in the Global Space'. In Pnina Werbner and Tariq Modood (eds), *Debating Cultural Hybridity*, pp. 90–105. London: Zed Books.

——(1998). 'The Global History of "Modernity"'. *Journal of the Economic and Social History of the Orient*, 41 (3), 285–95.

——(2001). *Imperial Encounters: Religion, Nation, and Empire*. Princeton: Princeton University Press.

——and Hartmut Lehmann (eds) (1999). *Nation and Religion: Perspectives on Europe and Asia*. Princeton: Princeton University Press.

Van Hear, Nicholas (1998). *New Diasporas: The Mass Exodus, Diepersal and Regrouping of Migrant Communities*. Seattle: University of Washington Press.

van Rooden, Peter (1996). 'Nineteenth-Century Representations of Missionary Conversion and the Transformation of Western Christianity'. In Peter Van der Veer (ed.), *Conversion to Modernities*, pp. 65–89. New York: Routledge.

Varouxakis, Georgios (1999). 'How "Cosmopolitan" Can Patriotism Be?' *ASEN Bulletin*, 16, 3–7.

Velie, Alan (1999). 'Ethnicity, Indian Identity, and Indian Literature'. *American Indian Culture and Research Journal*, 191–205.

Vertovec, Steven (1996). 'Berlin Multikulti: Germany, "Foreigners" and "World-openness"'. *New Community*, 22 (3), 381–99.

——(1999). 'Minority Associations, Networks and Public Policies: Re-assessing Relationships'. *Journal for Ethnic and Migration Studies*, 25 (1), 21–42.

——(2000*a*). 'Fostering Cosmopolitanisms: A Conceptual Survey and a Media Experiment in Berlin'. Oxford: ESRC Transnational Communities Programme Working Paper WPTC-2K-06 [www.transcomm.ox.ac.uk].

——(2000*b*). *The Hindu Diaspora: Comparative Patterns*. London: Routledge.

——and Robin Cohen (eds) (1999). *Migration, Diasporas and Transnationalism*. The International Library of Studies on Migration, 9. Aldershot: Edward Elgar.

——and Alisdair Rogers (1998). 'Introduction'. In Steven Vertovec and Alisdair Rogers (eds) *Muslim European Youth*, pp. 1–24. Aldershot: Ashgate.

Vincent, R. J. (1986). *Human Rights and International Relations*. Cambridge: Cambridge University Press.

——(1990). 'Grotius, Human Rights and Intervention'. In Hedley Bull, Benedict Kingsbury and Adam Roberts (eds), *Hugo Grotius and International Relations*, pp. 241–56. Oxford: Clarendon Press.

Vogel, U. (2000). 'Cosmopolitan Citizenship: Between Enlightenment and Romanticism'. Paper presented to the *Political Studies Association Conference*, London School of Economics, 11–13 April.

Wainwright, Joel, Scott Prudham, and Jim Glassman (2000). 'The Battles in Seattle: Microgeographies of Resistance and the Challenge of Building Alternative Futures'. *Environment and Planning D: Society and Space*, 18, 5–14.

Waldron, Jeremy (1992). 'Minority Cultures and the Cosmopolitan Alternative'. *University of Michigan Journal of Law Reform*, 25 (3), 751–93.

——(1999). 'What is Cosmopolitan?' *The Journal of Political Philosophy*, 8 (2): 227–43.

Waley, Arthur (1936). *The Analects of Confucius* (Book 12). New York: Vintage.

Wallace, William (1999). 'The Sharing of Sovereignty: The European Paradox'. *Political Studies*, 47 (3), special issue.

Wallerstein, Immanuel (1974). *The Modern World System* (Vol. 1). New York: Academic Press.

Walzer, Michael (1970). *Obligations: Essays on Disobedience, War and Citizenship*. Cambridge, MA: Harvard University Press.

——(1983). *Spheres of Justice: A Defence of Pluralism and Equality*. Oxford: Martin Robertson.

——(1994a). *Thick and Thin: Moral Argument at Home and Abroad*. Notre Dame Indiana: University of Notre Dame Press.

——(1994b). 'Spheres of Affection'. *Boston Review*, 19 (5), 29.

——(ed.) (1995). *Toward a Global Civil Society*. Providence, RI: Berghahn.

——(1996). 'Spheres of Affection'. In Joshua Cohen (ed.), *For Love of Country: Debating the Limits of Patriotism: Martha C. Nussbaum and Respondents*, pp. 125–7. Cambridge, MA: Beacon.

——(1997). *On Toleration*. New Haven: Yale University Press.

Weiler, Joseph (1999). 'To be a European Citizen: Eros and Civilization'. In *The Constitution of Europe*, pp. 324–57. Cambridge: Cambridge University Press.

Welch, Holmes (1967). *The Practice of Chinese Buddhism, 1900–1950*. Cambridge: Harvard University Press.

Werbner, Pnina (1999). 'Global Pathways: Working Class Cosmopolitans and the Creation of Transnational Ethnic Worlds'. *Social Anthropology*, 7 (1), 17–36.

Williams, Raymond (1958). *Culture and Society 1780–1950*. Harmondsworth: Penguin.

Williamson, Oliver E. (1975). *Markets and Hierarchies*. New York: Free Press.

——(1991). 'Introduction'. In O.E. Williamson and S.G. Winter (eds), *The Nature of the Firm: Origins, Evolution, and Development*, pp. 3–17. New York: Oxford University Press.

Wispe, Lauren G. (1968). 'Sympathy and Empathy'. In David Sills (ed.), *International Encyclopedia of the Social Sciences* (Vol. 15) pp. 441–7. New York: Macmillan Company.

Wolffe, John (1994). *God and Greater Britain: Religion and National Life in Britain and Ireland, 1843–1945*. London: Routledge.

Wolin, Richard (1997). 'Democracy and "Distinctive Status"'. *Dissent*, Winter, 135–41.

Yack, Bernard (1996). 'The Myth of the Civic Nation'. *Critical Review* 10 (2), 193–211.

Young, Iris Marion (1990). *Justice and the Politics of Difference*. Princeton: University of Princeton Press.

——(1999). 'Residential Segregation and Differentiated Citizenship'. *Citizenship Studies*, 3, 237–52.

Zachary, G. Pascal (2000*a*). 'Duelling Multiculturalisms: The Urgent Need to Reconceive Cosmopolitanism'. Oxford: *ESRC Transnational Communities Programme*, Working Paper WPTC-2K-04 [www.transcomm.ox.ac.uk].

——(2000*b*). *The Global Me: New Cosmopolitans and the Competitive Edge*. London: Nicholas Brealey.

Ziolkowski, Eric (ed.) (1993). *A Museum of Faiths: Histories and Legagies of the 1893 World's Parliament of Religions*. Atlanta: Scholars Press.

Zolo, Danilo (1997). *Cosmopolis: Prospects for World Government*. Cambridge: Polity.

Zürn, M. (1998). *Regieren jenseits des Nationalstaats*. Frankfurt/M: Suhrkamp.

INDEX

Lightning Source UK Ltd.
Milton Keynes UK
24 September 2010 .
160299UK00002B/28/P